P9-DNY-124

The American
Foreign Policy
Library

Edwin O. Reischauer, Editor

THE "TWO GERMANIES"
SINCE 1949

Map 1. The "Two Germanies" since 1949.

Germany
and the
United States

A "Special Relationship?"

Hans W. Gatzke

HARVARD UNIVERSITY PRESS
Cambridge, Massachusetts
and London, England
1980

Library of Congress Cataloging in Publication Data

Gatzke, Hans Wilhelm, 1915–
   The United States and Germany, a "special relationship"?

   (The American foreign policy library)
   Bibliography: p.
   Includes index.
   1. United States—Foreign relations—Germany. 2. Germany—
Foreign relations—United States. I. Title. II. Series.
E183.8.G3G37   327.73′043   79–15480
ISBN 0–674–35326–9

To
David W. Gregory

Foreword

Germany is without doubt one of the most important countries in the world, and its relations with the United States are of particular significance. The German people constitute the largest ethnic group in Europe west of the Russians. By the early twentieth century they had provided the United States with about a quarter of its population. The two great World Wars that focused around Germany drew the United States deeply into international affairs and threatened to bring down the whole edifice of Western civilization. Twice our bitter enemies, the Germans have at other times had relations of cordiality with the United States. Today West Germany alone ranks fourth in productive power in the world and is among the two or three staunchest and most important allies the United States has.

The story of modern Germany and its relations with the United States, thus, is a complex one. Germany has swung wildly between great successes and terrible failures. The relations between the two countries have gone through the same sort of rapid and violent fluctuations. Neither modern German history nor German-American relations are easy to analyze or describe in clear, coherent fashion. The task is made all the more difficult by the deep historical divisions among the German people, by the fact that their ethnic and political boundaries have never closely approximated each other, and by the present division of the core of Germany into two extremely distinct and basically hostile regimes, which have radically different relationships with the United States.

Professor Hans Gatzke presents this whole complex picture with extraordinary clarity and balance. His achievement is all the more remarkable because of the centrality of Germany in the politics and wars of modern Europe as well as in the great Soviet-American confrontation that has existed since World War II. The problem is further complicated by the deep emotions aroused by the memories of these wars, the terrible Nazi experience, and lingering Cold War tensions. German history and German-American relations can all too easily become so entangled with these wider themes as to lose all shape themselves. But Professor Gatzke, while always making clear the broader setting, keeps clearly in mind the specific story he is relating and makes it fully understandable to his readers.

Opinions on Germany and its relations with the United States, of course, vary widely and are often fiercely contested. It is by no means easy to maintain an evenhanded, fair approach to the contrasts between Hitlerian Germany and the more admirable aspects of the nation's past and present. The same is true of the treatment of the two current rival German regimes. A variety of viewpoints must be presented without bias, but also without producing a flavorless pudding, a series of mushy judgments expressed by statements beginning with "on the one hand" and followed by "on the other." Professor Gatzke presents the various problems clearly, crisply, and with eminent fairness. The result is not only very informative but most enjoyable reading.

Perhaps I am particularly struck by the judicious balance Professor Gatzke displays in this book, because I myself have written primarily about the country—Japan—which probably comes closest to Germany in the volatility of its modern history and relations with the United States, and therefore I can appreciate more than most the clarity and balance of his presentation. The contrasts between the German and Japanese cases probably are as striking as their parallels, but the problem of presenting both countries to the American public is very much the same.

In view of the great importance of Germany in modern history and more specifically to the United States today, the absence of a volume on Germany in the American Foreign Policy Library series has been a serious shortcoming. The passions aroused by World War II, the Hitlerian holocaust, and even the Cold War have made the writing of such a book difficult. But the time has obviously come when we can look at the whole German-American experience in better perspective, and this Professor Gatzke has done with great skill and soundness of judgment. I know of no other volume that in any way attempts to survey this whole story so fully and does so with such success. This is a book that has been worth waiting for, and the American Foreign Policy Library presents it to the public with great pride.

Edwin O. Reischauer

Preface

This book has been in the making for some time. Its original working title was "The United States and Germany." Only after completion was it changed to *Germany and the United States: A "Special Relationship"?* The answer to the question in the subtitle, as will be seen, is no. It should be noted, however, that the theme or thesis implied by the question emerged only as the book was being written. In other words, it was not a hypothesis from the start.

The book is intended for the general reader, primarily American, but also German. Though written by a historian, it is not merely a diplomatic history. Nor was it written for other historians, who are already familiar with much of what I say. The book is meant to be a reliable and balanced account of what the United States and Germany have meant to each other over the past two hundred years. In particular, I hope to dispel some of the myths, facile generalizations, and clichés that have grown up over the years to distort the image of one nation in the eyes of the other.

As an American of German origin—I first came to this country in 1934, as a young man of 18 years—I have lived in and am closely familiar with both countries. I have tried to be as objective as possible; but if I were charged with being more pro-American than pro-German, I would have to agree. I might compare myself to those authors who have written critically but sympathetically about their parents and who, while preferring one to the other, nevertheless realize that they are the product of both.

xi

There are other historians of similar ethnic and academic backgrounds who could have written a book on this subject. But it would probably have been quite a different book. So as not to be diverted from what I was trying to do, I kept very much to myself while writing and only occasionally consulted some colleagues on factual or bibliographical matters. Only when I had finished did I submit the manuscript to a few readers. I am deeply grateful to my friends David Gregory and Horst von Maltitz and to my friends and colleagues Professors Isabel Hull and Klemens von Klemperer, for their valuable criticisms and suggestions. I hope they will not mind that I did not agree with all the points they raised. They are certainly not to be blamed for any of the book's remaining shortcomings.

I have received help from other sources. For the final chapters, dealing with present-day Germany, the German Information Center in New York and its friendly staff, Hannelore Koehler and Inge Godenschweger, were most helpful in supplying me with factual information. Yale University, through a grant from its A. Whitney Griswold Faculty Research Fund, defrayed the cost of typing, which was capably done by Barbara Bouchard. Special thanks are due to the editors and staff of the Harvard University Press, notably Aida D. Donald and Camille Smith, who helped the manuscript to become a book. Peg Anderson did a superb job of smoothing some of its rough edges, Robert Forget supplied a set of excellent maps, and Ruth Cross prepared the index.

Finally, I should like to thank Professor Edwin O. Reischauer for inviting me to contribute to his series. I hope that my book will be worthy of the distinguished company it joins.

H. W. G.

Contents

	Introduction	1
1	Germany: The Land and the People	7
2	Germany and the United States, 1776–1914	27
3	World War I: A Turning Point, 1914–1918	52
4	The Weimar Republic: A Democratic Interlude, 1918–1933	75
5	Hitler and the "Third Reich," 1933–1939	103
6	World War II: The End of the German Reich, 1939–1945	126
7	One Germany or Two? Occupation, 1945–1949	154
8	The Germany of Konrad Adenauer, 1949–1963	179
9	From Adenauer to Brandt, 1963–1974	207
10	The German Federal Republic since 1974	230
11	The German Democratic Republic since 1961	258
12	Conclusion: A "Special Relationship"?	276
	Suggested Reading	284
	Index	303

Maps

1 The "Two Germanies" since 1949   frontispiece
2 The Unification of Germany, 1867–1871   34
3 Germany after 1919   79
4 Hitler's Empire at Its Greatest Extent, 1942   140
5 Occupied Germany, 1945–1949   155

Abbreviations

APO	Ausserparlamentarische Opposition
	Extra-Parliamentary Opposition
BHE	Block der Heimatvertriebenen und Entrechteten
	Bloc of Expellees and Disfranchised
BRD	Bundesrepublik Deutschland
	Federal Republic of Germany (West Germany)
CDU	Christlich-Demokratische Union
	Christian-Democratic Union
COMECON	Council of Mutual Economic Assistance
CSU	Christlich-Soziale Union
	Christian-Social Union
DDR	Deutsche Demokratische Republik
	German Democratic Republic (East Germany)
DGB	Deutscher Gewerkschaftsbund
	German Trade Union Federation
DKP	Deutsche Kommunistische Partei
	German Communist Party
DM	Deutsche Mark
ECSC	European Coal and Steel Community
EDC	European Defense Community
EEC	European Economic Community (Common Market)
FDGB	Freier Deutscher Gewerkschaftsbund
	Free German Trade Union Federation
FDJ	Freie Deutsche Jugend
	Free German Youth
FDP	Freie Demokratische Partei
	Free Democratic Party
HICOG	Office of the U.S. High Commissioner for Germany
JCS 1067	Joint Chiefs of Staff's Directive #1067
KPD	Kommunistische Partei Deutschlands
	Communist Party of Germany
MBFR	Mutual and Balanced Force Reductions
MLF	Multilateral Force
NDP	National-Demokratische Partei
	National-Democratic Party
NPG	Nuclear Planning Group

NVA	Nationale Volksarmee
	National People's Army
OEEC	Organization of European Economic Cooperation
OMGUS	Office of Military Government of the U.S. for Germany
OPEC	Oil Producing and Exporting Countries
RAF	Red Army Faction
SA	Sturm-Abteilung
	Storm Troops
SALT	Strategic Arms Limitation Talks
SDS	Sozialistischer Deutscher Studentenbund
	Socialist German Student League
SED	Sozialistische Einheitspartei Deutschlands
	Socialist Unity Party of Germany
SPD	Sozialdemokratische Partei Deutschlands
	Social-Democratic Party of Germany
SS	Schutzstaffel
	Protective Squad
SSD	Staatssicherheitsdienst
	State Security Service
USFET	United States Forces European Theatre

Germany
and the
United States

Introduction

The two bloodiest foreign wars fought by the United States have been against Germany and its allies. In both these wars, America's entry sealed Germany's defeat. If ever two nations were destined to be "eternal enemies," therefore, it should be these two. But the opposite has been the case. Not long after World War I, the United States began supporting Germany's attempt to get back on its feet economically and to revise some of the harsh terms of the Treaty of Versailles. Ten years after the war, Britain's ambassador to Berlin, Lord D'Abernon, commented on the "close and instinctive understanding between Americans and Germans," which he found "difficult to analyze and explain." His American colleague, Ambassador Jacob Gould Schurman, had no such difficulty. "Never in our history," he told a Steuben Day audience in New York in 1927, "have the political institutions and international ideals of Germany and the United States been as much in agreement as they are today. Both nations believe in government of the people, by the people, and for the people. Both are instinctively and unalterably opposed to dictators, no matter whether the dictator is an individual or a class." Six years later Adolf Hitler seized power.

In 1945, after Germany's second defeat, the United States appeared at first to be set on a less conciliatory course. To drive home to the Germans the totality of their defeat and to give symbolic expression to America's contempt for them, members of the occupying forces were forbidden even to shake hands with their recent enemies. But such nonfraternization did not last long. As the

1

shadows of the cold war fell across Europe and the world, contempt rapidly gave way to understanding, and soon there developed that astonishing "love affair" between the United States and Germany, which found its early culmination in Germany's admission, ten years after the war, into the western community of nations.

Relations between the United States and Germany have thus been somewhat erratic. But this has not discouraged people of good-will in both countries from speaking once again of genuine friend-ship between the two. That friendship, they claim, goes deeper than the mere dictates of cold war diplomacy; it is seen as not unlike the "special relationship" that developed during the nineteenth century between the United States and Britain. But such a friend-ship, as the American-British example shows, besides requiring com-mon interests, also calls for an underlying affinity and kinship be-tween the two partners; most important, it requires time in which to grow. Americans use the term friendship more readily and easily than most Germans. As the German saying goes, for a true and last-ing *Freundschaft* to develop, the prospective friends must first con-sume at least a bushel of salt together to give them time to get to know each other.

Considering the obvious interest of the two nations in each other and their sincere desire to become and remain friends, it is curious that no attempt has been made thus far to put their past relations in a wider historical perspective. Only by doing so can we understand the ambivalence that has characterized so much of their past attitudes. One of the reasons for the lack of such a compre-hensive overview has been that except during the major interna-tional crises of our century, relations between the United States and Germany on the diplomatic level have been quite uneventful. For most of the nineteenth century, it was not so much the official dealings between governments as the human contacts between their peoples that characterized the relations of the two countries. That was the century of the great Germanic migrations across the Atlantic; at the beginning of this century almost a third of the citizens of the United States had some ties, direct or through their parents, with the Father-land. The image that each nation formed of the other could not help being shaped by these personal contacts, although the resulting impressions were not always true to reality.

To help Americans better understand the Germany of today, this study first deals with the political rise and fall of that country and its interaction with the United States prior to 1945. These events are dealt with in the broadest sense, emphasizing in particu-lar those factors that help to explain the involvement of the two nations as the leading protagonists in the two world wars. The second half of the book deals in some detail with Germany, or better the Germanies, that have evolved from the collapse and breakup of Hitler's "Third Reich."

How many of these Germanies one recognizes depends on how permanent one considers the separation of the easternmost part of what was Germany in 1937, before Hitler embarked on his course of conquest (see map 3). The annexation in 1945, by Poland and the Soviet Union, of the former German lands beyond the Oder and Neisse rivers was for some time a source of much international tension and a standing threat to peace. It was only in the early 1970s that the majority of Germans began to acquiesce in the loss of these lands, in their minds at least, if not in their hearts. Accepting this adjustment to reality, I will consider here only what is left of Germany politically, the two Germanies—the West German Federal Republic (Bundesrepublik Deutschland, BRD) and the East German Democratic Republic (Deutsche Demokratische Republik, DDR). The reader must bear in mind, however, that through much of the period covered in this book there was a German Reich, both larger and more integrated than these artificial states born in the early days of the cold war. At the same time it is worth remembering that the Reich that came to an end in 1945 had existed for only seventy-four years, since 1871. What Bismarck had forged together then with "iron and blood," came apart again, also with iron and blood, and as a result of a war that Germany under Hitler unleashed against the rest of the world. In the final analysis, therefore, the Germans have themselves to blame for the states they are in.

Some other general thoughts occur as one looks back from the Germanies of the present to the Germany of the past. At no time in its history has the dream of uniting all the German-speaking people of Europe in one pan-German state been realized. Hitler came close to doing so, and had he won the war, a German or Germanic Reich would have lorded it over an enslaved continent. But the Greater Germany Hitler envisaged would have been not an organically grown political unit but an artificial conglomerate ruled by assorted German-speaking masters collected from all over Europe and the world. (Hitler, as we shall see, even hoped to entice the Germans in America into "coming home.")

The ethnic and the political frontiers of Germany, unlike those of France, Britain, or Italy, have never coincided and, again unlike these countries, Germany has never had a genuine capital, acknowledged as such by all its citizens. Berlin filled the role after 1871, of course, but never in quite the same way as Paris, London, or Rome. Through most of its history, Germany has been a country of many states and regions, each with its own political and cultural center. The desire for national unity has been a comparatively recent, nineteenth-century phenomenon. And even after it had been achieved, some of the regions, notably the Rhineland and Bavaria, at times tried to dissociate themselves from their fellow Germans. The issue of unity versus particularism has been and remains a major theme in German history.

Among the various states and regions of Germany, one has held a unique and commanding position. To some historians, the unification of Germany appeared as little more than the conquest of the German nation by its most powerful member state, the kingdom of Prussia. The antagonism resulting from the predominance of this reactionary and Protestant north German giant over the smaller, more liberal, and mostly Catholic states of the south could not help but affect the cohesion of the newly created Reich. This north-south split has not entirely disappeared, even though Prussia has been gone for more than a generation. Even today, particularist feelings still survive in the south, especially in Bavaria. There is some truth, therefore, in referring to the Main River, which separates north from south, as Germany's Mason-Dixon line.

Another dividing line that is sometimes mentioned by historians is the one running from north to south along the Elbe River. Its significance is more deeply embedded in German consciousness, having originated during the Middle Ages, when the Elbe separated the partly Romanized empire of Charlemagne from those regions to the east into which the German *Drang nach Osten* (drive to the east) slowly but steadily advanced against the Slavs. In more modern times, the Elbe divided Prussia's older provinces in the east from its more recently acquired territories in the west. The regions east of the Elbe, chiefly agrarian and dominated by the large estates of the Prussian Junker aristocracy, differed in many ways from the western parts, which became rapidly industrialized during the last century and were the stamping ground for that other stereotype of Prusso-German society, the industrial baron of the Ruhr. It would be an oversimplification to see a historic connection between the Elbe line of the past and Germany's east-west partition of the present, but the fact that a division existed before 1945 provides some perspective on the events since.

From what has been said it should be clear that Germany, even during its brief existence as a national state, was a far less coherent and monolithic state than its patriotic poets and propagandists tried to make their compatriots believe. Compared to the other countries of western Europe, Germany has always been a nation in flux, with ill-defined borders and changing territory. The drastic reduction in size and the division into two sovereign states that Germany has undergone since 1945 may thus be seen as merely another phase in that nation's effort to find its political identity, although in this case the effort was not voluntary but imposed by the harsh realities of history.

The sudden emergence a century ago of a politically united, economically powerful, and militarily aggressive German nation could not help but cause apprehension among people in the rest of the world. That apprehension in time gave rise to the well-known image of the militaristic German or Prussian, an image that events, especially between 1914 and 1945, seemed to confirm. As far as the United States was concerned, however, this unfavorable image did not develop until the eve of World War I, and even then it underwent frequent changes. On the whole, except in times of war, the picture that the average American has held of his German counterpart has been favorable, although, as the term "Dutchman," often erroneously applied to the Germans, denotes, it has been tinged with a certain condescension. It should be noted that this condescension was often reciprocated in Germany, where the term *amerikanisch* at times has had decidedly negative undertones. Such mutual patronizing, needless to say, has hardly been helpful to mutual understanding. Only in our own day, as common interests have drawn the United States and Germany closer together than they have ever been before, have the two nations developed an objective image of and a realistic attitude toward each other.

How long this American-German entente will last is impossible to predict, and the wishful thinking of Ambassador Schurman in 1927 should serve as a warning against undue optimism. Still, the similarities between the United States and West Germany, at least, are closer today than at any other time in their histories. Not only do the two nations share a common concern for the containment of communism, but their interests in most other respects—political, economic, and cultural—are closely related and complementary. The American-German rapprochement, moreover, has by now been going on for more than a generation and has survived a number of major and minor crises. There has been, and continues to be, mutual criticism, but criticism, if constructive, can be a firmer basis for lasting friendship than mutual admiration. American-German relations in the past have often been a tale of missed opportunities. The fact that both nations have learned from that past and seem to recognize their mutual interests holds much hope for the future.

1 | Germany
The Land and the People

GERMANY HAS ALWAYS BEEN an open country, with few natural and no clear-cut ethnic frontiers. Along all its borders, Germans live intermingled with the peoples of its various foreign neighbors, of which West Germany has eight, while East Germany has only two; this may explain why the latter is so far more parochial than the former. The Germans like to refer to their country as the "land of the middle," or more poetically, "the heart of Europe." This central location has its advantages and disadvantages. It can aid cultural and economic exchange, or it can lead to war. Germany throughout its history has been either a "bridge or battleground," usually the latter, as German historians like to point out. The effort to avoid thus being caught in the middle has been, and continues to be, one of Germany's major concerns.

In trying to convey some impression of what Germany and the Germans are like, one is constantly faced with the innumerable changes that World War II and its aftermath have brought about, not only in political, cultural, and economic life, but in physical appearance as well. First of all, there is the shrinkage in size. In 1937 Germany was almost a quarter again as large as the two present German republics together. Most of the lost territory, some 41,000 square miles (the size of Virginia), went to Russia and Poland, the countries that had suffered most from Hitler's aggression. The Federal Republic of West Germany today comprises a bit more than half the area of the 1937 Reich, close to 96,000 square miles, roughly

7

the size of Britain or Oregon. The German Democratic Republic in the East controls less than a quarter of the 1937 area, about 40,000 square miles, which is smaller than Cuba or just about the size of Kentucky. West Germany has not only the larger share of prewar Germany, but the more desirable part in every respect—economically, scenically, and even climatically.

Besides undergoing drastic territorial cuts as a result of the war, Germany also suffered untold human losses and sweeping demographic changes. The exact figures of German war casualties will never be known. To the more than four and a half million killed in battles, air raids, and other war-related acts must be added several million who died while fleeing the advancing Soviet armies or while being "resettled" (a euphemism for being expelled) from their former homes in Germany east of the Oder-Neisse line, Poland, Czechoslovakia, and other East European countries. The total number of German war victims probably comes close to eight million. Then there are the refugees or expellees who survived their ordeal; in 1950, four and a half million of them lived in East Germany and seven and a half million in the West. I shall deal with the fate of these uprooted peoples later on. They are mentioned here to give an idea of the war's effect on Germany's human geography.

A nation with its territory reduced by one-fourth and with a population more than decimated—that was how Germany awoke from the nightmare of war in 1945. What was left of the land and the people, furthermore, was in shambles. At the end of 1945, among a population of mostly women, children, and old people, there were 1.6 million disabled veterans, 1.2 million war widows, and 1.5 million orphans. Almost all the major cities lay in ruins from air raids, ground fighting, and the last-minute scorched-earth policy decreed by Hitler. That policy also was responsible for the blowing-up of virtually every bridge in the path of the advancing Allied armies. To say that one-fifth of Germany's total dwellings had been destroyed does not describe the utter desolation that reigned in cities like Berlin, Hamburg, Dresden, or Cologne, where anywhere from 70 to 90 percent of the houses lay in rubble or were severely damaged. Never has the saying that a country "lay in ruins" been more literally true than of Germany in 1945.

It is necessary to point to the ravaging effects of the war on the German landscape, physical and human, in order to bring home the fact that the Germany of today is not the result of an orderly and organic growth, that within recent memory the country and its people have undergone an ordeal, which in its severity and impact has been compared to the Thirty Years' War or, a more recent event, the Russian Revolution. But visitors to Germany today, who did not know the country before 1939 and did not see it in 1945, will find few signs, at least in West Germany, of the devastation just described. Bombed-out houses have been replaced by modern structures; bridges, roads, and railroads have been rebuilt, extended, and modernized; even the demographic wounds of World War II seem to be more than healed. There were sixty-seven million Germans in the 1937 Reich before Hitler launched his drive for a Greater Germany. In 1975, the populations of West and East Germany were sixty-two and seventeen million, respectively, or seventy-nine million in all.

This larger figure, it should be noted, is due not so much to the German birthrate, which is very low, as to the influx of refugees and expellees who had lived outside Germany's borders in 1937, mostly in Poland and Czechoslovakia. With many more people living on less land, the population density in West Germany is approaching 650 per square mile (by comparison, the population per square mile in the United States is 60). The German Federal Republic is thus a very crowded place, especially since in addition to the German citizens, it includes some two million foreign workers. Only Belgium, the Netherlands, and Japan are more densely populated.

For more then a century before Germany lost World War II, the German Reich and its Prussian predecessor had enjoyed the status of a great power. Those days are over now, but even in a world of powerful or potentially powerful giants—the United States, the Soviet Union, and China—the two Germanies still hold the leading positions, at least economically, in their respective spheres of western and eastern Europe. They do so through superior technological ability and skills and through close collaboration with their neighbors rather than through any inherent wealth of natural resources, which have never been abundant, although the Germans have long known how to make the most of what they have.

The only raw materials that Germany has in any quantity are bituminous coal in the West and lignite and potash in the East. Coal and lignite are used for a variety of derivative products and thus are of considerable industrial value. But as sources of energy they have gradually been overtaken by oil, which is more convenient and until a few years ago at least, cheaper. (West Germany has only a very small supply of its own oil.) West Germany is one of the world's leading producers of steel, but the iron ore must be supplied by Germany's French partner in the European Common Market. Both German states depend heavily on exports, which in some industries account for between 30 and 50 percent of production. I shall have more to say about the economic viability of the two Germanies later on. Neither is remotely self-sufficient; both urgently need imports, especially of raw materials and foodstuffs. As is the case with all countries in an advanced stage of industrialization, there has been a steady shift away from agriculture which, in the West as in the East, is the problem child of an otherwise thriving economy.

Thus far I have spoken mainly of the things that have changed in Germany as a result of the war. Many other recent changes are not peculiar to Germany but are the result of the fact that in the last twenty or twenty-five years, West Germany, at least, has become a thoroughly modern, highly prosperous, and very much consumer-oriented society, not unlike the United States. German cities, with their tall glass buildings, shopping malls, and traffic jams resemble American cities, especially those that have undergone a phase of urban renewal. The American tourist in search of the Germany he has seen advertised on travel posters—romantic castles, rustic villages, peasants in native costumes—may be disappointed upon arriving in Frankfurt to find that it looks pretty much like home. But if he ventures beyond the shopping and business districts of that most American of German cities, he will find some of the old sections of the town lovingly restored (including Goethe's house), allowing him to recapture some of the feeling of "what it was like." The same is true of most other cities. Because so much of their past has been wiped out, the Germans seem to appreciate what is left that much more. American visitors, therefore, need not worry—"Old Heidelberg" is still there, entirely undamaged by the war, and so is the Cologne cathedral. And while much of Munich looks different from what it did before the war, most of its architectural monuments have been restored.

Many of the changes in Germany's urban landscape are really no different from those in major cities the world over. Everywhere an increasingly industrial and technological age has concentrated large numbers of people in urban areas. A great deal has been done in Germany to relieve the congestion caused by such concentration, especially through improved transportation. The German railroads, traditionally a model of efficiency, today are a source of nostalgia tinged with envy to most Americans. Several cities now have subway systems, including Bonn, the capital of West Germany. As I have said, Germany has never had a natural capital. Berlin, which served that function for seventy-four years, is now a divided city, surrounded by the German Democratic Republic, and its eastern part serves as the capital of that state. The most logical capital for the Federal Republic would have been Frankfurt, but chiefly to please that state's founder and first chancellor, Konrad Adenauer, Bonn was selected instead. In the course of some thirty years, that sleepy university town has grown into a sprawling city, which still, however, lacks the function and flavor of a metropolis. It has been said that West Germany actually has several capitals—Bonn (political), Frankfurt (financial), Düsseldorf (industrial), and Karlsruhe (judicial). But that is really not much different from the situation in the United States, where some of the functions just described, as well as most of the cultural life, are centered in New York rather than Washington.

As one moves from the cities and their proliferating suburbs into the countryside, Germany still offers the tourist some of what he expects. Yes, there are hundreds of castles, and not just along the Rhine—large and small, preserved and ruined, inhabited or serving as museums. There are small towns with ancient town halls and picturesque marketplaces, and there are peaceful villages and hamlets with cobblestoned streets and half-timbered houses. There are also the many spas or watering places of which the Germans are so fond and where they go to recuperate from real or imaginary illnesses by taking the *Kur*. Some regions of Germany are more famous for their natural beauty than others. The northern plains are perhaps least attractive to visitors, except for the beach resorts along the North and Baltic seas. Here also is Hamburg, Germany's second-largest city after Berlin, with close to two million inhabitants, and one of the world's leading ports. At the western edge of the North German Plain, along the lower part of the Rhine, lies Germany's best-known and richest industrial region, named after the small river Ruhr that flows through it.

The Germans have a genuine and deep-felt love of nature, which is reflected in the care they lavish on their abundant forests. Most of the central and southwestern part of the country is made up of heavily wooded mountain regions, not unlike the Appalachians, of which the Black Forest is the most beautiful and the most popular with Americans. There are other such *Mittelgebirge* (medium-sized mountains, as the Germans call them), less well-known, but decidedly worth seeing: the Eifel and the Westerwald, not far from Bonn in the West; and the Harz and the Thüringer Wald in the East.

Most of southern Germany, east of the Neckar and south of the Main rivers, consists of a high plateau, with the old city of Nüremberg in the center and Munich, the capital of Bavaria, at the southern end. Both of these places were closely associated with the rise and heyday of Adolf Hitler, but they have successfully lived down their past. South of Munich and, before the days of smog, visible from there lie the Bavarian Alps, the small and very beautiful German part of that majestic mountain range, another major tourist attraction. Its best-known resort, Berchtesgaden, again was one of Hitler's favorite retreats.

One German region that deserves special mention is the Rhineland. Germany has a number of rivers, large and small, many of them navigable and most of them quite scenic. But among them the Rhine holds a special place, in the hearts not only of Rhinelanders, but of all Germans. No other river in the world, not even the Mississippi, has been celebrated as much in poetry and song as Father Rhine. It is a beautiful river, even in its present polluted state—"the biggest sewer in Europe." It also is one of the busiest arteries of traffic anywhere, with an endless succession of barges, pleasure and excursion boats. Because its source is in Switzerland and its mouth in the Netherlands and because for part of its course it constitutes the border between France and Germany, the Rhine is technically an international river. But there is no question in any German's mind that the Rhine is "Germany's stream, not Germany's border," as a German poet exclaimed more than a century ago when the French were casting longing eyes at it, as they have done repeatedly throughout history.

As a matter of fact, much of the Rhine's popularity may be due to the role it has played as a perennial issue in Franco-German relations. For almost thirty years after the French Revolution and during the Napoleonic period, the French extended their borders to the left bank of the Rhine. If they had had their way at the Paris Peace Conference in 1919, they would have done so again. But in the long run the repeated Rhineland occupations, from Roman times to the present, have had a beneficial effect. Subjected to foreign influences and ideas, the Rhinelander could not help but develop a different outlook from that of his countrymen—more rational, cosmopolitan, and pro-Western. The region also produces most of Germany's wine, which has probably helped to make its inhabitants easygoing and cheerful. The Rhinelander (like the Berliner) has the gift, rare among Germans, of being able to laugh at himself. Nowhere in Germany is the pre-Lenten Karneval celebrated with greater joy and abandon than in Cologne and Mainz.

This brief digression shows that regionalism is still a strong force in Germany. Like most Europeans, the Germans are much more closely attached to their native soil, their *Heimat,* than Americans. Despite the dislocations of World War II, the majority of

Germans still live not far from where they were born. Except for the brief span of Hitler's rule, Germany has never been a centralized nation. Even after Bismarck created a united nation in 1871, a German's first loyalty remained to his native state or Land—Bavaria, Württemberg, Saxony—or to his province or region—the Rhineland, Westphalia, the Palatinate. These native states have either disappeared today (Prussia), or they have been much reduced in size (Bavaria). Most of the ten Länder of the West German Federal Republic are artificially created administrative units rather than historically evolved states. The Democratic Republic in the East has abolished its Länder altogether and instead has divided the country into fourteen administrative districts. But this redistricting has not affected the individual German's regional attachment, his *Heimatgefühl.* He still thinks of himself first and foremost as a Westphalian or a Bavarian, or even as a Berliner or Hamburger. Regionalism pervades all aspects of life, from art and architecture to food and, in some areas, dress. And it seems to be more than skin-deep, shaping a person's entire character. A Rhinelander, as we saw, is considered easygoing and cheerful, a Westphalian stubborn and conservative, a Bavarian earthy and jovial, and so on. The fact that not all natives of these regions fit these stereotypes is less surprising than that quite a few do. But more on the German "national character" anon.

One of the most charming manifestations of regionalism is the native dialects. All Germans are taught high German, or *Hochdeutsch,* in school, which they use in writing and on all formal occasions, in speeches and such. In their everyday speech, however, their language is a blend of regional and standard German, a patois that is as noticeable and identifiable as, say, a Southern accent is in the United States. Dialects are spoken only by the less well-educated lower classes, workers and small farmers, and in their pure form they are incomprehensible even to Germans from the same region, unless they also are lower class. High German ranks sixth numerically among the world's languages, and it can be melodious and quite beautiful. In its written form, however, it often tends to be unnecessarily wordy, theoretical, and abstruse. The Germans have a penchant for interminable sentences made up of strings of subordinate clauses, crammed full of compound nouns and abstract verbs. The worst sinners muddying the linguistic stream have been Germany's professors, while some of the best German writing—lively, crisp, and clear—has come from journalists, especially since World War II.

Languages at all times are affected by their environment. The

Hitler period, aside from creating its own terrible jargon, also misused and thus tainted, probably forever, some perfectly good German words. The Germans, especially in the West, have worked hard at ridding their vocabulary of these linguistic additions and perversions. But meanwhile a similar adulteration is going on in East Germany, this one by Marxist and communist terminology. At present the main threat to the purity of German is seen by many people to be the growing infiltration of Americanisms into everyday use. Where these are untranslatable or where translation would change their meaning ("jeans," "test," "rock band"), their adoption will enrich the German language, but where a German word would do as well or better, the opposite holds true. In either case, the use of American terms, especially verbs, often leads to abominable new verbal creations. They may simplify communication, but they are offensive to anyone who is fond of and familiar with both languages.

The regions of Germany not only differ in landscape, people, and language, they vary in climate as well. Germany's overall weather is moderate, thanks to the Gulf Stream, with a mean temperature of fifty degrees Fahrenheit and an annual rainfall of twenty-seven inches. But behind these averages one finds considerable regional variations. While the North German Plain west of the Elbe River has cool summers, mild winters, medium rainfall, and much cloudiness, the Plain east of the Elbe has warm summers, cold winters that become more severe as one moves eastward, little rain, and few clouds. The river valleys of the West—Moselle, Rhine, Neckar, and Main—are dry and relatively mild in winter; spring comes early, and summers are hot. The central mountain regions and the Bavarian Plateau have the widest variety of weather, from dry and warm in the Bavarian lowlands, to wet and colder in the Black Forest. In the winter, there is ample snow in the Alps and in some of the *Mittelgebirge*. The reason for this climatic diversity is the country's intermediate situation between the mild and moist maritime climate of western Europe and the cold and dry continental climate of eastern Europe. Winters in West Germany tend to be cloudy, damp, and depressing, especially to Americans, who are used to frequent sunshine in all seasons. In compensation, however, the weather rarely gets bitter cold or scorching hot, as it does in much of the United States.

There is much more that one should probably say about Germany to give American readers an idea of what it is like. But the best way to find out is to go and see for yourself, as thousands of Americans do each year, and as millions have done since World War II. Never before have so many Americans known Germany firsthand, as soldiers, students, businessmen, or just plain tourists. The impressions they have formed differ from person to person. Not only have they seen the country, they have met the people, and while Germany is not all that different from its neighbors geographically, the Germans as a people are said to have a number of peculiarities, many unpleasant, that distinguish them from the people of other nations.

Before we embark on that favorite pastime of anyone who writes about Germany, explaining the German "national character," two observations: first of all, a nation's position in the international pecking order is not permanently fixed. In the early nineteenth century, the Germans were generally liked as peace-loving and idealistic, the direct opposite of the militarists and materialists they have supposedly become since. The question arises whether the German people, individually and collectively, have changed during the intervening period or whether the negative traits attributed to them in 1914 were already latent a century earlier.

Most foreign commentators on the Germans have held the view that the Germans have always been an obnoxious people and will remain so. But the drastic changes that Germany has undergone since World War II make one wonder if it is not possible for a people to change, to make a clear break with their past and start all over again? In 1945 the majority of Germans had been born before 1930 and had experienced the Nazi years as adults or adolescents. But now the reverse is true—the majority of Germans today were either not yet born while Hitler was alive or else were far too young to have possibly been involved in any Nazi crimes. So unless one applies Hitlerian criteria of inherent national (or racial, as he would have said) traits, one must acquit all but the older generation of Germans from having been involved in Nazism in any way.

It is understandable, if deplorable, that the generation that supported Hitler does not like to be reminded of that fact and tries to ignore the issue by refusing to face it. This unwillingness to overcome the past by trying to understand it also applied, at least during the early years after World War II, to the period before Hitler. Most foreign books about Germany, especially those written during the war, described the Germans as innately aggressive and presented Hitler as the last link in a long chain that included every national hero of the past, from Luther to Bismarck. For a German to write anything that would support such sweeping and simplistic indictments was condemned as "fouling one's own nest." When one of Germany's leading historians, Professor Fritz Fischer of Hamburg University, argued in the early 1960s that the two world wars, in their origins and aims, did prove a certain continuity in German history, he caused a major scandal, at least among his older colleagues. But

Fischer performed a valuable service, because since then a younger generation of historians has not been afraid to ask embarrassing questions about Germany's past. As a result some of the nation's traditional idols have tarnished, monuments have disappeared, and streets have been renamed; on the other hand, there are still many great men and women, especially outside the realm of politics, of whom the German people can justly be proud.

Most books on the "German problem" by outsiders, at least before 1945, were highly critical or outright hostile, with American authors contributing their share. The Germans themselves during that time made few attempts at self-examination or self-criticism. But the Nazi experience changed this, and now a number of Germans are making laudable efforts to understand themselves. Most critics of the German character emphasize its negative qualities, which a German writer has summarized as follows:

1. The Germans are inconsiderate toward the weak. 2. The Germans have much pity with themselves but little with others; love of humanity is alien to them. 3. The Germans are arrogant as long as they can get away with it; if they can't, arrogance changes to servile submissiveness. 4. The Germans glorify war. 5. The Germans live in extremes: hare-brained idealism or crassest materialism, uninformed stupor or overbred intellectualism. 6. Germans do not know real freedom, and they do not want it. 7. The Germans will never become democrats, but will always remain subjects.*

Nobody, of course, would claim that all Germans have shared all these traits at all times. But even the casual visitor to Germany will find evidence of some of them, and the Germans themselves admit that they are at least half true. The argument often made by their defenders, that other nations have similar or worse faults, is beside the point, as is the assertion that the Germans also have a number of admirable qualities, which no one would deny.

Still, the assignment of individual characteristics to a whole nation is open to the obvious criticism that it is wholly subjective, impressionistic, and impossible to prove. In an effort to reach more valid conclusions, social scientists since 1945 have used public opinion polls to test people's self-evaluation and have used the data thus obtained to gain insights into national character. In general these tests have shown that people's opinions of themselves change over the course of time and that national character, as already suggested,

* Rudolf Walter Leonhardt, *X-mal Deutschland* (Munich, 1961), pp. 15–18.

also changes. But self-evaluation polls undertaken on a cross-cultural level in six nations, including Germany, have also shown striking variations between the self-image of Germans and that of the other nations, findings that confirm that there is something special or peculiar about the Germans, that they *are* different.

Rather than saddle the Germans with an inherent and un-alterable national character, it would be more just and correct to say that they show certain characteristic patterns of behavior that differ from those of other peoples. But one must distinguish between out-ward customs and inner traits and remember that what is "normal" and good manners in one country may be considered bad manners, or cause ridicule, in another. "Typically German" behavior, such as the constant shaking of hands or the insistence on closing doors, is no more baffling to Americans than the obverse American customs are to Germans. Nor are the Germans in these respects very different from most other Europeans. While the Germans admittedly are among the world's rudest drivers, the French are hardly models of amiability. There are signs, actually, that some of the ingrained habits of the Germans, the incessant handshaking for instance, are giving way to more informal ways, changes that some observers at-tribute to American influence. Certainly the Germans today are far less rigid and more easygoing than their fathers were, though it remains to be seen how deep and lasting these changes will be.

In Germany as everywhere else, the institution that molds a person's character and influences his behavior most is the family. The traditional picture of the German family, an authoritarian father lording it over a submissive wife and a brood of browbeaten children, is today pretty much a thing of the past. There are several reasons for this democratization of German family life, one of which is the long absence or death of many fathers in the war. More impor-tant, perhaps, has been the feeling of guilt or shame for their Nazi past on the part of the older generation vis-à-vis the younger, which could not help but damage the authority of parents in the eyes of their children.

The absolute legal guarantee of equal rights for women has also played its part, although the actual implementation of women's rights has been less thorough in West Germany than in the East; the German Democratic Republic is far more progressive in this respect than the Federal Republic or, for that matter, the United States. Many women in the West and a large majority in the East hold paying jobs, which has further helped to change the family from a father-dominated, authoritarian institution into a more equal partnership.

As a result of these various factors, family life in modern Germany is not very different from that in the United States. In both countries much of the tenor of that life is determined by the teenage children and their tastes. One long-standing characteristic, however, German families have not lost: they are still quite self-centered and exclusive toward outsiders, less so than the French, but far more than the outgoing Americans. Judging by the divorce rate, which, although rising, is less than half that of the United States, German families are also more stable. The fact that until recently most Germans did not marry until their late twenties may have something to do with this.

Next to the family, the second most important character-forming institutions are the schools. Here there have also been many changes since 1945, although in the opinion of some Germans they have not gone far enough or been always for the better. Attempts at educational reform, at least in West Germany, are complicated by that country's federal constitution, which leaves education in the hands of the Länder. German education in the past has often been criticized for its elitism, with secondary and university training reserved for the middle and upper classes, and for its ethnocentrism, with Germany's history and *Kultur* dominating the curriculum. In both respects the situation has been much improved, though there are some important differences between the two republics. Although secondary education of some kind has been opened to all children in both Germanies, the quality and length of such education in the East is more uniform than it is in the West. At the university level in West Germany, only 5 or 6 percent of the students come from working-class families, compared to close to 40 percent in East Germany. As far as making education more democratic, especially at the top, the East German Republic thus holds a decided lead. In the West, on the other hand, the curriculum is broad, liberal, and cosmopolitan, not different from other western countries, but in the East it is narrow, science- and technology-oriented and, of course, Marxist. Nevertheless, in the sciences and related fields talented young East Germans can gain as good an education as their West German counterparts.

Because of their traditional role in German life, the universities deserve some additional comments. During the nineteenth century, the German universities commanded universal respect. They served as models for institutions of higher learning everywhere, especially in the United States. Since then their reputation has declined, especially as a result of the Nazi years. Within Germany, however, a university professor still enjoys tremendous prestige and ranks at the top of the social and economic ladder. All German universities are graduate schools; there are no colleges of the American or British type; and all of the universities are state institutions.

In the past the states usually allowed the universities to run their internal affairs, and there were few major conflicts between politicians and academicians. As was the case with most other German organizations until recently, the university was organized along hierarchical lines and run in an authoritarian fashion. It was an academic oligarchy in which full professors wielded virtually absolute power over appointments, promotions, curricula, and examinations. For more than twenty years after 1945, this state of affairs continued; then came the revolution.

The academic unrest in Germany in the late sixties and early seventies was part of a worldwide movement, and as such it had much in common with similar outbreaks in other western countries (there was little or no unrest in East Germany). The main academic target of the protesters, who as elsewhere constituted a minority within the student body, was the full professor, or *Ordinarius*. Giving way to mounting disruption and violence, most of the Länder finally made far-reaching and long-overdue academic changes, the most important of which concerned university governance. Although the situation differed from Land to Land, most adopted a system under which universities were run jointly by the full professors, the lower academic ranks, students, and employees, with the professors, who formerly exercised sole control, in the minority. The German inclination to go from one extreme to the other had thus won another victory. The results of this academic revolution were mixed. On the one hand, the influx of fresh blood and the reform of curricula relieved some of the stuffiness of the German academic scene. But on the other hand, the breakdown of discipline, together with vastly increased enrollments, seriously interfered with the universities' major functions of teaching and research and in general tended to lower academic standards. It took some time for German academic life to adjust to the changes so suddenly thrust upon it (see chapter 10).

Two institutions that once were influential in every German's life, the army and the churches, today have lost much of their significance. As we have seen, among the various characteristics attributed to the Germans, love of things military was one of the chief traits. The eradication of "Prussian militarism," therefore, was one of the prime Allied aims after World War II. As it turned out, however, there was not much left to eradicate: German militarism evaporated almost overnight, as the German people at long last had the bitter lessons of two lost wars driven home to them.

I shall discuss later the revival of the German army, largely under American pressure, during the 1950s. At that time it was feared by many non-Germans that with such an army, the specter of militarism might rise again. But thanks to the conscious efforts by the organizers of the Bundeswehr to make it truly a force of civilians in uniform and under civilian control, and because of the genuine pacifism of Germany's young, militarism today is definitely a dead issue, at least in the West. In the East where an attempt has been made to tie the Nationale Volksarmee to the more glorious phase of Germany's military past, such as the wars of liberation against Napoleon in the early nineteenth century, the younger generation is still being taught some of the so-called positive virtues of militarism— discipline, obedience, and courage. The eastern Volksarmee, as a result, is far more reminiscent of Hitler's Wehrmacht than is the western Bundeswehr.

When I said that the churches no longer played a large role in the life of the individual German, it does not mean that they have suffered a radical decline in membership. In the Federal Republic, some 95 percent of the population are still church members, about 50 percent Catholics and 45 percent Protestants; in the East the figures are roughly 10 percent Catholics and 80 percent Protestants. Since there is no separation of church and state, all Germans have to pay a church tax (about 10 percent of their total income tax), from which they are released only upon special application, a step few Germans have been ready to take. When it comes to participation in church affairs, however, the figures are far from impressive. It is estimated that only about half of the Catholics still go to church with any regularity, and for Protestants the number is only 20 percent in the West and still lower in the East. In the past relations between the two confessions in Germany have always been tense, more so than in any country except Ireland. But this mutual acrimony is much less today, and marriages between Catholics and Protestants are on the increase. During the Empire and the Weimar Republic, German Catholics had their own Center Party to protect their interests. Efforts to revive that party after 1945 were unsuccessful, and instead a new party emerged, the Christian Democratic Union (CDU), which is backed by both confessions. When it comes to assigning government positions, however, an elaborate proportional system is followed, a sign that the awareness of religious differences is still strong. There also are still parochial schools in all the

Länder. In East Germany, there has been a noticeable decline in the observance of the basic Christian rituals of baptism, communion or confirmation, and marriage, for each of which the state provides substitute ceremonies; only Christian burial is still the rule, probably as a kind of reinsurance.

One of the touchiest problems faced by both churches concerns their none-too-creditable role during the Nazi regime. Although there were individual heroic acts of resistance among the rank and file, the leaders, especially of the Catholics, opposed the regime only when church interests were at stake. For a while after 1945 it was hoped that the misery and despair of the early postwar years might spur a religious revival. But the everyday struggle for survival, followed by growing affluence, diverted people's attention to more worldly concerns. German Protestantism, in an effort to overcome the existing division among three separate confessions and some twenty-seven state churches, formed the united Evangelical Church in Germany (EKD) in 1945. Until the late 1960s, the EKD covered all of Germany, East as well as West, thus constituting the sole remaining bond between the two states, but this tie was severed in 1969. While it is clear that both the Catholic and the Protestant churches have lost their former hold over their members, as organizations they continue to thrive, disposing of vast funds for charitable purposes in Germany and in underdeveloped countries.

Compared to the large number of at least nominal Christians, the Jews in Germany have always been a tiny minority. When Hitler came to power in 1933, Germany's 564,000 Jews constituted less than 1 percent of the total population, and today there are only about 30,000 Jews left, most of them in the West. The Federal Republic has tried to atone for the atrocities committed against the Jews under Hitler by indemnifying the few survivors and by paying substantial reparations to the state of Israel. The East Germans, though they deny any responsibility for Hitler's crimes, also pay a modest pension to their small number of Jews. But no amount of money can ever compensate for mass murder, and even though the majority of Germans today are clearly innocent of the crimes committed or acquiesced in by their elders, relations between Gentiles and Jews remain delicate.

German anti-Semitism, its history and causes, has been the subject of numerous studies to determine why this universal disease took such particularly virulent forms in Germany. There is no doubt that Hitler had much to do with it, since hatred of the Jews was his most absorbing and abiding passion. But his hatred must have struck a sympathetic chord among many Germans, and the rest must have somehow been inured against feeling moral outrage at the crimes committed in their name. The latent nonviolent anti-Semitism of German society before Hitler may have contributed to this insensitivity, as may also some of the German characteristics mentioned above—lack of consideration for the weak and inability to feel pity or compassion for others. There is probably no more, but also no less, anti-Semitism in Germany today than in most other countries. That such nonviolent anti-Semitism may provide a ready soil for the more violent Hitlerian variety and that any kind of anti-Semitism is evil and immoral is a realization that unfortunately is still far from general, not only in Germany.

One point I wish to make in this admittedly impressionistic account of today's Germans is that they are quite different from what they were in 1945 and that in many ways they are not unlike other people, including Americans. There was a time when it was easy to spot a German. But today, except when they travel in large groups abroad (where German tourists are as unpopular as American ones), it is difficult to recognize a German until he opens his mouth. The ideal German, of course, blond and blue-eyed, was a figment of Hitler's imagination. Germany, it has rightly been said, is the melting pot of Europe. Even dress no longer reveals German origin, except among the older generation. Germans have always liked being taken for something else, preferably Americans, and today they quite often succeed.

Yet even though the Germans have changed in many ways, they have remained the same in others. One thing most Americans miss in everyday German life is an intuitive feeling for democracy. Germany has always been a hierarchical class society, where everyone "knew his place." Thanks to the ruinous and leveling effects of Hitler's Third Reich, that has changed, and there now exists a genuine opportunity for social mobility. Theoretically at least, Germany is an open society. But in practice there are still obstacles, not political, legal, or economic, but psychological, within each German, to an instinctive acceptance of the American truism that everyone is as good as everyone else. The German's belief in social differences makes him subservient to those above him and condescending or arrogant to those below. It manifests itself in many ways: Germans still insist on using titles, not only *Herr Professor* (the most esteemed) or *Herr Doktor* (the most common), but *Herr Generaldirektor, Herr Oberbürgermeister, Herr Intendant,* and so on. They are still impressed by nobility, and a name preceded by *von,* denoting a *Herr Baron,* even outranks a professor.

Germans are very status-conscious, and they do not expect

their betters to do certain tasks, manual labor being the most important. These quirks and customs would not be worth mentioning if they were merely holdovers from an earlier age. But now as then, they are signs of a deeply rooted belief in human inequality. One of its consequences has been a preference among Germans for having decisions made or conflicts solved for them. Social responsibility and good citizenship are not among the individual German's outstanding virtues.

Another German characteristic often noted by Americans is formality in everyday social intercourse. The German language makes a distinction between the formal *Sie* (you) and the informal *Du* (thou), and the change from *Sie* to *Du* is made only after a long and close acquaintance and sometimes even a special ceremony, the "drinking to brotherhood." To be on a first-name basis with Germans is not as difficult as it used to be, but this still means that the first name is coupled with *Sie* rather than *Du*. Friendship to Germans is a serious business, and the readiness with which Americans vault social and personal barriers, calling everyone by first names, is considered insincere, ill-mannered, and *typisch amerikanisch*. The fact that it is a sign of a basically democratic attitude and that it eases human contact and communication is understood only by Germans who have spent some time in America.

But enough of comparing Germans with Americans, especially since such comparisons always imply that Americans are really better. One problem with pinpointing a nation's peculiarities is that the outside visitor will be on the lookout for such peculiarities and, of course, will find plenty of examples. Any German who has been told that Americans are a superficial, crass, and materialistic people can certainly find sufficient evidence to verify his preconceptions. The best way for the people of two countries to become acquainted is not to read about each other but to meet and live together for awhile. For such contacts the many German-American exchange programs offer ample opportunities.

Even though I have tried as much as possible in this chapter to speak of Germany as a whole, that is, the two Germanies, my emphasis throughout has been on West rather than East Germany because Americans have most contact with the Federal Republic. For the first twenty-five years of its existence, the Democratic Republic kept itself hermetically sealed against the West. Even with the subsequent easing of restrictions, its government does not yet and probably never will permit the free access and close personal contacts that prevail in the West. The few American visitors to East Germany in its early days brought back accounts of a somber, gray, and gloomy country, where time seemed to have stood still and one could imagine oneself back in the 1920s, "an open-air museum of the German past." They told of a country where soldiers and bureaucrats ruled over a silent and hard-working people and where fun and laughter had ceased to exist.

All this has changed. While the German Democratic Republic still cannot compare with its sparkling and prosperous western counterpart, it has the highest living standard among Russia's eastern satellites and holds eighth place among the world's industrial nations. Its people, the majority of whom have never known anything but a divided Germany, have grown used to the restrictions of a socialized economy in which lack of freedom is compensated for by economic security. In some areas, as I have shown, conditions in East Germany are better than in the West, notably in education, women's rights, and social services such as health care. Most observers agree that the majority of East Germans today are loyal citizens of their country and would not leave it permanently even if they were permitted to, because, after all, it is their *Heimat*.

I shall have more to say on how the division of Germany came about after World War II and how the Soviet zone or the so-called DDR, as West Germans and Americans used to call the German Democratic Republic, became a full-fledged and internationally recognized sovereign state. The question I should like to consider here is whether, aside from being a separate state, East Germany has also become a separate nation, with its own feeling of national identity.

For almost twenty-five years after World War II, the question of German reunification was the most important issue not only between East and West Germany, but between the eastern and the western powers in general. During those years, the de facto separation of the two Germanies proceeded step by step. The zonal border soon became literally an iron curtain, as mine fields, barbed wire, and death strips made it the most impassable frontier in Europe. Its 841 miles cut through more than thirty railway lines and major highways and through hundreds of secondary roads. Only nine roads and railroad crossings, plus three air corridors, were left open for travel between West Germany and Berlin. Access to the former capital, as we shall see, became one of the hottest issues in the cold war. Before 1961, when the East German government built the notorious Berlin Wall, more than two and a half million East Germans escaped to the West via West Berlin. In retrospect, the building of the wall was the most important single event in the final partition of Germany. It allowed the DDR to complete its transformation into the first German socialist state, as it proudly calls itself, and to rally the majority of East Germans to its support.

Relations between East and West Germany have undergone a noticeable change since the early postwar years. As long as both parts of Germany were equally miserable, there was great concern among West Germans for their brethren in the East who had fallen under communist rule. This concern continued as West Germany became more and more prosperous in the early 1950s, and a constant stream of food and other packages went from West to East. Visits back and forth were restricted to family business, and until the mid-1970s only pensioners and invalids received permission from the East German authorities to visit the Federal Republic. In time, as the contrast between the two Germanies, so evident in the glitter of West Berlin and the drabness of the eastern sector, became more and more glaring, the East Germans began to resent the self-satisfied and condescending ways of their western relatives who after all had many advantages, such as American aid, which the East had never enjoyed. Government propaganda did its share to reinforce this all-too-human reaction. The constant stream of eastern refugees prior to 1961, meanwhile, tended to bolster the West's feeling of superiority. For those remaining behind, the hope of possible escape made life in the virtual prison of East Germany somehow more endurable.

The construction of the Berlin Wall killed that hope once and for all. But it also enabled the rulers of East Germany to ease some of their restrictions and to allow their people to enjoy some of the fruits of their hard work. A marked improvement in the East German economy, furthermore, showed that such work was finally paying off. The material well-being resulting from these changes could not help but affect the East Germans' attitude toward their state. Pride of achievement brought self-assurance, and this in turn made them more ready to identify with a regime that hitherto had been considered alien. After having been looked down upon for so long by their relatives in the West, the East Germans now felt that they were just as good, if not better. Not only had they proved that their system worked, they had created a society far more open and egalitarian than that of West Germany, made up of citizens who were far less selfish and materialistic than their western counterparts. Whether this self-image is true or not, the fact that it is believed is an important step on the road to a distinct East German national consciousness.

A thirty-year separation and widely differing political, economic, and social systems have thus inevitably brought about not only two German states, but two German peoples as well. Until the early 1970s this split was still thought of as temporary. Since then, however, most Germans on both sides have come to accept it as permanent. Germany is not the only country to be thus cut in two by ideological differences, nor is this the first time that there has been more than one German state. But never before have two states inhabited by Germans differed so widely and deeply as do the Federal and Democratic Republics today.

Whether there now exists a national consciousness in East Germany strong enough to counteract any surviving feelings of loyalty to a common German past is difficult to say. Observers who know the country say that there is such an awareness, and there are signs that the government is trying to foster it. One thing is certain; the confident expectation held for many years, especially by Americans, that if free elections were held in the German Democratic Republic tomorrow, a vast majority of the people would opt for the West, is no longer justified and has not been for some time. There have even been some East Germans who, having fled to the West, have become disillusioned by what they found and have returned to the DDR. A country that inspires such loyalty must have more to offer than outsiders can appreciate.

2 | Germany and the United States 1776–1914

TWO HUNDRED YEARS AGO when the United States was born, the region that later became known as Germany was still a collection of hundreds of sovereign territories, large and small, nominally organized as the Holy Roman Empire of the German Nation. Prussia and Austria were the most important members of this decrepit body, and Austria for centuries past had supplied its head. This "First Reich," as Hitler was to call it later, came to an end during the Napoleonic wars in 1806, when the Austrian emperor resigned the old Imperial Crown. At the same time Napoleon abolished most of the smallest territories, thus considerably simplifying the political map and indirectly contributing to the unification of Germany. From 1815 to 1866, what had been the Holy Roman Empire became the German Confederation, or Bund, a loose association of thirty-nine sovereign states, including four free cities, still under the presidency of Austria. In 1866 Austria was excluded from Germany after losing the brief war of that year with Prussia for leadership in German affairs. This left Prussia the dominant state in what was to become the "Second Reich," the German Empire, in 1871.

Relations between the new United States of America and the old disunited states of Germany at first were neither very active nor of great importance to either side. For various reasons the United States was closer to Prussia than to Austria, whose leading figure, Prince Metternich, made no secret of his contempt for the fledgling republic across the Atlantic. In their eagerness to show the contri-

butions made by Germans in founding this country, German writers
have sometimes strained the truth a bit, perpetuating legends or
exaggerating the importance of certain individuals. Americans would
be surprised to learn that the first German to set foot on the North
American continent was Leif Ericson's German foster father, in
1000 A.D. and that, had it not been for a single Congressional vote in
the 1790s, German would have become the official language of the
United States. Other claims are more valid: that it was a German
cartographer, Martin Waldseemüller, who in 1507 referred to the
New World for the first time as America; that Peter Minuit, who
bought Manhattan from the Indians in 1626, was born in Germany,
though he was probably of Walloon stock. Other legends have grown
up around the supposed mutual admiration between Frederick the
Great of Prussia and George Washington, and the decisive role
played by General von Steuben, to this day the patron saint of an
annual parade in New York City, as "drillmaster of the Continental
Army."

At the time of the American Revolution, an estimated 250,000,
or between 8 and 9 percent, of the colonists were of German descent.
There had been some Germans as early as 1607 among the followers
of Captain John Smith at Jamestown, but the first Germans to
organize permanent settlements in this country were groups from
various persecuted Protestant sects, such as the thirteen Mennonite
families from the Rhenish town of Krefeld, who settled in what
became Germantown, near Philadelphia, in 1683. There were some
noted figures among the early German settlers—Franz Pastorius, the
first burgomaster of Germantown; John Peter Zenger, who as editor
of the *New York Weekly Journal* successfully fought for a free press;
and Jacob Leisler, leader of an abortive insurrection in colonial
New York. The bulk of these first German immigrants settled in
New York, Pennsylvania, Maryland, and Virginia; few of them lived
in New England. During the Revolution most of them were anti-
British, and in the person of Molly Pitcher, née Maria Ludwig, they
supplied one of its folk heroines. The German mercenaries or Hes-
sians who fought on the British side were not colonists, but many of
them became so after the war.

What little intercourse there was at first between the United
States and the Germanies was mostly commercial and did not
amount to much. A trade agreement with Prussia in 1785 remained
stillborn, and subsequent attempts to put economic relations on
a regular basis did not bear fruit until 1828, when trade and nav-
igation treaties were concluded with Prussia and later with the
Hanseatic cities of Bremen and Hamburg. Prussia at that time was

sponsoring a customs union, the Zollverein, within Germany, and in 1844 the United States signed a treaty with that body, but it was not ratified. From the very beginning, American-German commercial exchange was hampered by protectionism on both sides, an obstacle that was to remain a permanent factor in relations between the countries.

The first major political event in Germany that aroused widespread interest on this side of the Atlantic and at least briefly brought the two nations closer was the revolution of 1848. Most of the German states at that time were still under the absolute or authoritarian rule of their various princelings; what parliamentary institutions there were had very little influence. There had already been several local uprisings against these feudal conditions, notably in 1830. As time went on, economic hardships and a growing desire for national unity added to the ferment. When revolutions broke out in other parts of Europe in the spring of 1848, the Germans felt that their day for freedom and unity had come as well. Within a few days in March, and after very little violence, most of Germany's rulers granted constitutions. In May, a popularly elected National Assembly convened in Frankfurt to draft a constitution for a united Germany.

Had the revolution succeeded, Germany's future, and Europe's, would doubtless have been happier. It failed because of lack of unity among its leaders, especially over whether the united Germany they hoped to create should include Austria, and because of the resumption of control, with the aid of their armed forces, by the rulers in Berlin and Vienna. By the time the Frankfurt assembly was ready to offer the crown of a small German (*kleindeutsch*) nation to King Frederick William IV of Prussia, the latter had sufficiently regained his command and conceit to refuse this gift "from the gutter." Historians have looked upon the failure of Germany thus to become united peacefully and democratically as one of the most tragic events in the nation's history.

When news of the revolution in Germany reached the United States, it was greeted with genuine sympathy. The American minister in Berlin, Andrew J. Donelson, illuminated his legation and later represented his government at the provisional central government in Frankfurt. Back home, money was collected to aid the revolutionaries, and a few volunteers went to Germany to fight on the barricades. There even was some debate about American intervention when it became clear that without outside aid the revolution would fail. The Germans very much hoped for such aid, especially to support a brief war they fought with Denmark during the revolution and to build a navy, which was one of the most cherished aims of the Frankfurt assembly. But except for some naval plans and a frigate constructed in Brooklyn, America gave mostly moral support, serving as inspiration and example in the constitutional debates of the Frankfurt parliament. When the revolution had failed by 1849, Americans were clearly disappointed and outspoken in their criticism of the "professors' parliament."

Today the revolution of 1848 is probably best remembered by Americans for the many refugees who found asylum and started a new life in the United States. To be descended from one of these "Forty-Eighters" is almost as good as having an ancestor who came over on the *Mayflower,* though claims to these distinctions are often equally dubious. Between the mid-forties and the mid-fifties, some 750,000 German immigrants entered the United States. Most of them, then as at all times except for the 1930s, came for economic reasons; others came to evade military service. Neither reason entitles them to the nimbus of political martyrdom usually associated with the term Forty-Eighter. The best-known bona fide political refugee was Carl Schurz, who was also the most admirable and certainly the most politically successful.

Few Germans had come to America between the Revolution and the 1820s. Religious persecutions in Germany had long ceased, and economic conditions were not as bad as they became soon after. The long voyage, six weeks or more under slave-ship conditions, and the harshness of pioneer life discouraged all but the most desperate or venturesome. In time a number of books acquainted prospective emigrants and travelers from Germany with what to expect in the New World. Thus began the fertile genre of *Amerikaliteratur,* which is still going strong but has yet to produce anything comparable to what Alexis de Tocqueville and Lord Bryce wrote about the United States. On the whole, these early books painted a far too favorable picture, inevitably causing the new arrivals to be disappointed.

German immigrants came from all parts of Germany, though more from the west than the east. In America, they tended to concentrate in the Middle West—Wisconsin, Illinois, Missouri, and Texas—where they settled in fertile, wooded regions reminiscent of home and stuck pretty much to themselves. In the early part of the nineteenth century, various "New Germany" settlements were planned to preserve the old ways on American soil. Americans of German descent were criticized by their compatriots for resisting Americanization and by their German cousins for becoming *amerikanisch* too fast. One can cite ample evidence to support both assertions. Assimilation was made more difficult as the number of immigrants increased, from 10,000 in 1832 to 215,000 in 1854, the largest annual figure until the record year of 1882, when close to 250,000 Germans came to live in this country. By 1900 more than 27 percent of Americans were of German stock, meaning that at least one of their parents was born in the old country.

What did the old and established Americans think of these newcomers? On the whole the impression was favorable; hard-working, ambitious, frugal, honest, independent—these are some of the qualities attributed to the Germans from that day to this. In contrast to this somewhat severe image, the Germans were also considered to be easygoing, or *gemütlich*, an untranslatable term that usually crops up when Americans speak of Germans—singing songs, drinking beer, and being jolly good fellows. As is often the case, however, these positive characteristics had their negative side. Depending on the eye of the beholder, hard work and ambition could be denounced as materialism, and the enjoyment of simple pleasures, in Puritanical eyes at least, could appear as licentiousness, especially on the Sabbath. Germans in America were often criticized for not assimilating, for continuing to speak their language and for refusing to intermarry. They supposedly thought of themselves as culturally superior, which they were not. The majority of German immigrants came from lowly farming, artisan, and later on, working-class backgrounds. Certainly the Germans in the United States, like other minority groups, including the Irish and Italians, were different from their Anglo-Saxon neighbors. But the fact that they remained so was not entirely their fault.

The increasing rate of immigration during the 1840s, not only from Germany but also from Ireland, gave birth to a nativist reaction in many organizations, subsumed under the term Know-Nothings. This movement reached its height during the early 1850s, just about at the peak of the post-1848 influx. Agitating in favor of Americanism and advocating restrictions on further immigration, the nativist movement forced the Germans in America to defend their rights. Up to this point, they had played hardly any role politically, and they continued to be passive citizens, followers rather than leaders. Few Germans reached high political office, and no person of recent German origin has ever been President. But from the mid-nineteenth century on, the Germans began to use their influence as voters, usually for the Democratic Party, and on issues they felt strongly about, such as the fight against Prohibition. From that time on we can speak of the hyphenated German-American, a term that was to cause much concern and bitterness during World War I. This self-conscious preoccupation with preserving their German heritage, or *Deutschtum,* in their schools, churches, and a proliferating German-language press, was touched off by the nativism of the forties and fifties and gained momentum as the emergence of a powerful empire in Germany gave German-Americans something to be proud of. Germanic nativism, of course, could serve as a potential link between the old country and the new, but in time of tension between the two, as we shall see, it could also appear as a potential threat to the cohesion and security of the United States.

The German-Americans actually proved singularly ineffective as a bridge between their old and adopted countries. For one thing, the German *Kultur* they tried to preserve had a decidedly petit bourgeois and dated quality. In an endless variety of clubs or *Vereine,* devoted to everything from gymnastics and shooting to singing and bowling, the German-Americans kept alive the pastimes their forebears had known rather than keeping up with more modern developments. When they told their families back home about the United States, furthermore, German-Americans rarely painted a realistic picture but instead presented stereotyped descriptions, either of a heaven-on-earth land of boundless opportunities (*Land der unbegrenzten Möglichkeiten*) or of an uncultured, artificial, heartless, and mechanistic society, bent merely on chasing the dollar. Both stereotypes have survived into our own day and have not contributed to better American-German understanding.

The 1860s was a most momentous decade in the history of both the United States and Germany. Both nations underwent major upheavals—the Civil War in America and the wars of unification in Germany—concerning the preservation or creation of national unity. By the time the American Civil War broke out, the nativist movement had split over the slavery issue, and the German-American element had helped elect Abraham Lincoln because he opposed nativism. The role of the German-Americans in the war itself has been overly praised by some German historians, who seem to forget that Americans of German origin had as much reason as other Americans to fight for their nation's unity. Close to 9 percent of the Union Army's enlisted soldiers were German-born, and Carl Schurz served as one of its generals. Sentiment in Germany, meanwhile, favored the North, especially over the slavery issue. Bismarck, whose star in Prussia was rapidly rising, advocated a "benevolent neutrality," influenced, no doubt, by his old friend of some thirty years, the American historian and diplomat John Lothrop Motley.

In 1864 while the United States was still engaged in its fratricidal struggle, the armies of Prussia and Austria invaded the small nation of Denmark. The issue behind the war was a complicated one; who should control the two German duchies of Schleswig and Holstein? The victory of Austria and Prussia left the territories under their joint control, but this solution merely provided added cause for the conflict between the two leading German states that had been going on intermittently for at least fifteen years.

When the king of Prussia had refused the crown offered him by the Frankfurt parliament in 1849, Germany had seemed to return to the prerevolutionary status quo. To be sure, the governments of some of the South German states became a bit more liberal, and even Prussia was given a constitution in 1850. But this document did not seriously curtail the power of the king, especially since a cleverly rigged franchise ensured that the influence of the conservative Junker aristocracy was maintained in the Prussian parliament, or Landtag. In its domestic policy Prussia remained one of the most reactionary states of Germany, but it was also clearly the natural leader in German affairs, at least north of the Main River. Frederick William's refusal of the crown, moreover, did not mean that he was averse to becoming emperor of a united Germany; all he wanted was to be asked by his fellow monarchs to assume that title. When he tried to engineer such an invitation in 1850, however, he was stopped by Austria, Prussia's chief rival.

It was at this point that Otto von Bismarck began to play a prominent part in his country's affairs. This Prussian Junker, then in his mid-thirties, had endeared himself to his king during the recent revolution by his ultraconservatism and outspoken monarchism. During the 1850s Bismarck represented Prussia at the Diet of the German Confederation in Frankfurt, where he frequently clashed with his Austrian colleague. His real influence, however, dated from 1862, when Frederick William's successor, William I, appointed him minister president of Prussia, a position he was to hold for the next twenty-eight years.

The reason for Bismarck's appointment was a governmental crisis that had arisen when the Landtag refused to vote the necessary funds for Prussian army "reforms," designed by King William to make the army even more of a reactionary tool than it already was. In Bismarck, the king hoped to find a man capable of coping with the recalcitrant Landtag, and in this he was not disappointed. Using specious constitutional arguments, Bismarck simply spent unauthorized funds to carry out the army reforms. Later when the Prussian victory over Austria in 1866 seemingly justified his actions, he asked the Landtag for an *ex post facto* indemnity. Bismarck's request put the liberal members of that body in a quandary: their principles

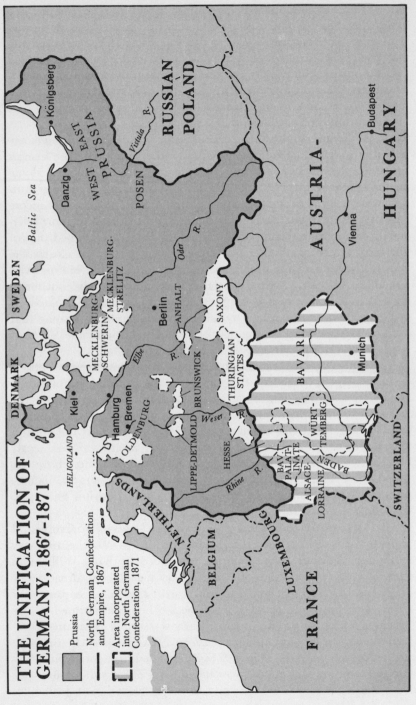

Map 2. *The Unification of Germany, 1867–1871.*

THE UNIFICATION OF
GERMANY, 1867-1871

☐ Prussia

▬ North German Confederation
and Empire, 1867

⬚ Area incorporated
into North German
Confederation, 1871

RUSSIAN POLAND

AUSTRIA-HUNGARY

• Budapest

• Vienna

EAST PRUSSIA

• Königsberg

WEST PRUSSIA

• Danzig

POSEN

Vistula R.

Baltic Sea

SWEDEN

Oder R.

DENMARK

HELIGOLAND

MECKLENBURG-SCHWERIN

MECKLENBURG-STRELITZ

ANHALT

• Berlin

SAXONY

THURINGIAN
STATES

BAVARIA

• Munich

Elbe R.

Kiel •

• Hamburg

• Bremen

BRUNSWICK

Weser R.

OLDENBURG

LIPPE-DETMOLD

HESSE

WÜRT-
TEMBERG

BADEN

BAV.
PALAT-
INATE

ALSACE-
LORRAINE

Rhine R.

NETHERLANDS

BELGIUM

LUXEMBOURG

FRANCE

SWITZERLAND

told them to refuse, but their patriotism urged them to give in. The result was a split in the ranks of Prussian, and later German, liberalism between the truly liberal Progressives and the compromising National Liberals. It was a split that was never healed, either under the Empire or during the Weimar Republic, and as such it perpetuated a deep inner weakness in German politics, which had fateful consequences and explains in part the unhappy course of German history culminating in the rise of Hitler.

If Bismarck's influence in Prussian and German domestic politics was thus far from beneficial, his role as architect of German unity was hailed by German historians, at least until 1945, as his proudest achievement. Since then it has been recognized that unification from below, as the delegates of the Frankfurt parliament had proposed, might have been preferable to the unification from above, by "iron and blood," which was Bismarck's method. I cannot here discuss in detail the manner in which the Prussian statesman's superb diplomacy maneuvered first Austria into war in 1866 and then France in 1870. Since then the question of responsibility for the Franco-Prussian War has been hotly debated by German and French historians. As is usually the case in such controversies, both sides now acknowledge a share of the blame. The final outcome of what the Germans long considered the most glorious period in their history was the founding, in January 1871, of a united German empire, with the king of Prussia as kaiser and Bismarck as chancellor of this "Second Reich."

These stirring events in Germany were watched with fascination by the rest of the world, most of which, including the United States, sympathized with Prussia, at least during the early phase of the war. The completion of a trans-Atlantic cable in 1867 had speeded up transmission of news from Europe, so the American public was able to follow the happenings closely. During the Prussian constitutional conflict, American sympathies had been with the Landtag rather than with the government. But while the Danish and Austro-Prussian wars were going on, the Civil War and its aftermath demanded all of America's attention, and during the crisis leading up to the war of 1870, tension with France and hatred of Napoleon III for his abortive intervention in Mexico put most Americans squarely on Prussia's side. Like many Americans, the American minister in Berlin since 1867, historian George Bancroft, had studied in Germany and was on friendly terms with Bismarck and especially with General Helmuth von Moltke, Prussia's military leader in the wars of unification, who had learned valuable lessons from the American Civil War on the use of railroads and the telegraph in modern war. When France became a republic again during the war, and Germany annexed the once-German, but now pro-French, provinces of Alsace and Lorraine, American sentiment became critical of Germany. But the American government, although it opposed the annexation, did not take an official stand.

The segment of American society most deeply affected by the developments in Germany were the German-Americans. Many of them had deplored the war against Austria as a struggle among Germans. But the war against France, Germany's hereditary foe (*Erbfeind*), was different. Like their relatives in Germany, the German-Americans were swept along on a wave of patriotic enthusiasm powerful enough to make them forget any misgivings they might have had about the victory of reactionary Prussia, not only over France but over the rest of Germany as well. Even the Forty-Eighters, men like Carl Schurz and Friedrich Kapp, cheered on the German armies and gloried in their victories. Some $600,000 was collected among German-Americans for German relief; victory parades and celebrations were held by the Germans in New York, Chicago, and elsewhere; and the German-language press outdid itself in praise for William I, Bismarck, and Moltke.

Not all German-Americans went so wild. Karl Heinzen, Forty-Eighter and radical journalist, referred to Bismarck as a "robber captain" in the employ of a "robber dynasty." "The victory over the hereditary foreign foe," he wrote to a friend in Germany, "has no value for me without a victory over the far greater hereditary foes within, of which the worst is servility." But his was an isolated voice. The majority of German-Americans, having felt inferior for so long, were now swelled with pride and filled with a new sense of importance as bearers of *Kultur* and missionaries of *Deutschtum* in America.

In fairness to the German-Americans who thus hailed the birth of the new Germany, it should be pointed out that many of them expected that nation to become more liberal in its government and more open in its society as time went on. But that hope was never fulfilled. The government that Bismarck gave his Reich may be described as absolutism concealed by a false parliamentary front. There was a popularly elected parliament, the Reichstag, but it had very few powers, and even those, notably over the army's budget, were often curtailed or circumvented. The main governmental power was vested in a federal council, or Bundesrat, made up of delegations from the various member states of the empire, according to population, which naturally assured the predominance of Prussia.

Executive power was given to a chancellor, until 1890 Bismarck, who was responsible only to the emperor. Ministerial responsibility to parliament was unknown in Germany. The main source of the emperor's and chancellor's power rested in their dual roles. The emperor was also king of Prussia, and the chancellor as a rule was also Prussia's minister president and as such Prussia's chief delegate to the Bundesrat. The emperor was supreme commander of the army; he appointed the chancellor, dissolved the Reichstag, declared war, formulated the nation's foreign policy, and filled high civil and military positions. The only way the Reichstag could make its influence felt was by debating, amending, or occasionally refusing to pass, the legislation put before it. Such limited tasks did not encourage the more able Germans to go into politics. In Prussia, as we saw earlier, the situation was still worse, because of the antiquated franchise adopted in 1850.

Yet the Reichstag, despite its weakness, was necessary for the orderly conduct of government, and Bismarck had to use much skill to assure himself of its support. Because no party ever achieved an absolute majority, coalitions were formed of two or more parties. The major parties in the German Empire from right to left were the Conservatives, the National Liberals, the Center Party, the Progressives, and the Social Democrats (SPD). The two parties Bismarck felt closest to most of the time were the Conservatives and the National Liberals. If those two groups had seen eye to eye on crucial issues, the task of Bismarck and his successors would have been easy. But because the Conservatives largely represented agrarian, and the National Liberals, industrial interests, their aims were often deeply antagonistic. The government could win their support only by making concessions to both, usually at the expense of the rest, that is the majority, of the population.

I cannot go into the details of the empire's domestic history here. It is important to understand, however, that its undemocratic system of government helped to discourage many Germans, but not all, from becoming politically active. Two groups in particular, the Catholics and the workers, who were singled out for persecution by Bismarck, struck back by forming the two best-organized parties in the empire. The Catholic Center Party arose in response to the so-called *Kulturkampf* (cultural struggle) of the 1870s, in which Bismarck tried to assert the power of the state against the Catholic Church. In time that party achieved great influence as a much-sought-after coalition partner by both right and left. The workers' party, the SPD, was radically Marxist in theory but moderate in practice. It was made the victim of governmental oppression in the 1880s, only to emerge stronger than ever in the 1890s. By 1912 it had become the country's leading party. Meanwhile the subjection of Germany's two largest minorities to official ostracism severely weakened the inner fabric of the Bismarckian Reich. The failure of his and successive governments to give the growing middle and working classes their due influence in the country's political affairs goes far to explain democracy's failure to take root in Germany.

While Bismarck's domestic policy is now generally recognized even in Germany as a major misfortune, his foreign policy is still accorded widespread admiration. Its keynote after 1871 was peace, not because the iron chancellor had suddenly turned pacifist, but because peace was what Germany needed to complete its process of unification and integration. I am here concerned mainly with the relations between the new German Empire and the United States, which during the 1870s were decidedly cordial. There was a noticeable shift in America's attitude toward Germany from a feeling of somewhat condescending benevolence to one of respect and even admiration. For the moment, Germany seemed the more important of the two. In an age when great-power status was still judged primarily by military and naval strength, the United States clearly belonged in the minor league, although there was little doubt that its vast economic resources destined it to a major role in world affairs. Both countries faced many of the same problems, stepped-up industrialization, rapid population growth, increased urbanization; and both were preoccupied with domestic affairs, the United States repairing the injuries of the Civil War and Germany learning to live as a united country.

Bismarck had considerable liking for America, which is surprising in view of his conservative background. I have mentioned his friendship with the historians turned diplomats, Motley and Bancroft, and he got on well with most other American diplomats. Bismarck even managed to charm Carl Schurz, who paid him two visits and came away much impressed. The chancellor did not approve of German emigration. "A German who discards his fatherland like an old coat," he told the Reichstag in 1884, "is for me no longer a German," but he recognized that the Germans in America presented a potential link and tried to remain on good terms with them.

There were more German-Americans than ever before, and the number continued to grow. More than two million Germans left the Vaterland during the twenty years after 1871, mainly for economic reasons. After a brief initial boom, depression had hit the German Empire, as well as the rest of the world, in 1873. An agrarian crisis in the eastern part of Germany further swelled the ranks of emigrants hoping for a farm of their own on the other side of the Atlantic under the provisions of the Homestead Act of 1862. Until the mid-eighties, this constant stream of immigrants was welcomed in America because most of them brought along not only their savings, but also a variety of skills. Only when economic crises hit the United States were there voices, especially among American labor, demanding the restriction of immigration. Certainly the vast majority of German immigrants continued to add greatly to American life. Some of their former countrymen back home actually began to deplore the loss of these valuable human assets, and various schemes were discussed in Germany for curtailing emigration or directing it to areas such as southern Brazil, where the German element seemed to maintain its identity better than in the United States. Although assimilation of Germans into American life had earlier been very slow, it now proceeded very rapidly, and the new arrivals overcame the stigma that clung to anyone who was not "100 percent American."

It is probably true that during this period Germany contributed far more to the United States than the other way around, not only by sending over millions of hard-working and thrifty new citizens, but intellectually, by providing inspiration and artists for the first American symphony orchestras and operas and by introducing German educational methods and practices to this country. To this day the term kindergarten commemorates the German origin of that institution, first established over here by Mrs. Carl Schurz in 1856. At the other end of the educational spectrum, the founding of Johns Hopkins University in 1876 introduced the German system of graduate education, later adopted by all major American universities. Since the beginning of the nineteenth century, it had been common for American academics to spend some time at a German university, and German professors had come to teach at American institutions. These academic relations continued; if there had been similar exchanges in the political sector, much subsequent misunderstanding between the two nations could have been avoided.

Beginning in the 1880s official relations between the United States and Germany became more active and foreshadowed some of their later difficulties. The most important areas of conflict between the two countries lay in commercial and colonial affairs. Both nations were entering an era of intensive industrialization, but while the United States enjoyed the advantages of abundant land, ample raw materials, and a vast domestic market, which it jealously guarded by protective tariffs, Germany was territorially restricted, less generously endowed with natural resources, and had a burgeoning population. Increasingly it depended on foreign trade to keep its industries going and to feed its workers. America's commercial relations with Germany continued to be guided by the trade agreement concluded with Prussia in 1828. But from the beginning there had been constant bickering over that treaty's reciprocity and most-favored-nation provisions, and these controversies became more frequent as time went on.

One of Bismarck's most significant acts was the introduction of the German protective tariff of 1879. Its main purpose was to shield Prussia's agrarian lords, the Junkers, from the competition of lower-priced agricultural goods from abroad. The result was a rise in German food prices, which hit the working class disproportionately hard. The American commodities primarily affected by German protectionism were wheat and meat, especially pork. When the German government stopped all imports of salt pork in 1883, tension between the two countries ran high and threatened to escalate into an all-out tariff war. The Germans, not without justification, cited inadequate American meat inspection as the reason for the ban. But American critics (among them many German-American farmers), also with some justification, saw the ban as an effort to kill American competition. The fact that the pork crisis coincided with a political incident involving Bismarck did not help matters. In early 1884 Eduard Lasker, a prominent Reichstag deputy and ardent opponent of Bismarck, died while on a speaking tour in the United States, and the United States House of Representatives sent its condolences to the German parliament. But Bismarck, in a not unusual fit of personal pique, refused to relay the message, thus causing considerable resentment among influential Americans. The pork crisis was not settled until after the United States adopted more comprehensive regulation of meat inspection in 1890. The simultaneous passage of the McKinley Tariff, however, opened up another front in the never-ending conflict between American and German economic interests.

In 1889 Germany, the United States, and Britain settled their ten-year-long feud over the Samoan Islands in the Pacific by agreeing on a tripartite protectorate for the area; the arrangement was changed to outright partition ten years later. Bismarck initially had opposed colonial ventures for Germany, but for various political and economic reasons, he changed his mind. In 1883 Germany began extending protection to its traders and missionaries in those parts of Africa and the Pacific that were not yet claimed by other powers. From that time on, Germany's clamor for a greater share of the world's colonial riches became a major cause of international tension. The United States was not worried over Germany's colonial ambitions in Africa, but in the Pacific, as the imbroglio over Samoa showed, the situation was different. The most sensitive area for the United States was the Western Hemisphere; German commercial expansion in South America and recurrent rumors of Germany's desire to obtain a naval station in the Caribbean caused growing concern. It was not until the turn of the century, however, that conflicting interests in the Pacific and South America led to direct confrontation between the two countries.

The dismissal of Bismarck in 1890 was a momentous event in the history of Germany and of Europe. It came about because the chancellor and his new emperor, William II, did not see eye to eye on a number of key issues in domestic and foreign affairs, and because the kaiser wanted to be his own chancellor. William, in his early thirties, had succeeded his father, Frederick III in 1888, when the latter died after ruling for only three months. Frederick had had a somewhat liberal reputation, and his death was seen as a major tragedy by Bismarck's Progressive opponents. William was anything but a liberal. More than any of his Hohenzollern forebears, William II believed that he was monarch by divine right and insisted on proudly proclaiming that belief on every possible occasion. He was an intelligent man of great charm, but he was also impetuous, loud-mouthed, and unstable. These latter qualities determined his public image and, by association, the image of his country as well.

Germany under William II remained as politically backward as it had been under his grandfather. Political reforms in the direction of more representative government were never undertaken, and as more and more people moved to urban areas, the equal franchise in Reichstag elections in fact became increasingly unequal. The men who succeeded Bismarck were well-meaning and less domineering or autocratic than the old chancellor had been, but they were also less able. The army continued to hold the central place in German society and politics, but it too was far from democratic. Socialists and Jews were barred from the officer corps, the upper ranks of which remained the preserve of the aristocracy. The kaiser's inordinate love of uniforms and his penchant for saber-rattling speeches strengthened the impression abroad of German militarism. Beginning in 1898 William II charged one of his most able advisers, Admiral Alfred von Tirpitz, with preparing plans for a vast expansion of the German navy, a project that could not help but alarm Britain as well as the United States.

More than in most countries, the chief preoccupation of Wilhelmian Germany was foreign affairs. Bismarck had been aware that the French would never forget their defeat of 1870–71 and would not rest until they had regained Alsace-Lorraine. He had tried to find security for his empire by keeping France diplomatically isolated through an intricate web of secret alliances and treaties so complicated that only the old master diplomat could hold it together. When he left, this web gradually came apart, and Germany, formerly the diplomatic center of Europe, found *itself* isolated. In 1914 on the eve of World War I, the only ally on whom Germany could fully rely was Austria-Hungary. Italy, though still nominally tied to these two powers, had long been veering to the rival camp organized by France. The French, to be sure, also had only one firm ally, Czarist Russia. But France and Russia were much more closely tied to England than their mere entente with that country seemed to imply.

The main task of German diplomacy during the Wilhelmian period should have been to find a *modus vivendi* with Britain, and efforts in this direction were made from both sides at the turn of the century and again before 1914. But there were a number of obstacles to an Anglo-German understanding, including commercial rivalry as Germany began to compete with Britain in areas where the latter had enjoyed a monopoly. There were political squabbles as Germany tried to use Britain's colonial crises, especially in South Africa, to win concessions for itself, which the British denounced as blackmail. And most important there was naval rivalry, as the shining new German fleet became a factor to be reckoned with in a future war. From Germany's point of view, there was no reason why it, as a great power, should not have a naval force commensurate with its strength. But as the British saw it, Germany did not need a navy straining its already tight military budget, unless it was intended some day to be used against Britain. Ironically, Germany's leaders felt that the potential threat of a large navy would make the British that much more eager to seek their friendship; they forgot that friendship does not exactly thrive in a climate of fear.

Knowing what happened in 1914, we tend to look at Germany before World War I primarily as a nation getting ready for the great showdown. To be sure, as one crisis gave way to the next in the Far East, Africa, and the Balkans, the thought of war began to permeate the international atmosphere. But we must also realize that the Germans at the time, although feared as warmongers, were much admired and envied as a people who excelled in virtually every field of human endeavor. Economically, Germany was rapidly catching up with and in some areas even surpassing Britain's traditional industrial and commercial leadership. German science and technology were acknowledged to be superior to those of any country except perhaps the United States. The German provisions for social welfare started under Bismarck were perfected under William II and served as a model for the rest of the world. German culture, always rich and varied because of its many regional centers, continued to thrive and in music at least remained unchallenged. Even the much-feared and maligned Prusso-German army was secretly admired and imitated, and it was agreed that the Prussian general staff had no equal.

If with all these achievements the Germans sometimes seemed bumptious, overbearing, and arrogant, we must remember that they had much to be proud of. The years before 1914 were the most intensely nationalistic in European history; although the Germans at times suffered from an overdose of *Hurrapatriotismus,* Britain had its jingoism and France its chauvinism. There were many similarities between Germany and the United States. Both nations were *nouveau riche* in every sense of that term; both were vibrantly alive and felt that the future belonged to them. The Germans differed in feeling that the world owed them something, that as latecomers they had missed out on many of the good things they were entitled to. Envy, which has been seen as one of Germany's national characteristics, can be a powerful motive in international affairs.

The ten years between 1895 and 1905 witnessed the climax of what has been called the new imperialism, that is, the scramble by nearly all the major countries for control of the few remaining colonial areas of the world. Conflicting interests during these years caused at least five wars involving one or two of the great powers and led to endless confrontations short of war, several between the United States and Germany. Continued commercial differences and disagreements did much to poison the air between the two. American tariff legislation during the 1890s was particularly harmful to German sugar interests, which led the German government to retaliate with renewed restrictions on the import of American livestock and meat. There were many other petty forms of discrimination, more by Germany against the United States than vice versa; when all was said and done, however, trade between the two nations increased rather than decreased in value, and Germany in particular was heavily dependent on imports of American oil, cotton, and foodstuffs.

It is against this background of continuous commercial squabbles that we must see the various colonial clashes between the United States and Germany, the most serious of which occurred during the Spanish-American War. That confrontation grew out of the simultaneous presence of American and German naval squadrons in Manila Bay at the time of the American assault on the Philippines. The Germans were not the only outsiders present; there were also British, French, and Japanese warships. But the German contingent was the largest, at least matching the American, and relations between its commander, Vice Admiral Otto von Diederichs, and America's Commodore George Dewey, while correct, were far from cordial. The Germans were there to see if they could pick up any Spanish possessions that the Americans did not want. But to the American press and public, Germany's intentions appeared more sinister, and it was chiefly because of American public opinion that a mere episode escalated into an international incident. Contemporary rumors claimed that America was saved from a German stab in the back only when Britain's Captain Chichester moved his ships between Diederichs and Dewey.

The Manila events brought relations between the United States and Germany to their most critical state thus far. The German ambassador in Washington reported that his was the country most hated by Americans, and Admiral Dewey was convinced that America's next war would be with Germany. Another aftereffect of the Manila Bay affair was that America's strained relations with Germany were balanced by a marked improvement in American-British relations. The British government had made clear its intention to do nothing that would displease the United States, and the British people, in contrast to the Germans, had wholeheartedly supported the American war effort. Half a year after the Manila incident, American-German estrangement continued in the Samoan crisis, which led in 1899 to the partition of the islands between the two countries, with Britain compensated elsewhere. That crisis further drew the United States and Britain together. America's secretary of state, John Hay, who until recently had been ambassador in London, was ardently pro-British and anti-German, which helped to turn America more and more away from Germany and toward England.

In 1900 there was a native Chinese uprising, the Boxer Rebellion, against the foreign legations in Peking, which many Americans blamed on the protectorate that Germany had established over the Shantung Peninsula the year before. A joint expedition sent by the great powers to put down the Chinese was criticized in the United States for its harshness, most of the blame going to the German contingent and its leader, Field Marshal Count Waldersee. The kaiser's admonition to the departing German soldiers, "Give no quarter, spare nobody, take no prisoners . . . Be as terrible as Attila's Huns," seemed to support this charge. It also presented the world with its favorite epithet for the Germans, Huns, which became very popular during World War I.

Many of the accusations and suspicions against Germany during these crisis-ridden years were unjustified, such as the rumor that the Germans put pressure on the Danes in 1902 not to sell the Virgin Islands to the United States. But as far as Germany was concerned, the American public seemed increasingly ready to believe the worst. This was demonstrated again during the Venezuelan crisis of 1902–1903, when the United States protested against a joint blockade by British, German, and Italian warships to support the claims of European creditors against that South American republic. The Germans bombarded Venezuelan ports and sunk some gunboats. But the storm of anti-German indignation that swept the American public and press was chiefly inspired by the fear that the Germans might try to gain a foothold near the projected Panama Canal. Even so, it was curious and unjust that American anger should have been directed so exclusively against Germany.

The German government was naturally concerned about its worsening relations with the United States. Efforts to mend fences by sending the kaiser's brother, Prince Henry, on a visit to America and by urging Washington to accept the gift of a statue of Frederick the Great failed to have the desired effect. The statue of the Prussian king was hardly a statue of liberty. Again and again Germany's ambassador, Speck von Sternburg, who was on most cordial terms with Theodore Roosevelt, wishfully thought that relations were improving. But he had to admit that the Manila affair had created "a latent animosity, and it will take a long time before this disappears." It was not until the Russo-Japanese War in 1904–1905 that relations improved, at least on the official level, because of the kaiser's support of Roosevelt's mediation efforts. During the subsequent crisis between Germany and France over Morocco, however, the president's role at the Algeciras conference in 1906, while outwardly neutral, in reality favored Germany's opponents, which the Germans failed, or did not want, to understand.

Some historians have seen a close connection between the American-German estrangement before 1914 and the simultaneous American-British rapprochement. In other words, in order to improve relations with the United States, Germany would first have had to be on better terms with Britain. Efforts were made at an Anglo-German understanding at this time, as we have seen, but most of them came from the British side and were motivated not so much by feelings of friendship as by feelings of fear. This fear, which was shared by the United States, helped draw the two Anglo-Saxon powers closer together. But it would be too simple to see apprehension of Germany as the only, or even the major, tie that bound the two nations together. Their entente at heart was one of sentiment and sympathy rather than of realpolitik. It was based on common language, common heritage, and common values.

The makers of German foreign policy were very aware of America's rapprochement with Britain, even though they tried to belittle it. When President Theodore Roosevelt stated in 1904 that America "was related to many different nations, but identical with none," the German foreign ministry interpreted it as being directed against "British jingoes." Ambassador Sternburg repeatedly poured cold water on the reports by his counterpart in London, Count Metternich, that Britain and the United States were becoming friends. Instead Sternburg reported that Roosevelt took a dim view of England and that there was growing sentiment among America's leaders to improve Anglo-German relations. Sternburg's successor, Count Bernstorff, held similarly disparaging views of the importance of an Anglo-American rapprochement. He realized the influence of the British press in America, but he felt that the majority of Americans remained "indifferent and neutral." Britain's "main purpose," he wrote in 1911, "to use the United States against Germany, will not succeed in the foreseeable future . . . if ever." On the eve of the war in 1914, Bernstorff assured his government that "Even an Englishman caught in the Anglo-Saxon delusion would hardly dare claim today that in case of an Anglo-German war (which, hopefully, is now impossible) the United States would join the British side."

Given this information, it is not surprising that the men in Berlin never adopted a clear policy toward the Anglo-American entente. They talked occasionally of a joint Anglo-Saxon and Germanic alliance, directed, as far as William II was concerned, against his major bogey, the "Yellow Peril." But at the same time, the kaiser seemed more interested in collaborating with the United States alone, preferably against Britain. And to compound the confusion, the emperor and some of his advisors also toyed with the idea of a "United States of Europe," including England, "against America." While this plethora of plans did credit to the German leaders' imagination, it was hardly a sign of statesmanship.

One reason why officials in Berlin did not take seriously the implications of an Anglo-American entente was that they expected the German element in the United States to serve as a counterweight to British influence. Germany's ambassadors spent much of their time attending German Day rallies in various Midwestern cities, addressing thousands of loyal sons and daughters of the Vaterland who listened bareheaded and with tears in their eyes to some message graciously sent them by the kaiser. In 1914 Bernstorff urged his superiors in Berlin "to keep the German-American weapon bright and sharp." But at the same time he warned against relying too much on the German-Americans, pointing out that they did not really carry much weight in American political affairs.

Some German-Americans made it their special task to serve as intermediaries between their adopted and native lands. While some of them, Harvard's Kuno Francke for instance, were very helpful, others, notably Harvard's Hugo Münsterberg, did more harm than good. The academic world, as we have seen, was a major area of contact between the two countries, and certain German universities, Göttingen in particular, were especially popular among Americans. In 1905 James Speyer, a New York banker of German origin, endowed a Theodore Roosevelt Professorship of American History and Institutions at the University of Berlin, where five years later a special Amerika-Institut was founded. There were German exchange and visiting professorships at American universities as well, but these academic connections affected only a small segment of the population, and they never really fulfilled the hopes of their sponsors. By 1914 the number of Americans enrolled at German universities had declined sharply, while the number of students going to England and France had increased. It seems that scholars, with a few exceptions, were not very interested in studying and interpreting each other's societies.

Another link between the United States and Germany that has often been overrated was the alleged friendship between Theodore Roosevelt and William II. Roosevelt's feelings toward the kaiser were at best ambivalent. In public the president went out of his way to express his admiration for the "great man," but in private he referred to him as "a bully who bluffs and then backs down," adding that he would regard neither William nor Germany as pleasant neighbors. The kaiser, on the other hand, seems to have been more consistent in his friendly feelings toward Roosevelt. It might be added that while some Americans shared the President's negative views, the kaiser was not as yet seen as the ogre he became during World War I. In 1913 when he celebrated the twenty-fifth anniversary of his rule, the American press was, on the whole, congratulatory. Roosevelt's feelings about Germany, as about its ruler, were mixed. He had considerable admiration for the country's achievements, but as time went on, this became overshadowed by apprehension, and it was that feeling rather than any pronounced Anglophilia that made him gravitate more toward England than Germany.

In general the importance of the various factors that supposedly created a favorable image of Germany in the United States— German-Americans, cultural exchange, and the Roosevelt-William friendship—has been exaggerated. Although fewer Americans had recently come from Britain (if one excludes the Irish) than from Germany, Americans of British origin certainly far outnumbered those whose ancestors were German. The continued vitality of Britain's cultural influence, moreover, made unnecessary any deliberate cultural exchange. And while Roosevelt was on far better terms with William II than with Edward VII, his relations with other prominent Englishmen, notably Britain's ambassador Cecil Spring Rice, were both closer and more significant than those with comparable Germans. In other words, to be truly meaningful, the study of Germany's image in the United States has to be set against a similar assessment of American sentiment toward Britain.

As for the German image of the United States, it tended toward extremes of admiration or condescension. The German press before 1914 was almost uniformly anti-American, a cause of much concern to Bernstorff, because German press attacks were faithfully reported in the United States. Of the various pressure groups clamoring for a greater Germany, the Pan-German League was particularly violent in its anti-Americanism. In 1912 its leader, Heinrich Class, after the usual jibes at America's *Unkultur,* concluded with foresight and conceit that "in the coming great war of the European powers" the United States "will certainly not join the German side; and if it did, what practical use would it be to us?" While the "classes," with the exception of some professors, thus persisted in arrogant ignorance of American views, the "masses" clung to an equally unrealistic view of the new world as a land of boundless riches and opportunities.

As we look at American-German diplomacy during the prewar decade, we find neither major conflicts nor much harmony. America's role at Algeciras was its deepest involvement in prewar European affairs. From that time on the United States again kept its distance, in part so as not to give the European powers a pretext for intervening on this side of the Atlantic. Compared to the mounting tensions between Germany and most of Europe, German relations with the United States were placid and even cordial. In 1908 Roosevelt wrote the kaiser: "I attribute the growing feeling of goodwill between the two nations more to your influence than to anything else." Roosevelt's successor, William Howard Taft, while close to England, also seemed well disposed toward Germany. Bernstorff in retrospect felt that "official relations between the German and American governments were never as good as between 1909 and 1913." In 1912 he reported that the last coolness remaining from the Manila affair had finally vanished.

On the popular level, however, feelings were less friendly. Whenever Germany became involved in a crisis at home or abroad, most of the American press took a strong anti-German stand, and anti-German books were quite common. In 1909 an American diplomat, Lewis Einstein, wrote a book on American foreign policy in which he called for close collaboration with Great Britain against the domination of Europe by a single power. The same year, Herbert Croly's *The Promise of American Life* called Germany "the chief menace to the international stability of Europe"; in 1912, Homer Lea's *The Day of the Saxon* described the impending war between Germany and the Anglo-Saxon powers; in 1913, Roland G. Usher's *Pan-Germanism* asserted that "the Germans aim at nothing less than the domination of Europe and the world"; and Admiral Dewey's *Autobiography,* published later that year, did much to keep alive the memory of Manila Bay, which Bernstorff thought had vanished.

Furthermore, if American-German relations just before the war were free from dramatic confrontations, they were not without underlying tensions, especially naval rivalry. Although it did not loom as large in America as it did between Germany and Britain, it nevertheless played an important role, both in American-German estrangement and American-British rapprochement. In a period of rapid American naval expansion, the threat of a German navy provided welcome propaganda for naval enthusiasts like admirals Mahan and Dewey, if only to get the necessary funds from an often-reluctant Congress. But there was more to it than that. As Britain withdrew its forces from the western Atlantic, the defense of that region naturally devolved upon the United States, and there seemed little doubt that such defense would be against Germany.

Closely related to America's fears of Germany's naval strength were its suspicions of German aims in the Western Hemisphere. Specifically these worries were German immigration in South America, especially in Brazil; the possible acquisition of naval stations, especially in the vicinity of the Panama Canal; and increasing German economic penetration into Latin America. In retrospect these fears may appear exaggerated, but Americans always suspected political motives behind Germany's economic drive, and rumors of German territorial ambitions never subsided.

A third issue that divided the United States from Germany was international arbitration and disarmament. That had not been much of a problem under Theodore Roosevelt, who shared the kaiser's dislike of international pacifism. Germany's ineptitude at the Hague conferences of 1899 and 1907 had given it some bad publicity among American pacifists but had not seriously affected official relations. However, that changed under the Taft and Wilson administrations, when America urged Germany to join the rest of the powers in signing arbitration treaties with Washington. Bernstorff thought that such treaties were "as useless as they were harmless," and he strongly pleaded for catering to the "self-delusion of a great people." But the German government demurred, distrusting the fairness of international arbitration and fearing that pressure to sign similar treaties with its neighbors would deprive Germany of the advantages of quick mobilization in time of war.

Besides these larger issues, the two nations also had numerous minor disagreements, many in the economic sphere, where haggling over tariffs, quotas, and prices continued. To ease economic relations, the Deutsch-Amerikanischer Wirtschaftsverband (German-American Economic Association) was founded in 1914, but the war intervened. More significant was the growing American-German rivalry on the world market. German competition was especially keen in Latin America, but it was felt elsewhere as well. The rivalry was sometimes a three-cornered one, with Britain as the third contestant. Often Britain rather than Germany was America's chief competitor, but it was Germany that both Anglo-Saxon powers feared, united against, and fought.

Woodrow Wilson, who became president in 1913, was more interested in domestic than in foreign affairs. His occasional references to Germany in the past had been quite critical. Unlike many other American scholars, he had never learned German or gone to Germany, although he respected German scholarship, knowledge, and enterprise. While Wilson was thus neutral at best on the subject of Germany, he was also decidedly pro-British. Most of his advisers were equally so, foremost among them Colonel Edward M. House.

The last diplomatic event involving the two countries before the outbreak of war was Colonel House's visit to Germany in the spring and early summer of 1914. House, far more than Wilson, was worried about the mounting tension abroad because he feared that it might involve the United States. The purpose of his trip to Europe was to achieve an understanding among the United States, Britain, France, and Germany, to maintain world peace through arms reduction and joint development of underdeveloped areas. His first stop was Berlin, where he had a long talk with the kaiser, of whom he gained a favorable impression; his subsequent talks with French and British leaders were less encouraging. Then the heir to the Austro-Hungarian throne was assassinated at Sarajevo, and soon after, the war began. House's mission is best remembered for his letter to Wilson, in which he described the European (not just the German) climate as "jingoism run stark mad." Had he taken his trip a year earlier, it might have been more successful.

It is significant that the heart of House's peace plan was an American-British alliance, surrounded by a wider entente with Germany, France, and some other countries. House thus ranked Germany behind Britain in America's order of preference, which shows the special relationship that had by then grown up between the two Anglo-Saxon powers. This did not mean that the United States would automatically take Britain's side against Germany. If possible, America hoped to avoid such a choice. What it *did* mean, however, was that America, if faced with the alternative of intervention, could not be expected to join Germany against Britain. If the need to choose sides arose, America would range itself against Germany.

3 | World War I
A Turning Point, 1914–1918

MORE THAN with any other war, the issue of responsibility for the Great War, as it was then called, has preoccupied historians from the days of its outbreak to the present. The number of books on the subject by now runs into the tens of thousands, and more are still being written. At first the answer seemed quite simple: each side felt that it was right and the other was wrong. Then, when the Central Powers lost the war, the victors put all the blame on the Germans, and their "war guilt" was officially proclaimed in the Treaty of Versailles. From then on, German historians saw as their major task disproving this accusation, and their Allied counterparts, substantiating it. In time as the passions of war subsided, it was possible for both sides to take a more objective view and to meet halfway. By the late 1920s, it was generally accepted that no power was wholly responsible and no power wholly blameless for what had happened in 1914, though most Allied historians still claimed that Germany bore the major share of the blame.

An exception was the so-called revisionists, historians who held that it was the other powers—Russia, France, Austria, or Serbia—rather than Germany, who were primarily responsible. The fact that the revisionists were echoing what their German colleagues had said all along, and that some of the most influential among them were Americans, notably Sidney B. Fay and Harry Elmer Barnes, could not help but improve American-German relations.

Until 1945, then, most Germans felt that they were less re-

52

sponsible for World War I than most non-Germans charged. Since then the debate about war guilt has reopened with a vengeance. I have already mentioned the Hamburg historian, Fritz Fischer, whose book, *Germany's Aims in the First World War,* first published in German in 1961, dealt with Germany's wartime ambitions; in an introductory chapter he also charged that his country was chiefly responsible for the war. Although Fischer's views did not particularly startle his readers abroad, they caused a major uproar in Germany. Violently attacked by his colleagues, Fischer spelled out his thesis in a sequel, *War of Illusions,** which held that Germany had planned an aggressive war for several years before 1914, not only to break out of the "encirclement" (*Einkreisung*) of Allied alliances and alignments but to gain its rightful place in the sun as a world power (*Weltmacht*), comparable in might and wealth with Great Britain and the United States. While Fischer's ultimate conclusions, especially his assertion of continuity in German history from Bismarck through Hitler, are open to criticism, the fact that he confronted one of the most sensitive issues in Germany's recent past has had a most stimulating and liberating effect on German historical studies in general.

The German people in 1914 believed what their government told them, that they were called on to defend their Fatherland against envious and aggressive enemies. They rallied to their country's cause with patriotic enthusiasm. Even those stepchildren of German society, the Social Democrats, pledged their support, and Germany's workers fought bravely and loyally through four long years of war. Nobody had any idea, of course, that the war would last that long; the general belief was that it would be all over by Christmas.

However, Germany's overall strategy, the Schlieffen Plan, which called for a knockout blow against the western Allies and subsequent concentration of Germany's forces against the Russians in the east, failed during the first weeks of fighting; after that a wholly new kind of trench warfare transformed the war into the bloody stalemate it remained, at least in the west, to the bitter end. As casualty lists rose to figures hitherto unheard of, and as hunger and cold became the common lot, except for farmers and the rich, enthusiasm turned to despair and dreams of victory gave way to hopes for peace. By late 1916 or early 1917 the majority of Germans would gladly have called an end to the bloodletting and gone back to the way things had been in 1914. But such a "peace without

* The German edition was published in 1969, the English edition in 1973.

annexations and indemnities" assumed that Germany's enemies were ready to forgo whatever they hoped to get out of the war and also presupposed that Germany's ruling classes would be content to renounce their own war aims, which they had begun proclaiming as soon as the war started.

The war aims question was the most important single issue in German domestic and foreign affairs during World War I. It divided German society at home, and it prevented the conclusion of a negotiated peace abroad. At one time or other, almost every German hoped for some gains from the war, so that their sacrifices would not have been in vain. But because the classes rather than the masses stood to profit most from these gains, they stubbornly clung to their expectations, even though chances for their realization dimmed, especially after the United States entered the war in 1917.

What did these "annexationists"—the industrialists, the large agrarians, the military—hope for? There were a great many different war aims programs, but they all agreed that Germany needed more territory. Some of that territory should be annexed outright: French and Belgian districts rich in iron ore and coal, a protective border strip (*Grenzstreifen*) against future Russian invasions in the East. The most important territorial gains, however, were to be in the form of protectorates: over Belgium and parts of northern France in the west and over the Baltic, Polish, and Ukrainian provinces of Russia in the east. The result of these open and veiled annexations would have been a central European empire, *Mitteleuropa*, dominated by Germany with Austria as a junior partner. This continental empire, moreover, was to be supplemented by a large colony in central Africa, *Mittelafrika*, to supply Greater Germany with raw materials not available on the continent.

Had these annexationist dreams come true, Germany would clearly have achieved hegemony over the European continent and would, in fact, have become a serious contender for world power. The question that has concerned historians is whether these far-reaching aims were merely the fantasies of greedy nationalists or whether they actually constituted official government policy. The German government during World War I was far less monolithic than it appeared from the outside. Wartime emergency enhanced, if anything, the authoritarian nature of the regime, leaving the Reichstag to play a decidedly secondary role. The emperor, in addition to his many other powers, became supreme warlord (*oberster Kriegsherr*) as well. But William II proved ill suited to provide effective leadership in wartime. At best he served as arbiter between the two factions contending for leadership, the civilian and the military.

The head of the civilian sector, Chancellor Theobald von Bethmann Hollweg, was a well-meaning and able bureaucrat, but he was entirely devoid of charisma and was given to indecision rather than action, a worrier rather than a doer. Before the war he had already incurred the displeasure of the nationalist and conservative groups that formed the backbone of the war aims movement. Bethmann's major concern was to keep alive the spirit of national unity that the outbreak of the war seemed to have created overnight. For that reason the chancellor avoided making any public statements on the divisive subject of war aims but that did not mean that he did not share and hope to realize some of the expansionist aims just described. Had he said so openly, however, he would have lost the support of the more moderate elements among the German people and, equally important, he would have supplied Germany's enemies with welcome propaganda material, thus closing the door to any possibility for a compromise peace settlement.

The decisive leadership that the civilian authorities failed to provide was taken by the military, though not entirely by default. Under German military law the army already had far-reaching powers over the civilian sector in time of war, including the right of censorship, which gave it effective control over public opinion. During the war the army became involved in economic affairs as well, as most industrial production became geared to the war effort. The most important agency within the army was its Supreme Command (Oberste Heeresleitung). Until the summer of 1916 the position of chief of staff was held by General Erich von Falkenhayn. But prior to that time the commander in chief on the eastern front, Field Marshal Paul von Hindenburg, had already emerged as the most popular military leader in Germany. Disagreements between Hindenburg and Falkenhayn over strategic decisions and the latter's failure to win the battle of Verdun on the western front finally led to Falkenhayn's dismissal and Hindenburg's appointment in his place. As the kaiser withdrew more and more into the background, Hindenburg became the de facto military commander of Germany, and because of the ineptitude of the civilian branch, he wielded increasing influence in nonmilitary matters as well. Hindenburg shared his power with his chief executive and close associate since 1914, General Erich Ludendorff. It was Ludendorff, by far the brighter and more ruthless of the two, who then became the virtual dictator of Germany, working behind Hindenburg's stolid and genial front. One of the team's first acts, as we shall see, was to pressure the government into declaring unrestricted submarine warfare in early 1917, thus precipitating the break with the United States. Later that year Hindenburg and Ludendorff played an active part in the dismissal of Bethmann Hollweg, whose tendency to procrastinate and compromise they had long disliked. He was succeeded by a complete nonentity, Georg Michaelis.

On the question of war aims, the military leaders took an unwaveringly annexationist stand, in part for understandable strategic reasons but also because they were in complete sympathy with the aims and ambitions of the middle- and upper-class advocates of expansion. Among this group it was especially the large industrialists who hoped, by conquering raw materials, production facilities, and markets, to increase their power within Germany and without. Yet there were other motives besides economic and patriotic behind the agitation of the annexationists.

On the eve of the war the clamor for domestic reform, that is, for a truly parliamentary regime in the Reich and in Prussia, had reached alarming proportions. During the war, this clamor became louder and actually led the kaiser to make some vague promises that all would not remain the same once the war was over. The fear of the upper classes, that Bethmann Hollweg was not the man to hold the line against these demands for and promises of change had been a major factor in his dismissal. The best way to prevent the growing discontent from coming to a head, the annexationists and the military felt, was to prove that the existing system worked, that it brought tangible rewards in the form of large annexations and huge indemnities, from which Germany as a whole stood to profit. If, on the other hand, there was nothing to show for all the suffering and misery of war, sweeping governmental reforms or worse yet, revolution, might be the result. Only if we realize how much was at stake for Germany's ruling classes—the whole basis of their power, their whole way of life—can we understand the obduracy and avidity with which they clung to their aims, even at the very end, when the tide of war had turned.

As the war dragged on without an end in sight, many Germans began to suspect, not without reason, that stubborn adherence to large war aims presented the major obstacle to a negotiated peace. There were innumerable peace feelers and peace efforts during the war, as both sides became more and more weary of fighting. In December 1916 President Wilson attempted to mediate between the two camps, and in August 1917 Pope Benedict XV tried the same. There were other such moves, official and unofficial, but each time the efforts broke down because the belligerents refused to state their war aims.

As far as Germany was concerned, the major stumbling block

to a negotiated settlement was the desire, even of moderate elements within the government, to retain some form of control over Belgium. By its own admission, Germany's invasion of that small country had been a breach of international law, so the Allies refused even to discuss a possible settlement unless Germany promised Belgium's unconditional restoration. While Belgium presented a hindrance to a possible separate peace in the west, Poland, which Germany had provisionally restored in 1916, played a similar role with respect to a separate arrangement with Russia. As an obstacle to reform at home and to peace abroad, Germany's annexationist aims thus had a most pernicious effect on that nation's affairs.

The second major issue in wartime Germany was submarine warfare, which was related to war aims in that the same people advocated both. The main significance of the submarine controversy was that it brought the United States into the war against Germany. But it is probably correct to assume, as some historians have, that America would have entered the war in any case, had there been a threat of total German victory and hegemony in Europe. The United States should have done so, not only for the moralistic, "make the world safe for democracy" reasons that President Wilson proclaimed, but because a German-dominated Europe might easily have presented a threat to, and ultimately have come in conflict with, America's own vital interests. The ideal solution, as far as President Wilson and the majority of the American people were concerned, would have been a deadlock between the two camps, leading to a negotiated peace, with America serving as arbiter. But such was not to be, largely due to German miscalculations and mistakes.

It is difficult to gauge exactly what Americans felt at the start of the war. The majority, most historians agree, did not seem terribly interested in what was considered primarily a European affair. Those Americans who did take sides at first were pretty evenly divided between supporters of the Central Powers and sympathizers for the Allies. But this balance soon began to shift, and by the middle of 1915 the majority of Americans clearly favored the Allied side. There were underlying as well as immediate reasons for this shift. Even before 1914 America's feelings about Germany had at best been ambivalent, a mixture of admiration and antipathy, like and dislike, hope and fear. We have seen that shortly before the war a number of books published in the United States and in England had warned of the potential threat of an aggressive Germany. In 1911 a German general, Friedrich von Bernhardi, in a book entitled *Germany and the Next War,* had foretold, so it seemed, the war that was now going on; needless to say, his prognosis proved a boon to Allied propaganda. A similar windfall for the Allied cause, also written by a German, was Friedrich Naumann's *Mitteleuropa* (1916), which advocated a kind of benevolent German domination over most of the continent after the war. There were other influential books, some by serious scholars, such as the American Bernadotte Schmitt's *England and Germany, 1740–1914* (1916), others by propagandists, like the several works on pan-Germanism by the French journalist André Chéradame.

It was among the cultural elite, the reading public, that pro-Allied and pro-British sentiments found their earliest and strongest echo. It has sometimes been held that British propaganda was chiefly responsible for turning the United States against Germany and thus was a major cause of American intervention. But Germany, although its initial propagandist efforts were more amateurish, was less handicapped than has often been assumed. The reason for the greater effectiveness of British propaganda was that the soil was already prepared and that as time went on the Germans seemed to live up to the negative image that many Americans had formed of them earlier. The invasion of Belgium, the execution of nurse Edith Cavell for aiding Allied prisoners, the death of women and children because of the submarine campaign, the deportation of Belgian workers for "slave labor" in Germany—all these were seen as evidence that the Germans deserved the epithets *boches* (swine) or Huns, with which the French and British propagandists, respectively, incited their audiences.

The Germans, however, did have a sizable constituency of potential sympathizers in the United States—the millions of German-Americans. According to the 1910 census, close to 8.3 million persons considered Germany as their land of origin; 2.5 million of these were born in Germany, 4 million were born in the United States of German parents, and the rest had one German parent. With their native penchant for joining associations, these Germans had formed innumerable local and regional organizations. In an effort to combine these heterogeneous groups into a more effective pressure group, Dr. Charles J. Hexamer of Philadelphia in 1901 had founded the National German-American Alliance (Deutsch-Amerikanischer Nationalbund), which in time counted some two million members. But the Nationalbund wielded far less influence than its large membership would lead one to assume, for it was as much interested in fighting Prohibition as in spreading Kultur. As Germany's ambassadors had repeatedly bemoaned before the war, the political interest and influence of the large German-American community was practically nil. Few, if any, Americans of German origin held important government positions, and the more economically influential among them—the Strauses, Speyers, Warburgs, and Schiffs—while interested in German cultural activities, wanted little to do with professional German-Americanism.

The outbreak of the war, as might be expected, found the majority of German-Americans squarely on the side of the Vaterland. The 537 German-language papers, 53 of them dailies, tried to counteract the generally pro-Allied slant of the American press. The Nationalbund passed a resolution blaming the war on the Allies, and there were numerous local demonstrations of loyalty, much singing of *"Die Wacht am Rhein"* and collecting of gifts and money for the German cause. But while individuals like Hugo Münsterberg, Kuno Francke, and George Sylvester Viereck, who had sung Germany's praises before the war, now felt that their hour had come, most German-Americans seemed perfectly content with President Wilson's neutral policy of keeping their country out of war, and many of them helped him win his narrow reelection in 1916.

Still, this potential fifth column (as it would have been called in World War II) was a cause for some concern, the more so because the anti-Allied sentiments of the German-Americans were shared by other "hyphenates," notably some four and a half million anti-British Irish-Americans and several million anti-Russian Jewish Americans. Before the war efforts had been made by these groups to bring about some collaboration between them, and during the war the German government tried to use Irish-American elements in its anti-British meddling in Ireland. Some German-Americans also became involved in the clandestine activities of German agents in the United States. But on the whole the German-Americans proved to be loyal citizens of their (or their forebears') adopted country.

This did not save many of them from ostracism or outright persecution, however, once their fellow countrymen became infected with the hysteria of war. Today, the switch from sauerkraut to "liberty cabbage" may seem a silly joke, but to German-Americans at the time it was merely one of the milder humiliations to which they were subjected because of their ethnic background. In the history of Germans in America, World War I constitutes the darkest chapter, but it also had positive aspects. By emphasizing the hyphen, the war helped to erase it. In 1918 the Nationalbund, then under Congressional investigation, dissolved itself, and the following year a new organization, the Steuben Society, began to improve American-German understanding by helping the Germans in this country become good Americans rather than remain German-Americans.

The sentimental attachment of the millions of German-

Americans to the old country was far less important in shaping American opinion and possibly policy than the views of what have been called "the professional custodians of culture" *—the leading writers, editors, publishers, college presidents, and such. Not that they were rabidly pro-British, though some of them were, but they were certainly anti-German and became more so as the war progressed. The fact that their counterparts in Germany rallied to the defense of kaiser and Kultur did not help the German cause in this country. Only a few American intellectuals were outspokenly pro-German; aside from Münsterberg, Francke, and Viereck, there were John W. Burgess of Columbia University, who had been the first Roosevelt Professor at the University of Berlin before the war; H. L. Mencken, "the sage of Baltimore"; and Oswald Garrison Villard, ardent pacifist and owner and editor of the *New York Evening Post*. But they were exceptions. Although most members of America's cultural elite were pro-Allied, they were not necessarily interventionist. They believed in the justice of the Allied cause and felt that it would triumph without American involvement. Friendly neutrality would suffice.

These sentiments were shared by the men who directed America's foreign policy. Most important among these were President Wilson and his close friend and political adviser, Colonel House. Wilson, while making sincere and initially successful efforts to remain neutral, was clearly more favorably disposed toward Britain than he was toward Germany, and the same may be said for House. The most genuinely neutral member of Wilson's cabinet was his secretary of state, William Jennings Bryan. But Bryan had little influence and, overshadowed by House, he resigned during the *Lusitania* crisis in May 1915. Bryan's successor, Robert Lansing, tried to keep an open mind, but he also favored the Allies. The American ambassador in Berlin, James Gerard, was openly anti-German, but he carried little weight.

Although the American people, including its government, became more and more anti-German, the majority nevertheless expected their country to stay out of the war. There were a few hawks, who called for America to join the Allies, most prominent of whom was Theodore Roosevelt, who hankered for a fight with his one-time buddy, "Kaiser Bill." We must keep in mind this continued isolationism of the United States when trying to understand Germany's blindness to the possible danger of American intervention. The

* Henry F. May, *The End of American Innocence: A Study of the First Years of Our Own Time 1912–1917* (New York: 1969), p. 363.

German people were too much preoccupied with events in Europe to worry about a country so far away and inhabited by millions of former Germans who, even if they could not help their cousins, certainly would see to it that America helped nobody else. The German government was far from united in its views of America's possible reaction to German provocation. Only Germany's ambassador in Washington, Count Bernstorff, was fully aware of the consequences that his government's policy might have. But while his warnings were understood and to some extent heeded by the civilian authorities in Berlin, notably Chancellor Bethmann Hollweg, they either were not understood or were ignored by the naval and military establishment, especially Admiral Tirpitz and the Supreme Army Command, Hindenburg and Ludendorff. The responsibility for the war between the United States and Germany thus clearly rests with Germany, and within Germany, with its military rather than its civilian leaders.

The most important cause for America's declaration of war against Germany on April 6, 1917, was the German resumption a few weeks earlier of unrestricted submarine warfare. There were other reasons for American intervention—British propaganda, American economic involvement with the Allies, German sabotage activities in the United States, and the notorious Zimmermann telegram (of which more anon)—but these were secondary compared to the overriding submarine issue.

The submarine question first became acute in the spring of 1915. Having scored some unforeseen successes with this still experimental weapon the previous fall, the German government in February 1915 imposed a submarine blockade against the British Isles, which was a perfectly justifiable countermeasure to Britain's surface blockade against Germany. To be effective, however, the German blockade, like that of the British, had to be directed against neutrals as well as belligerents. But while Britain's surface blockade followed the established procedure of seizing and searching neutral ships suspected of carrying contraband, Germany's submarines, because of their vulnerability to surface attacks, had to rely on sinking suspected vessels without warning. Moreover, because of their cramped space, submarines were unable to save any survivors. The United States and other neutrals had already taken strong exception to Britain's rigorous contraband restrictions, and American-British exchanges on this score had at times become acrimonious. But while British naval patrols captured only goods, Germany's submarines killed innocent civilians. That was the crux of the matter.

After Germany declared the waters around Britain a war zone,

President Wilson charged the German government with "strict accountability" for the loss of any American lives or property. The first American ship, the tanker *Gulflight,* was sunk without warning on May 1, 1915. But the climax of this first phase of Germany's submarine campaign came a week later on May 7, when the British luxury liner *Lusitania* was torpedoed off the coast of Ireland. The ship's cargo allegedly contained some arms and ammunition, but more important was the fact that among the 1,198 passengers who lost their lives were 139 Americans.

The sinking of the *Lusitania* caused a wave of indignation among the American people. Had it not been for Wilson's calm appraisal of the situation, the break with Germany might have come then and there. Instead, in a note to Berlin on May 13, the American government merely demanded reparation for the damages and assurance that there would be no similar incidents. The German government, grossly underestimating the seriousness of the situation, took two weeks to reply and then put the blame for the *Lusitania* incident on the British. Two more American notes, each firmer in tone, followed in June and July, but they received equally unsatisfactory replies, despite Ambassador Bernstorff's urgent warnings that his government give in to American demands. Meanwhile the German government had issued secret orders not to attack passenger ships, which prevented further incidents and helped ease tensions. But then on August 19, 1915, another British liner, the *Arabic,* was sunk with a loss of forty-four lives, including two Americans.

The *Arabic* affair rekindled the outrage felt among the American public over the *Lusitania.* This time it was chiefly because of Count Bernstorff's efforts that the incident did not escalate into war. By then the ambassador had been able to convince his civilian superiors in Berlin that Washington had reached the end of its patience. After first trying to explain away and evade responsibility for the *Arabic* incident, the Germans finally agreed to make the required reparation and promised not to attack any more passenger ships.

These concessions were made against the protests of the military and naval segments of the German government, which enjoyed wide support among the German press and public. As the hardships of war increased, submarine warfare came to be seen as a means not only of breaking the British blockade but of ending the war altogether. Chancellor Bethmann Hollweg, on this as on the war aims issue, pursued an indecisive course. As long as the army, that is, the chief of staff General Falkenhayn, opposed an all-out submarine campaign, the chancellor was able to prevail against the naval advocates of such a course. But when first Falkenhayn and later Hindenburg and Ludendorff joined the agitation for stepped-up submarine warfare, the chancellor gradually had to give in.

In February 1916, the German government announced that thenceforth all armed merchant ships would be sunk without warning. When this policy led to another crisis, however, the sinking of the British channel steamer *Sussex* on March 25, in which several Americans were injured, the Germans relented again. The Americans threatened to sever diplomatic relations unless Germany abandoned its campaign against passenger and merchant vessels, and the German government gave in. On May 4 it promised that no such ships would be sunk "without warning and without saving human lives." This *"Sussex* pledge" appeared to be a victory for the forces of moderation in Germany that were trying to avoid a collision with the United States. But it did not silence the clamor for resumption of all-out submarine warfare, which won out in the spring of 1917.

While the submarine crisis was gaining momentum, there were other causes for American uneasiness about Germany. From the start of the war German agents and officials in the United States had been engaged in activities, both open and secret, that gave rise to fears of a German conspiracy. Some of these activities were quite harmless, such as the elaborate efforts to sway American opinion in favor of Germany. In August 1914 the German government had sent the former colonial secretary Bernhard Dernburg to New York to open a German news agency. Whatever initial success this *Pressebüro* had in spreading German propaganda, its effectiveness became practically nil after the sinking of the *Lusitania*. While Ambassador Bernstorff carefully avoided associating himself with the agency's amateurish doings, he did try to gain control over some American newspapers, but the net result of his efforts was disappointing. The only English-language daily to come under German financial and editorial influence was the *New York Evening Mail*; negotiations to acquire the *New York Sun* and the *Washington Post* failed.

Besides trying to work through the press, the Germans also sought contact with other anti-Allied minority groups, especially the German-Americans. One of the most effective ways of aiding them was by supporting their press. The most respected German-language daily, the New York *Staats-Zeitung*, thus was bailed out of its financial difficulties by the German government, as was George Sylvester Viereck's less influential weekly, *The Fatherland*. In trying to influence the American Jewish community by appealing chiefly to Jewish Russophobia, the Germans were less successful. Presenting the war as a struggle between "German civilization and Russian barbarism" ignored the persistence of anti-Semitism in Germany, of which American Jews, especially those of German origin, were very much aware.

Other targets for German advances were the Irish-Americans. As with the German-Americans, the German war effort with the Irish in America often went beyond mere propaganda to encouraging Irish-Americans to use sabotage.

The story of German sabotage and related activities in the United States has never been fully unraveled and because of the secrecy surrounding it, probably never will. However, enough became known about these events at the time, chiefly through the carelessness of some of the agents involved, to poison further the tense atmosphere of American-German relations. Among the individuals involved in these sabotage activities, the best known was Franz von Papen. Until his expulsion from America late in 1915, he was military attaché at the German embassy. (Later, during the 1930s, he was one of the men most responsible for the rise of Hitler.) The offenses committed covered a wide range, from falsifying passports (to enable German reserve officers to return to Germany) to infecting defense workers with influenza bacilli. But the most widely publicized crimes were bombing war plants, causing explosions on ships carrying strategic goods, and fomenting strikes. Initially, most such acts were committed in Canada from American bases, but as the United States drew closer to war, activity shifted to American soil. One of the best-known blows was struck against the Black Tom Terminal in New York harbor in July 1916, when tons of war materials in freight trains and warehouses were destroyed. The saboteurs for these acts were frequently recruited from among German- or Irish-Americans. There also were schemes, never carried out, for invading Canada with a joint German-Irish force.

Although German sabotage measures clearly broke American laws, some of Germany's other activities merely abused American neutrality. In this category belong Ambassador Bernstorff's involvement with Irish revolutionary circles in the United States and with Sir Roger Casement prior to the Irish Easter Rebellion of 1916. The Germans also aided similar conspiracies against Britain's rule in India by supplying Indian revolutionary groups in America with weapons and funds. More dangerous to their host country were German schemes to keep tensions alive between the United States and Mexico, in the hope that involvement south of the border might divert America's attention and supplies from the European theater. Most of these machinations became known to American authorities and helped increase American distrust of Germany at a time when the submarine issue had already created a highly sensitive atmosphere.

As one after another minor German official and even the Austrian ambassador, Constantin Dumba, were declared personae non gratae for their unsavory activities, voices were heard calling for the expulsion of the German ambassador as well. But such an act would have caused a break and maybe war, which President Wilson hoped to avoid.

If America's relations with Germany became increasingly strained as the war went on and incidents multiplied, relations with the Allies and notably Britain were not exactly smooth. The majority of Americans, to be sure, favored Britain rather than Germany. To the age-old Anglo-Saxon affinities of culture and ideology had been added Germany's wartime mistakes, thus disposing Americans toward "friendly," pro-Allied neutrality. But there were also some causes for friction, chiefly because of Britain's high-handed disregard for the rights of neutrals under the British blockade. The blockade provisions of international law were at best controversial and vague, so there had been constant American protests since the beginning of the war concerning Britain's decisions on contraband, the use of blacklists, and other acts interfering with the rights of neutrals. The British government became less and less ready to listen to such protests. But the United States, while threatening countermeasures, usually acquiesced. One important reason was that American-Allied trade even under existing restrictions had become highly lucrative. After a near-depression at the beginning of the war, the United States was approaching a boom. Another reason for America to apply different measures to German and British violations of its neutral rights was that the former caused loss of life, while the latter involved only loss of property. Such moral considerations, though less tangible than economic ones, weighed heavily with the man who determined American policy.

The fondest wish of Woodrow Wilson throughout the war was to use his influence to conclude a negotiated peace that was short of total victory for either side. In this he found some support among his associates and full support from Ambassador Bernstorff. Wilson's first offer to serve as mediator was made as early as August 4, 1914, but the leaders in both camps had more pressing decisions on their minds. There followed various talks, first by Bryan and then House, with Bernstorff, in which the German ambassador showed himself far more eager than his superiors in Berlin to find a compromise. The culmination of this early phase of peace efforts came with Colonel House's first wartime visit to Europe in early 1915. Its results were nil, because neither side was willing to make the first move or even to state its war aims publicly. The British had insisted, as a precondition for negotiations, that Germany restore Belgium's full independence and pay reparations for damages suffered by that country. In view of Germany's far-reaching secret war aims, such a demand was wholly unacceptable. While in London, House learned of similar sweeping gains that the Allies hoped to make. Under those circumstances, peace negotiations were out of the question.

At that point, the *Lusitania* incident in the spring of 1915 pushed the submarine question into the foreground of American-German concerns. While Bernstorff continued to hope for American mediation, the refusal of both sides in the European war to make the slightest concessions made any compromise impossible. At the turn of 1915–16, House paid a second visit to Europe, but again it was fruitless. The Germans told him they might be willing to withdraw from the territories they had occupied in return for an appropriate indemnity, but the British continued to insist that it should be the Germans who paid the indemnity. By then the agitation in Germany for extravagant war aims had reached such heights that Bethmann Hollweg could no longer remain silent. "Can anyone believe," he told a cheering Reichstag on April 5, 1916, "that we shall give up areas which we have occupied in the west, on which the blood of our people has been spilled, without gaining complete security for our future? We shall secure real guarantees for ourselves, so that Belgium will not become an Anglo-French vassal state . . . Here, too, there will be no status quo ante."

In America both Wilson and House began to face the reality of a showdown with Germany. One way to avoid it might be for the United States to use its power to induce the Germans to come to the conference table. In February 1916 Colonel House proposed to Britain's foreign secretary, Sir Edward Grey, that America should invite the belligerents to a conference and added that if the Germans refused to come or proved unreasonable, the United States might join the Allied side. But the British government, believing that the submarine crisis would soon bring America into the war anyway, did not take up the suggestion. Besides, the British, like the Germans, feared that readiness to negotiate might be interpreted as a sign of weakness by the other side.

In the spring of 1916 the German high command tried to break the military stalemate on the western front by a massive offensive against the fortress of Verdun; but the effort, terribly costly in human lives, failed, as did a similar British offensive along the Somme River in the summer and fall. The only way to win a quick and certain victory, a growing number of Germans felt, was to resume unrestricted submarine warfare. There were still those, however, especially within the civilian sector of the government, who doubted the efficacy of the submarine solution and feared that it might worsen matters by bringing the United States into the war. To avoid that, Chancellor Bethmann Hollweg continued to show an interest in President Wilson's mediation efforts. But the German chancellor also worried that at the kind of conference Wilson proposed the United States might be aligned with Germany's enemies.

In part to forestall a move by Wilson and in part to make unrestricted submarine war unnecessary or, in case of Allied refusal, to justify its resumption, the German government on December 12, 1916, came forth with its own peace proposal. The moment was carefully chosen. The recent defeat of Rumania had shown that Germany acted from strength rather than weakness, and news of an impending statement from Wilson made German action urgent. The Germans hoped to initiate peace talks without American participation, preferably with one rather than all of the Allied powers. But because the German proposal contained no specific terms and was clearly intended to divide the Allies, the latter turned it down. A few days later, President Wilson publicized his own proposal for a general international conference to end the war, asking each side as a preliminary to state its aims. This the Germans refused to do, and when the Allies in turn refused to negotiate with the Central Powers on equal terms, Wilson's proposal fell through.

The failure of both the German peace efforts and his own did not discourage Wilson. In a speech to Congress on January 22, 1917, he again called for a peace "without victors and vanquished ... without annexations and indemnities." A week later the Germans, under American pressure, confidentially stated their peace terms to Washington, and the terms showed that Germany was far from ready to settle on the basis of the status quo ante. Any interest this communication might have had for the United States was overshadowed by Germany's simultaneous announcement that unrestricted submarine warfare was to be resumed on February 1. Thenceforth all suspicious ships were to be sunk without warning.

That fateful step had been decided upon at a crown council on January 9. Bethmann Hollweg had vainly tried to prevent thus challenging the United States, but he could not prevail against his naval and military colleagues, also supported by the kaiser, who clamored for action. As Bethmann Hollweg had foreseen, the United States severed relations with Germany on February 3. Still, President Wilson did not intend to declare war until the Germans committed an overt act. Bernstorff's efforts to have the submarine campaign postponed by a month failed, as did Wilson's suggestion that

American ships be exempted from German attacks. After several such attacks the United States had no choice but to declare war on Germany on April 5, 1917. The justice of America's cause was enhanced by the interception by the British of the famous Zimmermann telegram, in which the German foreign minister offered Mexico an alliance against the United States, promising the return of New Mexico, Arizona, and Texas as prizes of victory. To counteract any lingering Midwestern isolationism, the American government could not have asked for more.

America's entry into the war sealed the fate of Germany. But few Germans understood the significance of this event—Bernstorff and Bethmann Hollweg were exceptions. Misled by overly optimistic estimates, most Germans believed their economic and naval experts, who predicted that Britain would be defeated within five months or less, long before American aid could make itself felt. Because they were used to judging a nation's strength by the size of its army rather than by its economic potential, Germany's military leaders considered the United States of decidedly secondary importance. That this pacifist and isolationist country could be ready and able to train and ship to Europe an army of close to two million men was thought impossible, and in any case, Germany's submarines would see to it that no American troops would get across. As it turned out, only one transport was ever sunk, and as the convoy system was perfected, the submarine danger was gradually contained. The submarine war was a colossal gamble that can be understood only if we realize what its proponents—the military, the large industrialists and agrarians, the advocates of large war aims, in short, Germany's ruling classes—felt was at stake, namely, the perpetuation of a political, economic, and social order of which they were the chief beneficiaries. It was a question of all or nothing.

The history of Germany for the remainder of the war is a melancholy tale. Bethmann Hollweg was dismissed in the summer of 1917, chiefly because the military considered the chancellor too weak and vacillating in the face of growing demands for governmental reform at home and a moderate peace abroad. Demands for peace came out into the open in July 1917, when a majority of parties in the Reichstag passed a resolution asking for a negotiated "peace of understanding" rather than a "peace of victory." But as before, it was the military components of the government, rather than parliament, who determined German policy. The kind of peace that the real rulers of Germany favored became clear during the negotiations with the defeated revolutionary regime in Russia, concluded by the Treaty of Brest-Litovsk on March 3, 1918. Under its provisions, the new communist state was deprived of vast areas along its western borders, including all its Baltic provinces. A similarly harsh peace was imposed on Rumania at Bucharest on May 7, 1918. Neither of these settlements was protested by the Reichstag, where only the Socialist parties on the left dissociated themselves from their government's annexationist greed.

Had the Germans adopted a more enlightened policy toward these occupied areas in the east and had there been time to develop their economic resources, the Central Powers might have been able to hold out, if not until total victory, at least for a negotiated peace. But time was running out. In the spring and early summer of 1918, the Germans made a last desperate effort to win a decision in the west. It failed, chiefly because large German contingents remained tied up in the east and because American aid, material, and men had become fully effective. The tide turned in August when the German offensive, its force spent, came to a halt, and the Allied counteroffensive gained momentum. The German people, after four years of war, had reached the end of their endurance. Sporadic strikes, spawned by growing discontent with virtual military dictatorship, demanded food and peace. Unrest at home, reversals at the front, and the imminent collapse of Germany's Bulgarian, Turkish, and Austrian allies—all these combined to shake the nerve of General Ludendorff. On October 4, 1918, Prince Max of Baden, a reputed liberal, formed a new government and asked President Wilson to serve as mediator for an armistice based on the Fourteen Points, which the president had proclaimed earlier.

While armistice negotiations dragged on and the war continued, domestic discontent in Germany grew rapidly. There had been important constitutional changes under Prince Max, to be sure, which gave Germany for the first time in its history a truly parliamentary regime. But to the majority of Germans at home and at the front, things looked no different—the same breadlines, the same casualty lists, and the same military establishment suspected of unnecessarily prolonging the war. On October 28 mutiny broke out among the sailors at Kiel, who refused to set out on a final suicidal naval raid. From Kiel the revolt spread to other ports and then inland, and revolutionary workers' and soldiers' councils were set up. During the first week of November, revolution reached Munich and then Berlin. There had been growing demands for the abdication of William II, who was quite rightly considered an obstacle to an armistice. On November 9, finally, Prince Max took the initiative, announcing the kaiser's abdication and turning the government over to the Socialists under Friedrich Ebert. The same day, to forestall a threatened take-over by a small Spartacist (or Communist) faction, Ebert's party colleague, Philipp Scheidemann, proclaimed a German republic. The new regime almost immediately signed an armistice, and on November 11, 1918, at 11 A.M., the guns on the western front fell silent.

Germany thus had lost the war, had lost it on the battlefield, albeit after a heroic fight against increasingly heavy odds. But to many Germans, who had been told for years that their country would be victorious and that the sacrifices of war would not be in vain, the suddenness of the collapse came as a severe shock. The debate over who was responsible for Germany's fate started almost immediately. But instead of the blame being placed where it clearly belonged—on the ruling classes, especially the military, who bore a large share of responsibility for starting the war in the first place and then, because of their hopes for exaggerated gains, for not finishing it in time—there grew up what became known as the "stab-in-the-back legend" (*Dolchstosslegende*). This fabrication held that a radical and treasonous minority (soon to be labeled Jewish-Bolshevik), by fomenting revolution at home, had undermined and sabotaged the fighting spirit of Germany's armed forces, which militarily remained unbeaten. The fact that this legend was spread by the circles that stood to profit most from it, the military (notably Hindenburg), is hardly surprising. What *is* surprising is the readiness of so many Germans to believe it. The German Republic was thus slandered not only as the child of defeat but, with strange logic, also as the cause of defeat. That was one of the major birth defects of the new German state. Another was the peace treaty with which the fledgling republic was soon to be saddled, and in the making of that treaty, the United States played a decisive part.

President Wilson had taken his country into the war reluctantly, disappointed that his hope for "peace without victory" had not materialized. He was by no means ready, however, to relinquish his role as arbiter. He wanted to stand above the selfish national aims and interests that he had found in his dealings with both belligerent camps. There was nothing America wanted except to rid the world of war and to make it "safe for democracy." To show its aloofness, the United States fought as an "associated" rather than an Allied power.

The president and his advisers were told of the various secret agreements on war aims that the Allies had concluded, and their texts were published by the Bolsheviks in November 1917. But Wilson never took official notice of these treaties, so as not to bind his hands. When speaking of Germany, he was usually moderate in tone, careful to make a distinction between the German people and its government. "We are not the enemies of the German people . . . and they are not our enemies," the president said in a Flag Day address in June 1917. "The war was begun by the military masters of Germany."

The American people were less dispassionate. The majority backed the declaration of war against Germany, but quite a few felt that the war was unnecessary. To change their minds, Wilson asked George Creel, an overzealous journalist, to head a Committee on Public Information. Its purpose was not merely to propagandize America's cause, but in doing so to paint Germany's image in the most lurid colors. The committee's work proved useful in glamorizing the American war effort, but in fostering hysteria against people and things German, it also did great harm. The teaching of German was banned in American schools as a result of this hysteria, which is cause to be ashamed still. Other official actions were taken that violated civil rights in the cause of national security—the Espionage and Trading with the Enemy Acts of 1917 and the Sedition Act of 1918. These measures hurt many German-Americans and were also used to persecute other minorities. Americans, for better or worse, like to do things wholeheartedly.

America, as I said, wanted nothing for itself from the war, except to find a way of guaranteeing the freedom of the seas, which had been violated by both Germany and Britain. Wilson's main concern was to detect and correct the causes of the tensions and injustices that had led to war in 1914. To help him find out what they were, Colonel House in the fall of 1917 set up a committee of some 150 experts, primarily scholars, but also some public figures and noted journalists, including Walter Lippmann. This body, the Inquiry, supplied the information that went into the making of Wilson's own peace program, the famous Fourteen Points.

The need for such a program arose when the Bolsheviks, in their negotiations with the Germans at the end of 1917, popularized Lenin's formula for peace "without annexations and indemnities." It was a slogan that appealed to idealists and progressives everywhere despite, or because of, its simplicity. If adopted, it would leave boundaries pretty much as they had been before the war, which in Wilson's and his allies' minds was hardly desirable. Britain's prime minister, David Lloyd George, had come out with his own peace program, not unlike Wilson's, which was another reason for Wilson's speech to Congress on January 8, 1918, unveiling the Fourteen Points.

The President's program was a mixture of general and specific proposals. The first five points dealt with broad issues: open diplomacy, freedom of the seas, free trade among nations, reduction of armaments, and adjustment of colonial claims. The next eight concerned specific territorial questions to be settled according to the principle of self-determination: German evacuation of Russian territory, restoration of Belgian independence, return to France of Alsace-Lorraine, readjustment of the frontiers of Italy, autonomy for the peoples of Austria-Hungary, evacuation and restoration of the Balkan states, autonomous development for the peoples of the Turkish empire, and an independent Poland with secure access to the sea. The fourteenth and crowning point, finally, called for the establishment of "a general association of nations ... for the purpose of affording mutual guarantees of political independence and territorial integrity to great and small states alike."

It was this last point that was closest to Wilson's heart. The idea of an international organization, a league of nations to serve as guardian of peace and arbiter of international conflicts, had been in the air for some time. Wilson had first made public reference to it in June 1916 in an address to the American League to Enforce Peace, a body devoted to the idea of a league of nations, and he had reiterated his suggestion in subsequent statements, public and private. The league the president envisioned, to be effective, had to be universal, including victors and vanquished alike. Even after America went to war against Germany, he still looked for German membership in such a body. It was only pressure from America's allies abroad and from opponents of Germany at home that made Wilson abandon his universalist concept of the league.

Wilson's plan to include Germany in an international peace-keeping organization was based on the expectation that Germany, by reforming and democratizing, could redeem itself and thus be reintegrated into the family of nations. For that reason the president continued to draw a distinction between the German people and its rulers, at the same time hinting at the desirability of a change in government. "We have no jealousy of German greatness ..." he said in his Fourteen Points address in January 1918. "But it is necessary ... that we should know whom her spokesmen speak for when they speak to us, whether for the Reichstag majority or for the military party." In Germany a wave of strikes in late January seemed to bear out the president's hope for change. But soon thereafter the great spring offensive in the west and the Treaty of Brest-Litovsk in the east revealed that the situation remained much the same. The military was still firmly in control.

President Wilson's wish to serve as supreme arbiter came true in October 1918, when Prince Max's government asked him to initiate an armistice. The ensuing negotiations were complicated by the fact that Wilson had to deal not only with the Germans and the Allies, but also with the criticism of his Republican opponents at home during a crucial election campaign.

The Germans, in asking for an armistice based on the Fourteen Points, expected to carry out an orderly and gradual withdrawal of their forces, so that they could halt and continue fighting if peace negotiations proved unsatisfactory. But the Allies demanded a quick and total evacuation of all occupied territories and the surrender of vast quantities of war materials, submarines, ships, airplanes, rolling stock, and other implements of war, thus effectively crippling Germany's capacity to resist. General Ludendorff at one point advocated breaking off negotiations, but the civilian authorities turned him down, and he was forced to resign. Another issue that became a major stumbling block in the armistice talks was Wilson's insistence that William II abdicate and that a truly democratic German regime be established. That problem was resolved when the kaiser's hand was forced on November 9. He went to Holland the next day, where he remained until his death in 1941.

President Wilson's negotiations with the Allies were chiefly concerned with clarifying the vague and sometimes contradictory provisions of the Fourteen Points. The Allies had never formally endorsed the president's program, which he had elaborated and supplemented in various declarations. The French in particular found much to criticize in the American proposals as well as in Wilson's underlying hope of rehabilitating Germany. Their aim was the total defeat and disablement of their foe. To iron out these differences, Colonel House went to Paris during the armistice negotiations. As a result, the freedom of the seas issue was left open for discussion at the later peace conference, and the Germans were to be informed that they would have to pay reparations for all civilian damages they had caused.

While Wilson was negotiating with the Germans and House with the Allies, the armistice and future peace with Germany were the subject of heated debate in the United States. Plenty of domestic issues divided the two major parties, but because of Wilson's deep involvement in foreign affairs, the Republicans decided to take advantage of the popular passions aroused by everything concerning Germany. All along a strong faction within the party had opposed Wilson's concept of peace without victory. This group was led by Theodore Roosevelt, who had outdone himself in tirades against the Huns abroad and the "shadow Huns," the German-Americans, at home. The Fourteen Points he termed mere "high-sounding phrases of muddy meaning," and rather than negotiate with the Germans, he asked that they be served with a demand for unconditional surrender. The other leading Republicans, Henry Cabot Lodge and Howard Taft, while less violent than Roosevelt, nevertheless supported his demand for a tough line against Germany. To an American public fired by slogans of "Hang the kaiser!" and "On to Berlin!" the clamor for unconditional surrender had great appeal. How great was shown when, five days before the armistice, the Republicans won control of both houses of Congress, albeit in the Senate by only one seat.

Still, Wilson had won two of his most cherished aims: the war was over, and Germany had become a democracy. His next task was to see that the blueprint of the Fourteen Points became a reality, and to achieve this, the president decided to attend the peace conference in person, thus continuing in his role as *arbiter mundi*. The fact that his Republican critics challenged his right to speak for the American people did not deter him from what he truly felt to be his mission. Rather than speaking only for Americans, Wilson believed he was speaking for men of goodwill everywhere. He was soon to be disillusioned.

4 | The Weimar Republic
A Democratic Interlude, 1918–1933

THE FIRST GERMAN REPUBLIC has gone down in history as the Weimar Republic, named after the town made famous by Goethe and Schiller, where its constitution was drafted in the spring of 1919. The reason this was not done in Berlin was not so much to dissociate the new state from its predecessor, the Prusso-German Empire, as to protect the members of the constituent assembly from the intermittent riots and street fighting that had shaken the German capital from the day of the republic's birth.

The new republic, as we have seen, had been founded hastily to remove the kaiser and to prevent the proclamation of a more radical, communist regime. The specter of communism continued to haunt the new government. Its leading supporters, the Social Democrats, were by no means agreed on the kind of state they wanted. The majority looked to a parliamentary system with an elected assembly to draw up a democratic constitution. But meanwhile a minority, spearheaded by the party's radical faction, the Spartacists, who had split off during the war, hoped to use the spontaneous uprisings everywhere to bring about more sweeping changes, not merely political, but social and economic as well, following the example set by the Bolshevik Revolution in Russia a year earlier. The Russians gave ideological and material support to these German communists; all over Germany workers' and soldiers' councils were springing up along the model of Russia's soviets; and in Munich a Bavarian Soviet Republic actually came into being. All these events combined to make the threat of communist revolution appear quite real to non-Germans as well as many Germans. We know now that there was actually scant danger of a communist revolution in Germany, but we enjoy the benefit of hindsight.

The German government after the resignation of Prince Max was in the hands of a Council of People's Delegates, made up of Socialists. They were decent, devoted, and patriotic men, but they were wholly inexperienced in the affairs of state. They were faced, moreover, with problems that would have staggered a more expert body—the demobilization of millions of soldiers, their reintegration into civilian life, the feeding of a hungry population destitute after years of deprivation, and, they thought, the threat of a communist take-over. In their desperation to avoid utter chaos and possible Allied intervention, the government turned for help to the only experts at hand—the servants of the old regime, civilian and military.

There was no need to twist any arms to get the kaiser's bureaucrats and generals to serve the Socialists' republic. These men were patriots, and like most of their fellow countrymen, they prided themselves on being above politics, *unpolitisch*. As for the civilian officials, their continuation in office did not pose any real danger to the republic, except that their continued presence prevented any fundamental changes in attitudes and values, so that much of what had been wrong with the empire continued to be wrong with the republic.

But the continued influence of the traditional army in German affairs was even more pernicious. Friedrich Ebert, soon to become the first president of the Weimar Republic, asked General Wilhelm Groener, Ludendorff's successor, for help in putting down the disturbances in Berlin. Groener complied on condition that the army remain immune from attempts to change, that is, democratize it. Ebert, probably unaware of the consequences of his action, agreed, and he was present at Berlin's Brandenburg Gate to welcome the returning forces, bands playing and flags flying. It soon turned out, however, that the regular army of conscripts was unable to cope with the revolutionary situation; its soldiers wanted to go home. So in its place the government hired bands of volunteers, the so-called Free Corps (Freikorps), to defend the republic against its enemies on the left. After a series of bloody battles in December and January 1918–19, Berlin became pacified, although disturbances flared up again and again during the next few years. It was not long before these mercenaries turned against the republic they were hired to defend, because in their innermost hearts they hated it. The first

putsch against the Weimar Republic took place in 1920. When the
Free Corps were subsequently disbanded, many of their members
flocked to support one of their former comrades in the imperial
army, a private first class by the name of Adolf Hitler. The army,
meanwhile, now called Reichswehr, under the leadership of Hans
von Seeckt, a cool and clever general of the old imperial army, had
emerged as the most powerful single factor within the republic, a
state within the state.

The bureaucracy and the army were not the only institutions
that survived the change from empire to republic. Similar continuity
in personnel and attitudes prevailed in virtually all of the leading
professions—academic, judicial, and religious. The fact that the
Weimar Republic, socially, economically, and in some respects even
politically, did not fundamentally differ from the empire that preceded it has made historians question whether Germany really did
undergo a revolution in 1918. Ever since then, and especially since
1945, scholars have tried to discover what went wrong, why Weimar
was a republic without republicans.

The basic reason may have been that the empire, in retrospect, did not really look too bad to most Germans. Its political
weaknesses had been corrected, thanks to a new constitution that
was one of the most democratic in the world. But more than the
empire's weaknesses, people remembered its strengths—its thriving
economy, its military might, its world power. Compared to the
glamor and glitter of those good old days, the present seemed drab
and dreary indeed. From being one of the world's great powers,
respected and, better yet, feared, Germany had become a pariah,
despised and, worse yet, pitied. It has become the fashion among
historians to apply psychological criteria to their craft. Even if one
does not believe in combining two such disparate disciplines, one
would agree that the loss of the greatest war in its recent history
amounted to a truly traumatic experience for the German people.
The terrible truth and awesome extent of that loss were brought
home to them in May 1919, when they were presented with the bill
for the war, the Treaty of Versailles.

The peace conference had opened in Paris on January 18,
1919. The date was symbolic, for on that day in 1871 the German
empire had been proclaimed, at the same place where the treaty
was to be signed on June 28. That was another historic date, the day
when the Austrian archduke Francis Ferdinand had been assassinated five years earlier. While such minor insults to a beaten foe
may now seem gratuitous and in poor taste, they help to remind
us of the intense animosity harbored by the Allies against their erst-

while foes. To be sure, the Germans had changed their government, but had they changed their ways? The kaiser was gone, but Hindenburg was still in command.

Reading the German rightist press, one hardly knew the war was over. In May 1919 the army command took a poll to ascertain sentiment for resuming the fight. In June, while the peace conference was still in session, the German battle fleet, interned at Scapa Flow, was scuttled by its crews to keep it out of enemy hands. There was an air of truculence about the Germans that confirmed Allied suspicions and apprehensions. When the leader of the German delegation sent to receive the text of the treaty, Count Brockdorff-Rantzau, remained seated while delivering an arrogant blast at Allied injustices, he may have boosted his own and his countrymen's egos, but he did so at great expense to his country's image.

The date was May 7, another memorable day—the anniversary of the sinking of the *Lusitania*. Much has been made of the fact that the Germans on this occasion were presented with a treaty to which they could make their reactions known only in writing. This, they claimed, was a dictated peace, a *Diktat,* but it wasn't really. Quite a few of Germany's objections were subsequently taken into account, and the text modified accordingly. Nor was it unusual for a defeated nation to be faced thus with categorical demands. Bismarck's peace with France in 1871 had hardly been less of a *Diktat,* as Georges Clemenceau hinted when he referred to the document he presented to the Germans as "the second peace of Versailles."

The German delegation, even though they had some idea of what to expect, was staggered by what they were asked to sign. In the west Germany was to return Alsace-Lorraine to the French, from whom the Prussians had taken it in 1871. In the east it had to give up much of the territory that Prussia had taken from Poland in the eighteenth century, including some areas clearly inhabited by Germans. The fate of other border regions was to be determined by plebiscites. The total losses amounted to one-eighth of the nation's European territory, inhabited by some six million people, half of them Germans, and containing one-third of the country's coal and three-quarters of its iron production (see map 3). In addition, Germany was stripped of its colonies. Under the military terms of the treaty, the army and navy were to be reduced to the bare minimum needed to keep order at home, and all offensive weapons—planes, submarines, heavy guns, and such—were banned. Germany, furthermore, was to bear the total cost of the war, including pensions and allowances paid to dependents. To justify the demand for what

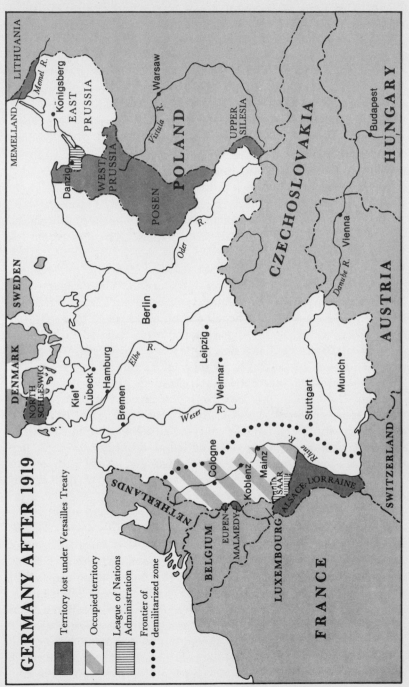

GERMANY AFTER 1919

Territory lost under Versailles Treaty

Occupied territory

League of Nations Administration

Frontier of demilitarized zone

Map 3. Germany after 1919.

LITHUANIA

MEMELLAND

Memel R.

Königsberg

EAST PRUSSIA

WEST PRUSSIA

Danzig

Warsaw

Vistula R.

UPPER SILESIA

POSEN

POLAND

Oder R.

SWEDEN

DENMARK

NORTH SCHLESWIG

Kiel

Lübeck

Hamburg

Bremen

Elbe R.

Berlin

Leipzig

Weimar

Weser R.

CZECHOSLOVAKIA

Vienna

Danube R.

AUSTRIA

HUNGARY

Budapest

NETHERLANDS

Cologne

Koblenz

Mainz

Rhine R.

SAAR

Stuttgart

Munich

BELGIUM

EUPEN

MALMEDY

LUXEMBOURG

ALSACE-LORRAINE

FRANCE

SWITZERLAND

amounted to unimaginable sums, the Allies prefaced the reparations clauses with perhaps the most famous provision of the Treaty of Versailles, Article 231, the war guilt clause, specifying Germany's responsibility for the war. And to make sure that Germany lived up to the provisions of the treaty, the Rhineland was to be occupied by Allied troops for fifteen years.

It is curious, though understandable, that the Germans reacted most vehemently to those and some other punitive clauses of the treaty, including the demand for the surrender of "war criminals," foremost among them the kaiser. The question of responsibility for the war, as we have seen, was then and remains a controversial issue. The Allies, in drafting Article 231, had not intended it to have the prominence it subsequently assumed, yet the more Germany protested, the more the Allies, especially France, insisted on it. Europe might have been spared much anguish if this clause, in its final wording by an American expert, John Foster Dulles, had been omitted.

The debate over whether or not to accept the treaty shook the still precarious republic to its foundations. The delegates who had received the treaty unanimously rejected it. The government, headed by Socialist Philipp Scheidemann and backed by a majority of Socialists, Liberals, and the Center Party, resigned rather than sign. What determined the final outcome was the army's estimate that resumption of hostilities by Germany could not succeed. The Allies, meanwhile, threatened that refusal to sign would result in invasion. Under such pressure, Germany finally complied, "giving way to superior force." The fact that it was once again the civilian authorities who subjected Germany to this humiliating "treaty of shame" (Schandfrieden) provided added ammunition to the domestic enemies of the republic. The responsibility of the military for both the armistice and the peace was overlooked or deliberately covered up.

The Treaty of Versailles was the heaviest burden that the Weimar Republic had to bear, the proverbial millstone around its neck. Opposition to it was the one issue on which all Germans, regardless of party or class, agreed. Even those leaders who had the courage to fulfill its conditions, hoped that by so doing they might put an end to it. For demagogues of the right, notably Adolf Hitler, the treaty provided their most effective propaganda weapon against the hated republic at home and Germany's "oppressors" abroad. Among the latter one man was singled out for German obloquy, and that was Woodrow Wilson. Of course, historians have found much to criticize about Wilson's policy during and after the peace conference, but only a small part of the criticism pertains to his actions toward Germany. The Germans, perhaps expecting too much from him, were disappointed when he did not deliver what they had hoped. But the epithet of hypocrite (*Heuchler*), which to this day they like to apply to the American president, is hardly justified.

Wilson's role in Paris was an extremely difficult one. Unused to contradiction and inexperienced in the arts of compromise, he had to negotiate with the European leaders, foremost among them Clemenceau and Lloyd George, who had definite aims of their own, and whose realistic national aspirations clashed with the president's lofty international ideals. On several occasions deliberations came close to the breaking point, once when Clemenceau accused Wilson of being pro-German! It must be remembered that Germany's future was only one of many problems before the conference, and if the Germans were unhappy with the results of the peace conference, so were the Austrians, the Hungarians, the Bulgars, the Turks, and even the Italians, the Poles, and the Chinese.

Wilson's thinking on Germany at Paris was ambiguous. On the one hand, he wanted to integrate the country into the community of democratic nations. He hoped that the change in government from empire to republic, for which he had been partly responsible, was genuine. He did not want that change to go too far, however, and to see Germany turn communist. The fear that the Russian "disease" might spread westward was omnipresent at the peace conference and was played upon by the Germans in their attempts to have the peace terms modified. Wilson and Lloyd George in particular were much concerned that too harsh a peace might drive the Germans into the arms of communism. But Wilson was also affected by the general atmosphere of Germanophobia at Paris. He wanted a just settlement according to the noble principles of his prearmistice pronouncements. When these principles had to be compromised, however, it was only natural that more often than not the president would side with America's friends rather than its recent enemies.

The attitude of Wilson's advisers varied. The most important of them, Colonel House, was somewhat more pro-Allied than his chief, while Secretary of State Lansing, who played only a secondary role, was more pro-German. Among the rest of the president's entourage, General Tasker Bliss, his chief military adviser, and Herbert Hoover, were favorably inclined toward Germany. Hoover was chiefly concerned with providing food relief for Europe, including Germany. German propaganda has made much of the fact that the Allied "hunger blockade" was not lifted as soon as the armistice was signed. The responsibility for this neglect, however, lay primarily with the Germans themselves, who were slow in providing the necessary ships and funds for the food program. It was not until March 1919 that the first American food ship arrived in a German port.

If we look more closely at some of the treaty's specific provisions, we find that Wilson was far from the villain the Germans made him out to be. It was chiefly through his efforts, for instance, that Germany did not lose the Saar region and the left bank of the Rhine, as the French demanded. Instead, the Saar was to be administered by the new League of Nations and its ultimate future decided by a plebiscite in 1935. In the interim the area became economically integrated with France. To compensate France for the Rhenish buffer state it wanted, but did not get, for protection against Germany, the United States and Britain promised to support the French against possible German aggression.

Wilson helped modify the demands of the Allied powers in other instances as well. He insisted on plebiscites for some of the regions ceded to Poland and on having the new states of eastern Europe sign treaties to protect German (and other) minorities. On the overall settlement in the east, however, the president agreed to terms that the Germans considered violations of the principle of self-determination. Wilson's pro-Slav sympathies, his desire to make up for past injustices, and pressure from his pro-Polish advisers help to explain his acquiescence. The restoration of Poland, after all, had been one of the Fourteen Points.

If the eastern settlement was closely supported by the French, the colonial issue was pushed by the British. That Germany lost its colonies proved a blessing in the long run, because it saved the Germans from the taint of colonialism and made for good relations between today's Germany and the third world. But that was hardly obvious in 1919. Germany was deprived of its colonies because of alleged maladministration—a charge that soon was successfully disproved. The Germans, if not the world's best colonizers, certainly had been no worse than the rest of the colonial powers. A nation already smarting from the "war guilt lie" now was saddled with another grievance, the "colonial guilt lie." Wilson, however, could have done little to prevent the seizure of the German colonies because they had been divided up during the war, chiefly among Britain and the Dominions. The most the president could do was to support an arrangement under which these territories were to be administered as mandates under the League of Nations, leaving open the possibility that Germany might some day obtain such a mandate.

Another territorial injustice Germany held against the peacemakers was that they had kept German Austria, as it was then briefly called, from joining its German cousins. There was strong sentiment for an anschluss on both sides of the border, and its denial by the statesmen in Paris was a clear violation of self-determination. In the long run such a solution might have benefited not only the two countries concerned but the peace of Europe in general. But it would have been expecting too much that the Allies would agree to the creation of a state larger and more powerful than Germany had been in 1914. Few Germans actually expected to be thus rewarded for losing the war, though they continued to agitate for anschluss throughout the twenties and thirties, until Hitler made their wish come true in 1938.

Among the nonterritorial issues, reparations proved the most troublesome, not only at Paris but as we shall see, throughout the postwar period. Wilson's compliance with the exaggerated claims of France and Britain rightly earned him the criticism of experts at the conference and after. The inclusion of pensions almost doubled the total amount of Germany's obligations. Furthermore, because no agreement could be reached on how much Germany would be able to pay, the exact amount and time limit were left to the decision of a Reparations Commission, which was to report by 1921. Had the United States been a member of that commission, some of the earlier mistakes might have been corrected. But the American Senate's refusal to ratify the peace treaty precluded participation.

Wilson realized that the peace he brought home was far from perfect, but he believed that the decisions reached at Paris need not be considered final and unalterable. After all, there was an agency to deal with international injustices and tensions that might lead to war. The League of Nations was the fulfillment of the president's fondest dream, and the adoption of its Covenant, much of it drafted by him, his greatest triumph. To emphasize the close relation between the League and the peace settlement, the Covenant was made an integral part of the treaty, even though Germany was not at first admitted to the organization. The exclusion of Germany had not been originally intended by Wilson, but circumstances, chiefly anti-German pressures at home and in Paris, had made it advisable to postpone its membership until the Germans had "redeemed" themselves. To the German people this was further cause for grievance. German Socialists and Liberals in particular had set great hopes on the League, and the Germans had submitted their own proposals for a Völkerbund. An organization that Wilson had envisioned as truly a universal body thus became initially little more than a continuation of the wartime coalition against the Central Powers.

The president's triumph in having his League accepted by its critics at the conference, notably the French, was shattered soon after, when the American people refused to endorse his achievement. This is not the place to recount Wilson's stubborn battle for acceptance of the treaty and his defeat, due in part to his unwillingness to compromise over the several Republican reservations against the Covenant. The League was an intensely personal, all-or-nothing matter for Wilson. For most Republicans it was merely a partisan issue, but they had grass-roots support among isolationists, who viewed the Covenant as an "entangling alliance"; among hyphenates —not only German-Americans but other ethnic groups as well—who were dissatisfied with what the peace treaty did or did not do for their old country; and among many Americans who were disillusioned by, and tired of, the war and wanted to return to normalcy, as the saying went. After the Senate refused to ratify the treaty, the Republicans won a resounding victory in the presidential elections of 1920.

The Treaty of Versailles was one of the most momentous events in modern history. It deeply affected not only international relations but domestic affairs in every country of Europe and beyond. The treaty has been the subject of endless analyses, explications, and criticisms, which started even before the ink of its signatures was dry. In 1919 one of Britain's economic experts at the peace conference, the young John Maynard Keynes, who had resigned in protest against the treaty, published *The Economic Consequences of the Peace,* a vitriolic attack upon the settlement in general and its economic terms in particular, and upon its makers, especially Woodrow Wilson. The book provided German critics of the treaty with some of their most effective ammunition. Historians, at least outside Germany, took a more detached view. Some of the treaty's more unwise or unworkable decisions, as we shall see, were revised during the twenties and early thirties, before Hitler tore it to shreds. Since then, much of the debate has centered on whether Versailles created Hitler, whether a milder peace, or perhaps a still harsher one, might have spared the world that scourge. The answer is, we do not know.

We do know that during the 1920s the Treaty of Versailles

permeated the life of Germany more than that of any other nation. The history of the Weimar Republic divides into three more or less equal phases: first, a period of intermittent unrest, culminating in the French invasion of the Ruhr region in 1923; then some five years of deceptive stability, ending with the death of the republic's most prominent statesman, Gustav Stresemann, in 1929, and with the coming of the Great Depression; and finally, the decline of German democracy and its destruction by Hitler's victory in 1933. The keynote of Weimar politics was instability. During its short life of fourteen years, the republic had twenty-one cabinets under thirteen different chancellors. The reason for the frequent changes was that these governments rarely enjoyed clear parliamentary majorities. In an attempt to be as democratic as possible, the Weimar constitution provided for proportional representation, a system that encouraged party splits and interest groups. At no time were there fewer than ten parties, and most of the time there were more than fifteen. Nearly all of the leading parties dated back to the empire, most clearly so the Social Democrats and the Catholic Center. The liberals were still split into a leftist Democratic and a rightist German People's Party. On the far right the pre-1918 Conservatives survived as the German National People's Party.

In addition to these traditional parties and a varying number of splinter groups, there arose during the 1920s two other parties at opposite ends of the political spectrum—the Communists on the left and the National Socialists, or Nazis, on the right. Both were violent enemies of the republic, but at first they did not pose any serious threat, because the Communists were too isolated and the Nazis too few. Since no party in the Reichstag ever gained an absolute majority, all of the Weimar governments were coalitions. Depending on the degree of affinity among their members, some of the coalitions were more effective than others, but on the whole, during the 1920s at least, the Weimar Republic was able to function.

During its first years, the republic was chiefly preoccupied with adjusting to the peace settlement. At a long series of conferences the Germans were charged with failing to live up to their treaty obligations, especially on disarmament and reparations. These charges were not unjustified. Germany was most reluctant to scale down its military force to the 100,000-man limit set at Versailles and by every possible subterfuge tried to evade its armaments restrictions. When the Germans showed similar reluctance about paying reparations, the Allies threatened to occupy Germany beyond the zone already held under the peace treaty unless they complied.

The best known of the early postwar meetings took place at

Genoa in 1922. It was intended not so much to deal with Germany as to find some general solution to the many economic difficulties that beset Europe as a whole, and for that reason a Russian delegation was invited to participate. This was a milestone of sorts, the first international conference attended by the Soviets. Their absence from the Paris conference had kept them from being part of the peace settlement, and like the Germans, they felt isolated. It was in large part to escape their isolation that Germany and Russia joined forces at Genoa, concluding the famous Treaty of Rapallo on April 16, 1922. The event caused a major stir in Allied circles and almost wrecked the conference. On the face of it, the treaty was an innocuous economic agreement rather than an alliance, as it has often been called. But economic collaboration helped open the door to other joint efforts, especially in the military field. These were highly secret, and the Allies did not learn of them until later, although they had suspicions at the time.

The most constant irritant in Allied-German relations throughout these years was reparations, and it was this issue that brought about the most serious crisis since 1918. Germany continued to default on its reparations deliveries of coal, so in January 1923 the French, supported by the Belgians and some Italians, occupied the Ruhr district, Germany's industrial heart. The fact that the British did not participate and actually protested this French "invasion" showed that Franco-British relations were not what they had been. Even during the peace conference the two allies had not always seen eye to eye. The French, primarily worried about their security, hoped to weaken Germany as drastically and permanently as possible. The British, on the other hand, having less reason to fear the Germans, wanted them to regain a measure of their economic strength, so that they could resume a mutually beneficial commercial relationship. Britain's disapproval of the Ruhr venture brought tension into Franco-British relations, from which the Germans hoped to profit.

Germany responded to the French occupation by proclaiming passive resistance; the government urged its citizens, in particular the coal miners, to strike, and they did. But by September that strategy had to be abandoned, for it had pushed the republic into total bankruptcy. Like most countries, Germany had suffered from growing inflation during and after the war, but more seriously because the German government had financed the war through loans rather than taxation. By 1923 devaluation of the mark had reached runaway proportions, causing utter economic ruin. The Germans blamed their inflation on reparations, but economists since then have charged that Germany's own faulty fiscal policy was responsible. As a result, savings were virtually wiped out. The middle classes were hit the hardest.

Added to this economic catastrophe and not unrelated to it were severe internal upheavals. In the west separatists were fighting for a Rhenish republic; in the east fear of a Polish invasion prevailed; in the south Adolf Hitler was getting ready to lead his nationalist bands in a march on Berlin; and in the Ruhr and elsewhere, communists were trying to take over. The man who saved Germany in this darkest hour from civil war and disintegration was its "chancellor for a hundred days" in 1923 and subsequently its foreign minister until 1929, Gustav Stresemann.

Stresemann was the leader of the rightist German People's Party. He had been a rabid nationalist and annexationist during the war, and in his heart he always remained a monarchist. But he was also a realist, and as such he had become a *Vernunftrepublikaner*, a "republican of the mind, if not of the heart." How genuinely his republican beliefs were, we shall never know. Stresemann was a superb politician, an ardent patriot, and a great statesman. The way he took charge, first in the disastrous crisis of 1923 and then in helping Germany regain a respected place among nations, entitles Stresemann to a place of highest honor in his nation's history, not unlike that of Konrad Adenauer after another war. To call off resistance in the Ruhr and embark on a policy of fulfillment of the hated *Diktat* of Versailles required great moral and even physical courage, because those policies had to be carried out against furious nationalist agitation, which did not shrink from murder to achieve its aims. Two leading German figures had already been assassinated by right-wing fanatics—Matthias Erzberger, the leading Centrist politician, who was hated because he had signed the armistice, and Walter Rathenau, foreign minister at the time of Rapallo, who was killed primarily because he was a Jew. Stresemann clearly risked being next on the assassins' list.

To return to normal conditions after 1923, Germany first had to find its way out of the maze of reparations, and in this Stresemann hoped for the assistance of the United States. German-American relations since the war had been uncertain; because America had not ratified the peace treaty, the two countries were still formally at war. This anomalous situation was resolved by a separate treaty in August 1921. The Treaty of Berlin was a revised version of the one signed at Versailles, minus the League Covenant and some other provisions but including all clauses that might affect the United States, directly or indirectly, especially those on reparations (including the war guilt clause). America, it has been said, thus assumed all the rights of the Treaty of Versailles and none of its obligations. Diplomatic relations with Germany were resumed in November 1921, and ambassadors were exchanged shortly thereafter. Since it was expected that most of their dealings would be economic, both sides appointed prominent businessmen. The first U.S. ambassador to Berlin, Alanson B. Houghton, proved a fortunate choice; he even knew German, having studied at Göttingen in his youth. The German ambassador in Washington, Dr. Otto Wiedfeldt, a director of the Krupp armaments firm, was less successful because of his nationalism and arrogance, but then, his task was not an easy one.

Anti-German feeling in America, which had reached its height at the end of the war, was slow to cool down. If during the war the Germans had to contend chiefly with British propaganda, afterward their chief competitors were the French. Those Americans who paid attention to European affairs were far more concerned with the reconstruction of France than with the recovery of Germany. Only among the farmers of the Middle West was there some pro-German feeling, in part because of their ethnic background. The hope for German-American support was slow to die, and Wiedfeldt tried, not without some success, to enlist it. The American press at best was neutral, but in times of Allied-German confrontations it resumed its anti-German stance. An exception was the Ruhr crisis in early 1923, when most papers sided with Germany. But soon the interest of the American public turned back to events closer to home.

The American government at first appeared indifferent to Germany's problems. The chief architect of American foreign policy, Secretary of State Charles Evans Hughes, while open to American involvement in Europe, shared the Francophile sentiments of the northeastern intellectual elite, and on several occasions both he and President Warren G. Harding declined Germany's requests for American mediation in the reparations controversy.

The only real friend the Germans had was Ambassador Houghton, and it was due to his influence that the United States played a more active part in German affairs. But Secretary Hughes also came to realize that the economic recovery of Germany was essential for the recovery of the rest of Europe and thus was of interest to the United States as well. He had expressed such views before the French move against the Ruhr, most clearly in a speech in New Haven on December 29, 1922, in which he proposed that a conference of experts, including Americans, should address itself to the reparations problem. But the French, led at the time by Raimond Poincaré, were poised for the Ruhr invasion and thus not inclined to listen.

The United States, like Britain, strongly disapproved of the Ruhr venture and in protest withdrew its occupation forces from the Rhineland. The inconclusive outcome of that venture, however, finally made the French give way to British and American pressure, and the conference that Hughes had suggested took place in early 1924. It was notable for the leading role played by the American delegation, led by Charles G. Dawes, prominent banker and subsequently vice-president under Calvin Coolidge, who gave his name to the reparations plan worked out by the experts.

The Dawes Plan did not solve the reparations problem, but by taking reparations out of politics, it helped ease tension and aid recovery. Germany was to pay specific annual amounts geared to its economic capacity. Payment and transfer abroad were to be controlled by a committee headed by a young American banker, Parker Gilbert, who emerged as a key figure in American-German relations. To ensure availability of funds, Germany's central bank, its railroads, and some key industries were placed under foreign supervision. As an aid to Germany's economy and to get the plan off the ground, the Germans were to be granted a pump-priming loan of $200 million, more than half of which came from the United States. One issue the Dawes Plan did not tackle was the relation of reparations to inter-Allied debts. While Germany owed vast amounts to the Allies, the latter owed large amounts to each other and ultimately to the United States. Allied efforts to establish a link between the two, making relief to Germany dependent on commensurate American relief to themselves, were staunchly resisted by the American government, which feared that the United States would end up paying for the war.

That, of course, was in effect what happened. As Germany underwent a spectacular economic revival after 1924, American loans began to flood the German market, enabling the German government to pay its reparations promptly and in full. Much of the American money went into nonproductive rather than capital projects, especially by German municipalities, and many of the loans were short-term. When the stock market crashed in the United States in 1929, these loans were recalled, and when the depression hit Germany, the German debtors defaulted. Since payment of reparations had been made possible largely through the influx of those American loans, their cessation and withdrawal after 1929 once again moved the reparations problem to center stage. Efforts to cope with it through a revised scheme, the Young Plan of 1929–30, again named after an American expert, Owen D. Young of General Electric, remained stillborn. After two more years of agony, moratoriums, and standstill agreements, the reparations issue was finally buried at an international conference at Lausanne in 1932. By that time the Germans had paid only a fraction of what they owed, and most of that had come from the United States. No wonder Winston Churchill called the reparations story a "sad story of complicated idiocy," the sadder because its ultimate outcome had been foreseen.

But this has taken us beyond the era of sweetness and light that the Dawes Plan supposedly inaugurated in 1924. Much of Germany's energy over the next five years went into foreign affairs, with Stresemann steadily refurbishing his country's image. Every one of his diplomatic achievements, however, had to be won not only against continued suspicion abroad but against nationalist opposition at home. How powerful the antirepublican right had become was shown during the presidential elections of 1925. Friedrich Ebert, who had recently died, had been a good president, respected, fair-minded, and patriotic, but colorless. In his place the German people elected Field Marshal Paul von Hindenburg, then seventy-seven years old. Under the Weimar constitution the president wielded considerable power, so Hindenburg's election was a fateful step, as became clear in 1933. Outside Germany the election of this avowed monarchist and relic of imperial days at first inspired fear of a resurgence of German nationalism. But it soon appeared that "the old gentleman" intended to take his constitutional oath quite seriously.

There were other causes for foreign uneasiness: reports of continued German disarmament violations, in particular of collaboration between the Reichswehr and the Red Army; agitation in favor of reintroducing the former imperial colors and against confiscating the property of the former princely houses; and a large number of paramilitary organizations like the Stahlhelm (Steel Helmet), a veterans' association, and Hitler's SA (Sturmabteilung). These and other signs of continued monarchism and militarism made Stresemann's search for détente more difficult. But the country's increasing prosperity diverted most Germans from some of their earlier grievances and made them adopt a more positive attitude toward their new state. Except among the Socialists, however, genuine enthusiasm for, or even understanding of, democracy was still rare.

The best known of Stresemann's international agreements were the various treaties negotiated at Locarno, chiefly with his

French and British counterparts, Aristide Briand and Austen Chamberlain, in the fall of 1925. To understand the background of these treaties, we must recall France's concern for security at the peace conference, which had led Wilson and Lloyd George to promise Clemenceau an alliance against possible German aggression. America's failure to sign the peace treaty, however, had made that promise invalid. The Germans recognized that France's fears had led, among other things, to the Ruhr invasion. Even before that calamity, therefore, Germany had proposed a scheme by which the powers immediately concerned, Germany, France, and Belgium, would agree to the territorial status quo in the west, while the other two western European Allies, Great Britain and Italy, would guarantee the inviolability of these borders. This, substantially, was what the Locarno pact did: Germany gave up its claim to Alsace-Lorraine, and France agreed not to invade the Ruhr again. But there was more to Locarno than that. For one, Germany was at long last to become a member of the League; for another, Stresemann made it quite plain that he was not ready to conclude a similar agreement for Germany's eastern frontiers.

Germany's joining the League of Nations was more complicated than it appeared. Ever since the Rapallo Treaty in 1922, the special relationship between Berlin and Moscow had been an asset to German diplomacy, because the fear of Russo-German collaboration never quite left the western Allies. The Russians, on the other hand, were equally afraid of collaboration between Germany and the Allies. Locarno seemed to bear out the Russian fears, and they tried by all possible means to deter the Germans from attending the conference, even going so far as to offer them an alliance against Poland. But Stresemann was able to secure the best of both worlds. At Locarno he agreed to join the League on condition that Germany would not have to participate in any League action against the Soviet Union. To calm any remaining Russian fears, Germany in 1926 concluded another Treaty of Berlin, this time with the Soviets, reaffirming the friendship first proclaimed at Rapallo four years earlier. Polish opposition delayed Germany's entry into the League until September 1926.

Which brings us to the second point, Stresemann's refusal to balance the western security pact with an "eastern Locarno." Among Germany's territorial grievances, the settlement in the east, especially the Polish Corridor separating East Prussia from the rest of Germany, hurt the most. To sanction the eastern borders by treaty would have been suicidal for any German government. All Stresemann agreed to at Locarno, therefore, was to settle future differences with Poland and Czechoslovakia by arbitration, which meant that territorial revision in the east was left open.

Historians have long wondered about Stresemann's ultimate aims, and some have accused him of playing East against West for the gradual erosion of Versailles, but that judgment is only partially correct. There can be no doubt that the German foreign minister hoped to free his country from the "shackles of Versailles," but he intended to do so by enlisting the backing of the democratic West, rather than the support of the communist East. Although in his day-to-day diplomacy, Stresemann was not above courting both sides, in his innermost heart he was a westerner, not an easterner.

One of the basic issues in Europe during the 1920s, as during the 1950s, was for the two "hereditary enemies," France and Germany, to find a *modus vivendi*. But where Adenauer and de Gaulle succeeded thirty years later, Stresemann and Briand failed. Shortly after Germany was admitted to the League in the fall of 1926, the two statesmen had their famous heart-to-heart talk at Thoiry, from which Stresemann carried away far-too-optimistic hopes for the future of Franco-German relations. Having achieved Germany's western reintegration at Locarno, he next hoped to free the Rhineland from foreign occupation and perhaps obtain some other concessions—return of the Saar, a colonial mandate, anything to convince the German people of the benefits of "fulfillment." At Thoiry the two foreign ministers discussed a scheme under which Germany would aid France economically by completing its reparations payments, in return for which France would leave the Rhineland ahead of schedule. The financial part of their plan ultimately depended on America's readiness to join in the commercialization of the German reparations debt. When such American support was not forthcoming, the dream of Thoiry dissolved. Disappointment and some bitterness remained between the two partners.

The United States watched the emergence of the Spirit of Locarno with a mixture of benevolence and indifference. American feelings toward Germany, improved during the Dawes negotiations, had suffered a temporary reversal as a result of Hindenburg's election. Once its effects had worn off, however, America became increasingly pro-German, though never as wholeheartedly as some Germans imagined. Ambassador Houghton was transferred to London in 1925, where he continued to be solicitous toward Germany's interests. His successor in Berlin, Jacob Gould Schurman was, if anything, even more pro-German than Houghton had been. As I mentioned in the introduction, it was Schurman who delivered the glowing tribute to

American-German friendship in his Steuben Day address in 1927.

Ambassador Wiedfeldt had also been replaced. His successor, Baron Ago von Maltzan, was one of Germany's top diplomats, a sign of the importance Berlin attached to the Washington post. The American government during this period, at least President Coolidge and Secretary of State Frank B. Kellogg, took a friendly view of Germany. William R. Castle, head of the State Department's western European division was somewhat more critical. There were few major diplomatic issues between the two countries. America played a key role in the area of reparations, but the experts who participated in the Dawes and Young Plans did so in a private capacity. In 1923 America and Germany signed a commercial and in 1928 an arbitration treaty, both of which removed points of friction that had existed before 1914. When America took the lead in the negotiations of the so-called Kellogg-Briand Pact, or Pact of Paris, which outlawed war, Germany immediately became one of its sponsors. The treaty, signed in 1928, did not fulfill the hopes of its signers; it did not increase America's interest in Europe, and it did not prevent war, of course.

More important than what the government felt about Germany was the attitude of America's bankers and businessmen, because it was they who managed the steady flow of money to that country. When news was bad, as during the Hindenburg campaign, the market for German investments slowed down. There were also some warnings about the unproductive use of these loans from observers in Berlin, such as America's Parker Gilbert and Germany's Hjalmar Schacht, president of the Reichsbank. But on the whole the market for German bonds and securities remained bullish until that black Thursday in 1929. Between 1924 and 1930 German industries and municipalities borrowed close to $1.5 billion in long-term loans, and the annual average of short-term loans was estimated at nearly $23 million. In addition, some seventy-nine American concerns established branches in Germany, foremost among them the automobile industry. There were close relations and combines in the chemical (IG Farben and Dupont), electrical (AEG and General Electric), and shipping (Hapag and Harriman) industries, as well as in banking. Some German nationalists opposed this *Veramerikanisierung*, but they were a small minority.

Along with this economic rapprochement, American-German relations also became closer in the cultural field. Although it lasted only a bare fourteen years, the Weimar Republic produced a distinct culture of its own. This Weimar culture was not really all that new; its roots were in the last decades of the empire. But trends in the arts, literature, music, architecture, and the theater, which had been barely tolerated before the war, now flourished. Germany was the most innovative, progressive, and exciting country in Europe, and Berlin the Mecca of the international avant-garde. That ugly, sprawling big town had a particular attraction for American writers— Thomas Wolfe, Sinclair Lewis, Dorothy Thompson, Katherine Anne Porter, and a host of others. Probably the majority of Germans, it might be added, did not share this admiration for Weimar culture and the city in which it thrived. To them it was somehow *fremd* (alien), un-German, even degenerate; it was, as the Nazis were soon to say, *Kulturbolschewismus,* associated in their minds with a republican and democratic *System,* which they hated. Americans at home were not much affected by this German cultural quickening either. Few German authors were read in the United States and those few, like Thomas Mann and Erich Maria Remarque, chiefly in translation. The teaching of German in public schools, discontinued during the war, was slow to come back.

Of more interest to the average American were Germany's technical achievements and records—the first east-west airplane crossing of the Atlantic by a German team, Köhl and von Hünefeldt in 1928, followed the same year by the airship *Graf Zeppelin,* forerunner of the ill-fated *Hindenburg,* whose crash in 1937 ended trans-Atlantic lighter-than-air service soon after it had begun. The chief mode of transportation between the United States and Europe in the twenties and early thirties was still the ocean liner, with each line and country trying to make the voyage as quick and comfortable as possible. In this international speed competition, Germany's luxury liners *Bremen* and *Europa* both won the coveted "blue ribbon of the Atlantic" and were seen as symbols of German recovery.

With quicker, cheaper, and more comfortable transportation, more and more people traveled back and forth. There had been many prominent American visitors to Germany in the past, from Thomas Jefferson and Mark Twain to Teddy Roosevelt. But American tourism, as we understand the term, did not really begin until the 1920s, and even then it was a far cry from what it is today.

One sphere in particular in which the exchange of persons and ideas became active again after the war and its aftermath was the academic world. The reputation of German universities was still as high as it had been before the war, especially in the sciences, and the exchange of professors and students, although far less common than today, made for valuable human contacts.

One issue that aroused special interest among scholars in both countries was the question of war guilt. In Germany it was easily the central concern of historians, regardless of their special field, and it diverted research from other, perhaps more burning, problems in Germany's past. But in the United States, too, there was a strong desire to discover the truth behind the assertion, in the peace treaty, of Germany's responsibility. Revisionism in this country went through various phases; the "divided guilt" thesis was stated most effectively in 1922 by Lewis S. Gannet's slogan in *The Nation*, "They all lied," and summed up in a more scholarly fashion by Sidney B. Fay in *The Origins of the World War* (1928). The assertion that, of the great powers, Russia and France had been solely and directly responsible for the war was put forth in Harry Elmer Barnes's *The Genesis of the War* (1929).

But the debate about revisionism was not confined to academia. It was brought to the attention of the general public through innumerable magazine articles and discussed on the floor of the Senate. The revision of American opinion on German guilt became one of the prime concerns of the Steuben Society from its founding in 1919. Some Germans saw America's modified position on the war guilt question as a sign of growing pro-Germanism, but that was not necessarily so. Revisionism was merely one phase of the general disillusionment about the war that Europe had dragged the American people into. As such, the realization that "they all lied" tended to foster rather than counteract American isolationism.

Still, it is safe to say that America's image of Germany ten years after the war was far more favorable than it had been in 1918 or even in 1914. If there were some lingering fears about German nationalism and militarism, they focused on the traditional monarchism of the German National People's Party and the Stahlhelm, rather than on the still-insignificant Nazis. The German republic was considered securely established, and the death of Stresemann in 1929, while sincerely mourned, was not seen as the turning point it appears in retrospect.

Germany's image of the United States, while on the whole favorable, was somewhat more complex. Stresemann and his main assistant, Staatssekretär Carl von Schubert, were fully aware of America's importance for German recovery and acted accordingly. Stresemann had a genuine interest in the United States, which he had visited in 1912. In 1914 he had been instrumental in founding the German-American Economic Association, which had survived the war. As foreign minister, he was on very cordial terms with America's ambassadors in Berlin and got on well with secretaries of state Hughes and Kellogg. In 1928 the simultaneous award of honorary degrees by the University of Heidelberg to Stresemann and

Ambassador Schurman was hailed by both recipients as symbolic of German-American friendship. Stresemann was always careful not to offend the United States. When Ambassador Wiedfeldt refused to fly the German embassy's flag at half-staff on the occasion of President Wilson's death in 1924, he was recalled shortly thereafter. Also, when Germany seemed to be drawing closer to France at Locarno and Thoiry, Stresemann insisted that the rapprochement was not to affect Germany's close economic relations with the United States.

If we turn from the makers of foreign policy to the German people at large, attitudes toward America become more varied. Anti-Wilson feeling remained strong, not only among the right but even among liberal circles, and some of the disdain for this "hypocrite," "traitor," and "charlatan" could not help but rub off on America as a whole. There were some countervailing factors, however: first, America's relief activities right after the war, which were connected with the name of Herbert Hoover, and then the influx of American loans from 1924 to 1929.

The loans kindled a marked interest in America and American ways among Germans of all classes. From production methods to jazz, American influence was felt probably more strongly in Germany than in any other country in Europe. Although few people could afford to visit the United States, American movies for the first time allowed the average German to catch a glimpse of the "land of boundless opportunities." Few realized that daily life in America was quite different from what they saw on the screen. The 1920s was also a fertile period for *Amerikaliteratur,* that is, books about America written by Germans who rarely had spent much time over here. One of the most successful of this genre was Manfred Hausmann's book *Kleine Liebe zu Amerika* ("A Bit of Love for America"), a charming and exotic, but hardly accurate portrayal of American life.

Germany's image of America thus continued to be ambivalent. On the one hand there was great admiration, especially for America's technical and economic achievements—*The American Economic Miracle (Wirtschaftswunder)* was the title of a book published in 1926. Henry Ford's autobiography, translated in 1923, became an overnight best seller, and *Fordismus,* the American version of social capitalism, became the ideal not only of liberals, but of many socialists as well. In 1925 a delegation of German labor leaders visited the United States and brought back not just the usual tales of economic and social injustices, but praise for America's higher wages and living standards. Many Germans wondered if the answer to their country's economic ills lay in the adoption of American methods of rationalization and automation. They did not ask whether these were suitable to Germany's different economic and social situation. Much of the American money lent to Germany in the 1920s thus helped, ironically, to modernize German industry for Hitler's use in the 1930s.

Along with admiration for American efficiency, however, went its opposite, a contempt for what the Germans called *Amerikanismus,* a preoccupation with material things, business, money, at the expense of "finer things" and more noble concerns. America's was a mass civilization in which the individual counted for nothing—it was mechanistic, materialistic, conformist, and superficial, in brief, *Zivilisation* rather than *Kultur,* a distinction popularized by Oswald Spengler's *The Decline of the West* (1918). This view of the American people as a *kulturlose Herde* (cultureless herd) was not unique to this period. There were examples of it before the war, it reached its highest point during the Nazi years, and there are still more than just traces of it today. Just as there will always be Americans who think of the Germans as incurably militaristic, so there will always be Germans who consider the Americans innately materialistic.

Some Germans, motivated no doubt by wishful thinking, tried to make German-American relations appear much closer than they actually were. In 1929 a well-known Berlin professor and publicist, Ernst Jäckh, delivered a series of talks on Germany and the United States over the German radio, subsequently published as *Amerika und Wir : Amerikanisch-Deutsches Ideenbündnis* ("America and Ourselves: American-German Alliance of Ideas"), and dedicated to Owen D. Young, "the ideal American." Jäckh proudly quoted the phrase of "the two sister republics," which he attributed to ambassadors Houghton and Schurman, and asserted that "the American heart of the world" and "the German heart of Europe" both "beat in the same rhythm, the rhythm of an ideology first thought of by a few minds born in Europe and Germany, and then realized by Europeans turned Americans." Few Americans, or even Germans, would have agreed with this sweeping claim of American-German kinship, but it does show the false hope held by a few men of goodwill in both countries, that the rapprochement between their nations might some day grow into genuine friendship. Had Germany's recovery continued, that might have happened, but at this point the Great Depression intervened.

The Weimar Republic did not suddenly die, it slowly passed away. I have already mentioned some of its ailments—the failure to undergo a real social revolution; the heavy burden of the Versailles Treaty; flaws in the Weimar constitution—and there were others, as we shall see. But in 1928 nobody could foresee that democracy in Germany was on the verge of dissolution. In the spring elections that year, the prorepublican parties won a clear majority, and for the first time in eight years, a Socialist, Hermann Müller, was once again chancellor. But there were also some dark clouds.

The National People's Party, smarting from defeat at the polls, now reorganized itself under a new leader, Alfred Hugenberg, who was one of the most embittered opponents of the republic. His first chance came in 1929, when Germany negotiated the Young Plan, which brought some relief on reparations but also called for payments until 1988. Here was the issue the right had been waiting for—*Schuldknechtschaft,* debt slavery for generations to come. In collaboration with other radical rightists, including Hitler, Hugenberg organized a national referendum against the Young Plan, which diverted attention from the concessions Germany had gained by it, especially the final evacuation of the Rhineland five years ahead of schedule. The referendum failed, but meanwhile Hugenberg had brought Hitler out of obscurity into the limelight and given him the recognition and respectability he needed.

There were other alarming developments. Stresemann's death in October 1929 deprived Germany of its most capable leader at the most critical time, and shortly afterward, the Wall Street crash accelerated an already evident decline in Germany's economy. Its most graphic indicator was growing unemployment. In trying to cope with it, the Müller government faced a split between its left wing, the Socialists, who expected industry to bear the mounting burden of unemployment insurance, and its right wing, the German People's Party, which wanted the workers to do their share. It was over this issue that the last truly democratic government of Weimar Germany came to grief. In March 1930 Chancellor Müller resigned, and Hindenburg appointed Heinrich Brüning, leader of the Center Party's parliamentary delegation, as his successor.

Brüning to this day remains something of an enigma. At forty-five, he was the youngest person ever to become chancellor. He looked like and was an intellectual, and like all the republic's leaders, he utterly lacked charisma. The new chancellor was a loyal supporter of the republic, but he had also been a front-line officer in World War I and afterward briefly a Free-Corps leader. It was that phase of his past that endeared him to President Hindenburg. Because of the economic emergency with which he had to cope and the absence of parliamentary support, Brüning by necessity (but also by inclination, because he was an authoritarian) depended on the president's power to rule by decree. To solve Germany's desperate depression, the chancellor adopted a strictly deflationary policy of cutting expenses and raising taxes. As under his predecessor, however, the question remained: who should pay, business or labor, the rich or the poor? When the Social Democrats, advocates of the workers and unemployed, refused to support Brüning's policy, the chancellor asked Hindenburg 'to dissolve the Reichstag. The elections of September 1930 raised the curtain on the drama that ended with Hitler's becoming chancellor in January 1933. The moderate parties lost, and the extremists gained, the Communists increasing from 54 to 77 seats, and the Nazis from 12 to 107. National socialism suddenly had become a force to be reckoned with.

Brüning's main efforts during his two-year tenure (the longest in Weimar history) were devoted to foreign affairs, where he hoped to find the popular support that eluded him at home. But his successes did not materialize until after his dismissal in May 1932 and thus were reaped by his successor. The two chief problems were still reparations and disarmament. On the former issue the Brüning government obtained the one-year Hoover moratorium in June 1931, which postponed all payments of intergovernmental debts for one year. But by July 1932, when the Lausanne Conference virtually scrapped reparations, the Brüning government had fallen. Also on disarmament, Germany's fight to have its right to equality in principle (but not yet in practice) recognized by the Geneva Disarmament Conference was won only after Brüning had gone. Brüning's endeavor, finally, to negotiate a customs union with Austria in 1931 was torpedoed, chiefly by the French, who saw it as an attempt to bring about an anschluss.

Wherever Brüning turned, he faced defeat; whatever the "hunger chancellor" touched seemed to fail. With unemployment skyrocketing, with Nazis and Communists battling each other in the streets, and with Reichstag debates turning into shouting matches or worse, Germany was on the verge of chaos. This was not what Hindenburg and the Reichswehr, which had put Brüning into office, had looked for. They had expected him to be the strong man the hour demanded. Because of the president's emergency powers, Germany was ruled by Hindenburg and the men who had his ear; as long as Brüning remained one of them, his position was secure. But Hindenburg's presidency would run out in 1932, and the only way to prevent Hitler from gaining that office was to have Hindenburg run again. It took all of Brüning's influence with the prorepublican electorate, especially the Socialists, to assure Hindenburg's reelection. For Hindenburg to owe his victory to the left rather than his own people on the right, however, was a bitter disappointment, and this contributed to Brüning's fall six weeks after the election.

Hindenburg, eighty-five years old and verging on senility, had always in his heart remained a monarchist. Even Brüning, especially the soldier in him, would not have been averse to a limited monarchy. However, he needed the support of the Socialists, who respected him, but their aims were anathema to Hindenburg and his advisers. The chancellor thus was caught in the middle. When his government tried to aid the economy by a moderate land reform in eastern Germany, Hindenburg's agrarian friends cried "agrarian Bolshevism," and Brüning's fate was sealed. On May 31, 1932, Franz von Papen was asked to form a new government.

It is not necessary to recount the final agony of the Weimar Republic. Its last eight months were a sordid succession of intrigues, plots, and conspiracies, chiefly among Hindenburg's entourage, of which Papen was a member. We have already seen his ill-fated role as German military attaché in Washington during World War I (see chapter 3). Other members of this camarilla were General Kurt von Schleicher, who succeeded Papen in December 1932 as head of the last cabinet of the republic, and the president's son Oskar. They all were enemies of the republic, narrowly selfish, class oriented, and antidemocratic. Papen's aim was a corporate state favoring the rich, while Schleicher hoped for an alliance between the army, organized labor, and a dissident wing of the Nazis. In either case, parliamentary democracy would go.

Since neither Papen nor Schleicher had any parliamentary support, they continued to rule by decree. When the Reichstag refuse to endorse the *faits accomplis* put before it, it was dissolved. In 1932 there were two federal elections, plus the presidential and several state elections, which did little to enhance democracy in the eyes of the German voters. The first Reichstag elections in July gave the Nazis a landslide victory. With 230 seats and 37.4 percent of the votes, they were the strongest party, able to subvert all parliamentary action. In the second elections in November, the Nazis lost 34 seats, but together with the Communists, they were still able to block all legislation.

To bring about a change other than by violence (an alternative seriously considered by both Papen and Schleicher), Nazi participation in the government was clearly necessary. This was the most important issue during the final months of the republic. Hitler was ready to negotiate, but on his own terms. After his abortive putsch in 1923, he had abandoned his aim of gaining power by revolution and he had recently declared his intention to gain power only by legal means. But he was not ready to play second fiddle, even after his fortunes seemed to have turned in the November elections. He was to be chancellor, or nothing. Any government, to be workable had to be a coalition, and the only two possible partners were the Center or the National People's Party.

The extended negotiations between Hitler and both these groups need not detain us. Suffice it to say that Hugenberg finally consented to become Hitler's *Steigbügelhalter* (stirrup holder), thus joining Papen, Schleicher, and Hindenburg as the gravediggers of the republic. What made this wily conservative throw his party's support behind a man he really despised was that he thoroughly underestimated Hitler. Hugenberg had courted him during the campaign against the Young Plan in 1929, and he did so again during a much-publicized meeting of a "National Front" at Harzburg in 1931. What impressed Hugenberg was Hitler's ability to attract the masses. Here was the drummer, as the saying went, to rally the German people to the banner of the nationalist revolution, which would be led and masterminded by Hugenberg and his kind. The old tycoon was not the only one to indulge in such daydreams; everyone who helped Hitler gain power, other than his own Nazis, did, but they were soon to learn better.

The only other hurdle in the road to the Third Reich was Hindenburg. The president was deeply suspicious of the rabble-rousing Austrian demagogue, both instinctively and because of some of Hitler's aims. It took all of Papen's persuasive charm to overcome the old gentleman's scruples and have him consent to swearing in the Nazi leader as chancellor on January 30, 1933. It did not seem an earthshaking event. Hitler, even though he was head of the Reichstag's largest party, contented himself with minimal Nazi representation in his cabinet. He did have a large private army, the SA, but that was hardly a match for the Reichswehr. Papen, who was especially dear to Hindenburg, was to serve as vice chancellor. And then there was the president himself, whose popularity, as the recent elections had shown, far surpassed Hitler's. So let the "Bohemian Pfc." show what he can do. If he did not work out, the president who had appointed him could dismiss him. Wishful thinking indeed!

American-German relations during these crucial last years of the Weimar Republic were uneventful, except in the financial sphere. Both countries were too deeply involved in domestic difficulties to pay much attention to each other. President Hoover enjoyed considerable popularity in Germany because of his postwar relief work, and both Brüning and even Hindenburg had a favorable press in the United States. In the summer of 1931 Secretary of State Henry L. Stimson paid a visit to Berlin, where he "talked as a soldier" with the two German leaders. He was impressed with and liked them both, although he felt that Brüning lacked confidence. A year later, when Hindenburg appointed Papen, Stimson was shocked, though he blamed the appointment on the president's senility. America's ambassador in Berlin, Frederic M. Sackett, likewise was favorably inclined toward the Germans, but they were not overly impressed by his naïveté. His German counterpart in Washington, Baron Friedrich Wilhelm von Prittwitz und Gaffron, despite his forbidding aristocratic label, was a true democrat of the heart (rather than the mind), which he proved by resigning shortly after Hitler came to power. He was the only major German diplomat to do so.

The United States government and American financiers were deeply and, from Germany's point of view beneficently, involved in burying the reparations issue. There even were occasional voices in favor of further revisions of the Versailles settlement, especially on Germany's eastern border, as French Premier Pierre Laval discovered to his consternation during a visit to Washington in 1931. Hoover and Stimson broached the subject of treaty revision in private, and Senator William E. Borah, chairman of the Committee on Foreign Relations, in a public press conference suggested that the Polish Corridor be returned to Germany! The Germans, needless to say, were overjoyed.

This brings us to the end of Germany's first, short-lived experiment with democracy. Much has been written about the causes of the Weimar Republic's failure, which were underlying and immediate, foreign and domestic, political and economic, personal, social, and even psychological. Given the many things that were wrong with it, historians have asked whether the republic's demise was inevitable. Most would agree that it was not inevitable from the start, and many would say that it was not even at the end. To gain a more complete picture of what happened both before and after 1933, we must take a closer look at the man and the movement that put an end to the republic.

5 | Hitler and the "Third Reich" 1933–1939

NONE OF THE thousands of books written about Adolf Hitler have fully explained him, and none are likely to. An undistinguished, common person, he appeared to his early contemporaries semieducated and preoccupied with megalomaniac schemes to remake Germany. Yet before he was through, he had done just that and more. While he was alive, the fashion was to make fun of him, as Charlie Chaplin did in his classic film, *The Great Dictator*. The film was very funny and had some shrewd insights, but by making us underrate "the little man with the silly moustache," it may have done more harm than good. Hitler was not a little man; quite the contrary. If not used as an accolade, the term *great*, intended ironically in the movie's title, might well be taken at face value. Historians now realize this and no longer treat Hitler as a mad paperhanger or *Teppichfresser* (carpet-chewer). The puzzle is that the man who inspired more hatred and loathing outside of Germany than any figure in recent history, aroused more admiration and affection among the German people than any other national hero. To explain this contrast by referring to the German national character does not hold, because Hitler also aroused admiration among some non-Germans, from David Lloyd George and Arnold Toynbee to Charles Lindbergh.

Although historians today agree on Hitler's villainy, and their research into every phase of his life has unearthed much new material, there are still areas about which we know very little. Hitler was a highly secretive individual. He wrote few personal letters, kept no diary, and had no confidants. Most of what we know about him is second hand, although some of the legends surrounding him have now been corrected. He did not have a disadvantaged childhood, for instance, but came from quite comfortable middle-class circumstances. He was never a paperhanger or house painter, but an amateur artist of some talent. Although not formally well educated, he had read widely, albeit selectively and tendentiously. About other aspects of his life, however, we know next to nothing. There has been much interest, especially among psychohistorians, in Hitler's sex life. He has been charged with all sorts of perversions, but there is no reliable evidence for any of them, and it may well be that he was not very active in this sphere; after all, he had other things to do. But even if more came to light on this subject, how would it help us understand the man's veritable genius for doing evil?

Most people who met Hitler, including foreigners, seem to have liked, and been impressed by, him. He could be affable and is said to have exuded a certain magnetic charm. How much of this was genuine and how much put on, we do not know. At the same time the führer had an ugly side; he was extremely self-centered, domineering, and given to temper tantrums, like a small child who does not get what he wants. There can be no doubt that Hitler was sick, both in mind and, as he grew older, in body. But again our evidence about his mental and physical health is slim, and probably millions of people the world over suffer from whatever ailed Hitler, without committing any of his monstrous crimes.

To understand the Hitler phenomenon, it is necessary to look beyond the man and take into account his environment, the social and political climate that gave birth to his movement and permitted it to thrive, as discussed in the previous chapter. The major reason for Hitler's success was that he intuited and gave voice to the manifold grievances, real or imaginary, that afflicted the German people during the Weimar Republic, from defeat in war through the Versailles *Diktat* and inflation to the depression. To aid his agitation, Hitler invented scapegoats for these grievances—the Jewish-Bolshevik *Novemberverbrecher* (November criminals), that is, the men who allegedly made the revolution in 1918 and ruled the republic thereafter. And finally, Hitler offered simplistic solutions to Germany's problems, promising something to almost everyone. It has been said, especially in Germany, that the Germans in the 1920s suffered a series of catastrophes that were not shared to quite the same degree by any other country. True, but other nations at other times have passed through similar times of trouble without producing a regime as inhuman as that of Hitler.

Here we are back in the touchy area of responsibility. To blame what happened between 1930 or 1933 and 1945 on an unfortunate combination of uncontrollable circumstances, which were taken advantage of by an unscrupulous maniac, would absolve the majority of contemporary Germans from guilt for the Nazi nightmare. But it would also be a gross oversimplification, as untenable as the opposite thesis, that the Third Reich was but the culmination of German history since Bismarck, or Frederick the Great or Luther or "Herman the German." Yet anyone familiar with Germany's past knows that certain trends in the nineteenth century, although not leading directly to Nazism, were akin and pointed the way to it. The label used for these trends is *völkisch,* an untranslatable word, as nebulous as the ideology it describes.

The völkisch fog has shrouded the German political landscape for much of the last century; and although it has now lifted, it may descend again. The main tenet of this weltanschauung was the assertion that Germany was different from and better than the rest of the western world, that German *Kultur* (to borrow again from Spengler) was superior to western *Zivilisation.* At the root of this difference lay the dichotomy of western rationalism against German romanticism, of head against heart, of intellect against instinct. It was a backward- rather than a forward-looking philosophy, more suitable to an agrarian than an industrial age. As a reaction against Germany's rapid industrialization at the end of the century, this conservative protest gained many followers. The prophets of the Germanic Ideology, men like Paul de Lagarde and Julius Langbehn, preached a revolt against modernity, a return to the values, institutions, and traditions of the German *Volk.* They glorified the soil-bound peasant and guild-bound artisan over the rootless industrial worker. They preferred country life to city life. They attacked democracy as atomistic and instead called for a more traditional, organic, hierarchical society ruled by a leader. The völkisch ideology gained momentum during World War I, when some of Germany's leading intellectuals, including Thomas Mann, extolled the superiority of German culture over that of the west. During the Weimar Republic, "neoconservatism," as it was called, developed into almost a conservative revolution, as a large number of writers—Oswald Spengler, Moeller van den Bruck, and Ernst Jünger were some of the most influential—refurbished the Germanic Ideology as an antidote to the prevailing Weimar *System.* By the early 1930s plans were underway to translate thought into action, to replace an alien and artificial democracy with a home-grown, organic, "corporate" state. Both Papen and to some extent Schleicher, if they had had their way, would have launched such a conservative revolution.

What did all this have to do with Hitler? Few, if any, of these men ever were Nazis and some, like Spengler and Jünger, turned against Hitler once he rose to power. But there was a close kinship between the Germanic and Nazi ideologies; both were völkisch. The neoconservatives did not supply Hitler with his ideas, that was not necessary. He had imbibed most of them in his youth in Austria, where völkisch thought was widespread. What the neoconservatives did was prepare the German public, including the intelligentsia, for the more vulgarized version of the völkisch philosophy spouted by Hitler and his disciples. If Hugenberg helped to make Hitler respectable politically, the neoconservatives made him acceptable ideologically. More important, by spreading their antidemocratic gospel, they helped to discredit and weaken the Weimar Republic and thus hastened its overthrow. Only when it was too late did they realize that this was not the Third Reich Moeller van den Bruck had called for in his book by that title, and Hitler was not the messiah they had all dreamed of.

Hitler's weltanschauung had other elements that were not necessarily neoconservative. He was a strong believer in Social Darwinism, a doctrine that history is a struggle for existence among nations or, in Hitler's case, among races. Hitler was above all a racist; he accepted the assertions, first made by the French Count Joseph Arthur Gobineau in the middle of the nineteenth century and later elaborated upon by the British writer Houston Stewart Chamberlain, that the white race was superior to all the rest and that among the whites, the Nordic, Teutonic "Aryans" were destined to rule.

In the racist hierarchy the most dangerous and destructive people were the Jews. Anti-Semitism was an ingredient of the völkisch creed, though not every one of its followers accepted it. As shown by the authors just mentioned, anti-Semitism was not confined to Germany, but it found its most abhorrent manifestation there under Hitler, in the cold-blooded murder of some six million Jews. How this unheard-of crime was possible and to what extent the German people were involved has been and will continue to be a subject of study and debate, as mentioned in chapter 1. Among Hitler's aims, the solution of the "Jewish question" was the most basic and abiding. Whether he foresaw at the start the logical conclusion of his hatred of the Jews, the "final solution," we do not know.

About Hitler's early life I must be brief. He was born in Austria in 1889, son of a stern father, a customs official, and an overly indulgent mother. Young Adolf wanted to be an artist and architect, but he failed the entrance examination to art school. He subsequently became a drifter, first in Vienna and then in Munich, where he absorbed most of the notions and prejudices, including anti-Semitism, that later made up his weltanschauung. The happiest moment in Hitler's early life came in August 1914, when he enlisted in the Bavarian contingent of the German army. He was by all accounts a model soldier, not very popular with his comrades, because he liked to harangue them with his völkisch nostrums, but he was wounded twice and decorated for bravery.

If Hitler's spirits soared in 1914, they reached their nadir four years later during Germany's defeat and revolution. It was then, in Germany's darkest hour, as he said later, that he decided to enter politics. Starting out as an army informer on revolutionary activities within its ranks, he soon advanced to propagandist for the nationalist cause. One of Hitler's greatest assets was his oratorical skill. Much of his later success was due to his uncanny hold over, and appeal to, mass audiences. The guttural voice, staccato gestures, the foaming at the mouth, so ludicrously parodied by Charlie Chaplin, might amuse foreign listeners, but they mesmerized the Germans and chilled those few outsiders who understood what was being said.

In 1919 Hitler joined one of the innumerable small völkisch cliques in Munich, the Deutsche Arbeiterpartei (German Workers' party), forerunner of what became the Nationalsozialistische Deutsche Arbeiterpartei (NSDAP) or Nazi party. Before long he became its leader and main attraction, filling local beer halls with crowds of anti-Prussian Bavarians, disenchanted veterans, and enemies of the republic. By 1923, the year of the Ruhr crisis, the time seemed ripe for action. The little Pfc. of World War I was ready to march on Berlin, arm in arm with General Ludendorff. But the venture went awry, because it was ill conceived and ill prepared.

Hitler turned his subsequent trial for high treason into a personal triumph by assuming full responsibility for the abortive putsch and proclaiming himself public enemy number one of the Weimar Republic, a role he stuck to for the next ten years. He went to prison briefly, where he wrote his autobiography and magnum opus, *Mein Kampf* (1925), one of the world's truly terrible best sellers. He was released in 1924 and spent the next six years rebuilding his party, making it into a national rather than merely south German movement. In doing so he proved himself to be not only a charismatic leader and accomplished propagandist, but a superb politician as well.

When the depression hit Germany in 1930, the Nazi party was still a negligible force. Much study has been made of what groups helped Hitler win the Nazi victories in the elections of 1930 and 1932. His main support came from the disenchanted and fearful: the lower middle class, fearing the descent into the proletariat; the young, at sea in a time of economic crisis; and the well-to-do, afraid of the threat of communism. As we have seen, Hitler won his victory by legal means, a fact that counted for much in a country that valued de jure appearances over de facto realities.

The *Machtergreifung* (seizure of power) by the Nazis is well known, so I will be brief. Its key practice was *Gleichschaltung* (co-ordination), a term borrowed from electricity, denoting the conversion of alternating into direct current. It was applied in every sector —political, economic, and cultural; the Third Reich was a truly totalitarian state. A month after becoming chancellor, Hitler ordered another election, hoping that it might bring him an absolute majority. But despite an all-out campaign of propaganda mixed with terror, the Nazis received only 44 percent of the vote. Hitler then pressured the Reichstag into passing an Enabling Act, giving him (or his cabinet) absolute power. Everything had to be *legal*. Shortly thereafter one party after another was forced into dissolution. In May 1933 the labor unions were "converted" into a national Labor Front. And so it went; one domain after another was *gleichgeschaltet*, with little or no resistance. The Nazi conquest was far easier than Hitler had dreamed. In a wave of national enthusiasm, democracy in Germany committed suicide.

By early 1934 only three rallying points of potential opposition remained: President Hindenburg, the army, and a disaffected faction of Hitler's party, concentrated in the SA. The first of these posed no problem. When Hindenburg died in August 1934, Hitler had the offices of president and chancellor merged, assuming the title of *Führer und Reichskanzler*. At the same time he gained a firmer hold over the army by having its members swear an oath of personal allegiance to him. Hitler's final ascendancy over the armed services came in 1938, when he used a scandal involving his war minister, General Werner von Blomberg, to take over personal command of all the Reich's armed forces.

Hitler's differences with the SA called for more drastic action. There had been earlier troubles with the party's paramilitary branch, headed by one of Hitler's oldest cronies, former army captain Ernst Röhm. Some members of the SA objected to Hitler's reliance on legality; instead, they wanted some "heads to roll." Others had taken the socialist component of national socialism seriously and expected socioeconomic changes. Many of the *alte Kämpfer* (old fighters) who had been SA members before 1933 felt that not enough was being done for them. Whether this grumbling might ultimately have led to a second revolution we do not know, because Hitler struck before there was a chance. On June 30, 1934, alleging an SA conspiracy, he staged a bloody purge, relying chiefly on the much smaller and more elitist SS under Heinrich Himmler, and on the secret police, the Gestapo, under another one of his henchmen, Prussia's minister president, Hermann Göring. In two days of savage executions, Hitler settled his score not only with the dissidents in the SA, but with an assortment of other opponents, real or suspected, as well. It was a truly barbaric spectacle, revealing to the German people and the rest of the world what Nazism and its leader were really like. But there were few protests. Many Germans secretly welcomed the "cleansing" of the Nazi party, and people abroad could hardly be expected to become excited over Nazis killing Nazis.

What the outside world *did* get excited about was Hitler's persecution of the Jews. As we saw, anti-Semitism was a prime ingredient of Hitler's philosophy and of his party's program. One of his first acts after the Nazis came to power was to dismiss all Jews from political and cultural positions. Economic boycotts of Jewish shops, on the other hand, did not prove very effective, since many Germans refused to cooperate. In September 1935 the now totally nazified Reichstag passed the so-called Nuremberg Laws, demoting the Jews to second-class citizens and prohibiting their intermarriage with "Aryans." Anti-Semitism in Germany did not become overtly violent until November 1938, when the assassination in Paris of a German embassy official by a young Polish Jew was taken as pretext for a "spontaneous" pogrom of violence and vandalism against Jewish persons and property. It was organized, we now know, by Hitler's master propagandist, another of his old comrades, Joseph Goebbels. Those Jews who had not yet emigrated, almost half of the original 564,000, were then subjected to increasingly stringent economic and social restrictions, which did not run their full course— from segregation to expulsion and finally extermination—until the war.

Germany's persecution of the Jews made a particularly deep impression on the United States. Adolf Hitler's victory coincided with that of Franklin D. Roosevelt in America, and while the two were worlds apart in background, outlook, and policies, they tried at first to get along. Hitler in particular, despite his inward contempt for the United States, went out of his way to be civil to the American president, congratulating him on the first anniversary of his presidency and ordering the German press to write favorably about him. This moderation continued until the late thirties, despite the fact that American-German relations by then had become quite strained. Hitler was clearly motivated by realpolitik, the desire to not antagonize the United States, rather than by genuine sympathy. As his ambassador to Washington, he sent exchancellor Hans Luther, who had been until recently president of the Reichsbank, a humorless but agreeable man, not a Nazi, who was obviously intended to project a solid and dependable image.

Roosevelt tried as best he could to reciprocate this show of goodwill. In 1933 he invited Hitler to visit America, which Hitler declined, and on several occasions he spoke favorably of the führer. The president remembered Germany from extended stays during his youth, and he read and understood German. But he also shared the prejudices of the northeastern elite against "Prussian militarism" and Germany's incapacity for democracy. As time went on, Roosevelt was very influenced by the anti-German attitude of his advisers, notably Secretary of the Treasury Henry Morgenthau, Secretary of the Interior Harold Ickes, and Undersecretary of State Sumner Welles. Of equal influence was his ambassador in Berlin, William E. Dodd. When the Chicago historian returned to Germany (he had been a student at Leipzig), he was eager to help improve German-American relations. But what he saw of the New Germany soon disillusioned him, and he became one of Hitler's bitterest critics.

Dodd's change of attitude was typical of many Americans. At first people were ready to give Hitler a chance, saying that perhaps he would become more moderate once the situation in Germany settled down. We must also remember that America at this time was experiencing its own kind of revolution, the New Deal, and attention was focused on events at home. Only the persecution of the Jews caused widespread protests, especially in the eastern part of the country. But after these protests seemed to make Hitler modify his anti-Jewish policy, a more neutral American attitude toward Nazi Germany returned. The German government tried its best to sell the new regime through widespread propaganda in America and through such efforts as that splendid propaganda spectacle, the summer Olympics of 1936. It was only when Hitler embarked on his road to war that the majority of Americans turned against him.

Some people in America, however, took a clear-cut stand for

Hitler throughout the Nazi years. Most of the pro-Nazis were of recent German origin. The 1930 census listed some 1.6 million German immigrants; 400,000 had come since World War I, and 300,000 were still German citizens. World War I had been a deep shock to most German-Americans, and as soon as they recovered from it, Nazism revived the issue of divided loyalty. There were 178 German newspapers, 12 of which turned pro-Nazi and 36 anti-Nazi; the rest were anywhere from neutral to pro-German. Hitler, like the kaiser before him, counted heavily on the German element in the United States to counteract "Jewish propaganda," even though his diplomatic representatives repeated the warnings of their predecessors before World War I, that he should not expect anything from these former Germans. They had become thoroughly assimilated and were immune to völkisch ideas.

But there were some exceptions. There is no need here to go into the Yorkville follies of the League of the Friends of the New Germany (Bund der Freunde des Neuen Deutschland), led by a Nazi worthy named Heinz Spanknöbel, and its successor, the Amerikadeutscher Volksbund (American-German People's League), under its führer, Fritz Kuhn. Kuhn, a naturalized *alter Kämpfer* and former Free Corps fighter, was jailed in 1939 for embezzling his organization's funds and was sent home to the Fatherland after the war. The Bund's membership was estimated at anywhere from six thousand to more than a hundred thousand; it probably was around ten thousand. But what it lacked in numbers, it made up for in noise. German Day celebrations of some twenty-five thousand members and sympathizers in Madison Square Garden, complete with swastika flags, Hitler portraits, and shouted slogans like: "To a free, Gentile-ruled United States and to our fighting movement of awakened Aryan Americans, a threefold FREE AMERICA! FREE AMERICA! FREE AMERICA!", could not help but attract public attention and cause official concern.

The more respectable German-American cultural organizations kept away from these beer-swilling rabble-rousers. But the Steuben Society, under its president Theodore Hoffman, did not keep the distance from Hitler's Germany one might have wished, nor did that simon-pure purveyor of German *Kultur,* the Carl Schurz Memorial Foundation. Still, the fear of a German-American fifth column never materialized, and the Bund's agitation harmed rather than aided the Nazi cause in the United States. German-America passed its loyalty test in World War II as it had in World War I. The relatively few Nazi sympathizers were exposed, sometimes in an overly sensational fashion, by watchful Congressional committees.

Among the most dedicated guardians against Nazi infiltration were America's Jews, fortified by the influx of recent refugees from Germany. They were the most consistently anti-Nazi group. The definitive history of these German refugees and their impact upon American life and American-German relations remains to be written. Between 1933 and 1941 some 105,000 German-speaking immigrants entered the United States, more than 90 percent of them Jewish, at least by Hitler's standards. For Germany their exodus constituted a "brain drain" the like of which no nation has suffered before or since; for the United States it was an unprecedented cultural windfall. A list of only the most famous names, men and women like Thomas Mann and his brother Heinrich, Albert Einstein, Hannah Arendt, Paul Hindemith, Paul Tillich, Kurt Weill, Lotte Lenya, Bertolt Brecht, Emil Ludwig, Max Reinhardt, and hundreds more, would fill many pages.

Most of these exiles became and remained Americans, some returned to Germany after the war. It was not easy, except for the more prominent among them, to make a new start in a strange and not always hospitable environment. The most famous easily merged into the kind of milieu, academic, artistic, or, more rarely, literary from which they had come. Except for the outgoing efforts of some of their American colleagues—Alvin Johnson, George N. Shuster, Nicholas Murray Butler, Robert M. Hutchins, and others—they might never have found the positions they deserved. Private universities and colleges (especially the New School for Social Research), on the one hand, and the movie industry, on the other, were most receptive to this influx of talent, justifying one refugee's observation that "the cemeteries of Hollywood contain a large part of the Weimar Republic."

A majority of the German exiles were on the left politically. The most prominent official was exchancellor Heinrich Brüning, who kept himself consciously aloof from his former compatriots, hoping no doubt to make a political comeback in Germany once Hitler was overthrown. There was little unity among these individualists; common adversity did not create togetherness. Quite the contrary—the backbiting squabbles and petty jealousies within the refugee community present a most disillusioning spectacle. Politically, in helping shape American policy vis-à-vis Hitler, the refugees played a very minor role. A few, Emil Ludwig and Konrad Heiden for instance, wrote books against Hitler, often equating the German people with their leader. This did not endear the *Emigranten* to their former countrymen, despite the fact that the refugees as a group did more than any other to bridge the gap between the

United States and Germany, helping to prepare the cultural and intellectual climate for the close collaboration between their new and old countries in the years after World War II.

What did the German people think of the United States during the Hitler years? We do not really know, since they were not allowed to speak freely. What counted was what Hitler thought, and much has been written about the führer's image of America. Like that of most Germans in the past it was ambivalent, a mixture of admiration and contempt. *Mein Kampf* contains few references to the United States, but in his *Second Book,* written in the late 1920s, but not published at the time, Hitler had some positive things to say. What impressed him most were America's scientific and industrial achievements, in particular its automobile industry and mass production methods. Quite typically he explained these achievements in racial terms, viewing the United States as a predominantly Nordic country, made up of the best elements from the nations of northern Europe, including Germany. But any feelings of admiration did not survive the depression. Throughout the thirties and early forties, Hitler's references to the United States, in private at least, ranged from patronizing condescension to utter disdain. He felt then that America was a mongrel society, "half Judaized, half negrified, with everything built on the dollar." He discounted any role the United States might play in European affairs, sharing the widespread belief in American isolationism, seemingly confirmed by the various neutrality acts from 1935 on.

As for America's military potential, Hitler waved it aside as mere bluff. "What is America," he asked one of his America "experts," the half-American Harvard graduate Ernst "Putzi" Hanfstaengl, "but millionaires, beauty queens, stupid records, and Hollywood?" Hitler's failure to gauge the decisive importance of the United States was not due to lack of information. Hanfstaengl and a number of others, including Germany's diplomatic representatives in Washington, tried to open his eyes to America's real power. But as always, Hitler ignored any advice he disagreed with and listened only to that which confirmed his preconceived notions.

The German foreign ministry did not share Hitler's misapprehensions concerning the United States, at least not until 1938, when the aggressive and amateurish Joachim von Ribbentrop succeeded the more cautious and professional Constantin von Neurath as foreign minister. But the Auswärtiges Amt and its representatives abroad came to play a less and less important part in making foreign policy. In ruling the "Third Reich," Hitler preferred to have in every sphere a number of competing organizations, official and unofficial, state and party, so that final decisions rested only with himself. The overlapping of conflicting agencies and authorities was particularly marked in the conduct of foreign relations and in propaganda for foreign consumption, which was one of the chief activities of Germany's representatives abroad. Even though Hitler had nothing but scorn for the United States, the importance of public opinion and its possible economic effects could not be ignored. Germany, therefore, launched a massive propaganda campaign in the United States, using its official diplomatic apparatus and enlisting a wide variety of private (though government-controlled) organizations to enlighten the American people about the achievements of Nazism, to bolster isolationist sentiment, and to remind German-Americans of their heritage, urging them to work for the Nazi cause or even to return to the Fatherland, where they would help to ease the growing labor shortage on the eve of the war. Some of these activities were open, such as the German Information Library established in New York in 1934. Others were clandestine, such as the agitation of George Sylvester Viereck, who resumed the propaganda work he had carried on before and during World War I and whose failure to register as a Nazi agent eventually landed him in prison.

Yet all these various efforts to sell Nazi Germany to the American people failed, in part because too many agencies were involved. Only after the outbreak of war, when the Auswärtiges Amt was given sole charge of German propaganda in the United States, did it have some effect among isolationists. Another impediment was lack of funds. Hermann Göring, in charge of Hitler's rearmament program, was interested more in spending Germany's dwindling supply of foreign currency on vital raw materials rather than on using it to sway American opinion. But the most important obstacle to effective German propaganda was Hitler's growing threat to peace, which made it impossible any longer to present national socialism as purely a German domestic concern. Meanwhile the seemingly all-pervasive nature of German propaganda, combined with the activities of America's native Nazis, worked to poison the atmosphere between the two countries long before they went to war once again.

Hitler never made any secret of his foreign policy aims. Much of his mass appeal was due to his never-ending tirades against the Treaty of Versailles. In *Mein Kampf*, furthermore, he had quite openly proclaimed France and the Soviet Union as Germany's natural enemies, and England and Italy as Germany's potential friends. He also repeatedly stressed the need of the German people for more living space, lebensraum. But then, most Germans and many non-

Germans shared Hitler's feelings about the Versailles settlement. As for *Mein Kampf,* few Germans and even fewer foreigners had ever read, or, if they did, believed it.

Aware of the apprehension his assumption of power had caused abroad, Hitler at first proceeded with great caution in his foreign policy. True, Germany walked out of the Geneva Disarmament Conference and the League of Nations in October 1933, but Hitler could claim that there had been provocation for these steps. He made up for them by such decidedly peaceful moves as concluding a concordat with the Holy See, renewing the Berlin Treaty of 1926 with the Soviet Union and, most startlingly, concluding a ten-year treaty of nonaggression with Poland. More than anything else, this conciliatory gesture toward another of Germany's natural enemies seemed clear proof of Germany's peaceful intentions. Hitler, or Nazism, suffered a reversal in the summer of 1934, when an attempt by a band of Austrian Nazis to seize power in that country failed, but since Germany had not been officially involved, it was only an indirect defeat. Moreover, the Austrian debacle was compensated for in January 1935, when the population of the Saar region, in a plebiscite conducted under League of Nations auspices, voted to return to Germany. It was a triumph of German nationalism rather than Nazism, but Hitler took credit for it.

Thus far Germany had done nothing that openly violated the Treaty of Versailles. But that changed on March 16, 1935, when Hitler stunned the world by denouncing the disarmament clauses of the Versailles Treaty and announcing the formation of a German air force. This was only the first of a series of unilateral acts that in retrospect appear as so many stepping-stones to World War II. We need not here review this series of crises, since the major events are well enough known: the reoccupation of the Rhineland in March 1936; Germany's involvement in the Spanish civil war; the invasion and annexation of Austria in March 1938; the dismemberment of Czechoslovakia in September of that year and the occupation of the remainder by German troops in March 1939; and finally the invasion of Poland on September 1, 1939, followed by the declaration of war by Britain and France two days later, thus officially starting World War II. Two interrelated questions, however, deserve a brief discussion. First, to what extent did Hitler plan his policy in advance and follow a blueprint for war? Second, how was it possible for him to get away with what he did for as long as he did?

The first question has caused some debate among historians, touched off by a controversial book by one of Britain's leading historians, A. J. P. Taylor, *The Origins of the Second World War* (1961). The author depicted Hitler as a rather traditional statesman who advanced his nation's cause by opportunistically profiting from the mistakes of his opponents rather than by following a predetermined course of conquest. Professor Taylor's thesis has by now been pretty well demolished. No one would argue, or ever did, that Hitler followed a carefully prepared timetable; that was entirely foreign to his impulsive nature. To say, on the other hand, that he pursued a wholly pragmatic, hand-to-mouth foreign policy is equally wide of the mark.

A careful scrutiny of Hitler's utterances throughout his career shows that he adhered unswervingly to certain basic aims, which went far beyond what he seemed bent on when he invaded Poland in 1939. First there was the revision of Versailles, which he accomplished after winning the Polish campaign and beating the French and, for the time being at least, the British, in his blitzkrieg in the west in 1940. His hope before the war and during its early phase was to find a *modus vivendi* with Britain that would enable him to go beyond a mere revision of the Versailles settlement and gain lebensraum in eastern and southeastern Europe, which he considered his prime mission. From what evidence we have, and we must remember that Hitler's secretive nature did not let anyone share his inner thoughts, there is sufficient proof that he would have been perfectly content to divide the world between two superpowers, Germany and Britain. The former would rule the Eurasian continent, and the latter would maintain its overseas empire, except perhaps in the Mediterranean and parts of the Far East, where Germany's junior partners, Italy and Japan, were to enjoy satellite status.

But there remained one other power to be dealt with, the United States. Hitler felt, or daydreamed, that once Germany and Britain had divided the world between them, these two Nordic nations would join forces against the United States, or if Britain refused to go along, Germany would first defeat the British and then dispose of the United States as well. If these schemes sound like the mad hallucinations of a megalomaniac, they were, of course, but to Hitler they were quite real. They certainly were not the calculated aims of a traditional statesman like Bismarck or Stresemann.

The second question—how was Hitler allowed to get to the point where his dreams might possibly have come true—divides into two separate issues. Why did the rest of the world let him have his way until 1939? And why did the German people allow itself to be used as the instrument of the führer's mad adventures?

The first issue centers around what is called appeasement, another much-debated subject among historians. The roots of appeasement go back to the years before Hitler. Some scholars see the Locarno agreements of 1925 as the first instance of it. Appeasement of Hitler began in 1935, when Britain, after first joining France in protesting Germany's violation of disarmament, signed the Anglo-German naval agreement, which implicitly sanctioned that violation. From that time on, every one of Hitler's surprise moves was greeted with protests but, except for the showdown over Poland, never with action. Historians lay most of the blame for appeasement at Britain's door, probably rightly so, because after Germany reoccupied the Rhineland, France became the more vulnerable and thenceforth had to follow Britain's lead in dealing with Germany.

The two Allies of World War I had never seen eye to eye on the German problem. Even before 1933 many Britishers thought that Germany had been treated unfairly at the peace conference. Now they felt that some of Hitler's aims were not wholly unjustified, and Hitler cleverly exploited these signs of Britain's guilty conscience. Another sentiment conducive to appeasement, pacifism, was likewise more pronounced in England than in France. Both countries, however, were open to the fear of communism and ready to listen to Hitler's assertion that Nazi Germany was the most effective bulwark against its westward spread. These were some of the feelings and fears that helped create the climate in which appeasement could thrive.

There were also more tangible causes, most important among them Britain's military unpreparedness. The trough of the depression was hardly the time to embark on a major expansion of armaments. Furthermore, because of Britain's global responsibilities and the continued economic recession at home, the navy usually won at the expense of the army, and overseas commitments at the expense of continental ones. Finally, in trying to understand appeasement, we must not forget the clever way in which Hitler played on the fears and hopes of his opponents, following each of his territorial coups with assurances that this was the last surprise he had in store. As time went on he became more reckless, correctly gauging his adversaries' reluctance to go to war. Fear of war, especially from the air, was probably the most potent ingredient in the climate of appeasement, coupled with the hope that Hitler would become reasonable once he got what he wanted. It was such everyday hopes and fears that moved the men who were responsible for appeasement, and it is only fair to say that these emotions were shared by the majority of their countrymen. Had Hitler been more reasonable and had appeasement succeeded, he, together with Neville Chamberlain and Édouard Daladier, might well have been awarded the Nobel Peace Prize, as Stresemann, Briand, and Chamberlain's half-brother Austen had been after Locarno. But Hitler, alas, was not a reasonable man.

If Hitler's foreign adversaries did nothing to stop him, why should and how could the German people have done so? This brings us to the second issue mentioned above, once more a controversial one, the problem of German resistance to Hitler, or the absence of it. There can be little doubt that up to the outbreak of war Hitler and his foreign policy had the full endorsement of the majority of Germans. After all, the führer had created in six years and without bloodshed what their forebears had dreamed of for generations—a Greater Germany. It should be added, however, that it was not the German people who pushed Hitler into these conquests and ultimately into war; it was Hitler who did the pushing. Nor did the Germans greet the war, when it first stared them in the face during the Munich crisis in 1938 and when it finally broke out a year later, with anything like the enthusiasm their fathers had shown in 1914; quite the contrary. But they went, obediently at first and, as victory followed upon victory, even eagerly, believing what their führer told them, that Germany's hour had come.

There were some Germans, however, who did not join in the general acclaim of the "Third Reich" and its leader. How many, we will never know, since only those involved in actual conspiracies were recorded and their number, while in the thousands, was only a minute fraction of the total population. Added to them, however, must be those hundreds of thousands who went through Hitler's infamous Gestapo prisons and concentration camps, mostly for political offenses. And there were probably millions who, while not openly anti-Nazi, were so in their hearts, even though they paid lip service to the regime. It is impossible for outsiders to imagine what it was like to live in a police state such as Hitler's, where the failure to say "Heil Hitler" or to salute the swastika flag could land one in a concentration camp. In time mere neutrality, the failure to show overt enthusiasm for the "Thousand-Year Reich," became a form of resistance.

We are here chiefly concerned with the resisters in high places, whose positions in the foreign ministry or the army (the two organizations chiefly involved) gave them an opportunity to sabotage Hitler's aggressive designs. During the Czech crisis in 1938, courageous men in both agencies collaborated to warn the western powers of the führer's intentions, declaring their readiness to help overthrow Hitler if Allied refusal to give in to his demands led to war. But these approaches did not receive the attention they deserved, and by once again acquiescing in Hitler's schemes at Munich, so it has been charged, the powers missed their last opportunity to subdue the Nazi menace before it got out of hand. The relations at that time between the German resistance and the western powers remain a controversial subject. The Germans involved, although opposed to Hitler, were nevertheless German nationalists who had supported the führer in his expansionist ventures up to that point and were reluctant to give up some of the earlier gains, especially the Austrian anschluss. Their proposals to overthrow Hitler before and again during the war were thus received with considerable skepticism abroad, where they were seen not so much as an attempt to get rid of Hitler but as an effort to replace him with a conservative but equally militaristic, rather than liberal and peaceful, regime. In retrospect this reluctance to deal with the resistance may seem regrettable. But the fact that Nazism was considered not a deviation from, but in the mainstream of, German history also makes this reluctance understandable. The question remains open whether the plans of the resistance, had they been given a chance, would have succeeded, considering the firm control that Hitler held over the minds of the German people. All this should not detract, however, from the admiration one feels for those brave men and women, many of whom paid with their lives for their convictions.

One other factor, aside from Allied appeasement and the wholehearted support of the German people, encouraged Hitler in his drive toward war: the seeming reluctance of the United States to become involved in European affairs. The führer's opinion of this country, as we have seen, was very low, and there is no evidence that he worried about possible American involvement when making his plans. The war was to be a short one, so there would be no chance for American intervention in any case. Besides, Hitler shared the general belief in American isolationism, which would tie President Roosevelt's hands, should that "warmonger" try to bring his country into the war. The repeated warnings of Germany's ambassador in Washington, Hans Dieckhoff, who replaced Luther in 1937, that America would fight, were ignored in favor of the misleading reports by General Friedrich von Bötticher, Germany's military attaché, about the inadequacies of America's military establishment. Hitler's miscalculations concerning the United States were shared by most of his lieutenants, especially Ribbentrop. Only Göring, it seems, had some inkling of the American danger.

German-American relations since 1933 had on the whole been

uneventful. There were no major crises, only a gradual deterioration of the good feeling that had developed between the two countries during the Weimar Republic. Most of their everyday diplomatic business dealt with economic affairs—debts, tariffs, and trade. The key figures in these matters were Foreign Secretary Cordell Hull, and on the German side Dr. Hjalmar Schacht, president of the Reichsbank since 1933 and minister of economics from 1934 to 1937.

Schacht's major task was to find money for German rearmament. In doing so, he was often given to sharp practices, which did not make him many friends in America. He visited the United States in 1933, the only high-ranking German official to do so during the Nazi years. His main purpose was to obtain a moratorium on the interest payments on the huge loans American investors had made to Germany during the 1920s, claiming that his country lacked the necessary foreign exchange to make these payments. Since the Germans were spending large amounts of their scarce dollars on propaganda in America and on buying strategic materials, this claim was clearly false. The real purpose of Schacht's move was to drive down the price of the securities covering the original loans, so Germany could buy them cheap and use the resulting profits to subsidize German exports and ultimately German rearmament. That was a prime example of Schacht's renowned wizardry, but it did not fool the Americans, as both Roosevelt and Hull told him.

The main tensions between Germany and America in the economic sphere arose over trade and tariffs. In 1934 Schacht inaugurated a New Plan that imposed tight controls over exports and imports to derive maximum benefits for the German economy. The plan called for individual arrangements with each country, preferential tariffs, barter deals, and such, and it ultimately envisaged a German-dominated *Grossraumwirtschaft* (large-scale economy) in central and southeastern Europe. Schacht's scheme not only ran counter to the commercial treaty with the United States that had gone into effect in 1925, it was the direct opposite of Secretary Hull's favorite program of reciprocal trade agreements, designed to lower economic barriers and thus to ease international tensions. When the U.S.-German trade treaty ran out in 1935, Germany did not renew it. As it turned out, that was a mistake, because the United States began using countervailing tariffs to offset German export subsidies. The total effect of this economic guerrilla warfare was to cut ties that in the past had helped draw the two nations together. There were other economic annoyances, such as the running battle over the so-called mixed claims resulting from damages suffered by individuals, mostly Americans, during the period of American neutrality in World War I.

But more important for their effect on American opinion than these economic imbroglios were the repressive acts that the Nazis committed on their home ground. I have discussed American reaction to anti-Semitism. From time to time the victims of persecution were American citizens, which invariably provoked sharp protests from Washington. Other events incensed Americans—the burning of books, the purging of the universities, the oppression of the churches, and the control of all the news media. The American public was kept well informed of what went on by a group of unusually able foreign correspondents, men and women like Edgar Ansel Mowrer, Dorothy Thompson, and William L. Shirer, several of whom were expelled for reporting too truthfully what they saw and heard.

Still, many Americans returned from visiting Germany with glowing tales of the wonders Hitler was performing in ridding his country of unemployment and instilling a sense of pride and purpose in the German people. The warnings of German refugees that Hitler's final achievement would be war found few listeners before 1938. There was much wishful thinking in America, as in Europe, that Hitler was not really as bad as he was made out to be and that once his demands were met, he would become easier to deal with. The counterpart of European appeasement was American isolationism. Some historians in recent years have questioned the validity of the term and instead have stressed America's many overseas interests and commitments. But isolationism describes the prevailing mode and mood of American foreign policy at that time very well. The most palpable manifestations of it were the neutrality acts of 1935, 1936, and 1937, designed to keep the United States from becoming entangled in foreign wars by placing an embargo on arms shipments and imposing cash and carry restrictions on other strategic materials. These measures were initially aimed at staying clear of the Ethiopian and Spanish wars. But as the threat of a general European war loomed larger in 1939, it became clear that the arms embargo effectively prevented the United States from providing the British and French with the implements they so desperately needed. The failure of Roosevelt's efforts in the summer of 1939 to have the embargo repealed was taken as further proof by the Germans that they had nothing to fear from the United States.

During the first years of his regime, as we have seen, Hitler was careful to avoid any confrontation with the United States. Some of his initial moves, such as the departure from the Disarmament Conference and the League of Nations, German rearmament, and the reoccupation of the Rhineland, did not cause much official reaction from Washington, in part, no doubt, because these actions did not lead to anything more than verbal protests from America's former European allies. Some historians see Roosevelt's "quarantine the aggressor" speech of October 5, 1937, as a turning point in American-German relations. But it was primarily aimed at Japan and did not have any violent repercussions in Berlin. In the fall of 1937 one of Hitler's close associates, Captain Fritz Wiedemann, on a trip through the United States, was alarmed at the extent of anti-German sentiment he found, and subsequently Germany made clear its separation from the activities of the American Bund. Hitler nevertheless continued to count on the sympathy of the German-American element in this country, and America's fear of a Nazi underground contributed appreciably to the deterioration of American-German relations.

The American fear of Nazi infiltration applied to the southern half of the Western Hemisphere as well. American-German rivalry in Latin America was of long standing (see chapters 2, 3), and there German activity proceeded along two lines. One aim was to gain control over the sizable German community of the region, estimated at anywhere from 800,000 to well over a million, concentrated chiefly in Argentina and Brazil. The other effort was economic. Because of the depression, the ailing economies of South America appreciated any opportunity to find markets for their raw materials, especially if in return their various strong-man regimes obtained welcome supplies of arms. German officers, including the former chief of Hitler's SA, Captain Röhm, had long played an active part as military advisers and instructors in various South American countries. As a result of Germany's aggressive commercial policy, its trade with Latin America almost doubled during the first three or four years after 1933, while the United States trade in that area remained the same. With Germany's Lufthansa controlling much of South America's commercial aviation, there was also fear of a possible threat from the air to the Panama Canal in case of war.

To counteract Germany's advances in Latin America, President Roosevelt pursued a policy of hemispheric solidarity, which on the whole was successful. At the Lima conference in 1938, the twenty-one American republics adopted a declaration opposing any foreign intervention in the Western Hemisphere, thus making the Monroe Doctrine a concern of all nations, rather than of just the

United States. Shortly after the outbreak of war, in October 1939, another Pan-American conference at Panama proclaimed a 300-mile maritime safety zone along the whole length of the Americas. Germany's request to send an observer to that conference was turned down. In 1942 at Rio de Janeiro the twenty-one republics passed a resolution calling for the severance of all relations with the Axis powers. Compliance was not always what one might have wished, especially on the part of Argentina, where German influence was strongest. It was not until March 27, 1944, six weeks before D-Day, that Argentina declared war on Germany and Japan.

This has taken us beyond the period we are concerned with here. By early 1938 the majority of Americans were considerably more anti-German than they had been in 1914. Reaction to the conquest of Austria in March of that year was far more violent in the United States than in Britain or France. Washington immediately denounced its trade agreements with Austria and continued to demand payments of that nation's debts. Both at the time of the anschluss and again during the May crisis over Czechoslovakia, Ambassador Dieckhoff warned his superiors that in case of war the United States could be expected to join the anti-German camp. These warnings were repeated during the critical weeks before Munich. When war appeared imminent in late September 1938, Roosevelt urged Hitler to call a general conference on Czechoslovakia. But when the führer did, it was in reply to pressure from Mussolini rather than from the American president.

The results of the Munich conference were greeted in America with the same relief that was felt by most Europeans—a second world war had been avoided. The American government, having had no part in the dismemberment of Czechoslovakia, took a noncommittal stand, thus confirming Hitler's and Ribbentrop's belief in American isolationism. It was not long after Munich, however, that American relations with Nazi Germany received a major jolt. I have mentioned the sudden pogrom against Germany's Jews in November 1938, and American reaction to what the Germans, with sick humor, called the *Reichskristallnacht* (Reich's Crystal Night), because of the many Jewish shop windows smashed, was fast and furious. Ambassador Hugh Wilson, who had succeeded Dodd in early 1938, was immediately recalled, and Ambassador Dieckhoff left Washington, permanently as it turned out. Berlin, afraid of possible economic sanctions by the United States, made some conciliatory gestures concerning American Jews living in Germany, but the damage could not be repaired. As the American press stepped up its attacks on Nazi barbarism, the Germans, led by Reichspropagandaminister Joseph Goebbels, repaid in kind. Even President Roosevelt, hitherto protected at Hitler's instigation, became a target of the mud slung by the Nazi press.

The beginning of the end of appeasement came in March 1939, when German troops occupied what was left of Czechoslovakia. For the first time Hitler had taken territory containing few ethnic Germans, thus revealing to the world that his aims went beyond the mere revision of Versailles or the unification of all Germans in a Grossdeutschland. Largely because of popular pressure, the British and French governments warned that they would not stand by while Germany prepared to move against its next likely victim, Poland. The United States, meanwhile, refused to recognize the demise of Czechoslovakia and applied various economic sanctions against the Reich, including a 25 percent tax on all imports from Germany. In April 1939 Roosevelt decided to put both Hitler and Mussolini on the spot. In a letter to the two dictators, he suggested that as an earnest of their peaceful intentions they promise not to attack some thirty specified European and Middle Eastern states for the next ten years. The president also proposed, and promised American participation in, international discussions on the reduction of armaments and the improvement of international trade. America, it seemed, was ready to come out of its isolation.

Hitler, by all accounts, was furious at thus being called to task by that "madman" and "imbecile" Roosevelt. At first he decided not to reply, but then he changed his mind. He had his foreign ministry elicit from the various countries mentioned in Roosevelt's letter statements that they did not feel in any way threatened by Germany. Then he went on the air, and after first denouncing the 1934 nonaggression pact with Poland and the 1935 naval agreement with Britain, he lit into the American president. In a voice brimming with scorn and sarcasm, he derided Roosevelt's meddlesome concern for countries that did not feel any need for such concern; in other words, let America mind its own business. The speech was heard not only in Germany but in the United States as well. It was a superb performance by a master propagandist, who clearly won that round.

Roosevelt, in the meantime, tried to improve America's chances of aiding Hitler's adversaries by having Congress revise the Neutrality Act of 1937 and by calling for a repeal of the arms embargo. But after more than three months of deliberations, the House of Representatives, by a two-vote margin, defeated such revision. Both the president and Secretary of State Hull decried this isolationist victory as a stimulus and encouragement to war, but it is doubtful that a change at that late date would have made much difference.

I will not recount the mounting crisis over Poland in the summer of 1939. Americans shared the alternating hopes and fears of people the world over. When Hitler pulled off the biggest stunt of his prewar diplomacy, the pact with Stalin on August 22, some still hoped that by discouraging Britain and France from going to the aid of Poland, a major war might be avoided. But that was not to be. On August 24 Roosevelt, even though snubbed by Hitler four months earlier, made a last-minute appeal to the German leader to refrain from war and instead resort to arbitration. The führer did not reply until a week later, saying that he "greatly appreciated" the president's message. Early the next morning, the German Wehrmacht crossed the Polish border.

In a fireside chat on the evening of September 3, after Britain and France had declared war on Germany, President Roosevelt told the American people that he would try his best to keep the nation out of war. But he warned, "When peace has been broken anywhere, peace of all countries everywhere is in danger." America, he said, "must remain neutral, but I cannot ask that every American remain neutral in thought as well . . . Even a neutral cannot be asked to close his mind or his conscience." 1939 clearly was not 1914.

Most Americans agreed with their president, probably more than he realized. There were still some Nazi sympathizers, and some Communists turned pro-German after the Hitler-Stalin pact, but the majority of Americans were clearly anti-German, or anti-Nazi. This did not mean that they were pro-British or pro-French, ready to help the western powers. Yet if one believes the results of the now-common Gallup polls, most Americans were aware that their country might become involved in the European war. Isolationism, while not dead, was on the wane. What is surprising is that the Germans, or their government, did not seem to understand the critical significance of this fact.

6 | World War II
The End of the German Reich, 1939–1945

WORLD WAR II had many similarities with World War I, and some historians see it as merely a continuation of the earlier conflict. The underlying cause of both was the German problem —how to find for that restless and self-assertive nation the place in the world it demanded and, perhaps, deserved. The question of responsibility for the second war is less controversial than for the first. It was clearly Hitler's war; without him there would not have been a war, or at least not that kind of war. However, this fact does not free the rest of the powers, including the United States, from the secondary responsibility of not having done all they should to prevent Hitler from almost reaching his goal. Had it not been for the intervention of the United States in both conflicts, in 1917 and again in 1941, the kaiser's Germany might have become a weltmacht, and Hitler's Germany might have become *the* weltmacht. If World War II saw the end of the German Reich, it also witnessed the emergence of the United States from isolation and its assumption, however reluctantly, of leadership in European and world affairs. The role Hitler had envisaged for himself thus fell, ironically and by force of circumstance, to Roosevelt and his successors.

During the first two years of the war, Germany's successes exceeded even Hitler's expectations. The main events are well enough known, so I will only briefly recapitulate. All of Hitler's campaigns were based on a blitzkrieg (lightning war) strategy. The war against Poland gave the world a first taste of the combination of overwhelming power and frightfulness characteristic of this new mode of warfare. It was all over in four weeks. If the French and British had taken some initiative in the west, they might not have saved Poland, but the war would have taken a different course. Instead they adopted a wait-and-see attitude, thus encouraging Hitler to make some peace overtures, which failed, however.

The "phony war" came to a sudden end on April 9, 1940, when in one of the war's most brilliant surprise attacks, the German Wehrmacht occupied both Denmark and Norway. The British and French, expecting a German move in the west, were taken entirely by surprise. They had barely recovered when Hitler launched his Blitzkrieg im Westen. Repeating history by violating the neutrality of Belgium and also of the Netherlands, German troops and tanks overran these small countries in record time, driving deep into northern France, and within a week reaching the English Channel. The British expeditionary force, cut off from the French, was able to stage a mass escape from Dunkirk while the Germans advanced toward Paris. On June 17 Marshal Henri-Philippe Pétain, who had taken over the French government the day before, asked for an armistice. It was signed five days later on June 22 at the same place, Compiègne, and in the same railroad car where the previous armistice had been concluded in 1918—revenge must have its due! Under the armistice terms, France had to disarm and surrender three-fifths of its territory to German occupation.

The fall of France was a terrible blow to the morale of the free world, including the United States. With Britain now the only obstacle to a Nazi triumph, aid to that embattled fortress became the prime concern of the American government. Hitler, meanwhile, pursued a curiously halfhearted course in his preparations for Operation Sea Lion, the invasion of the British Isles. There is some reason to suspect that at the bottom of his hesitation was still the hope of reaching a *modus vivendi* with the British (see chapter 5). But there were also more concrete considerations. Neither Germany's navy nor its much-feared Luftwaffe were quite ready for the combined operations required for an invasion of Britain. Germany's all-out air offensive during the summer and fall of 1940, the Battle of Britain, while inflicting great hardship on the British people, did not break their will to resist. Led by one of the war's greatest leaders, Winston Churchill, and buoyed by the hope for American aid, the British stoutheartedly lived through their "finest hour."

Germany was no longer fighting alone. On June 10 when Hitler's victory in the west was assured, Mussolini had come off the fence to join his Axis partner. I have said little thus far about Italy and its leader, because they are peripheral to our main story. Early relations between the two dictators had not been overly cordial, chiefly because Mussolini considered himself the lord protector of Austria's independence. But after the Ethiopian and Spanish wars, the two had drawn closer, concluding first the Rome-Berlin Axis in 1936 and later an alliance, the Pact of Steel. Hitler always felt genuine admiration for Mussolini, even though the Duce was often more hindrance than help to him. Woefully ill prepared, Italy had stayed out of the war at the start. But now that the end seemed in sight, Mussolini was in a hurry to gather some laurels for himself. His "parallel war" in the Mediterranean, however, soon turned out a fiasco, and the Germans had to bail him out. The invasion of Greece and of Egypt by Italian forces in the fall of 1940 led to resounding defeats, which could be repaired only by massive German intervention the following spring. This diversion of forces, together with the need to subdue Yugoslavia in April 1941, seriously interfered with Hitler's timetable for his next major move, the invasion of the Soviet Union.

Russo-German relations during the early Hitler years, despite the ideological gulf separating the two countries, had on the whole remained correct. Their military collaboration, profitable for both during the 1920s, had been terminated with some show of regret in 1934. But diplomatic contacts and some economic exchanges continued. The Russians at long last had joined the League of Nations in 1934, where they were the most vocal advocates of collective security. In 1935 they had concluded alliances with France and Czechoslovakia, which seemingly drew the Soviet Union into the anti-German camp. But mutual suspicion among these powers, which was not unjustified if viewed objectively, proved a hindrance to the closing of ranks against Hitler. In the contest for Stalin's favor on the eve of the war, the Germans had won out, chiefly because they had more to offer—a free hand for Russian westward expansion, as delineated in the Hitler-Stalin pact of August 22, 1939.

The implementation of that pact at first proceeded smoothly, as the Soviets helped themselves to a large slice of eastern Poland, to the Baltic states, and to part of Finland (although the latter occurred only after the plucky Finns gave the Red Army a severe mauling in the Winter War of 1939–40). The Russians, furthermore, lived up faithfully to the economic provisions of their deal with the Germans, supplying them with vital raw materials for their war industries.

But there was growing friction between the two partners, chiefly over their respective spheres of influence in eastern Europe. Germany's advances into the Balkans, especially its increasing influence in Rumania, and its sympathy for Finland were viewed with alarm by Stalin, who had his own plans for these regions. That was one reason why Hitler turned against the Soviet Union; he believed that conflicting interests made an ultimate showdown inevitable and that Germany, still at the peak of its military strength, stood a better chance to win then than later. Of equal or greater relevance was Hitler's undeviating opposition to communism, only temporarily suspended during the pact with Stalin. Furthermore, the lebens-raum for the German people, which he considered it his mission to secure could be won only in Russia, where Hitler's grandiose schemes called for the German master race to lord it over the inferior Slavs. Some historians hold that there is still another reason why Hitler turned against the Soviet Union when he did. Unable or unwilling to take the British Isles by frontal assault, he believed that the only way to force the British to give in was to deprive them of whatever hope they might have for a Russo-German showdown. In other words, like Napoleon before him, Hitler felt that the road to London went through Moscow. He was quite certain that the superiority of his mechanized forces would enable him to defeat Stalin's armies, which were ill prepared, as the Winter War had shown, in a few crushing blows. The war against the Soviet Union was to be a super-blitzkrieg.

In retrospect Germany's invasion of Russia on June 22, 1941, appears as perhaps Hitler's greatest mistake, but only because it failed. Military historians do not consider that such failure was inevitable. Had the offensive not been delayed by some crucial months because of Germany's involvement in the Balkans and had Hitler refrained from assuming the supreme direction of the campaign, it might well have succeeded. But in addition to looking upon himself as the world's greatest political genius, the führer now also was sure that he would go down in history as "the greatest military leader of all time," another Alexander or Napoleon.

It is strange that in making his decision to strike against Russia, Hitler did not include the United States in his calculations. By the middle of 1941, America's influence in the European war was increasingly felt. America's progression from neutrality via non-belligerency and semibelligerency to war has often been described. The sympathy of the American government was clearly with England and France, as was shown shortly after the beginning of the war in the creation of the hemispheric maritime safety zone (see chapter 5), and in the revision of the Neutrality Act of 1937, lifting the arms embargo. Neither of these measures was directed specifically against the Germans, but in effect they both favored the British and

French. The debate over the repeal of the arms embargo still revealed widespread isolationism within Congress and the country at large, so the administration was careful not to mention this last fact. But the isolationists charged, quite rightly, that the repeal constituted an act of intervention that would lead to further such acts and ultimately to war.

The fall of France brought home to all Americans the need to give maximum aid to the Allied cause. A Committee to Defend America by Aiding the Allies soon had more than three hundred chapters engaged in a nationwide campaign to "stop Hitler now." With France out of the war, Britain's defense became the major cause for concern, and the most urgent need was for the British navy to repair the massive losses it had sustained from German submarines. In September 1940 President Roosevelt, still hesitant from fear of arousing the isolationists, authorized the exchange of fifty overage American destroyers for ninety-nine-year leases by American air and naval bases on British possessions in the Western Hemisphere. Two weeks later Congress passed the first peacetime Selective Service Act in American history. The shadow of war was reaching across the Atlantic.

The destroyer deal, which marked the transition of the United States from neutrality to nonbelligerency, was supported by a large majority of Americans, although they still opposed any direct intervention in the war. That issue loomed large in the presidential contest of 1940. The Republican candidate, Wendell Willkie, was a warm supporter of aid to Britain. The major attacks on the president's foreign policy, therefore, came from Republican isolationists and from the America First Committee, which had been organized to counteract the agitation of interventionist pressure groups. President Roosevelt steered a careful but equivocal course, advocating all-out aid to Britain, but at the same time assuring the American people that their boys were "not going to be sent into any foreign wars." His position won him reelection to a third term, though not by an overwhelming margin.

Britain was holding on, its RAF downing German bombers at home, and its desert forces in North Africa pushing the Italians back into Libya, but all this cost money. Again it was America's turn to come to the rescue. Although under existing neutrality legislation, loans to belligerents were out of the question, Roosevelt found a solution—lend-lease. America, he told the American people, must become "the great arsenal of democracy." To do this, he asked Congress for power "to sell, transfer title to, exchange, lease, lend, or otherwise dispose of" any war materials to "the government of any country whose defense the President deems vital to the defense of the United States." The lend-lease bill ran into violent isolationist opposition, but it was passed by both houses of Congress. Beginning in March 1941 Britain was able to obtain from the United States anything it needed in its fight for survival. America had taken another step toward war.

The next problem was transportation across the Atlantic of the materials the United States had virtually offered to give. German submarines were taking a disastrous toll of British merchant shipping, and the task of protecting trans-Atlantic convoys was becoming more than the British navy could handle. For the United States to become involved in this task, however, was extremely dangerous. After all, it had been the sinking of American ships by German submarines in World War I that had led America into that conflict. The slogan of the isolationists in Congress that "convoys mean war" still found a widespread echo in the country, so Roosevelt for the moment postponed the convoy question. Instead he asked the American navy to step up its patrols in the Western Hemisphere, which he interpreted now as extending halfway across the Atlantic. In April 1941, furthermore, the United States placed Greenland under its protection, arranging for naval and air bases there, and in July did the same for Iceland.

Germany's invasion of the Soviet Union added another candidate for receiving American aid. To many Americans, Hitler's Russian venture made a German move against the Western Hemisphere, and thus America's entry into the war, far less likely. Isolationism was still strong, as shown by the fierce debate over the extension of the Selective Service Act and the narrow margin by which it was passed. In August 1941 Roosevelt and Churchill secretly met off the coast of Newfoundland, the first of several meetings during the war. That meeting is chiefly remembered for the Atlantic Charter, a set of noble principles confirming Anglo-American ideological solidarity. But it was just words; what was needed were ships.

Roosevelt finally came to grips with the convoy issue in September. Using the attack of a German submarine on an American destroyer as the occasion, he accused Germany of seeking to create "a permanent world system based on force, terror, and murder." He then announced the inauguration of American convoys. On September 16 the first fleet of British merchant ships protected by American destroyers left Canada for a rendezvous near Iceland, where British destroyers took over. This activity could not help but lead to incidents. On October 17 the American destroyer *Kearney* was attacked, and two weeks later the *Reuben James* was sunk. These acts facilitated the president's next move, a further revision of neutrality legislation to allow the arming of merchant ships and their entry into the European war zone. The Neutrality Act of 1941 was passed by Congress in November. As before, in the spring of 1917, the United States and Germany stood face to face, with war a virtual certainty. But when it came, it was not in the Atlantic but in the Pacific.

American foreign policy for some time had been concerned with two major fronts, Europe and the Far East, and with two potential enemies, Germany and Japan. I will not go into the details of Japanese-American relations except to say that American resistance to Japan's expansion, first on the Chinese mainland and more recently in Indochina, had led to growing tension between the two countries. America's anti-Japanese policy had taken the form of export restrictions on vital raw materials, especially oil and scrap iron. In July 1940 Washington had imposed a limited embargo on these commodities, hoping thus to keep Japan from signing a military alliance with Germany and Italy. But the attempt failed. On September 27, the Tripartite Pact was signed in Berlin, clearly aimed at scaring America out of entering what might easily become a global conflict.

Japan, however, suffered increasingly from the American embargo and continued to try to reach a compromise. But extended negotiations during the first six months of 1941 failed, chiefly because Washington was not ready to acquiesce to Japan's plans for a New Order in Asia. In July President Roosevelt froze all Japanese credits, thus initiating a full-scale embargo in which Britain and the Dominions joined. Japan faced two alternatives: to give in to American conditions and forgo all plans of conquest or else fight. When last-minute attempts to break the deadlock through a summit conference between President Roosevelt and Japan's Prime Minister, Prince Konoye, failed because of Secretary of State Hull's opposition to such a meeting, war became inevitable. It is doubtful that a conference could have resolved the fundamental differences between the two governments, although it might have delayed the final collision until a more propitious time. Diplomatic negotiations continued up to the eve of the Japanese strike against Pearl Harbor on December 7, the groundwork for which had been laid weeks before. To the very end, the United States insisted on Japan's withdrawal from China and Indochina in return for American trade and financial assistance. Such compromise, in Japanese eyes, was equivalent to defeat and thus was unacceptable. On December 8 the United States declared war on Japan, and there was some question of also declaring war on Germany. That was resolved three days later, when Germany and Italy declared war on the United States.

Hitler's attitude toward the United States during the first two years of the war has rightly been called paradoxical. On the one hand, the führer told anyone ready to listen that he was wholly unconcerned about possible American intervention, but at the same time he gave strict orders to his navy to avoid any incidents that might provoke such intervention. He clearly continued to underrate America's enormous potential, but nevertheless did not want the United States to join the fight before the Russians had been defeated, because that might overtax Germany's already strained resources. For that reason Hitler welcomed the growing tension between the United States and Japan. Why, then, did he not continue his efforts to keep America neutral a while longer? I shall suggest some answers to this question a bit further along.

While everything was going his way and his blitzkrieg strategy succeeding, it was not surprising that Hitler paid little attention to the United States. The repeal of the arms embargo did not worry the Germans, because they felt that America's own defense needs would leave few surplus weapons for export. Attacks on Roosevelt in the Nazi press were again barred, and the social ostracism of American diplomats that Goebbels had decreed before the war was lifted. American ships at sea were to be spared, and during the invasion of Scandinavia strict orders were given not to interfere with American ships and planes in the area. Hitler was well aware of the American government's pro-Allied sympathies, but he was confident that isolationist sentiment would prevail and keep America neutral. This assumption was confirmed by the reports of General von Bötticher, his military attaché, who claimed to have close contacts with the American military establishment, which, he said, opposed America's entry into the war. On occasion Hitler showed some concern over what the United States might do if the war should be a long one, but he planned to have it be over before American aid could make itself felt.

American efforts to aid the British, as we have seen, became more urgent after the fall of France and during the Battle of Britain. The significance of the destroyer deal was not lost on the Germans, but the press was ordered to continue its moderate tone, and Hitler refused to give in to the urgings of his naval chief, Grossadmiral Erich Raeder, who wanted his submarines to start attacking American ships. Hitler's foreign minister and most obedient servant, Joachim von Ribbentrop, shared and encouraged his führer's unconcern about a possible American danger. The foreign ministry was now in charge of propaganda in the United States and pursued a strongly anti-British line, conjuring up and then believing all sorts of differences between the two Anglo-Saxon powers. Indications of Anglo-American solidarity, such as the Atlantic Charter were, in Ribbentrop's words, nothing but "a great big bluff." Germany's chargé d'affaires in Washington, Hans Thomsen, referred to the charter more accurately as an "international New Deal." However, as before the war, his reasonable voice went unheard.

By drawing closer to Japan, Germany hoped to discourage the United States from entering the European war; this was the purpose of the Tripartite Pact. It was not the first treaty between Nazi Germany and Japan; there had been the Anti-Comintern Pact of 1936, largely a propaganda gesture. The Tripartite Pact, however, seemed to strengthen rather than weaken America's determination to oppose Japanese expansion. The situation was further complicated by Hitler's invasion of Russia in June 1941, of which Japan had not been warned beforehand. Germany's hope of turning the Japanese against the Russians failed, because Japan had recently concluded a neutrality pact with the Soviet Union. So the Germans urged their allies to move toward southeast Asia, where they would soon collide with the United States. At the same time, Berlin watched with concern for any signs of détente or compromise between Washington and Tokyo.

Relations between Berlin and Washington became increasingly hostile as America stepped up its aid to Britain. Roosevelt's reelection in November 1940 caused little comment, although German propaganda in America had tried to prevent it. The Lend-Lease Act in early 1941 was seen by the Germans as more serious. Hitler made retaliatory threats to sink American ships, but they were still only verbal. He ordered the press to attack lend-lease as Jewish-inspired, but the German navy, eager to be turned loose, he kept in check. In March the führer extended the combat zone for German U-boats to Icelandic waters, but he resisted Admiral Raeder's request to operate within the hemispheric security zone, even after Roosevelt had broadened it to include Greenland.

The führer's main concern was with the Russian front, where a German victory, he hoped, would scare the United States away from further involvement in Europe, especially while tension with Japan was building up. To prevent any untoward incidents, Hitler gave renewed instructions that American ships were not to be attacked, even though they were soon to take up convoy duties. Hitler's attitude toward the United States during these crucial months was no longer nonchalant. He clearly realized the danger of possible

American intervention and wanted at all cost to avoid it, at least until the Russians were disposed of.

The United States during this time pursued a more aggressive policy. It seized all Axis ships in American ports, froze Germany's and Italy's assets, and sent their consular agents home. These measures were chiefly aimed at counteracting Germany's widespread propaganda efforts in the United States. Before the war these efforts had not been very effective (see chapter 5). But they improved at the start of the war, once they were coordinated by the foreign ministry. German propaganda took many different forms. First, the several official white books, of which thousands of copies were distributed, intended to prove Germany's innocence and Britain's responsibility for the war. One of them went even further. Based on captured Polish documents, it purported to show that American officials had urged Poland, France, and Britain into the war against a peace-loving Germany. The book caused a sensation among isolationists, leading one Congressman to accuse the State Department of trying "to fool us into another war so that the Star of David may embellish the White House as the insignia of a world union." Another German publication was *Facts in Review*, a skillfully edited monthly, sent by the hundreds of thousands to the news media and other influential organizations and individuals.

In addition to these official printings, large numbers of German books in translation and original works in English by Americans, surreptitiously financed, were circulated. In one of the cleverest propaganda schemes, excerpts from these writings, together with speeches by isolationist congressmen, were inserted in the *Congressional Record* and then, via the franking privilege, anywhere from 50,000 to a million copies were sent to unsuspecting recipients.

Except for the usual attacks on the Jews and, after Pearl Harbor, on Roosevelt, the main tenor of German propaganda in this country was anti-British, hoping to cash in on any latent Anglophobia that remained among ethnic minorities, especially German and Irish, and among enemies of British imperialism. Two white books specifically dealt with alleged British designs on Norway and the Low Countries. Just as in World War I, however, such anti-British agitation was more than neutralized by the favorable press that Britain enjoyed in America. When discussing their own country, the Germans stressed the certainty of their victory and the advantages that a peaceful and economically unified European continent would offer to all concerned, including the United States. Another ingredient was *Kulturpropaganda,* stressing the achievements and continuity of German culture.

The main target of Germany's propaganda was the isolationists. There were many clandestine relations between the Nazis and members of the America First organization, although this did not mean that America's isolationists were Nazi sympathizers. It was common opposition to Roosevelt rather than support for Hitler that brought about such collaboration. Some isolationists, like Fulton Lewis, Jr. or George Sylvester Viereck, were aware and did not seem to mind that they were aiding Hitler. Others, like the historian Charles A. Beard, while strongly isolationist, were outspokenly anti-Nazi. Charles Lindbergh, whom the Germans ranked highest among potential sympathizers, was primarily isolationist, but he was also pro-German. German propaganda clearly played an important role as a secret accomplice of American isolationism. To say, however, as some historians have, that isolationism, aided by German propaganda, might have kept the United States out of the war had it not been for Pearl Harbor, ignores the extent to which America had already become a de facto belligerent before December 8 or 11, 1941.

One segment of the American people whose pro-German sympathies Hitler took for granted was the German-Americans, and to the extent that they were organized, as in the Steuben Society, they were staunchly isolationist, at least until Pearl Harbor. After that the society's motto, "Our country first, last, and all the time," testified to the patriotism of its members. Some German-Americans had returned to the Fatherland, enticed by Hermann Göring who, as head of Hitler's economic Four-Year Plan, hoped to exploit their skills. Several thousand had answered the call in the late thirties, mostly workers, artisans, and small businessmen. To take care of these returnees the Germans had founded a special organization, the Kameradschaft USA (Comradeship USA). But most of them found it difficult to reacclimatize, and a few actually went back to America. During the war Heinrich Himmler, in charge of the resettlement of ethnic Germans, worked out plans for settling these and future remigrants from America in the conquered regions of eastern Europe, but the Russians put an end to such "Wild West in the East" schemes. The exodus from America of these malcontents and the proscription of the German-American Bund (see chapter 5) did much to purge the German-American community, if one can still use that term, of its more unsavory elements. There was no German-American problem in World War II, as there had been in World War I.

To return to the eve of the German-American war. President Roosevelt's "shoot on sight" speech of September 11, 1941, in which he announced the beginning of American convoys, and the revision of the Neutrality Act a few weeks later, made the eventual involvement of the United States a virtual certainty. To postpone it, Hitler continued to restrain the German navy. At the same time he welcomed the breakdown of American-Japanese negotiations, not realizing that Japan had already made preparations for its surprise attack on Pearl Harbor. The Tripartite Pact did not cover such acts of aggression, so Hitler could have continued his policy of postponing the showdown with the United States. Yet he chose to declare war on America while still tied down in Russia, thereby committing what some historians consider the greatest single mistake of his career. Why did he do so?

Several explanations come to mind; Hitler probably felt America was already doing all it could for the Allied cause with all-out material aid. As in the previous war, the role of an American expeditionary force, if not ignored, was at least underrated. Also he believed that by immediately ordering full-scale submarine attacks on all American shipping, maximum damage could be inflicted on the American-Allied cause. In addition, if Germany failed to join Japan, it would not only damage relations with that country and end all hope for Japanese help against the Soviet Union, it might also lower Germany's reputation among its satellites and the still neutral nations. As always, Hitler's decision to declare war on the United States derived from a combination of rational and irrational motives. Among the latter may have been fear of being thought a coward, afraid of Roosevelt. At long last he could tell the world what he really thought of the American president, and that by itself was worth a declaration of war.

The two nations were thus at war once again, less than twenty-five years since the last time. Their reasons for being at war, both long-range and immediate, were not unlike their earlier reasons. Whatever rapprochement had taken place during the 1920s had not proved enough to withstand the divisive effects of Hitler and Nazism. In neither war could the United States stand aside while Germany threatened to become the master of Europe. National interest called for American intervention in both cases, even though Americans preferred to see themselves in the role of crusaders for freedom and democracy against tyranny and dictatorship.

America's entry into the war gave rise to the expected propaganda campaigns and mutual recriminations. In Germany such agitation was largely government-inspired. We do not know how much the average German was affected by this hate-America campaign, but judging from the reception given America's occupation forces after the war, it was not very much.

In America during the 1930s there had been some excellent and incisive studies of Nazi Germany. Now, under the impact of a war which to many people seemed but a repetition or continuation of what had happened twenty-five years earlier, a new genre of writing tried to place the Hitler years in the wider context of German history. The result was an oversimplified view of Germany's past, in which historical truth was often ignored in a desire to prove continuity. Some of the more reputable of these works were by respected scholars: Peter Viereck's *Metapolitics: From the Romantics to Hitler* (1941), W. M. McGovern's *From Luther to Hitler* (1941), and R. Butler's *The Roots of National Socialism* (1942). But there were many others by less qualified writers, with titles like *The Thousand Year Conspiracy, The Junker Menace, Is Germany Incurable?, Germany: Jekyll and Hyde,* and *Germany Will Try It Again.* Never had the American reading public been so deluged with books on Germany's history and national character. What all these writings did was to revive the many prejudicial clichés about the Germans, popularized in World War I and now confirmed by World War II. The fact that collective condemnation of a whole people smacked dangerously of Hitler's sweeping ethnic and racial prejudices was overlooked. The image of the innately and incurably bad German was thus perpetuated, and its influence is still felt today (see chapter 1).

Although many Americans equated Germans and Nazis, they did so only for those living under Hitler. The hysteria against Germans and their culture in the United States, which had been such a distasteful spectacle in World War I, was not repeated. There were rumors that German agents were at large, and there was some fear of a German fifth column. But the FBI kept a watchful eye out for the occasional spy or saboteur set ashore by Nazi submarines. In an effort to avoid vigilantism and witch-hunts, the government introduced a strict system of registration of "enemy aliens," under which even known opponents of Hitler were classified as such. Most of these recent immigrants had taken out their first citizenship papers, however, so they were also subject to the draft, and shortly after joining the army they were granted citizenship. The majority of these new Americans were proud to fight for their country, and few had any scruples about helping to overthrow Hitler and liberate their former countrymen. Those who did could apply for service in the Pacific. On the whole, America showed tolerance and understanding in dealing with its German minority, quite in contrast to the harsh and unjust treatment of its citizens of Japanese origin.

At the time America went to war, Germany was at the height of its wartime power—virtually all of continental Europe was under

Nazi domination. There were still a few islands of neutrality, but most of them, such as Spain and Portugal, tended toward Hitler rather than his enemies. Some of Germany's allies—Finland, Hungary, Bulgaria, and Rumania—were allowed continued independence, for the time being at least, while Slovakia and Croatia (both Hitler's creations) were already dependencies of the German Reich. Italy, of course, was gradually changing from partner to satellite.

The organization and administration of Germany's vast wartime empire proceeded by improvisation rather than by any master plan (see map 4). Some regions were annexed outright, especially those that had been part of Germany before 1919, and their inhabitants became German citizens. Those that were on the periphery of Greater Germany and partly inhabited by Germans were placed under chiefs of civil administration and earmarked for future annexation: Luxembourg, Alsace, Lorraine, northeastern Poland, and northwestern Yugoslavia. A third category was a belt of "appended areas" in the east: Bohemia-Moravia, the Baltic States, the Government General of Poland, Byelorussia, and the Ukraine. These were also under German civil and/or military administration and clearly destined for de facto domination, if not de jure incorporation. Finally there were the occupied countries of western Europe: France, Belgium, the Netherlands, Denmark, and Norway. There hopes for independence were kept alive by native administrations under German supervision, intended to facilitate control and encourage collaboration against the Soviet Union.

There were collaborators in every country the Germans overran, most of them native fascists and anticommunists, some of them realists, trying to save themselves and their country through collaboration, and a few misguided idealists hoping for a United Europe. If Hitler had won his war, these western and northern Europeans might have been invited to participate in Germany's "civilizing mission" in the east, as some were already doing as members of Hitler's Waffen-SS, thus leaving the Germans to help themselves to the more lucrative areas vacated by their Germanic cousins.

While we can only speculate about the territorial and political organization of a German-dominated continent, we can gain some impression of what life under Hitler's New Order would have been like from the policies that were pursued by the Germans during the war. To realize Hitler's dream of lebensraum, the conquered lands of eastern Europe had to be cleared of their Slavic inhabitants and colonized by ethnic Germans or Volksdeutsche. In 1939 the führer appointed Heinrich Himmler as "Reich Commissar for the Strengthening of German Folkdom," and it fell to the deadly efficient head

Map 4. *Hitler's Empire at Its Greatest Extent, 1942.*

HITLER'S EMPIRE AT ITS
GREATER EXTENT, 1942

"Greater" Germany

Axis nations

Axis occupied

Allied nations

The Eastern front,
Fall, 1942

of the SS to carry out his leader's demographic schemes. Removing Poles and Russians by deportation or death was less trouble than finding enough Volksdeutsche to take their place. The German minorities dispersed over much of eastern and southeastern Europe and even in the United States were asked to come home to the Grossdeutsches Reich. But even when supplemented by those Reich Germans willing to start a new life, there hardly were enough pioneers to populate the vast plains of the east. Additional candidates had to be found, not only among the Baltic peoples, but even among those Poles, Ukrainians, and Czechs whose *Rassenmerkmale* (racial characteristics) showed them capable of becoming "re-Germanized." This Nazi ethnic policy gone berserk brought untold suffering not only to the millions of Slavs who had to make room for the "master race," but also to many of the Germans used as pawns in Hitler's and Himmler's *Rassenpolitik*.

The society of Hitler's thousand-year Reich was clearly to be one of masters and slaves. The keynotes of his policy were extermination and exploitation. In the west, these were pursued more quietly, because the führer wanted to win the cooperation of these skilled and civilized peoples in the colonization of the east. In the east Nazism could let itself go. High on the list of Himmler's extermination teams or *Einsatzgruppen* were the political and intellectual elites of Poland and the Soviet Union, with special attention to the latter's political commissars. As for the population at large, a less systematic but equally deadly policy of neglect and exploitation fulfilled its purpose. Of some five million Soviet prisoners of war and three million eastern slave laborers deported to Germany, more than half did not survive the war. The most horrible fate was suffered by Europe's Jews. The isolated regions of eastern Europe provided Hitler and his fanatics with the ideal environment to carry out the "final solution" (*Endlösung*) of the "Jewish problem." In six specially designed extermination camps, the most efficient of which, Auschwitz, could dispose of twelve thousand bodies per day, between four and six million Jews lost their lives. Thousands of Germans and many non-Germans were involved in the process of rounding up the victims, transporting them to eastern ghettos, and finally murdering them. The enormity of such crimes is almost impossible to comprehend. There have been some attempts to put the "final solution" into perspective by comparing it to other wartime acts that killed large numbers of innocent people, such as the devastating air raids on German cities and the atomic attacks on Japan at the end of the war. But such acts, deplorable or even reprehensible as they may have been, are not remotely comparable in motive, severity, and method to the mass murder of millions, decreed by Hitler in cold reason and carried out by his people in cold blood.

If the lives of non-Germans and especially Slavs were worth very little in Nazi eyes, the same was not true for their property. As Hermann Göring, head of the Four Year Plan, told German occupation officials in 1942, "In the old days, the rule was plunder. Now, outward forms have become more humane. Nevertheless I intend to plunder, and plunder copiously." Germany's exploitation of the occupied areas was dictated by shortsighted greed rather than far-sighted planning. Since the war was to be brief, the Nazis saw no need for long-range employment of Europe's resources in an extended war effort. Only during the latter part of the war, under the direction of Albert Speer, did Germany's economy become fully and effectively geared toward maximum war production. By that time, however, large-scale dismantling of industries in the east had cut the productive capacity of once-booming industrial districts in Poland and Russia.

In the west, the Germans pursued a more subtle policy of acquiring control over industry through purchase with valueless German marks or through jointly owned mixed companies. One of Germany's main economic problems, in this as in the previous war, was shortage of manpower, which was solved by employing some seven million foreign workers and prisoners of war, 20 percent of Germany's work force by 1944. Additional labor came from the innumerable concentration camps dotting the German landscape, whose inmates were farmed out to various enterprises where they often worked alongside regular workers. The treatment and living conditions of these forced or foreign laborers were such as to hasten their demise. Extermination through exploitation, a Nazi dream come true.

Some historians have speculated that a more humane policy on Hitler's part might have rallied the peoples of Europe to Germany's side in an anticommunist crusade. The führer tried to present his Russian campaign in that light, of course, and German troops in the east were supported by contingents from Germany's allies and even a small Russian force. Had Hitler gone to Russia as a liberator rather than a conqueror, events might have proceeded differently. As it was, no amount of idealistic jargon about a New Order spouted by Hitler's minions could hide the ugly facts of a continent gradually being enslaved.

The military events of the last years of the war need not concern us in any detail. Hitler's hope to deliver a blitzkrieg knock-out to the Soviet Union failed when the earlier-than-usual winter of

1941–42 halted his mechanized forces almost within sight of Moscow. The Germans resumed their offensive and made some spectacular gains in 1942, but in the fall the tide began to turn, as the Russians mounted successful counteroffensives on several fronts, culminating in the siege and German surrender of Stalingrad in February 1943. By that time American and British forces, having invaded North Africa the previous November, were moving into Tunisia, where the Axis powers met their final defeat in May 1943. Next the invasions of Sicily and southern Italy led to Mussolini's forced resignation in July and to the surrender of his successor, Marshal Pietro Badoglio, in September. This did not end the Italian campaign, however, as German forces were rushed in to resist the Allied drive up the peninsula.

The main efforts of the western Allies were concentrated on the buildup of the Anglo-American invasion force, which finally crossed the channel on June 6, 1944. From then on, except for a desperate last-minute German counteroffensive in December 1944, the Battle of the Bulge, it was downhill for the Allies on all fronts. In January the Russians took Warsaw; in February the western Allies launched their final push into Germany; in March American forces crossed the Rhine; in April the American and Russian armies met on the Elbe River; and shortly thereafter, German resistance in northern Italy ceased. On April 30 Hitler committed suicide, and a week later Germany's military leaders surrendered. May 8, 1945, was officially declared Victory Day in Europe (V-E Day). The nightmare was over, or so it seemed.

The question of what to do with Germany once it was defeated had been the subject of repeated yet inconclusive debates during the war. The Allies' primary concern had been to beat Hitler, and the western Allies and the Russians had frequently disagreed on how this aim might best be accomplished. The most persistent cause of east-west differences throughout the final years of the war had been the postponement by the Anglo-Saxon powers of their cross-channel invasion, from which Stalin expected relief of German pressure in the east. Stalin's fears of a possible deal between the western powers and Hitler, as well as western suspicions of Russia's postwar aims, had further added to tensions within the Grand Alliance. Plans for Germany's future could not help but be affected by these tensions.

The most important deliberations concerning Germany took place late in the war during three summit meetings, at Teheran in November 1943 and at Yalta and Potsdam in early 1945. Even before that time it had been made clear that the Germans themselves were to have no part in deciding their destiny. In January 1943 Roosevelt and Churchill, meeting at Casablanca, had proclaimed the famous and controversial "unconditional surrender" formula for the defeated Axis powers. Intended to dispel Soviet suspicions aroused by the recent Anglo-American deal with the pro-Nazi French admiral Jean Darlan, the formula freed the Allies from the kind of obligations vis-à-vis the vanquished that Wilson's Fourteen Points had imposed at the end of World War I. But the demand for unconditional surrender also provided grist for Goebbels' propaganda mill, who countered it with "victory or death" slogans. It has been held, therefore, that unconditional surrender, by bolstering Germany's will to resist, helped prolong the war. This assertion cannot be proved, however, and one can point to any number of instances —the German surrender at Stalingrad, continued attempts on Hitler's life (including the almost successful one on July 20, 1944), and Germany's several feelers for a separate peace with either the west or the Soviet Union—to show that unconditional surrender did not necessarily rally the Germans to last-ditch support of the Nazi regime.

A word should be said here about the final and finest hour of the German resistance to Hitler, the futile attempt to kill the tyrant in his heavily guarded headquarters at Rastenburg in East Prussia. The events themselves are well enough known. It was an amateurishly organized conspiracy, but even so it might have succeeded, had it not been for a combination of circumstances that first spared Hitler's life and then enabled him to take terrible revenge. I have already discussed the earlier instances of resistance to Hitler (see chapter 5), but this last effort was more drastic and desperate than previous ones. The conspirators hoped to escape utter defeat and chaos by killing the man responsible for it all. As with the earlier schemes, the motives of the conspirators have been questioned by outsiders, who charge that it was only the prospect of a lost war that spurred the plotters to action. Doubtless those thoughts were in the minds of some members of the resistance, especially the military. But looking at most of the heroes of the July 20 tragedy, one cannot help but be moved by their deep moral commitment and their genuine conviction that theirs was a fight of decency against corruption, of good against evil.

There remains the question of what would have happened if their coup d'état had succeeded? Would the Allies have been ready to deal with a German regime that had cleansed itself of the Nazi stigma? The answer is no. Five long years of war had erased whatever distinction had once been made between the German people

and their Nazi leaders. But even assuming that all had gone as the resisters hoped and that they had been able to build a new Germany, would it have been the free and democratic society that we find today in the German Federal Republic? Most likely not. In the words of Ralf Dahrendorf, one of the most insightful commentators on his country's search for democracy: "German resistance against Hitler is a leaf of fame in German history; but it is not a step on the path of German society toward the constitution of liberty . . . the resistance against his [Hitler's] regime acted in the name of a social tradition that could provide a basis only for authoritarian rule." *
In other words, the leaders of the German resistance looked to a better future, but their concept of what Germany should be like was shaped by the ideas and ideals of the past. Had they succeeded, they would have turned the clock back rather than forward. All of which does not diminish the feelings of respect and admiration for these courageous people, who were ready to die for what they believed. If they had lived, they would no doubt have been a valuable human asset to a nation in despair, despite their political conservatism.

To return to Allied planning for the future of Germany: by the end of 1943 there was general agreement on the outlines of future policy. Germany must be thoroughly denazified and demilitarized, its war criminals must be punished, its war industries dismantled, its territory reduced, and its government decentralized. Furthermore, reparations must be paid for all the damages caused by Hitler's war, and to carry out these policies, the country must remain occupied. When it came to implementing these general principles, however, considerable differences among the major Allies had already appeared during the war, and many of them had not been resolved by the time the fighting was over.

There was no disagreement about punishing the major war criminals, however, and their trial at Nuremberg in 1945–1946 was one of the few joint Allied measures carried out as planned. Denazification at the lower levels, on the other hand, was carried out separately and with varying success and severity in each occupation zone (see chapter 7). The assignment of these zones had been basically worked out by the fall of 1944. Britain was to occupy northwestern Germany, the United States the south (along with an enclave surrounding the northern port city of Bremen), France the southwest, and Russia the eastern 40 percent of what had been Germany in 1937, part of which was to be administered by Poland (see map 5).

* Ralf Dahrendorf, *Society and Democracy in Germany* (Garden City, N.Y., 1967), p. 391.

There was to be a four-power Allied Control Council in Berlin to determine joint occupation policies. The fact that the German capital was left some hundred miles inside the Soviet zone caused some concern at the time, but nobody foresaw the many problems this arrangement was to cause throughout the postwar period.

The territorial losses Germany should suffer and the extent to which the rest of the country should be decentralized or even dismembered caused much inter-Allied controversy during the war. There was no doubt that Germany would have to give up the regions acquired by threat of force before the war—Austria and Czechoslovakia. And there was also agreement among the Allies in principle that the Poles should be compensated with German territory for their eastern regions that the Russians had occupied under their treaty with Hitler in 1939 and which they now refused to relinquish. At the Teheran conference in November 1943, the Big Three had agreed that Poland's borders might move westward as far as the Oder River. But when Stalin in February 1945 at Yalta wanted to push Poland's frontiers still farther west to the western Neisse, both Roosevelt and Churchill objected. By the time the last summit conference convened at Potsdam in July and August 1945, the Russians and Poles had driven out many of the remaining Germans who had not already fled from the contested areas, thus presenting the western powers with a *fait accompli*. President Truman, who had succeeded Roosevelt, and Prime Minister Attlee, who had replaced Churchill, therefore reluctantly agreed to designate the region east of the Oder-Neisse line as under "Polish administration," its final status to be determined by the future German peace treaty. At the same time the western leaders also agreed that the northern half of East Prussia, including the city of Königsberg, would become part of the Soviet Union. About a quarter of Germany's pre-1938 territory, home of some nine million Germans, was thus lost in fact, if not as yet in law.

Plans for the dismemberment of Germany, by dividing what was left of the country into separate and independent states, never materialized, but they were the subject of endless wartime debates. At Teheran in late 1943, the Big Three had agreed on the general principle of dismemberment, but they had differed on the form it should take. As was often the case with issues affecting the future of Germany, a decision was postponed until the question could be studied more carefully. Meanwhile, disagreement within the United States government over partition further complicated matters. Secretary of State Cordell Hull and Secretary of War Henry Stimson feared that too drastic a weakening of Germany would leave the

Soviet Union the dominant power in Europe, but Secretary of the Treasury Henry Morgenthau advocated the partition and deindustrialization of Germany as the surest means of preventing the resurgence of Prussian militarism. I shall say more about the Morgenthau Plan below. Because of the importance of his office under lend-lease and his friendship with Roosevelt, the plan received a friendly hearing, and the deindustrialization (though not the partition) proposal was endorsed by Roosevelt and Churchill during a meeting at Quebec in September 1944.

The question of German dismemberment continued to be debated in Washington as well as by the inter-Allied European Advisory Commission in London. The State Department continued to oppose it, while Roosevelt preferred to postpone a final decision. "I dislike making plans for a country which we do not yet occupy," he told Hull in October 1944. When the Yalta conference took place in February 1945, however, American troops had taken a small corner of Germany and were poised for their final push. Still, nothing definite was done at Yalta about the partition of Germany. Stalin again proposed it, but for various reasons Churchill was reluctant to commit himself, and Roosevelt took a position in between. As a result, the question was postponed once again. By the time of the Potsdam conference in the summer of 1945, Stalin had settled the issue by announcing, at the time of the German surrender in May, that the Soviet Union did not intend "either to dismember or to destroy Germany." The Russian leader had realized that not only Britain but also the United States was opposed to German dismemberment. At Potsdam, therefore, the Big Three agreed to treat what remained of Germany as a unit. Events soon proved that that intention would be increasingly difficult to carry out.

On the related issues of reparations and deindustrialization, finally, deliberations by the Big Three remained quite inconclusive. It was over the reparations question that the first open break between the western and eastern Allies was to occur after the war. The Morgenthau Plan, calling for the dismantling of German industries and the transfer of equipment as reparations, ran into heavy opposition from both Stimson and Hull. To Stimson it was "fighting brutality with brutality," and Hull later called it a plan of "blind vengeance." For Nazi propagandists it was a godsend, of course, because it showed the German people what to expect from unconditional surrender—"a satanic plan of annihilation" inspired by Jews. However, it was not so much the understandable vengefulness of Morgenthau's program that deserved to be criticized, but its economic shortsightedness. To make Germany, as the plan said, "a country primarily agricultural and pastoral," would not only be punishment for the Germans, but it would chain Britain (and the rest of Europe), as Churchill had pointed out at Quebec, "to a dead body." In other words, the elimination of German industry would have dire economic consequences not only for Germany but for the rest of the world. As it turned out, the Morgenthau Plan was never officially implemented, but some of the thinking behind it survived and found its way into the regulations governing America's early occupation policy after 1945.

By December 1944 Roosevelt himself agreed that Germany should be permitted to "come back industrially to meet her own needs," and he warned at the same time against reparations, no doubt remembering the troubles they had caused after World War I. At Yalta, however, Morgenthau's proposals found a warm supporter in Stalin. The Russians insisted that Germany should surrender $20 billion in reparations, half to the Soviet Union, and that the bulk of this should come from the removal of Germany's heavy industry. Since Britain and the United States were very concerned about leaving the Germans enough to support themselves, no agreement was possible, and the problem was referred to a Reparations Commission for further study. At Potsdam the Big Three still could not agree on how much of German industry should be dismantled and removed. It was decided that each power should take reparations from its own occupation zone, a practice on which the Russians had already embarked with gusto. But since most of Germany's industry was located in the British and American zones, the Soviet Union was to receive an additional 25 percent from these areas, 15 percent of it in exchange for foodstuffs and raw materials from the predominantly agrarian Soviet zone.

The Potsdam conference ended the wartime phase of Allied planning for Germany, and its results foreshadowed many of the problems that were to make Germany the main battleground in the cold war that followed. With Germany defeated and shortly after Potsdam, Japan as well, the Grand Alliance lost its *raison d'être*, and differences that had been suppressed in favor of a common war effort now burst into the open.

The history of World War II is a favorite playground for purveyors of hindsight, and there has been much criticism of the policy of postponement that characterized inter-Allied negotiations during the war. If only the western powers had forced Stalin to agree to their postwar program while Russia was still fighting for its life (presuming that a victorious Stalin would have kept the promises he made under duress); if only the western powers had invaded the Balkans, thus preventing the Russians from taking over and communizing that area (but enabling them to move farther west in Germany, perhaps as far as the Rhine); or if only the western armies had made a dash for Berlin (forgetting that by the time such a feat became possible, the German capital had already been assigned to the Soviet zone).

President Roosevelt's dealings with Stalin have been variously described as treasonous, shortsighted, and naïve. This is not the place to argue the case of the traditional liberal historians versus the revisionist radical historians. But the following are some factors that may help us understand the American policy, in retrospect not very farsighted, on the future of Germany.

First of all, we must remember that the Grand Alliance was an accidental and far from harmonious coalition, held together solely by the common dread of Hitler. It was beset by suspicions, especially on Stalin's part, who remembered prewar appeasement and did not discount the possibility of an anti-Russian western deal with Hitler. The western Allies, on the other hand, never quite forgot the Russo-German pact that had helped unleash the war. In this atmosphere of distrust, any disagreement that might weaken the tenuous cohesion of the Grand Alliance had to be avoided. The members of the Alliance, furthermore, differed greatly on the postwar Europe they envisaged. Stalin's foremost concern was the security of the Soviet Union: hence his desire to weaken Germany as much as possible. But there was also a nationalist element in Russian policy—the hope to regain the territories that the Czarist empire had held in 1914 and that Stalin had temporarily regained under his pact with Hitler. To what extent the spread of communism was Stalin's aim, or when it became his aim, we do not know; it is safe to assume that it was always there, at least in the back of his mind.

The western leaders, Roosevelt more so than Churchill, in their desire to get along with the Russians and aware of the sacrifices the Russian people were making in the anti-Hitler cause, interpreted Stalin's aims as solely security and traditional nationalism. Only at Yalta in early 1945, when it was already too late, were they suddenly faced with the ingredient of communist expansion in Stalin's policy, when the Russian leader insisted that his country's security required the presence of friendly, that is communist, states on its borders.

The western Allies wanted to disable Germany permanently to prevent another war, but they did not want to see Russian, any more than German, hegemony on the continent. Churchill envisaged the future of Europe pretty much along traditional lines.

Overestimating Britain's and France's continued strength and underestimating the potential power of the Soviet Union, the British prime minister foresaw a continental balance of power in which Soviet expansionism would be checked by the western powers. Churchill was ready to recognize east-central Europe as primarily Russia's sphere of influence, but he failed to realize that to Stalin, influence was synonymous with control.

As for President Roosevelt, he thought of peace and security in worldwide rather than merely European terms. The only way a third world war could be avoided was through continued cooperation among the wartime Allies. His favorite scheme was that of the "four policemen"—America, Britain, the Soviet Union, and China—maintaining peace and order through the sheer weight of their superior power. In time, and under the influence of Cordell Hull, the idea of the United Nations replaced the great powers as a peacekeeping agency in Roosevelt's mind, but even within that body the word of the Big Four was to be decisive.

Far more than Churchill, Roosevelt believed, or wanted to believe, that Stalin was a reasonable and realistic statesman, not unlike his western partners. Much of this misconception was doubtless based on wishful thinking, like the view that the appeasers had held of Hitler. But unlike the appeasers, Roosevelt was convinced that the only way to avoid another war was through collaboration rather than confrontation with Russia, which was realistic, given the conditions at the time and the dependence of the western powers on Soviet help in defeating Germany. Also Roosevelt realized that the majority of the American people were not yet ready to forgo their isolationism. Despite much talk of One World (the title of Wendell Willkie's famous book) among a small group of internationalists, most Americans hoped for disengagement from Europe after this war, as after the previous one. Roosevelt may have been naïve in his belief that cooperation with Stalin would be possible. But given the situation in which he found himself at Yalta, with most of eastern Europe under Soviet control, with the final invasion of Germany about to begin, and with the war against Japan far from over, and given the expectations of the American people that at long last this was the war to end all wars, it is difficult to see how the president could have followed any other policy.

That policy, we must realize, was not concerned just with Germany. Military planning, the future of eastern Europe, the organization of the United Nations, the collaboration of Russia in the final defeat of Japan—all these and many other questions crowded the agendas of the various summit and sub-summit meetings in the final phase of the war. The future of Germany, in retrospect, was easily the most crucial of all these issues, but it did not appear so at the time. Nobody, at least among the top-echelon western leaders, seems to have given much thought to the drastic consequences inherent in the total defeat of Germany and the sudden emergence of a power vacuum in central Europe. But then, those were hardly days for quiet contemplation of long-range issues. Too much was happening too fast—the death of Roosevelt, the execution of Mussolini, the suicide of Hitler, the surrender of Germany, the defeat of Churchill, the dropping of the atomic bombs, and the surrender of Japan—all of these events took place within a span of only four months. Events were moving so fast it was impossible to assess their significance.

Meanwhile, the occupation of Germany brought Americans face to face with not only German soldiers but with civilians as well. On the eve of the final invasion, each American soldier was given a set of "Special Orders for German-American Relations." As a reminder of how Americans felt about the Germans, they deserve extensive quotation:

> We are now fighting on German soil, and we are in contact not only with the soldiers of our enemy but also civilians of Germany. As conquerors, we must now consider our relations with the people of Germany.

> It is imperative that you do not allow yourself to become friendly with Germans, but at the same time you must not persecute them . . . The occupational forces are not on a good-will mission . . .

> For most of the past century, Germany has sought to attain world domination by conquest . . . The German has been taught that the national goal of domination must be attained regardless of the depths of treachery, murder and destruction necessary . . .

> There will be appeals to generosity and fair play; to pity for victims of devastation; to racial and cultural similarities; and to sympathy for an allegedly oppressed people. There will be attempts . . . at proving that Nazism was never wanted by the "gentle and cultured" German people . . .

> We must bring home to the Germans that their support of Nazi leaders, their tolerance of racial hatreds and persecutions, and their unquestioning acceptance of the wanton aggressions on other nations, have earned for them the contempt and distrust of the civilized world. We must never forget that the German people support the Nazi principles . . .

American soldiers must not associate with Germans. Specifically, it is not permissible to shake hands with them ... Experience has shown that Germans regard kindness as weakness ...

Firmness must be tempered with a strict justice. Americans do not resort to gangster methods in dealing with any people. Remember, your fair but firm treatment of the German people will command the proper respect due a member of a conquering nation.

In their mixture of self-righteousness and indiscriminate contempt for a whole people, some of these instructions today make rather painful reading. But it is worth remembering that they did not seem unjustified or uncalled-for at the time they were issued.

7 | One Germany or Two?
Occupation, 1945–1949

T HE EARLY POSTWAR YEARS of what had been until May 8, 1945, Grossdeutschland were among the most troublous and turbulent in that nation's history. In their attempt to bring some order into the chaos left by the collapse of the Third Reich, the wartime Allies soon found themselves at odds over what kind of new Germany they hoped to build on the ruins of the old. As time went on, the German people, at first mere pawns of Allied policy, began to play an active part in the East-West struggle over their country. To disentangle these various interacting and often conflicting events, I shall first discuss the rising inter-Allied tension over Germany, which culminated in the Berlin blockade of 1948–1949; then I shall deal with the varying policies of the four occupying powers, especially the United States, vis-à-vis Germany; and finally I shall trace the revival of German domestic politics and the emergence of two quite disparate German states.

However, we must remember that the falling out between the western powers and the Soviet Union over that country was only one, albeit the most important, of several conflicts that together made up the cold war. The first differences among the wartime Allies had actually arisen in the final months of the war, not so much over the future of Germany as over that of Poland, where Stalin was busily establishing a Soviet satellite. Further Russian encroachments, not only upon eastern and southeastern Europe, but in the Near East as well, in Greece, Iran, and Turkey, gave the impression of a relent-

153

less communist advance, which in turn gave rise to western efforts to contain that expansion.

I will only briefly recall the major stages in the escalation of the cold war. When Britain in early 1947 announced its inability to give further aid to Greece and Turkey in their efforts to resist Russian pressure, the United States stepped in, and under the Truman Doctrine of March 12, 1947, took over the burden hitherto carried by the British. The Marshall Plan followed in June of that year, involving America still more deeply in the affairs of Europe. Out of the Marshall Plan grew the Organization for European Economic Cooperation (OEEC) the following year.

The Soviet Union, meanwhile, having refused America's invitation to participate in the Marshall Plan, gathered the communist states of eastern Europe behind the Cominform (a revival of the Comintern, which had been dissolved in World War II). In February 1948 the communist coup in Czechoslovakia further accelerated western fears of communism and led the western European nations to consolidate their military forces behind the Brussels Treaty Organization. All this time each of the major western powers was also involved in extra-European crises—Britain in southern Asia (India, Pakistan, Ceylon, and Burma), France in Indochina, and the United States in China. It was the victory of Mao Tse-tung on the Chinese mainland and the proclamation of the Chinese People's Republic in October 1949 that brought home the global nature of the cold war. In that war the potential power of Germany was still a major prize, which is the reason why the East-West struggle over Germany was fought with such tenacity.

I HAVE ALREADY DESCRIBED the utter desolation and despair that reigned in Germany after its surrender (see Chapter 1). This time defeat was truly total; there would be no "stab in the back" legend as there had been after World War I. Since there was no longer any German government, the Allies, by official declaration on June 5, 1945, assumed supreme control of the country, an unprecedented opportunity, but also an awesome responsibility. It soon became clear that the Allies had done little to prepare for this takeover. An Allied Control Council had been provided for, but it did not start functioning until the end of July, almost three months after the German surrender. By then the military governors in the four occupation zones had embarked on their separate policies of coping with the emergencies they faced. The decisions of the Control Council required unanimity, and its effective functioning depended on agreement among the powers it represented, but such agreement

DENMARK

North Sea

Baltic Sea

Kiel

MECKLENBURG

Schwerin

Hamburg

Bremen (U.S.)

LOWER SAXONY

Elbe R.

SOVIET

POLAND

BRANDENBURG

BRITISH

Berlin

Potsdam

NETHERLANDS

Hannover

Weser R.

ZONE

Bielefeld

ZONE

Oder R.

SAXONY-
ANHALT

NORTH RHINE-

Düsseldorf

Kassel

Halle

Erfurt

Leipzig

Dresden

Neisse R.

WESTPHALIA

SAXONY

Bonn

HESSE

THURINGIA

BELG.

Rhine R.

Frankfurt

RHINELAND-

LUX.

PALATINATE

R.

Main R.

CZECHOSLOVAKIA

FRENCH

SAAR

Nuremberg

Heidelberg

AMERICAN

WÜRTTEMBERG

Regensburg

Baden-Baden

Stuttgart

BADEN

BAVARIA

FRANCE

Freiburg

ZONE

Augsburg

ZONE

BADEN

Munich

AUSTRIA

OCCUPIED GERMANY
1945-1949

Map 5. Occupied Germany, 1945–1949.

was rare. Initially it was the French rather than the Russians who freely used their veto to prevent implementation of the provisions for central German administrative departments agreed on at the Potsdam conference, from which France had been excluded. As a coordinating body, therefore, the Control Council proved a major disappointment. Its activities were finally suspended sine die on the eve of the Berlin blockade in 1948, when its Russian member walked out in protest against the German policy of the western powers.

One important measure carried out jointly as planned was the trial by an inter-Allied tribunal of the major war criminals at Nuremberg in 1945–1946. Some of the most odious of them—Hitler, Goebbels, Himmler, and Ley—had already committed suicide, and Göring did the same while in prison. Among the rest, eleven, including Ribbentrop and Seyss-Inquart, were condemned to death; three, including Speer and Dönitz, were given life sentences; and three, including Schacht and Papen, were acquitted. Additional trials of Germans in various categories (diplomats, doctors, SS functionaries, and industrialists) were carried out by American tribunals under Control Council authority between 1946 and 1949. These were not the only attempts to eradicate the Nazi past, of course. There remained the far more cumbersome and lengthy denazification hearings and trials, which were carried out separately and with varying success in each occupation zone, as discussed later in this chapter.

The Nuremberg trials have come in for a good deal of justified criticism. They were conducted by a court that could hardly be called unprejudiced, and they were based on laws that were mostly *ex post facto*. In retrospect a neutral or even a German tribunal would have been preferable. Also, the fact that at least one of the governments sitting in judgment, the Soviet Union, had committed crimes not unlike those charged to the accused (for example, the Katyn Forest Massacre) hardly inspired confidence in the court's impartiality. Finally, by condemning whole groups of Germans for belonging to certain Nazi organizations and making them liable to prosecution implied a charge of collective guilt to which most Germans objected. As a means of showing the German people the errors of their ways, the Nuremberg proceedings were far from successful.

By the time the Nuremberg trials came to an end, the German policies of the various Allies had taken quite different directions. Russia, after a brief surge of revenge, settled down to steady exploitation and the collection of reparations, not only from its own zone but from the rest of Germany, as had been agreed at Potsdam. Looking to the future, the Soviets favored a centralized German state,

hoping that it would facilitate a communist take-over. Like the
Soviets, the French also wanted the Germans to pay to the limit.
But for reasons of security they advocated a loosely federated and
partially dismembered rather than high centralized Germany, with
the Saar region going to France, the Ruhr under international control, and an independent Rhineland serving as a buffer state. These
aims were not unlike those that France had pursued at the end of
World War I. At this stage any attempt to treat Germany as an economic or political unit was vetoed by the French representative on
the Allied Control Council on the grounds that it would lead to a
revival of German strength.

    The United States and Britain, while differing in some re-
spects from each other, were united in their opposition to the French
and Russian policies and plans. Since their zones were more heavily
populated and less agricultural than the Russian zone, they not only
had to support their own occupation forces (while the French and
Russians lived off the land), they also had to import large quantities
of food to keep the Germans alive. Both Britain and America initially favored a large-scale reduction of German industry. But they
soon realized that the only way in which the Germans could help
support themselves was by expanding, rather than reducing, German
industrial production and by treating the country as the "single economic unit" that had been agreed on at Potsdam. As for the political
future of Germany, the Anglo-Saxon powers favored a federal rather
than a unitary system, halfway between the solutions proposed by
the French and the Russians.

    Between 1945 and 1949 inter-Allied deliberations on German
affairs were carried on at a series of six Council of Foreign Ministers'
meetings. None of these brought any positive results on the German
question. The first conference in London, in September and October
1945, dealt chiefly with the peace treaties to be concluded with
Hitler's satellites and discussed Germany only peripherally. A fol-
low-up meeting of this first conference, in Moscow in December, remained indecisive, because French Foreign Minister Georges Bidault
did not attend. The other two western ministers, however, Britain's
Ernest Bevin and America's James F. Byrnes, used the occasion to
protest the drastic economic measures in the Soviet zone of occupation as destructive and detrimental to the German economy as a
whole.

    At the second Council of Foreign Ministers' meeting in Paris,
in April and in June and July 1946, Germany became the center of
increasingly acrimonious debate. Secretary of State Byrnes proposed
a twenty-five-year disarmament pact for Germany as a demonstra-

tion of continued Allied unity and a guarantee of future security. But Russia's Vyacheslav Molotov criticized the Byrnes plan as inadequate and called for the "democratization" of Germany, presumably on the model of the Soviet zone. Molotov reiterated his government's demand for $10 billion in reparations, and he joined the French in demanding four-power control over the Ruhr industrial region. Both Byrnes and Bevin, on the other hand, insisted that Germany's economy should be considered in toto and allowed to recover, not only for Germany's, but for Europe's sake. Byrnes also called for an early German peace conference, but Molotov wanted a central German government first, which the French in turn objected to.

The Paris meeting widened rather than narrowed the four-power differences over Germany. At the next foreign ministers' conference in New York, in November and December 1946, Molotov refused even to discuss the German problem, and negotiations were postponed until the following spring in Moscow. By that time, however, events in the western occupation zones had begun to show a definite trend toward the ultimate division of Germany. On September 6, 1946, Secretary of State Byrnes delivered his famous speech before a German audience in Stuttgart, signaling a wholly new phase in America's policy toward Germany. After reviewing various aspects of the Allied occupation, Byrnes sharply criticized the Allied Control Council for "neither governing Germany nor allowing Germany to govern itself." In particular he singled out the Council's failure to take the necessary steps to enable the German economy to function as an economic unit. "If complete unification cannot be secured," the secretary of state announced, "we shall do everything in our power to secure the maximum possible unification." The first step in partial unification had been taken the previous day, when the American and British military governments had agreed to join their two zones economically, establishing what came to be called Bizonia, a merger that went into effect on January 1, 1947. In retrospect that was the first move toward what later became a separate West German state, but it is important to note that this was not the intention of its sponsors at the time. "This policy of unification," Byrnes emphasized, "is not intended to exclude the governments not now willing to join. The unification will be open to them at any time they wish to join."

This was the situation when the foreign ministers met for their fourth conference in Moscow in March and April 1947. The preceding winter had been a particularly harsh one, and the German people had suffered because of it. It was urgent, therefore, to make some headway on the German question, but because the participants were unwilling to change their basic positions, little was achieved. The Russians once again repeated their $10 billion reparations demand and said they would agree to economic unification only in return for four-power control of the Ruhr. The western powers made specific proposals for the gradual political revival of a unified Germany, to which the Russians made specious counterproposals. As Secretary of State George Marshall, who had recently replaced Byrnes, wrote in his report: "The patient is sinking while the doctors deliberate." The announcement of the Truman Doctrine two days after the conference opened did not improve its atmosphere. The only agreement reached was on the official liquidation of the state of Prussia, its virtual dissolution having already taken place. It was hardly an enlightened decision.

The Moscow conference has been seen as a turning point for the future of Germany. From then on the emergence of a West German state and its integration into the western bloc appeared as a clearly discernible, though still not irrevocable, possibility. In June 1947, six weeks after Moscow, Germany's three western zones were invited under the Marshall Plan to participate in planning for European recovery. In August the American and British military governors announced a revised level-of-industry plan for Bizonia, substantially raising the level of production of steel The measure was attacked by the Russians as a violation of the Potsdam agreements and circumvention of the Control Council. To counter the ceaseless anti-American tirades in the eastern German press, the American military governor, Lucius D. Clay, lifted the ban against anticommunist attacks in the West German press, and the war of words was on. When the Council of Foreign Ministers met again, in London in November and December 1947, Molotov charged that the United States and Britain were using the Marshall Plan to "enslave" Germany and using the Ruhr as an arsenal for an "imperialist war." The western powers again made various suggestions for the integration of the four zones, and Marshall invited the Soviets to join their zone to Bizonia. But Molotov refused. The London conference followed the scenarios of earlier meetings. Shortly after the delegates departed, without setting a date for their next get-together, General Clay put a final halt to all reparations deliveries to the Russians from the American zone. Four-power efforts to solve the German problem, for the time being at least, had come to an end.

The next eighteen months were easily the most dramatic and decisive in the history of post-World War II Germany. As we shall see, they witnessed the formation of two separate German republics and, on the international level, the first East-West confrontation over Berlin. The Russians, deeply worried by events in the western zones, hoped to use the vulnerable and exposed position of the western powers in the former German capital to win by pressure the concessions they had been unable to obtain at the conference table. As a first move, the Soviet delegate to the Allied Control Council in Berlin, Marshal Sokolovsky, walked out on March 20, 1948, charging that the western powers were violating the quadripartite administration of Germany. Ten days later, the Russians began interfering with rail traffic between Berlin and western Germany. The western occupying countries, meanwhile, were meeting in London with the three Benelux nations to discuss the transformation of Bizonia from an economic into a political entity. The results of their deliberations were announced on June 4. There was to be close integration of the three western zones and the convocation of a German constituent assembly; the Ruhr was to come under international control; Germany was to participate in the European recovery program; and there was to be an Allied military security board. In addition, the western authorities two weeks later decreed a currency reform for their zones to spur economic recovery. This last measure gave the Russians the excuse they had been waiting for; to keep the new currency out of Berlin, a total ban on all rail and road traffic to the western zones was imposed on June 24. The Berlin blockade had started.

The four-power status of Berlin and the delineation of the occupation sectors had been worked out in November 1944, but no provision had been made for free access across the Soviet zone. The Russians claimed that with the termination of the Control Council's activities, there was no longer any need for the western powers to be in Berlin, but the latter disagreed. The first Berlin crisis, like succeeding ones, was a contest of strength. Until November 1948 the city had a unified municipal administration. In citywide elections in 1946, the Soviet-sponsored and communist-dominated Socialist Unity Party (SED) had won barely 20 percent of the vote, while the Social Democrats had gained close to 49 percent. Berlin was thus a testing ground for the comparative appeal of the eastern and western occupations. The story of the western, largely American, reply to Soviet provocation, the Berlin airlift, is well known. When the Russians finally realized, in the spring of 1949, that their competitors could not be dislodged, they gave in and signed an agreement calling for the end of travel restrictions and the convening of another Council of Foreign Ministers' meeting. The Berlin blockade was officially lifted on May 12, 1949.

During the blockade important developments had taken place elsewhere in Germany, mostly to implement the decisions reached at the six-power London conference the year before. In January 1949, a Military Security Board was established to "prevent the rebirth of any military or paramilitary organization or of the militarist outlook." In April the French zone was merged with Bizonia, thus completing the economic unification of West Germany. Later that month the Ruhr Statute for international control of that region was signed. More important still, on May 8 a German constituent assembly, which had been set up eleven months earlier, adopted a constitution for the western German Federal Republic; at the same time elections in East Germany prepared the way for the establishment of the German Democratic Republic. The most important development during this period, however, was the signing in Washington, on April 4, 1949, of the North Atlantic Treaty, a defensive alliance of twelve western nations, including the United States, Britain, and France. The integration of the new West German state into the North Atlantic Treaty Organization (NATO) was to be the principal task of the next few years.

The sixth and last meeting of the Council of Foreign Ministers got under way in Paris on May 23. The cast of characters had changed—Dean Acheson had replaced Marshall, Robert Schuman had succeeded Bidault, and Andrei Y. Vishinsky had taken over from Molotov; of the old guard, only Bevin remained. The Russians, still trying to arrest the development of a separate and already flourishing West German state, proposed an all-German council (Staatsrat) to be created out of already existing economic organs in the western and eastern zones. Such a body would have been merely an economic and administrative agency rather than a true German government, and for that reason it was unacceptable to the western powers. Instead, Secretary of State Acheson suggested that the recently proclaimed West German constitution, the Grundgesetz (Basic Law), be extended to the Soviet zone and that free elections be held in that area. For the first time "unification through all-German free elections," which remained the basic western demand in all future negotiations, was thus injected into the East-West debate over Germany. That solution, for obvious reasons, was unacceptable to the Russians.

The conference ended on June 20, 1949, and like all the earlier ones it had achieved little or nothing. In September the West German Federal Republic was launched, and a month later the East German Democratic Republic followed. The occupation phase of German postwar history was over.

SINCE EFFECTIVE four-power control in Germany was never established, the reconstruction of the country and the restoration of self-government were carried out separately and often quite differently in each occupation zone. I am here chiefly concerned with American military government, but I will also note how it differed from the activities of the other three occupying powers.

American policy toward Germany, as we have seen, was in large measure determined by and in reaction to Soviet policy, but not entirely so. The United States also had its own interests at heart, though perhaps not so exclusively as some revisionist historians claim, who see America's main motive as transforming Germany and western Europe into a virtual American colony. There can be little doubt that concern for its security, desire for economic gain, and maintenance of free enterprise were important factors in the American government's German and European policy. The average American, on the other hand, knew and cared little about what went on in Germany. Isolationism, for a while at least, was once again the prevailing mood of the United States. Bringing the boys home and reintegrating them into America's life and economy had first priority. Added to these sentiments were continued animosity and contempt for the recently beaten foe. It was only in 1947 that isolationism gradually gave way to internationalism, due not so much to idealistic altruism as to realistic anticommunism.

It is difficult to say at what point America became reconciled to the idea of a long-lasting or even permanent partition of Germany. During the fifties and early sixties German reunification was the professed aim of American foreign policy, but reunification had to be on free-world, that is, American, terms. There was always a third possibility between a liberal-democratic or authoritarian-communist state, a neutralized Germany, free from either Russian or American influence. Such a solution was proposed repeatedly, even before the division of Germany became a fact in 1949. But withdrawal of American and Soviet forces from German soil would have given the Soviet Union an overwhelming advantage, because all its military might was still close by in eastern Europe.

For the first two years after the war, America's planning for Germany was ambivalent. President Truman was too preoccupied with domestic problems to give the matter much thought. There were still men in influential positions—Henry Morgenthau, Bernard Baruch, Henry Wallace, Sumner Welles, and others, who advocated for Germany the punitive treatment provided for in the Joint Chiefs of Staff's directive #1067 (JCS 1067), which was the rulebook for America's occupation forces. But by late 1945 a more realistic appraisal of Germany's economic situation led to a gradual change of policy. Some of the proponents of that change were Herbert Hoover, serving, as he had after the previous war, as coordinator of American food relief; General Marshall, secretary of state after January 1947; John J. McCloy, assistant secretary of war until November 1945, U.S. military governor in 1949, and the first high commissioner for Germany from 1949 to 1952; and General Lucius Clay, at first deputy military governor, and from 1947 to 1949 in full control of the American zone. The first public statement of this change in America's attitude was Secretary of State Byrnes's Stuttgart speech of September 6, 1946.

American military government in Germany was not as successful as one might have wished, and to say that it was better than its Russian counterpart is hardly praise. It is generally agreed that the British performed better, while the French, though more tolerant in some ways, were a heavy burden on the Germans, because their occupation forces brought along their often large families. But then, like the Russians, the French had suffered from years of German occupation.

Many of America's mistakes were caused by lack of experience and proper preparation. Some specialists were trained, and target groups formed for occupation duty, but the available personnel were not always well suited for the tasks they faced, and they were often deficient in their knowledge of German affairs and of the German language. Only about 5 percent of American military government personnel knew enough German to function without an interpreter. One of the army's most laudable programs during the war, the Army Specialized Training Program (ASTP), had produced large numbers of GIs who were fluent in German and knew a great deal about Germany, but before they could apply what they had learned, many of them were shipped to the Pacific. One small contingent that played a highly beneficial role during the occupation was the refugees from Hitler's Germany who had either fought in the American army or returned as civilian employees of the military government. Contrary to the opinion of some Germans, who blamed the punitive aspects of the early occupation on these *Emigranten,* the latter did much to help prevent hardships resulting from misunderstandings between their present and former countrymen. Unfortunately, very few of these Americans of German origin achieved leading positions in American military government.

There were other difficulties that beset American occupation policy. Many of the specialists who had been recruited for work in Germany soon returned to the United States, either because they were discouraged by the difficulties or because their services were needed back home. Their replacements were often inferior, and while the top echelon of military government continued to be of uniformly high quality, the lower ranks in time were taken over by what one critic has called the "wine, women, and song" boys. Besides lack of qualified personnel, there were constant rivalries among the several agencies involved in military government and frequent differences between the aims of military government and the activities of the American tactical forces stationed in Germany. Germans frequently blamed the former for acts committed by the latter. In the early days of the occupation military government policy had to proceed through "channels," which was an added annoyance and impediment in what was already a troublesome and thankless task.

Initially there were two American military government agencies in Germany—the U.S. Group, Control Council for Germany, and the G-5 (civil affairs–military government) section of the U.S. Forces, European Theater (USFET). Because there was much overlapping and friction between the two, they were merged in the fall of 1945 in the Office of Military Government of the United States for Germany. The headquarters of OMGUS, as it was usually called, were in Berlin, though in time much of its work was shifted to the American zone, with Frankfurt as the main center. At its height, OMGUS had some 12,000 officers and enlisted men, less than half the number of the British Control Commission. But the United States, far more than the British, also employed large numbers of Germans, a practice necessitated by financial considerations. OMGUS consisted of a number of functional offices and divisions, which dealt with political, economic, cultural, and a wide variety of other affairs. It lasted until June 6, 1949, when its functions were taken over by the Office of the U.S. High Commissioner for Germany (HICOG), a civilian agency under the State Department.

Below OMGUS were four regional military government offices in the states, or Länder, that made up the American zone—Bavaria, Württemberg-Baden, Greater Hesse, and Bremen. Each state had its own military governor, who were, with few exceptions, undistinguished and often uninformed men. The form of military government most visible to the Germans was the detachments in the field, carrying out the regulations and decisions made higher up. Here again the quality of personnel varied greatly. In the emergency phase immediately after surrender, a great deal was accomplished. Getting the rubble cleared, utilities working, food distributed, and streetcars running appealed to the American do-it-yourself spirit and did not require much knowledge of German. When it came to finding suitable German officials, however, to whom to impart some of this spirit, the field detachments were less successful. They sometimes picked the very Nazis they were there to replace. Some of the blame must be shared by those Germans who knew better and could have helped, but who lacked the civic courage or sense of responsibility to do so. Once daily life was back to normal, the next step was to set up a German administrative hierarchy to take over. Americans then had to relinquish control to the Germans, a self-denial that many of them found difficult. By early 1946 military government detachments were officially restricted to advisory and liaison functions.

The single most important figure in the American zone of occupation was its military governor. The position was held by four men: Dwight D. Eisenhower until November 1945, Joseph T. McNarney until March 1947, Lucius Clay until May 1949, and John McCloy until the end of military government in September 1949. But only one of these men left an indelible stamp on Germany during this crucial period—General Clay, first as deputy to Eisenhower and McNarney and then in full control from 1947 to 1949. He was truly America's proconsul in Germany.

One would not have predicted the importance of Clay's role in Germany, given his engineering background, lack of foreign experience, and limited knowledge of German affairs. But he worked hard, was ready to learn, and did not shrink from taking decisive action. Although at times of somewhat imperious manner, Clay was a kind and sensitive man to whom the Germans owe a great deal. His basic concern was to get Germany back on its feet, not because he was pro-German, but because he realized that continued American presence would not be acceptable to the taxpayers at home. At the outset Clay was hampered by JCS 1067, the wholly negative and vengeful directive that forbade fraternization and inhibited any American aid in the rebuilding of German industry. But Clay bypassed and in fact often sabotaged many of the directive's provisions, until in July 1947 it was superseded by the more lenient and constructive JCS 1779.

The three most important and controversial activities of military government involved denazification, reeducation, and the dismantling of industry, all of which, in retrospect, left much to be desired. Denazification had been the most constantly reiterated common aim of the Allies during the war, but when the time came to carry it out, all sorts of difficulties arose. The first problem was the sheer numbers involved. In the American zone alone, some ninety-five thousand persons had been arrested outright, and subsequently, more than thirteen million *Fragebogen* (questionnaires), consisting of 133 questions about past political activities, were filled out by former members of the Nazi party and its sixty or so affiliated organizations. Processing these documents required thousands of trained analysts. In August 1946, in order to make some headway, military government granted an amnesty to all persons born after January 1, 1919, thus ruling in effect that "crime begins at twenty-six." At Christmas the same year, a second category of "little offenders" and disabled was let off. But even these highly debatable measures still left some two million cases to be decided. Meanwhile, on June 1, 1946, the responsibility for denazification had been handed over to the Germans themselves. German tribunals in the American zone tried some 930,000 cases, with categories ranging from major offenders to mere followers. Of these, 9,000 went to prison, 22,000 were barred from public office, 25,000 lost some or all of their property, and more than 500,000 were fined. As time went on sentences became more lenient, so that some "little" Nazis who were tried early were treated more harshly than some criminal ones whose cases were delayed. Denazification also differed from region to region. It was strictest in the American zone and more lenient in the British. The French, who considered all Germans equally guilty, showed less zeal in ferreting out Nazis. The most expeditious were the Russians, concentrating on major rather than minor offenders, executing some, and transporting the rest to Soviet labor camps. The Soviets also made use of former leading Nazis, however, when it suited their purpose.

Denazification has been criticized as both too severe and not severe enough. A more speedy procedure, concentrating on high-ranking and criminal, rather than small and innocent Nazis, certainly would have been preferable. As it turned out, total denazification proved impossible, and when it came to rebuilding Germany, perhaps even undesirable. In the early years of the Federal Republic, the majority of the judiciary and many members of the foreign ministry had a Nazi past, and by 1966 it was possible for Kurt Georg Kiesinger to become chancellor, even though he had joined the Nazi party in 1933. In addition denazification created an embittered minority of second-class citizens. But the fact that it fell short of its goals does not mean that this cleansing process was not necessary. Not to have attempted denazification would have been indefensible and unthinkable to most Americans at the time.

Reeducation, intended as a positive counterpart to denazification, also has come under attack. It took many forms, and under the broader rubric of reorientation included not only school and curriculum reform, but also, under American control, revival of the various information media, the publication of books, German-American exchange programs, the establishment of America Houses, and similar cultural activities. The term reeducation has a somewhat hypocritical or patronizing ring, and for that reason it was resented or made fun of by many Germans, who denied that they were in need of reeducation or that Americans were qualified to provide it. Under the terms of JCS 1067, the American military government was directed to prepare "for an eventual reconstruction of German political life on a democratic basis." Its sequel, JCS 1779, was careful to point out, however, that the intention was not to impose American forms of democracy on German society. On the whole this rule was followed, and the carping criticism by some Germans of American cultural efforts during the occupation period was highly uncalled for. American policy, moreover, compared favorably with that of the other occupying powers. Only the French did as much or more to establish contact with the Germans, especially among the younger generation.

In the narrower field of education, the most immediate task was to reopen the schools. Since about 80 percent of the teachers had been Nazis, screening was essential; and since most textbooks had become infected by Nazi ideology, new ones had to be found. A small group of dedicated American educators accomplished a great deal in the early reconstruction phase of the occupation, and schools in the American zone, which had closed during the invasion, started again on October 1, 1945. In the later phase, beginning in 1947, when education became a major concern of OMGUS, ambitious schemes for reeducating the Germans were drawn up by a larger, though less able, staff. According to JCS 1779 military government was to "require the German Länder authorities to adopt and execute education programs designed to develop a healthy, democratic educational system which will offer equal opportunity to all according to their qualifications." I will have more to say about German education in chapter 10. It suffices to say here that American influence on German education was felt more by indirection than by direction, as was quite natural in an area where the Germans were not exactly amateurs, although Americans thought that they still had much to learn.

The German press and radio also were quickly reactivated, not only to serve the occupation authorities but also to provide education and entertainment. Of the newspapers published by military government, only *Die Neue Zeitung* survived beyond 1945, although its circulation dropped from a high of two million to a few thousand when native German papers began to compete with it. Until May

1949 newspapers required a military government license, the first issued in July 1945 to the *Frankfurter Rundschau*. Because the licensees were chosen for their political convictions rather than journalistic expertise, the press did not really begin its rise until after licensing ended. Like the press, radio in the American zone remained under military government control until 1949, although the staff and direction of the three zonal stations had become wholly German before that time. Since broadcasting was government controlled—it had been Hitler's most effective propaganda instrument—its personnel had to be completely replaced, and a new system of governance devised. In these various changes, the Information Control Division of OMGUS made valuable and lasting contributions.

Much of America's reorientation program, a term that implies more planning than actually took place, depended on bringing the Germans in contact with American ways and American culture. But many Germans were convinced that American culture did not exist, so much resistance had to be overcome. This was done by sponsoring translations of American books, exhibitions of American art, and performances of American plays and music, all of which were received more readily by the young than the old. If ever a country experienced a generation gap, it was Germany after World War II. Two innovations in particular helped to further Germany's understanding of the United States—the America Houses set up in major cities, first in the American zone and later elsewhere, and the many exchange programs that began soon after the war and still continue today. Their basic aim was mutual understanding rather than one-sided reeducation, and more than anything else they helped the Germans to outgrow their past parochialism. It should be noted that the British and, even more, the French made similar efforts at intellectual and cultural rapprochement with equally positive results.

Of the various activities carried out by the occupying powers, the one most widely criticized by the Germans was the dismantling of the factories, a policy decided upon during the war and reaffirmed at Potsdam. Its purposes were to destroy Germany's war industries and to provide reparations. To these two motives German critics added a third—the desire to permanently weaken German competition. The wartime destruction of German industry had been far less than expected, only 10 to 20 percent of most key industries. Under a four-power agreement in 1946, German productive capacity was to be restricted to half that of 1938, with certain industries prohibited outright (aircraft, arms and ammunition, shipbuilding) and others strictly limited (machine tools, chemicals, steel). To keep Germany from regaining its former power and to repay Germany's enemies for the losses they had suffered, various reparations measures were adopted: the merchant fleet was divided among the wartime Allies; industrial patents were confiscated; and German prisoners of war were detained for compulsory labor.

The bulk of reparations, however, was to come from the dismantling of factories. This deindustrialization was most extensive in the French and Russian zones and more extensive in the British than in the American zone. It is difficult to give any reliable figure for the amount of damage resulting from dismantling, but estimates range in the vicinity of a billion dollars, at least. This was a most shortsighted policy, of course, which severely retarded German recovery and thus imposed a continued burden on the occupying powers. The Russians were the first to realize this fact and instead began helping themselves to reparations from current factory production. For the Germans, dismantling had the long-term advantage of modernizing their industrial plants, with outmoded equipment exchanged for more up-to-date machinery. But it was not viewed that way at the time. Dismantling led to a number of strikes and other protests and was resented more deeply than any other occupation measure, including denazification. As Germany became more closely allied with the western powers after 1949, dismantling was abandoned, though it did not officially terminate until 1954. By that time another set of controversial economic measures—the decartelization and deconcentration of Germany's large industrial combines, such as IG Farben and the large concerns of the Ruhr—had been only partially carried out, because these measures did not find much support in the American business community.

The only occupation act that the majority of Germans approved of was the currency reform of June 1948. Up to that time the heavily inflated reichsmark (RM) had impeded economic exchange and encouraged a black market on which cigarettes rather than money served as the generally accepted currency. The new deutsche mark (DM) was officially set at one-tenth the value of the old, but in fact the Germans received only 6.50 DM for any 100 RM they exchanged. The currency reform constituted a most brutal act of deflation, but it had the desired effect. Almost overnight the shelves and show windows of West Germany's stores once again displayed food and consumer goods, for which the destitute masses provided an unlimited market. All they had to do was work hard, and that they were ready to do.

Although most of Germany's *Wirtschaftswunder* (economic miracle, of which more in chapter 8) was due to the efforts of the Germans themselves, it also owed much to American help in many forms, from official Marshall Plan aid to unofficial charity. Without the millions of CARE and other packages that Americans sent to Germany during the desperate early postwar years, the people's suffering would have been infinitely greater than it was. The Germans' appreciation of this help was not all one might have expected, and much that was done for them they took for granted. The German capacity for self-pity far outweighed the inclination toward gratitude, and their forgetfulness of the wartime suffering they had inflicted on others was virtually total.

Relations between occupiers and occupied in the American zone were better than one might have anticipated. The nonfraternization rule, which was not applied in other zones, soon broke down, as American soldiers availed themselves of the readily offered companionship of the German fräuleins. The number of illegitimate children resulting from these liaisons has been estimated at more than ninety thousand. Discipline among American troops often left much to be desired, and during the early days of the occupation many instances of looting and some of rape were reported. The most common misdeed was black marketing, which led to a large loss of revenue for the German authorities and cost the American taxpayers millions of dollars. There were other sources of friction between Germans and Americans, sometimes due to misunderstanding. No nation enjoys being occupied, and the Germans were no exception. They objected to having their houses requisitioned, their woods used for hunting, their water supply chlorinated, and submitting to the other "injustices" the conquerors inflicted.

Grumbling and resentment were doubtless widespread. But most Germans refrained from showing their feelings, and most Americans were oblivious to them, so relations on the whole remained correct and in some instances even became cordial. Over the years thousands of Americans met thousands of Germans, which could not help but lead to better mutual understanding. Unfortunately, the self-segregation of the Americans in ghettolike "Little Americas" prevented still closer social relations after the nonfraternization ban had disappeared. Given the past German tendency toward xenophobia, it is remarkable that there was never much resentment against those Germans who collaborated with the recent enemy.

Although the occupation policies of the three western powers differed in some respects, they were sufficiently alike to enable their zones to become joined together into a single state. The same did not hold for the activities of the Soviet Military Administration (SMAD) in its eastern zone. There events from the start pointed toward a radically new and different political, economic, and social system.

As early as April 30, 1945, a group of ten exiled German communist functionaries, headed by Walter Ulbricht, had been flown into East Germany from Moscow to prepare for a German administration under Soviet auspices. Other communist veterans, among them Wilhelm Pieck and Johannes R. Becher, soon followed. On June 10, one day after the official launching of the Soviet military government, the formation of "antifascist parties" was permitted. The next day the German Communist Party (KPD) was the first to reconstitute itself, followed in subsequent weeks by the Social Democratic Party (SPD), the Christian-Democratic Union (CDU), and the Liberal-Democratic Party (LPD). On July 14 these four formed the Bloc of Antifascist-Democratic Parties. The Soviet authorities clearly intended to maintain at least the appearance of democracy. Of the two leftist parties, the SPD was much stronger than the KPD. To correct this imbalance, the two parties were merged in April 1946 into the Socialist Unity Party (SED), with Communist Wilhelm Pieck and Socialist Otto Grotewohl as joint leaders. The first elections in the Soviet zone were held in September and October 1946. While the SED emerged as the strongest party in each of the five Länder, it did not receive a majority anywhere. Beginning in 1947 the transformation of the SED into a Communist party along Stalinist lines was undertaken in earnest, and by the time the German Democratic Republic (DDR) started in October 1949, the process was complete.

Along with this political *Gleichschaltung* went Soviet-sponsored infiltration by KPD or SED functionaries of all key positions in East Germany's local and regional administrations. A "democratic school reform" in the fall of 1946 introduced a uniform school system for the whole Soviet zone, "to propagate the great worldhistorical teachings of Karl Marx and Friedrich Engels as well as the ideas of humanism and international friendship." The judicial establishment was completely overhauled and denazified, resulting in the replacement of some four-fifths of all former judges by hastily trained "people's judges."

The most far-reaching changes took place in the economic sphere. In July 1945 all banks were nationalized. In the fall, a drastic *Bodenreform* (land reform) program not only confiscated the real estate of all war criminals and Nazis, but appropriated without compensation all properties exceeding 100 hectares (about 250 acres). This affected some 7,000 owners of large estates, including most of Prussia's Junkers. The lands were subsequently divided among more than 330,000 agricultural laborers and small peasants. In the industrial sector, the Soviet military government converted about 10,000 leading industrial and commercial establishments into people's enterprises, and some 25 percent of them into *Sowjetische Aktiengesellschaften* (Soviet stock companies) to yield reparations for the Soviet Union.

Taken as a whole, the changes just described amounted to a veritable political, economic, and social revolution, which left East Germany fundamentally different from the West. The more firmly these changes became embedded, the more difficult the creation of a united Germany would become. Meanwhile the steady stream of refugees from East to West testified to the lack of support the East German people's democracy found among its subjects. The East German example helped to reconcile many West Germans to the temporary, as it still seemed, partition of their country.

THE REVIVAL of German self-government in the western zones was a gradual development, hastened by economic pressures and the mounting tensions of the cold war. It was most rapid in the American and slowest in the French zone. German administrative appointments at first were made and unmade by military government fiat. Thus the former lord mayor of Cologne, Dr. Konrad Adenauer, who had been fired by the Nazis in 1933 for political unreliability, was reappointed by the Americans in March 1945, only to be fired in October by the British, this time for "incompetence." A similar fate befell Dr. Fritz Schäffer, who was appointed minister president of Bavaria in May 1945 by the American military government and dismissed four months later. They were not the only German officials to be treated high-handedly.

The renewal of political parties began sporadically at the local level. In the summer of 1945 the first political organizations were permitted in the British and American zones, while the French waited until early 1946. The resulting parties followed the four main orientations that still prevail at the present time: The KPD and SPD on the left and the Freie Demokratische Partei (FDP) and the CDU (or CSU, Christlich-Soziale Union, in Bavaria) in the center. The first two are successors to parties that existed before 1933. The CDU-CSU, or Christian Democrats, in contrast to the old Center Party, includes Protestants as well as Catholics; and the FDP, or Free Democrats, are best described as traditional liberals. Except for the brief appearance of some smaller splinter groups in the 1950s and 1960s, there has been no major right-wing nationalist party. The Germans obviously have learned their lesson.

The first elections in the American zone took place in 1946, first for local assemblies, then for the constituent assemblies in the various Länder, and finally, late in the year, for the state parliaments, or Landtage. Comparable elections in the French and British zones were not held until the following spring. In most states the resulting governments were four-party coalitions, with authority still limited chiefly to economic and welfare matters. To broaden the scope of German participation in the overall administration of the American zone, a Länderrat (Council of States), consisting of the minister presidents of Bavaria, Württemberg-Baden, and Hesse, with headquarters in Stuttgart, was set up as early as October 1945. Although its powers were chiefly advisory, it was gradually assigned responsibilities of its own and was a positive step toward German self-government on a zonal level. The British zone's counterpart, the Zonenbeirat (Zonal Advisory Council), established in February 1946, never played quite the same role. As for the French zone, the first joint conference of minister presidents was not permitted until April 1948.

In the summer of 1946 a noticeable change took place in America's policy toward Germany. Its outward manifestation was Secretary Byrnes's Stuttgart speech of September 6, usually considered a turning point in American-German relations. The address heralded the impending economic unification of the American and British zones and held out hope for a better German future. "The American people," the secretary told his German audience, "want to return the government of Germany to the German people. The American people want to help the German people to win their way back to an honorable place among the free and peace-loving nations of the world." This was clearly intended as a conciliatory gesture and was received as such. Together with the Berlin airlift two years later, the Stuttgart speech did much to prepare the psychological climate for future American-German collaboration.

The Germans, although welcoming the change from retribution to reconstruction, were nevertheless concerned about developments that might deepen and perpetuate the East-West division of their country. In April 1946 members of the Länderrat and Zonenbeirat, meeting in Stuttgart, expressed their hope for German unity. Encouraged by Secretary Brynes's speech, a conference of the minister presidents of all four occupation zones was scheduled in Bremen for early October. However, the minister presidents of the French and Russian zones were refused permission to attend by their respective military governments. It was not until June 1947 that an all-German meeting finally took place in Munich. Even then, the French allowed their minister presidents to go only on condition that the question of German unity would not be discussed. The delegates from the Soviet zone, on the other hand, had strict instructions to advocate the creation of a central administration for all of Germany.

At the conference the western minister presidents, led by the meeting's organizer, Bavaria's Hans Ehard, insisted that the first and foremost issue to be taken up should be an economic one—"How will we get through the next winter?" The minister presidents of the five eastern Länder, however, stuck to their demand that the question of political unity should take precedence. When they did not get their way, they left. The remaining delegates then addressed themselves to a number of specific economic issues, reiterating at the same time their faith in a united Germany. In the eastern zone several people's congresses were subsequently held to demonstrate in favor of German unity, and a referendum was even sponsored on the subject. Their agitation found some echo in the West, chiefly among communists.

Meanwhile, the launching of Bizonia on January 1, 1947, offered further opportunity for German participation in the economic affairs of the region. In June 1947 a legislative Wirtschaftsrat (Economic Council), consisting of fifty-four delegates from the eight state parliaments of the American and British zones began its work in Frankfurt, together with an Exekutivrat (Executive Council), representing the governments of the eight Länder. In addition, five Verwaltungen (administrations or departments) were set up for specific economic and related tasks. These new agencies soon began to overshadow the existing zonal organizations (Länderrat and Zonenbeirat). After undergoing several changes in the direction of further democratization, the structure of the economic government of Bizonia in early 1948 foreshadowed the outlines of the West German Federal Republic soon to come.

The founding of the separate state, which in retrospect appears as a logical consequence of earlier developments, was not due to any long-range planning but rather to immediate circumstances, including the mounting tensions of the cold war, the failure of the Council of Foreign Ministers to agree on the future of Germany, and the need to integrate western Germany in the European Recovery Program. Because of the Marshall Plan, the United States more and more took the lead in the German policy of the western powers. The decision to ask the West Germans to set up a government of their own was reached at the London six-power conference in June 1948. On July 1 the three western military governors instructed the minister presidents of the eleven West German Länder to convene a constituent assembly for a new German state not later than September 1.

The German minister presidents thus were given a decisive role in the founding of the new republic, but some of them were not overly happy with this responsibility. They felt that the German people were not yet ready to give themselves a new constitution, and they went out of their way to stress the provisional nature of their decisions. Instead of an elected constituent assembly, the minister presidents proposed a Parlamentarischer Rat (Parliamentary Council) of delegates from the eleven Landtage; instead of a Verfassung (constitution), that body was to draw up a Grundgesetz to be adopted, not by popular referendum, but again by the various state assemblies. Today these semantic exercises may seem unimportant, but they show the reluctance with which the Germans approached anything that might prevent reunification of their country. The military governors objected to some of these reservations, but on the whole the minister presidents had their way, and on July 26, 1948, agreement was reached on a Parlamentarischer Rat, which was to begin deliberations on September 1.

At this point decision making shifted from the minister presidents to the various parties of the sixty-five delegates who were to make up the Parliamentary Council. Even though they considered themselves representatives of the people as a whole, the delegates' views could not help reflecting their party affiliation. The two major parties in particular, the Christian Democrats and the Social Democrats, differed on a number of key issues, necessitating frequent compromises. The fact that the meetings of the Parlamentarischer Rat took place in Bonn and were chaired by Konrad Adenauer, then head of the CDU in the British zone, were omens of the future. The draft of the Basic Law was completed and sent to the military governors in mid-February. The latter again raised several objections, and further negotiations followed. Final acceptance of the Grundgesetz by the Parlamentarischer Rat took place on May 8, four years after Germany's unconditional surrender. After ratification by the various Landtage, the new constitution went into effect on May 23, 1949.

The new state thus established, the Bundesrepublik Deutschland (BRD) is "a democratic and social federal state." Its head is a mostly, though not entirely, ceremonial federal president, who is chosen every five years by a federal convention rather than by popular vote. The executive head of the federal government is the federal chancellor, who is elected by the Bundestag, or Federal Parliament. The Bundestag has close to five hundred members, elected every four years by all citizens over eighteen years of age under a dual voting system that combines the features of plurality vote and proportional representation. The Bundesrat, or Council of Constituent States, has forty-five members, delegated by and representing the Länder. It shares in the legislative process and, when controlled by the parliamentary opposition, can play an important role. Finally, there is a Bundesverfassungsgericht, or Federal Constitutional Court, which rules on constitutional issues, conflicts between the two houses of parliament or between the federal government and the states, the legality of parties, and other basic issues.

Given the manner in which it was drafted, with pressure and interference from the occupying powers and without popular sanction, it is remarkable how satisfactory and workable the Grundgesetz turned out to be. This is quite in contrast to the Weimar Constitution which, though drawn up without outside interference and by a popularly elected assembly, was never really accepted by the majority of Germans. The Weimar Constitution was much on the minds of the authors of the Grundgesetz, and while the two documents have some similarities, the Basic Law consciously tried to correct the shortcomings of its predecessor. This is shown particularly by the weaker role it assigned to the president and the stronger one given the chancellor. It is shown by the way these two are elected and by the safeguards against the rapid turnover of governments, which so plagued the Weimar Republic. Under the Bonn constitution, before a chancellor can be forced to resign by a vote of no confidence, a successor must have been elected. As a result of these and other stabilizing factors, the Federal Republic in its first twenty-eight years has had eight governments, while the Weimar Republic had twenty-one in half the time.

The Grundgesetz has many other positive features. It spells out in admirable detail the *Grundrechte* (basic rights) of each citizen, including equal rights for women, the right of conscientious objection to military service, and the rights of illegitimate children. It furnishes, in the Federal Constitutional Court, a strong arbiter and protector of its terms. And it includes such progressive provisions as the possible transfer of sovereignty to an international collective security system; a ban on aggressive war; the constitutionality of socialization in return for proper compensation; and the unconstitutionality of capital punishment. In its already long life of thirty years, the Basic Law, intended according to its preamble for only a "transitional period," has been amended many times, but its original structure and provisions have been little changed. It has proved itself a solid basis on which to build a successful state.

The first Bundestag was elected on August 14, 1949, by 78.5 percent of the eligible voters, a record figure by American, though not by German, standards. The Christian Democrats won 139 seats, the Social Democrats 131, the Free Democrats 52, and the Communists 15. The rest of the seats were divided among some seven small parties, including the moderately rightist Deutsche Partei (DP), which received 17 seats. Since no party obtained an absolute majority, a coalition had to be formed. There were two alternatives, a two-party government made up of CDU-CSU and SPD, or a three-party one consisting of CDU-CSU, FDP, and DP. The decision rested chiefly with Konrad Adenauer, chairman of the CDU and already the dominant figure of the nascent republic. Differences between Adenauer and the leader of the SPD, Kurt Schumacher, on most political and economic issues precluded the first solution, so the second was adopted. On September 15 the Bundestag elected Adenauer chancellor by a single vote (his own). Three days earlier, Professor Theodor Heuss, a prominent member of the FDP, had been elected Bundespräsident. On September 20, Adenauer and his cabinet took the oath of office, and the German Federal Republic was launched.

In East Germany events followed a parallel course. In March 1948 a second People's Congress in East Berlin established the Deutsche Volksrat (German People's Council) as a provisional all-German government. By October a draft constitution was completed, which was officially adopted by the Volksrat on March 19, 1949. Two months later, the constitution was endorsed by a third German People's Congress, and a second Volksrat was set up. All these moves, it will be noted, were taken well ahead of parallel actions in the West. Only the final act was postponed until after the Federal Republic was proclaimed. On October 7, 1949, the Volksrat constituted itself a provisional parliament, or Volkskammer (People's Chamber), and asked Otto Grotewohl to serve as minister president and Wilhelm Pieck as president of the new Deutsche Demokratische Republik (DDR).

It is not necessary here to go into the details of the East German constitution, since it never assumed the central significance of its western counterpart. The DDR calls itself "a socialist state of German nationality." Its highest authority, in theory, is the Volkskammer, consisting of five hundred delegates. It is "elected" on the basis of a single list (*Einheitsliste*) of candidates, agreed upon beforehand among the several parties and mass organizations represented in the parliament. The list is usually endorsed by close to 100 percent of the voters. The Volkskammer in turn elects the executive, or Ministerrat (Council of Ministers). Despite some clumsy devices used to hide the fact, the decisive voice in each of these and all other governmental agencies belongs to the Socialist Unity (or Communist) party, the SED. The members of the Politburo and the first secretary of that party, therefore, exercise the real power in the DDR. In this respect East Germany is no different from any of the other people's democracies, including the Soviet Union. From 1950 to 1971 the first secretary of the SED was Walter Ulbricht.

Germany had thus been split in two. What Bismarck had joined together eighty years before had come apart, though as all Germans East and West fervently believed, only temporarily. Each of the two Germanies still considered itself the custodian and spokesman of the whole, and each adopted as its national colors the black, red, and gold of the Weimar Republic. For the next ten to fifteen years, reunification remained the single most burning issue in German domestic and foreign policy.

8 | The Germany of Konrad Adenauer
1949–1963

T HE FIRST FOURTEEN YEARS of the German Federal Republic were dominated by the solid and stolid figure of Konrad Adenauer. More than anyone else, the Rhenish statesman helped his country regain the international trust and respect it had lost during the Hitler years. The former lord mayor of Cologne, seventy-three years old when he took over the reins of government in 1949, was only a year younger than Bismarck had been when he retired. Like Bismarck's, Adenauer's main achievements were in foreign policy, a field in which he had had no previous experience. He had spent most of his adult life in the service of his native city. He had traveled little, and he spoke no foreign languages. *Der Alte* ("the old one," as the Germans called him with a mixture of affection and respect) was an uncomplicated person, a devout Catholic and a devoted family man. He was deeply anti-Prussian and genuinely pro-French, both rather uncommon sentiments among Germans of his generation.

He also was ardently anticommunist. The dominant aim of Adenauer's foreign policy was to gain the confidence of the western powers, especially the United States, and in so doing to win back his country's sovereignty. In this he was wholly successful. Much of his success was due to circumstances—the West's need for Germany's help in the containment of communism. Adenauer also brought to the task certain qualities that aided his efforts. He was a superb politician, always shrewd, sometimes sly, and often stubborn, but he was also reliable, steady, reasonable, and forthright. He had the

179

ability, rare among earlier German statesmen, of seeing his adversaries' points of view. In this respect Adenauer was not unlike Stresemann thirty years earlier. But while Stresemann was never quite free from suspicion of ulterior motives, there was no such distrust in the case of Adenauer.

Somewhat of an authoritarian and quite reserved in manner, Adenauer had few, if any, close friends among his German associates. It is the more surprising, therefore, that he was able to establish very cordial relations with a number of Americans. Among them was the first U.S. high commissioner to Germany after 1949, John McCloy, who was warmly pro-German and whose wife, a distant cousin of Adenauer's late wife, did much to aid the renascent German women's movement. McCloy's successor and, after 1955, first American ambassador to the Federal Republic, James B. Conant, although less close to the chancellor, was equally effective and, because of his background as former president of Harvard, much respected by the Germans. The closest ties, amounting to genuine friendship, developed between Adenauer and John Foster Dulles, American secretary of state during most of the crucial 1950s. The two men were drawn together by mutual sympathy, a deep faith in Christian principles, and their strong opposition to communism. Dulles's implicit trust in Adenauer was one of the greatest assets for close German-American relations.

The overture to such relations occurred in 1953, when Adenauer paid the first of many visits to the United States, the first German chancellor to do so while in office. The theme of the visit was friendship, almost as though the Hitler experience had been forgotten. Instead, the memories of a friendly past were stressed, from General Steuben to Carl Schurz, to give substance to what was still mostly wishful thinking. There were the usual bestowals of honorary degrees, addresses to German-Americans in the Middle West, and, most memorable to Adenauer, his wreath-laying ceremony at Arlington National Cemetery, which he viewed somewhat too confidently as "for the dead of both nations," restoring the honor of "our own dead German soldiers." "It had been a long and hard road," the chancellor later recalled, "from the total catastrophe of the year 1945 to this moment of the year in 1953 when the German national anthem was heard in the national cemetery of the United States." *

Adenauer's rule, which lasted as long as the Weimar Republic and two years longer than Hitler's, was not without its critics, more

* Konrad Adenauer, *Memoirs 1945–64* (Chicago, 1966), p. 456.

numerous at home than abroad. The majority of Germans, at least
during the 1950s, clearly approved of his policy and continued to
vote for the coalition parties that supported him. But there was
much dissatisfaction with the often high-handed and autocratic manner in which the chancellor conducted affairs and with his exclusive
emphasis on integration with the West, which to many Germans
made reunification more difficult, if not impossible.

The most ardent and able of Adenauer's opponents was the
leader of the Social Democratic party, Kurt Schumacher. Even
though he died in 1952, he deserves to be remembered as the only
figure who might have taken Adenauer's place. As a matter of fact,
during the early postwar years it was Schumacher, leader of the
largest, oldest, and most disciplined of Germany's parties, who
seemed destined to head the new republic. Schumacher's greatest
contribution was his stubborn resistance to the merger of the Socialist and Communist parties on the model of the Soviet zone. Like
Adenauer, Schumacher was staunchly anticommunist, but that was
the only issue on which they saw eye to eye; on almost everything
else they differed. Not only was Schumacher a Marxist and free-
thinker, both anathema to Adenauer, but he made a conscious effort
to free his party from the stigma of "fulfillment" that had clung to
it since Weimar days. He advocated instead a strongly nationalist
line and accused Adenauer at one point of being the "Chancellor of
the Allies." The two men had fundamentally different personalities
—the old but spry Adenauer, intelligent but hardly an intellectual,
pragmatic and unemotional, and Schumacher, twenty years younger
but a physical wreck after ten years in Nazi concentration camps, an
intellectual and ideologist, excitable and sharp-tongued. The remark
just cited about Adenauer cost him a temporary suspension from the
Bundestag. Besides disagreeing on most essential issues, the two
rivals also heartily disliked each other. Nevertheless, Schumacher's
death was a major loss, even though his continued opposition would
have made Adenauer's life more difficult than it already was.

The German Federal Republic, officially recognized by the
three western powers on September 21, 1949, was far from being a
sovereign state. In law, though less and less in fact, the occupation
continued until 1955. Under an Occupation Statute, the Allied
powers reserved to themselves far-reaching controls over military,
economic, financial, and even political matters, including the conduct of foreign policy. Adenauer's foremost task was to whittle away
these remaining restrictions.

He did this by patient negotiation, trading German concessions for gradual relief from foreign control. The first such exchange,

freely negotiated with the three high commissioners, was the Petersberg Agreement of November 22, 1949. In return for Germany's
joining the International Ruhr Authority and the Council of Europe, the western powers agreed to the almost complete cessation of
industrial dismantling, to Germany's direct participation in OEEC,
and to the opening of German consulates abroad.

The Petersberg provisions ran into violent opposition from
Schumacher and the SPD, who objected to Germany's acquiescence
in the international control of the Ruhr and in the separation of
the Saar, already economically tied to France, which was to be given
separate membership in the Council of Europe. But Adenauer would
not be diverted from his declared course of conciliation with France
and integration of the Federal Republic into the free world. An encouraging sign that his policy was bearing fruit came a few months
later, on May 9, 1950. In a letter from its foreign minister, Robert
Schuman, France proposed the formation of what became, after extended negotiations, the European Coal and Steel Community
(ECSC). Beginning in 1952 ECSC in effect superseded the Ruhr Authority. The Saar problem continued to becloud Franco-German relations for some time longer, but it too was eventually resolved.

The most important single event affecting the future of Germany occurred not in Europe but on the other side of the globe—
the invasion of South Korea by North Korean forces on June 25,
1950. The similarities between Korea and Germany were obvious:
both were divided nations, and the eastern DDR, with its people's
police, had a rudimentary army that might spearhead an invasion
of West Germany. Adenauer had long been concerned over his country's security, and for some time he and others had hinted at the
desirability of some kind of German participation in the defense of
western Europe. The Korean War injected a note of urgency into
the situation and gave the chancellor an opportunity not merely to
broach the question of West Germany's security, but also to gain
further concessions from the western powers. This double motive
became clear in two memoranda that he delivered to the high commissioners on August 29, 1950. One dealt with the creation of a
federal police force and a possible German contribution to the defense of western Europe, the other with the revision of Germany's
relations with the occupying powers.

The chancellor's initiative, taken without consulting his cabinet, caused a storm of indignation chiefly, though not exclusively,
among the SPD. Adenauer's minister of the interior, Gustav Heinemann, left the government in protest (and years later joined the
SPD). It was not only the chancellor's acting on his own to which

his critics objected. There was a genuine aversion to remilitarization among many Germans, especially the rank and file of the SPD. Throughout the drawn-out debate over rearmament during the next five years, the SPD maintained its firm opposition to the government's policy. Although the opposition was a major headache for Adenauer, it was also of indirect advantage to him in gaining concessions from the western allies and in strengthening his position in the eyes of the German people.

Adenauer's August memoranda were discussed by the three western foreign ministers at a meeting in September 1950 in New York. Both America's Dean Acheson and, to a lesser extent, Britain's Ernest Bevin favored the German security proposals, but France's Robert Schuman, for obvious reasons, objected to the revival of a German army. The foreign ministers, however, did agree to liberalize further the Occupation Statute, Adenauer's chief concern. A month after the New York conference, moreover, French Minister President René Pleven proposed a kind of military counterpart to the economic Schuman Plan then being negotiated, an integrated European army in which national contingents, including a German one, would serve under a European minister of defense. Here was the basis for what was soon called the European Defense Community (EDC). Its details were worked out at Paris with German participation throughout 1951, and by May 1952 the EDC treaty was signed. All that was needed was ratification by the parliaments of the participating powers.

Meanwhile the liberation of the Federal Republic from the remaining limitations of occupation had made rapid progress. The BRD was now recognized as speaking for the whole of Germany; the state of war between Germany and the western powers was officially terminated; virtually all economic restrictions, especially on the production of steel, were lifted; the Bonn government was permitted to establish diplomatic relations abroad; and most important, it was given the right to conduct its own foreign policy, free from the tutelage of the western powers. Adenauer personally assumed the post of foreign minister, which he kept until 1955. These various concessions were codified in the Bonn treaty or Generalvertrag (General Treaty), signed at the same time as the EDC treaty and scheduled to go into effect at the time of the latter's ratification.

The impending rearmament of Germany was viewed with growing alarm by many people in Germany and elsewhere. Aside from having felt twice in one generation the consequences of their own militarism, many Germans feared, quite rightly, that their country's military integration with the West would postpone indefinitely the chance for reunification. They were not ready, therefore, to accept their chancellor's argument that only a show of strength would bring the Soviets to the negotiating table. Liberals outside Germany shared these apprehensions and in addition were shocked by the realpolitik of their governments, which only a few years earlier had vowed to ban forever the evils of German militarism.

The people most worried by German rearmament were the Russians, and in view of their experiences in two world wars, understandably so. To halt the threatening military revival of West Germany, Stalin in March and April 1952 addressed two notes to Bonn, proposing reunification, conclusion of a German peace treaty, and subsequent withdrawal of all occupation forces, in other words, the neutralization of Germany. The western governments objected that the Russians did not include free elections as a precondition for reunification and insisted that such elections must be held under UN auspices. The Soviets, in their second note, conceded the elections, but not the UN supervision. The western powers, including the BRD, interpreted the Russian moves as intended to interrupt the negotiations for the EDC treaty then nearing completion and for that reason did not take them as seriously as some German critics did at the time and later. The charge of these critics was that Adenauer, subservient to American pressure, did not sufficiently try to ascertain what concessions the Russians might have been willing to make toward German reunification in return for western Germany's abstention from rearmament and agreement to neutralization. This charge of having missed a serious opportunity for reunification in 1952 was to haunt Adenauer for years to come, although in the opinion of most western historians it was unjustified.

Once the EDC treaty was signed, the German question was temporarily overshadowed by other events—the American election campaign, the Korean armistice negotiations, and the death of Stalin, which resulted in an East-West "thaw." That and the proposals of Winston Churchill, who had been returned to office in the fall of 1951, for a Big Four summit conference caused Adenauer some concern that an East-West détente might interfere with his own plans for German integration with the West. But the cordial reception and assurances he was given during his Washington visit dispelled his fears. In the summer of 1953 West Germany once again urged reunification through free elections, and shortly thereafter the western powers suggested that the Council of Foreign Ministers, which had last met in 1949, be reconvened to discuss the German problem.

The foreign ministers met in Berlin in January and February

1954. Like their previous six conferences since 1945, this one also ended in failure. Each side had elaborate plans for German reunification from which it would not budge. The western powers again insisted on free elections as a sine qua non, but it was quite obvious that the Russians would not agree to any scheme that might affect the status quo in East Germany. Molotov, who once again represented the Soviet Union, proposed a general European security plan, aimed more at getting America's armed forces out of Europe than at protecting the rest of the powers against future German aggression.

All this time the ratification of the EDC treaty was going through its tortuous phases. Its most difficult time and final defeat came, ironically, in France, where the Pleven Plan had originated. On August 30, 1954, the French National Assembly voted against ratification, thus delivering a serious blow to European integration. The decision, while deplorable, was understandable. Three times within the last century, the Germans had invaded France, and to collaborate with the hereditary enemy was to most Frenchmen unthinkable. Even more important, with the bulk of France's forces tied up overseas, mostly in Indochina, the Germans, backed by a rapidly expanding economy, could not help but assume the leadership in EDC.

Anthony Eden, Britain's foreign secretary, broke the impasse created by France's refusal to ratify EDC by proposing that the Federal Republic make its defense contribution within the framework of NATO. The necessary negotiations proceeded without major incident in the fall of 1954, and the resulting agreements were signed in Paris and Bonn on October 23. In addition to calling for German accession to NATO, the Paris treaties included far-reaching provisions for the final normalization of relations between West Germany and the western powers, following the lines laid down in the Generalvertrag of 1952. The occupation was officially terminated, and the powers thenceforth were to be represented by ambassadors rather than high commissioners. But even though the relevant agreement stated that the Bundesrepublik now enjoyed "the unrestricted power of a sovereign state over its domestic and foreign affairs," Germany was still subject to certain limitations. It could not produce ABC (atomic, bacteriological, and chemical) weapons; it had to tolerate the continued presence of foreign troops, albeit as NATO partners rather than as occupation forces; and the western powers reserved for themselves any remaining quadripartite rights concerning Berlin and a final German peace treaty. These limitations, however, did not present any problems. The Federal Republic, for all practical purposes, was a fully independent state once the Paris treaties were ratified.

Again there was much debate before ratification could take place. The Russians stepped up their agitation against German participation in NATO and instead proposed reunification and even free elections. Their appeals found ready listeners among the SPD, whose delegates in the Bundestag voted against the Paris treaties. But the government stood its ground, and the treaties were ratified in February and went into effect on May 5, 1955. Four days later Germany attended its first session of the NATO Council. The Soviet Union, meanwhile, granted "sovereignty" to its East German satellite, and on May 14 the nations of the communist bloc, including the DDR, concluded the Warsaw Pact as a counterweight to NATO.

The major portion of Adenauer's program, the integration of a fully sovereign Federal Republic into the western camp, had thus been accomplished. His second aim, rapprochement with France, also made marked progress with the resolution of the Saar issue. One of the Paris agreements had called for the Europeanization of the Saar following a plebiscite among the region's population. But the referendum held on October 23, 1955, showed that the overwhelming majority of the Saarlanders wanted to remain German; after extended negotiations, the Saar was returned to the Bundesrepublik on January 1, 1957. This removed the last major obstacle to Franco-German friendship. The European Coal and Steel Community already had led to close economic cooperation between the two. The scope of ECSC was widened during talks in 1956 and led to the Rome treaties of March 28, 1957, establishing the European Economic Community (EEC), or Common Market, which became effective on January 1, 1958. The fact that its first president was Dr. Walter Hallstein, Staatssekretär in the German foreign ministry and a close associate of Adenauer's, testified to the acceptance of the Federal Republic within the western community.

This acceptance, however, had as its reverse side the widening gulf between the two Germanies. As a sovereign state, West Germany now was free to conduct its own foreign policy, but thus far its relations had been exclusively with the West, and they continued to be so for some time. Under the so-called Hallstein Doctrine, named after the Staatssekretär, who had nothing to do with it, the Bonn government refused to deal with any state that recognized the DDR. It was an unfortunate and obstructive policy, but it showed that the Federal Republic took seriously its claim to represent all of Germany. The only country excepted from the Hallstein rule was the Soviet Union. In September 1955 Adenauer paid a visit to Moscow, where it was decided to establish diplomatic relations between the BRD and the USSR. The Russians thus recognized the Federal Republic, but neither Bonn nor its western allies reciprocated by recognizing the DDR, which was still referred to as the Soviet zone. Other than diplomatic relations and the possibility of commercial contacts, Adenauer's visit netted only a Russian promise of returning some ten thousand German prisoners of war who were still held in Soviet camps. On reunification, results were nil.

The same had been true of the first postwar summit meeting held at Geneva in July 1955, with Eisenhower, Nikolai Bulganin, Eden, and Edgar Faure attending. The Russians no longer seemed very interested in German reunification and insisted that it was a matter to be decided by "the two German states." The western powers, either from conviction or from loyalty to their West German ally, continued to demand reunification through free elections, realizing, however, that the Soviets would never agree to any settlement that weakened their hold over East Germany. Russia's determination to maintain the status quo was brought home to the free world by the brutal repression of the Hungarian revolution of 1956. At the same time the Suez crisis diverted the attention of the powers to still another tension spot, the Middle East. The German problem was clearly losing its central role in the cold war.

During the last years of the Eisenhower administration, one of Washington's main concerns was disarmament, especially after the launching of the first Sputnik in 1957 cut short America's invulnerability to nuclear attack. Numerous schemes were advanced to lessen the threat of an atomic war in Europe. The best known of them originated with Poland's foreign minister, Adam Rapacki. The Rapacki Plan called for an atomic weapon–free zone on both sides of the iron curtain and was not unlike proposals made earlier by western as well as Russian observers. After western criticism that the plan was too narrow, its scope was widened to include conventional as well as atomic weapons. But before the discussion could go much further, another major crisis was unleashed in November 1958, when Nikita Khrushchev, now in full control in the Soviet Union, delivered his ultimatum on Berlin.

In a speech on November 10 and in subsequent notes to the western powers, the Soviet leader declared that four-power control over Berlin had come to an end. The western allies would henceforth have to negotiate access to West Berlin with the East German Democratic Republic. Should they refuse to do so within six months, the Soviet Union would conclude a separate peace treaty with the DDR. As with anything the Russians do, we can only speculate about

Khrushchev's motives. He clearly intended to strengthen the DDR and, by forcing its recognition, create dissent within the western camp. He may also have wanted to force another summit conference to discuss not only Berlin but other East-West differences as well. And finally, he may have wished to gain prestige in the eyes of the communist world by disproving China's charges that post-Stalinist Russia had gone soft.

If Khrushchev had hoped for disarray among the western allies, he succeeded, even though much of it was due to other circumstances. American-German relations, for the first time since 1949, showed real signs of stress, partly because of personal factors, such as the death of John Foster Dulles in May 1959. From the beginning of the Berlin crisis, the American secretary of state had not always stood as firm vis-à-vis the Russians as Adenauer wished, but then, Berlin was only one of several battlefields in the cold war. However, the friendship and mutual trust between the two men lasted until the end. Dulles's successor, Christian Herter, was far less experienced and had no personal ties with Adenauer.

More important than the death of Dulles was the change of president that took place halfway through the Berlin crisis. John F. Kennedy, while a senator in 1957, had stated rather bluntly that, "Adenauer's time is now over. The main question . . . must now be the name of Adenauer's successor," a judgment that hardly endeared the young president-to-be to the old chancellor. Their difference in age alone, some forty years, impeded closer relations. Two other changes worried the old man: Democratic control of the Senate and the advent of William Fulbright, a known advocate of East-West détente, as chairman of the Senate Foreign Relations Committee.

In our age of summit diplomacy, changes at the top are always important. There were no major shifts in Germany during this period, although Adenauer, for reasons I shall discuss later, was gradually losing ground. But a radical change took place in France with the return in 1958 of Charles de Gaulle as head of a drastically revamped fifth republic. For Germany the advent of the vainglorious general had far-reaching consequences. It completed the rapprochement of the two countries, but at the price of temporarily loosening Bonn's ties with Washington. Adenauer's wish for friendship with France was genuine and of long standing, and in time a warm personal relationship grew up between the French and German leaders, far closer than that between Stresemann and Briand thirty years earlier. Adenauer and de Gaulle met for the first time in September 1958 and from the start found that they agreed on many basic issues. De Gaulle's overriding aim was to regain for his country some of the "grandeur" it had lost as a result of two world wars and to free both France and Europe from the tutelage of the Anglo-Saxons. In pursuit of this policy he embarked on a gradual withdrawal from NATO, development of an independent nuclear force, and unification of western Europe under French leadership. Germany, he hoped, would help him reach these goals.

Adenauer shared some of de Gaulle's feelings about the Anglo-Saxon powers, who seemed far too ready to negotiate on the German issue rather than hold the line against the Russians. He was grateful, therefore, for the unvarying support of his newfound friend at various international conferences dealing with the German question. But this assistance was given at the price of having to support de Gaulle's own schemes. As far as NATO was concerned, Adenauer shared some of the general's reservations concerning America's dominant role within the alliance, but on the whole he continued the policy of German integration begun in 1955. On European unification, Adenauer seemed more willing to follow de Gaulle's lead. In the early 1960s, the possibility was discussed of extending European economic integration to achieve some form of political integration. The question was how far such integration should go, how much sovereignty the members should give up. In the ensuing negotiations it became clear that de Gaulle was opposed to any kind of supranational political authority and instead advocated a confederation of European states, not including Britain, which was disqualified because of its "special relationship" with the United States. De Gaulle's limited vision of European unity was shared by Adenauer up to a point, but it was opposed by the Benelux countries as well as by Italy. As a result, talks among the six members of the Common Market broke down in early 1962.

Meanwhile relations between Paris and Bonn had become ever closer, as de Gaulle continued to back Adenauer's stand-firm policy on Berlin. During the summer of 1962 the two leaders exchanged much-publicized state visits that prepared for the culmination of their efforts to bury an unhappy past, the Franco-German Treaty of Friendship, signed in Paris on January 22, 1963. A week later, the Brussels conference that had been deliberating Britain's accession to the Common Market was adjourned; de Gaulle had vetoed the accession.

Relations between the United States and Germany during the last years of Adenauer's administration were certainly not as good as they had been earlier. Adenauer, egged on by de Gaulle, feared that the Americans might make a deal with the Russians over the heads of their European allies, while many Americans felt that their nation's freedom of action was unduly circumscribed by Adenauer's rigid stand on German reunification. There were other mutual annoyances—the Federal Republic's unwillingness to share America's European defense costs; America's alarm about incidents of overt anti-Semitism in Germany; and occasional instances of economic friction due to competing business and agricultural interests. But the main concern, at least in Germany, continued to be over the future of Berlin and the rest of Germany.

The reply by the three western powers to Khrushchev's Berlin ultimatum of November 1958 was worked out in consultation with West Germany during the spring of 1959. The results, the so-called Herter Plan, were presented at another Council of Foreign Ministers' conference in Geneva between May and August 1959, with advisers from both German states participating. The drawn-out meeting was intended to deal with the whole complex of European issues dividing the two sides—Germany, security, and disarmament. But the subject of Berlin monopolized the discussions. Again no concrete results were achieved, except that the six-month time limit of Khrushchev's original demand was silently dropped. In late September the Russian leader visited President Eisenhower at Camp David, and the two agreed to resume the Berlin talks at a next summit conference, scheduled for May 1960 in Paris. But that meeting was torpedoed at the last minute by Khrushchev's outburst over the U2 affair, the downing of an American spy plane over Russia. The Russians vetoed further talks, at least until after the American elections.

The new administration of John F. Kennedy and Secretary of State Dean Rusk inherited a global list of problems, of which the confrontation in central Europe was merely one. The administration got off to an inauspicious start with the Bay of Pigs fiasco in April 1961, which weakened the president's position for his first meeting with Khrushchev early in June in Vienna. The meeting was mostly exploratory, but the Russians did present Kennedy with a memorandum suggesting that the German situation be formalized by a general German peace treaty and that the situation in West Berlin be normalized. A month later the western powers, in separate notes to the Russians, reaffirmed their right to remain in and have free access to Berlin. They also said they were ready to discuss an overall solution of the German question on the basis of self-determination, in other words, free elections.

As these exchanges show, neither the Russian nor the western position on the German question had changed much since the Paris treaties in 1955; the Russians still insisted on a peace treaty with both Germanies (implying the recognition of the DDR), and the western allies countered with reunification through free elections. On August 13, 1961, another surprise move, again in Berlin, touched off what seemed at first a further escalation of the crisis. On that day the infamous Berlin Wall was suddenly thrown up as a barrier between the eastern and western sectors of the city. The wall was built by the East Germans, but Khrushchev took full responsibility for it. The motives for this challenge were probably not unlike those for the original ultimatum three years earlier, but there was an added reason for this shocking event. In the past the western part of Berlin had served as a vestibule to freedom for thousands of East Germans fleeing from communism. That escape route, a steady human drain from the DDR, was now sealed off.

The western powers, caught completely unprepared, protested but took no countermeasures. President Kennedy, to show his concern, sent Vice-President Lyndon B. Johnson to visit Berlin, followed by General Lucius Clay, now retired, the hero of the Berlin airlift. In addition, the American garrison in West Berlin was strengthened, but those were mere gestures; the West Germans had expected more. As it turned out, the construction of the wall inaugurated the end rather than an escalation of the Berlin crisis. On November 7 Khrushchev announced his readiness to postpone settlement of the Berlin question. Both he and Kennedy clearly wanted to avoid any further showdown, and their ambassadors in Moscow and Washington, in talks with Foreign Minister Andrei Gromyko and Secretary of State Rusk, continued their efforts to find a *modus vivendi* on Germany.

Meanwhile some important changes had taken place in Bonn. In the September elections, Adenauer's CDU-CSU had lost its absolute majority, and the chancellor once again depended on a coalition with the FDP. One of the FDP's conditions was that Foreign Minister von Brentano be dropped from the cabinet. Gerhard Schröder, who took over in November 1961, was welcomed by Washington as more open to a possible East-West détente than his predecessor had been. At the same time, Adenauer's term of office was limited by his party to two more years, ending in October 1963.

The grand old man was beginning to show his age—he was eighty-five—and during his last two years in office he came increasingly under the influence of de Gaulle. Also during this period contacts between West Germany and the Soviet Union became more active, on the initiative of Bonn's ambassador to Moscow, Hans Kroll. The details of these feelers, envisaging ultimately a visit to Bonn by Khrushchev, need not concern us here. At one point Adenauer suggested a ten-year *Burgfrieden,* or truce, on German reunification, an indication that he was becoming reconciled to the status quo of a divided Germany. The Soviets turned down the proposal.

The United States, although not happy with the Adenauer–de Gaulle entente, welcomed the chancellor's more open attitude toward Moscow. In other respects, however, relations between Washington and Bonn became more strained than ever before. Adenauer thought Kennedy's policy too flexible and directed by "too many cooks," while Kennedy found the old chancellor "hard to please and hard to budge, and his government hard put to keep a secret." The German ambassador in Washington, Wilhelm Grewe, confirmed the impression of inflexibility and finally had to be recalled. As for the inability to keep a secret, the latest such incident occurred in mid-April 1962 when a set of American proposals intended for the Russians, on European security, Germany, and Berlin, which had been submitted to Bonn for approval, was promptly leaked to the press. This, the State Department charged, was "a flagrant breach of diplomatic usage," causing "incurable harm" to relations between the two countries. Adenauer, meanwhile, publicly dismissed as unworkable Kennedy's and Rusk's efforts to reach an understanding with the Russians and urged that they be broken off.

The tension leading to the Cuban missile crisis of October 1962 seemed to support the chancellor's criticism. The events of the crisis lie outside the scope of this book and are well enough known. It had no direct effect on the German situation, although Khrushchev's diplomatic defeat in Cuba could not help but discourage further adventures in Berlin. The confrontation over Cuba, far from interrupting further dialogue between Moscow and Washington, actually encouraged them to settle their differences. One of the first results was the nuclear test ban treaty of August 5, 1963, which later included most of the powers except France and Communist China.

The Federal Republic's signing of the test ban treaty on August 19 was an indication that Bonn was not unconditionally tied to France's lead. Another such sign was the simultaneous discussion about a Multilateral Force (MLF) proposed by the United States to counter the complaints, chiefly by de Gaulle, of unilateral American control over nuclear forces within NATO. The American scheme was turned down by the French leader, who preferred to go it alone in the nuclear field. There was some support for the French position among what came to be called the German Gaullists, men like Adenauer's minister of defense, Franz Josef Strauss, who had been dismissed in December 1962 over the *Spiegel* affair. But Adenauer favored the MLF idea, since it would enhance his country's standing within the western alliance and give Germany a say in nuclear decision making.

As the Adenauer era drew to a close, therefore, American-German relations were beginning to recover from their low of the previous year. Washington's need to compete with de Gaulle for the German chancellor's goodwill had something to do with this change, as did the pro-American attitude of Gerhard Schröder, whose relations with the Kennedy forces were excellent. The impending departure of Adenauer and the high respect in the United States for his designated successor, Ludwig Erhard, also played a part. In June 1963 Kennedy made a trip to western Europe to assure his European allies of America's continued commitment to their defense. His four-day visit to Germany was a triumphal tour, best remembered for the president's ringing assertion to a frenzied Berlin audience, *"Ich bin ein Berliner!"* Relations with Adenauer on that occasion were correct rather than cordial. Three months later the old chancellor stepped down, and two months after that, the young president was assassinated. The Adenauer and Kennedy eras ended almost simultaneously.

Adenauer's decline had begun several years earlier, for domestic rather than foreign reasons, mostly of his own making. In 1959 the term of the Federal Republic's first president, Theodor Heuss, had come to an end. The genial and gifted Swabian had carried out his largely ceremonial duties with great dignity and tact and had earned universal respect at home and abroad. Adenauer, meanwhile, in his eighties, realized that the end of his own career as chancellor was also drawing near. Adenauer's most natural successor was Ludwig Erhard, the architect of the economic miracle of the 1950s. Yet the chancellor had little faith in his economics minister's political ability, especially in the area of foreign affairs, where Adenauer felt that Erhard lacked the necessary experience and toughness. To ensure his own continued control in this area, therefore, Adenauer decided to have himself made president; but after having startled everyone by his decision, he realized that the powers of the presidency were quite limited. So he reversed his course and announced that he would remain chancellor after all. The cavalier way in which the old man manipulated his country's highest office and his vindictive treatment of Erhard were seen as a most blatant example of Adenauer's authoritarian brand of "chancellor democracy" (*Kanzlerdemokratie*). The president finally chosen, Heinrich Lübke, of far lesser stature than Heuss, was hardly the man to restore the prestige that the presidency had lost.

Adenauer's open dislike of Erhard and the latter's strong support within the CDU weakened their party. The loss of its absolute majority in the elections of 1961, however, and the gains by the Socialist opposition, were due as much to the SPD's changed image (as the result of the Godesberg program, see below) as to Adenauer's dwindling popularity. The largest gains were actually made by the FDP. Since no other party had won the five percent of the total vote required under German election law for admission to the Bundestag, Adenauer had to enter into a coalition with the Free Democrats. As mentioned earlier, they were willing to join the Christian Democrats only on condition that the chancellor replace his faithful foreign minister, Heinrich von Brentano, with the more independent Gerhard Schröder and, more important, that Adenauer step down halfway through his next term. Adenauer had no choice but to agree.

The chancellor's last two years in office were far from happy. His main concern continued to be with foreign affairs. At home he kept up his petulant sniping at Erhard, whom he accused of being anti-European and too "Atlantic-minded." Shortly before he left office, Adenauer had to face another major domestic crisis, the most serious of his career—the *Spiegel* affair. *Der Spiegel* ("The Mirror"), one of Germany's leading weeklies, was edited by the journalistic enfant terrible Rudolf Augstein and known for its fearless exposition of governmental and other abuses. In the fall of 1962 the magazine published an article that was highly critical of the West German army, the Bundeswehr. In retaliation, the police occupied its offices, and the author of the article and Augstein himself were arrested and charged with high treason. In the process many judicial and constitutional principles were violated, and parliament, the press, and the public in general rose in protest. The main culprit in the affair turned out to be Minister of Defense Franz Josef Strauss, who was forced to resign from the cabinet. But Adenauer himself had been more involved than he admitted. This was a further blow to his prestige, and when the time came for him to resign a year later, few of his countrymen were sorry to see him go.

This was hardly just, because they owed him so much, especially in the realm of foreign affairs. Like Bismarck, to whom he has often been compared, Adenauer was far more gifted and more successful in international than in internal matters. In this respect he was the direct opposite of the man who succeeded him and whom he continued to criticize. Ludwig Erhard was not a great chancellor, because he lacked what Adenauer called *politische Eigenschaften* (political qualities). Yet Erhard's decline in the sixties, like Adenauer's, should not make us forget the great contributions both of them made during the fifties. The much-acclaimed *Wirtschaftswun-*

der of the Federal Republic had many causes, not least among them American aid and German hard work. But the underlying economic policy in which these ingredients were employed was largely the work of the republic's first minister of economics.

Erhard referred to his policy as *soziale Marktwirtschaft,* which can be loosely translated as a "free market economy with a social conscience." It was not his own invention, having been worked out years earlier by a number of economists, notably Walter Eucken, Wilhelm Röpke, and Friedrich Hayek. For a noneconomist, it is easier to understand what social market economy was *not* than what it *was.* It was not old-fashioned laissez-faire capitalism, nor was it modern *Planwirtschaft* (planned economy). It might be described as a kind of economic togetherness, in which the state played the role of a benevolent guardian or umpire over the free competition of economic interests, mitigated by consensus. The most striking feature of Erhard's policy was its emphasis on free competition. Even before the founding of the Federal Republic, while he was still the director of economic affairs in Bizonia, Erhard decreed the end of all economic and price controls. His critics predicted a major disaster, but they were proved wrong. After an initial increase, prices began to level off, and everyone who was willing to work hard was able to share in the growing affluence of the German economy.

Other factors aided the *Wirtschaftswunder*—Marshall Plan aid, the boom touched off by the Korean War, the almost limitless capacity of the domestic market, the enforced modernization of German industry due to wartime destruction and postwar dismantling, and (although it did not seem helpful at first) the influx of millions of expellees and refugees from the East. But the most important element in Germany's economic recovery was the industry and self-discipline of its people, eager to slave and save in order to pull themselves out of their economic abyss. The government did its part through tax and other incentives to encourage reinvestment and to foster the rising wave of exports, the barometer of recovery.

Even more than political integration with the West, economic progress has been the secret of the Federal Republic's success, just as lack of it had been the cause of the Weimar Republic's failure. I will not go into the details of that progress; they are well enough known and statistics are dull. Just a few facts and figures: between 1950 and 1963 total industrial production almost tripled, exports increased nearly sevenfold, automobile production rose twentyfold, and Germany's merchant marine grew to more than seventeen times its former size. By 1963 the Federal Republic was economically the strongest power in Europe except for the Soviet Union; it was the world's second-largest exporting country; and it held third place in the world's steel production. All of this amazing growth was achieved without major inflationary or other crises, in part because of the constant influx of additional manpower from the East, which helped to maintain a balance between wages and production. There was still unemployment at first, but by 1963 virtually full employment had been achieved. The cost of living index during the 1950s rose by a little over 20 percent, while wages more than doubled. Much of the additional income went into savings or long-range investments, especially housing, of which close to seven million new units were built before 1963.

The one sector that did not share in the general boom was agriculture. As in most other highly industrialized countries, including the United States, agriculture has been the problem child of the economy. The kind of controls and subsidies it required were incompatible with Erhard's belief in free enterprise. Germany's main agricultural regions before World War II had been in the East, the area now held by the German Democratic Republic or annexed by Poland and the Soviet Union. In the West holdings were generally too small and scattered to encourage the use of agricultural machinery. The government tried its best to help agriculture become competitive, but in a world of agrarian giants with food surpluses, such as the United States, this was a hopeless task. As in earlier phases of American-German relations, even before World War I, protecting the German farmer from his American competitor was the source of a great deal of minor friction.

Much of the credit for Germany's economic success belongs to the workers and the unions that represented them. Germans have always had a reputation for being thorough, dependable, industrious, disciplined, and obedient, and the early years of the Federal Republic showed that they deserved it. One of the remarkable features of Germany's rapid rise to riches was that it came about without any major instances of labor unrest. In Britain in the decade before 1963, an annual average of twenty-seven days per hundred workers was lost due to strikes, while the comparable figure for Germany was slightly less than five. But one need not cite national characteristics alone to explain the splendid performance of German labor. There are other explanations: the recent Nazi experience and the incentive of being able to start a new life; the absence of social grievances because of a long tradition of social legislation, begun by Bismarck and continued under Adenauer; most important, a powerful, enlightened, and efficient system of union representation.

Labor unions on the local level were the first German organizations sponsored by the occupying powers in 1945. They were intended as training grounds for democracy, and this has remained one of their foremost tasks and achievements. Unionism on the federal level was launched in 1949 with the founding of the German Trade Union Federation or DGB (Deutscher Gewerkschaftsbund). Its first head was Hans Böckler, a broad-minded and statesmanlike Social Democrat, whose close relations with Adenauer helped smooth the early years of labor relations. By the mid-fifties membership in the DGB had risen to around six million. There were also separate smaller organizations for white collar workers and civil servants. The DGB was a federation of sixteen separate unions, each concerned with wage and working agreements in its particular area. Strikes were rigidly regulated, and wildcat actions were ruled out. Because of the low incidence of strikes, the DGB and its member unions were able to amass large reserves of capital from dues. These fortunes not only strengthened organized labor vis-à-vis the employers, making the mere threat of a strike an effective weapon in the bargaining process, it enabled the unions to engage in a number of lucrative enterprises, such as banks, shipping companies, housing, and cooperatives. The DGB spent a large share of its money on cultural and educational ventures, such as the annual Ruhr Festivals, and training academies for its functionaries.

One of the chief concerns of the DGB was the workers' role in the management of industry. The catchword or slogan was *Mitbestimmung* (codetermination). In contrast to the SPD's demand for nationalization of at least the basic industries, the DGB advocated giving workers a share in determining their companies' policies. This aim was partly achieved, for the mining, iron, and steel industries only, by a law passed in 1951. It was hailed at the time as a major step toward industrial democracy, but it remained a first step. The DGB's efforts to broaden the workers' participation from social and personnel matters to economic management and to extend codetermination to other industries did not succeed during the Adenauer years. This did not seem to bother labor's rank and file, however, who were enjoying their affluent society (*Wohlstandsgesellschaft*), with its prospects of seemingly limitless prosperity.

Much of the average worker's contentment with life under Adenauer was due to the way his government was taking care of him in times of trouble—unemployment, sickness, old age. It is ironic that at a time when free competition was the keynote of West Germany's economy, the country entered on a road toward what can be called a welfare state. Germany looked back on a long and laudable tradition of social legislation. When Bismarck launched the program some seventy years earlier his motive had been to upstage the Social Democrats, and there may have been a similar, though unconscious, attempt in this case to keep up with the East German communists. The aftermath of war, of course, required drastic government action in the field of social policy, but those early emergency measures set a hand-to-mouth pattern that made it difficult later to work out a long-range social security package. This Adenauer left for his successors to do.

It is unnecessary here to spell out the details of Germany's welfare program. Compared to that of other industrialized nations, including the United States, it was most impressive. Between 1950 and 1963 the total outlay for social services in the Federal Republic increased almost fourfold, from $3 billion to more than $11 billion, or an equivalent of 13 percent of the gross national product. The financial burden was shared equally by employers and employees, with additional subventions from the state. Beginning in 1957 pension benefits were automatically adjusted to inflation, and the government provided substantial housing subsidies. The obligations thus assumed and the expectations raised were to become in time a tremendous burden, especially when economic growth began to slow down.

One issue related to welfare that was not faced by any other country was the responsibility thrust upon the Federal Republic for some twelve million expellees and refugees from beyond what was then called the iron curtain. This human wave not only posed a staggering economic problem, it also presented a major threat to European and world peace (one need only look at the Palestinian situation to realize the magnitude of that threat). Yet for the Federal Republic to absorb and assimilate these millions might imply acquiescence in the loss of German territory beyond the Oder and Neisse and recognition of Germany's partition. Resolving this dilemma required both courage and a sense of realism.

The German refugees and expellees from the East, for understandable reasons, were loath to give up their identity. In a dozen or so expellees' organizations, they proclaimed their continued loyalty to and kept alive memories of their former *Heimat,* including the Sudetenland, which had never belonged to Germany except under Hitler. As a potential political force, the newcomers were courted by the government, and at first their various pressure groups were able to wield considerable influence. The most important of these, the Bloc of Expellees and Disfranchised (BHE), tried to widen its influence by appealing to former Nazis as well. Between 1953 and 1957 the BHE joined the Adenauer coalition, and one of its leaders,

Professor Theodor Oberländer, became minister of expellees. The BHE later became a victim of the 5 percent requirement, however, and its influence declined.

The fate of the BHE was symptomatic of the gradual integration of the expellees, which was primarily an economic process. To defray the cost of indemnifying the victims of war in Germany and elsewhere, the Bundestag in 1952 decreed a sweeping "equalization of burdens" (*Lastenausgleich*), calling for a levy of up to 50 percent on all property that had survived the war, to be paid over a period of thirty years. The main beneficiaries of the law were the expellees and refugees, to whom it gave assistance in making a fresh start. The economic boom did the rest by providing employment for everyone. As the newcomers became assimilated, most of them came to accept their displacement as permanent.

To outsiders the most striking feature of the Federal Republic was its stability, due largely to economic causes, but there were other reasons. The proliferation of parties that had plagued the Weimar Republic was not repeated. By 1961 only three parties polled sufficient votes to enter the Bundestag. Extremist groups found little or no following. Under the constitution the neo-Nazi Sozialistische Reichspartei was outlawed in 1952, and the Communist party in 1956. The leading party until at least 1961 was Adenauer's CDU, which commanded an absolute majority after 1957.

Its main rival, then as now, was the SPD, which celebrated its one hundredth birthday in 1963. For the first seventeen years of the Federal Republic, the SPD remained in opposition to the ruling Christian Democrats. The death of Kurt Schumacher in 1952 deprived the party of its only leader who was a possible match for Adenauer. Schumacher's successor, Erich Ollenhauer, was an able functionary rather than a potential statesman, and it was only in the late fifties that Willy Brandt, then mayor of Berlin, emerged as his party's front runner. During the 1950s, the SPD was highly critical of the government's policy, especially on rearmament and integration into NATO, but the continued stagnation of the party in national elections finally led a reforming element within the SPD to reassess and drastically revise its platform. Under the Godesberg program of 1959, the SPD shed its traditional Marxist image and transformed itself from a class party into a people's party. It gave up its antireligious position, accepted the need for national defense, and in general endorsed the government's foreign policy. In economic affairs the program called for "competition so far as possible—planning so far as necessary."

The main architect behind the program was Herbert Wehner,

ably assisted by Fritz Erler and Willy Brandt. All three, in their late forties or early fifties, were excellent men and proof that the party did not lack talent. The change in program achieved what it was supposed to do. During the ten years after 1961 the share of SPD votes steadily rose by a total of almost 10 percent and finally over-took the CDU in the elections of 1972. The Godesberg program assured the stability and continuity of German policy in the event of an SPD electoral victory.

This brief discussion of German domestic affairs under Adenauer cannot possibly touch on every aspect, and I shall reserve some subjects, such as education and cultural affairs, for later. A few words should be said, however, about the new German army, the Bundeswehr, since it was the cause of much heated debate, already mentioned, during the fifties. The fears voiced then that a revival of the armed forces would bring a renascence of militarism fortunately proved false. The reasons for this may be found both within German society and within the Bundeswehr itself. For the general public, militarism, that is, admiration for the military establishment and its alleged values and virtues, was a thing of the past (see chapter 1). This became obvious during the mid-fifties, when Socialists, Protestants, and liberal intellectuals joined forces in denouncing rearmament. The young in particular were vehement in asserting their *ohne mich* (include me out) position.

These sentiments were taken into account by the founders of the new Bundeswehr. It was a great help that in contrast to the Weimar Republic, when the Reichswehr had proudly proclaimed itself the heir of the imperial army, the Federal Republic was able to make a fresh beginning and determine the type of army it wanted. Uppermost in the minds of the Bundeswehr's planners was to ensure continued civilian control over the armed forces. This was achieved in several ways: first, supreme command was vested in the minister of defense in time of peace and in the chancellor in time of war; second, a defense committee of parliament was given far-reaching powers of investigation; third, a special defense commissioner of the Bundestag was to serve as watchdog and ombudsman, to make sure that the basic rights of soldiers were observed and to listen to their complaints if they were not; and fourth, a personnel evaluation committee was charged with checking the credentials of applicants for high commissions to see that they were qualified to serve in a democratic army.

On the whole these safeguards fulfilled their purpose, and the emerging Bundeswehr, army, navy, and airforce, was radically different from the Wehrmacht that had surrendered ten years earlier.

Its founders, however, were concerned not only with matters of organization, but with the general nature and spirit of the new army as well. One of the key figures in this seemingly paradoxical exercise of creating a nonmilitaristic German army was a Prussian Junker and former officer in Hitler's Wehrmacht, Wolf Count von Baudissin. In spite of what his background might suggest, although he was a good soldier, he was also a humane, thoughtful, open-minded and Christian gentleman. Count Baudissin was chiefly responsible for the two concepts that ruled the Bundeswehr—"citizenship in uniform" and *innere Führung*. The former needs no explanation and was hardly a novelty outside of Germany. *Innere Führung,* which has been translated as "leadership and character training," referred to the educational philosophy that was to underlie German military training. Its emphasis was to be on citizenship rather than military drill, initiative rather than obedience, and self-discipline rather than discipline imposed from above.

These aims could hardly be put into practice overnight. But even though imperfectly realized, such ideals made for a more democratic army than the Germans had ever known. The early years of the Bundeswehr were beset by many difficulties, including shortage of trained officers and NCOs, lack of materiel, and problems of morale. Germany's youth were no more enthusiastic about being drafted than young people elsewhere. Much of the credit for coping with these difficulties belonged to Franz Josef Strauss, who served as minister of defense for six years before he disgraced himself in the *Spiegel* affair. By 1963 Germany contributed some 404,000 men to NATO, the largest contingent next to that of the United States.

My account of the Adenauer years has purposely dwelled on the positive side of the story—successful integration into the West, the economic miracle, a contented working class, a democratic army —because these were the developments that were important for the years to come. But this does not mean that there were no negative or even ugly events. At the time it was often Germany's shortcomings rather than its achievements that made headlines abroad, something that many Germans complained about, because they themselves were only too ready to forget their recent past.

The failure to come to grips with the Nazi past lent an air of uncertainty to the Federal Republic. Allied efforts during occupation to induce a feeling of collective guilt through reeducation had not been very successful (see chapter 7), and "collective shame," a term coined by President Heuss, was rarely shown. Much was done to inform the German people, especially the young, about the evils of the Hitler years. A Federal Office for Political Education (Bundeszentrale für politische Bildung) published an excellent weekly paper, *Das Parlament,* and sponsored numerous historical works, while organizations like the Institut für Zeitgeschichte (Institute for Contemporary History) in Munich conducted and published important research on the Nazi period. In most German schools, moreover, instruction in recent history and civics was made compulsory. But with an older generation refusing to admit its involvement with Nazism, these efforts were not very effective.

Adenauer was surprisingly insensitive to the shadows cast by the Nazi era. One of his closest collaborators, Hans Globke, had written the official commentary of Hitler's infamous Nuremberg laws (see chapter 5), but that did not disqualify him for government service in the chancellor's eyes. Theodor Oberländer, his minister of expellees, also had a Nazi past and had to be dismissed in 1960. There were other unfortunate choices for important posts, such as Minister of Transport Hans-Christoph Seebohm who, although not a Nazi, was a rabid nationalist. In fairness, however, these indiscretions in personnel matters must be balanced against Adenauer's sincere efforts to make amends for the crimes Germany had committed against the Jews under Hitler. According to an agreement signed in Luxembourg in 1952 and passed by a large majority of the Bundestag in 1953, the state of Israel was to receive $715 million in goods over a number of years.

The treaty with Israel was only one of many acts of restitution for the sufferings inflicted by the Nazis. The circle of recipients of the *Wiedergutmachung* (restitution) was drawn wide and included even those Nazi civil servants who had lost their jobs in 1945 and now claimed a pension. In some instances these former Nazis were treated more generously than the people they had victimized. There were other such inequities, especially in handing out light sentences to Nazis convicted of capital crimes. The fact that some 80 percent of the Federal Republic's judges at the start were former Nazis helps explain this leniency. On the other hand, it was German rather than Allied courts that conducted the trials, and their proceedings were widely publicized in the German press, which did much to bring home the terrible lessons of the Nazi experience. This was particularly true during the so-called Auschwitz trial, which began in Frankfurt just before Adenauer's departure in 1963 and lasted for two years. There were other events to make people remember the Nazi nightmare: the boycott by the general public of the movies of Veit Harlan, remembered for his anti-Semitic films under Hitler; the amazing success of the publication of *The Diary of Ann Frank*

(400,000 copies in two years) and the cult of the little Jewish girl developing from it; the institution of a "week of brotherhood" among Christians and Jews; and the Peace with Israel movement inaugurated by Erich Lüth. But there were also signs of continued anti-Semitism, especially during the winter of 1959–60 when, as often before, Jewish cemeteries were desecrated and synagogues smeared with swastikas. To some outside observers these acts were more than mere hooliganism; they were a sign that the Nazi virus was not dead and that the disease might flare up again. Time would tell.

Before turning to Adenauer's successors and their relations with the United States, we must take a brief look at developments in the East German Democratic Republic, or the Soviet Zone, as West Germans still insisted on calling it. If Konrad Adenauer was the architect of the Federal Republic, Walter Ulbricht had that role in the East. *Walterchen* ("Little Walter") as his countrymen patronizingly called him, was certainly far different from *der Alte*. He was sixteen years younger than Adenauer, was born a worker, and had been a Marxist and a Communist most of his life. He had spent the Nazi years in exile in Moscow and returned in 1945 to help in the communization of East Germany (see chapter 7). Ulbricht had a genuine admiration for Stalin, and he remained the Soviet Union's most willing agent throughout his long career, longer than that of almost any statesman in this century. He was an unimpressive little man, devoid of charisma, who viewed himself as the father of his country and had himself built up as such in a personality cult not unlike that of Stalin. But he was also a superb organizer, a ruthless (though not cruel) dictator, and an opportunist. In 1950 he became first secretary of the central committee of the SED, the most powerful position in the DDR. Ten years later, upon the death of the Democratic Republic's first president, Wilhelm Pieck, a Staatsrat (Council of State) replaced the presidency, and Ulbricht became its chairman and thus the head of state. This position he held until his death in 1973, although he relinquished the secretaryship of his party two years earlier.

Political and economic developments in the German Democratic Republic during the 1950s continued along the lines indicated earlier. The initial phase of an antifascist democratic front, which gave parties outside the SED (and the SPD within it) some voice, came to an end by 1952. Thenceforth the DDR was to be a genuine people's democracy ruled by the SED. There still were periodic elections for a pseudoparliament, the Volkskammer, but it was little more than a debating society, if that. Some former Nazis were allowed to hold government posts, if they had not committed notorious crimes, and a National Democratic Party (NDP) catered to the rank and file of Hitler's followers.

The SED was conceived of as an elite or "cadre" party, limited to about 10 percent of the population. The masses were enrolled in and kept in line by various auxiliary organizations, such as the Free German Labor Union or the Free German Youth. These organizations, together with the remainder of the CDU, the Liberal-Democratic Party (LDP), the NDP, the German Peasant Party (DBP) and, of course, the SED, were represented in the Volkskammer, thus giving it the appearance of democracy. The keynote of DDR policy was centralization. In 1952 its five Länder were structured into fourteen districts, and various central planning and control commissions were charged with directing every phase of the country's political and economic life. The SED adopted a strict line of Marxism-Leninism-Stalinism, and any sentiment in favor of an "own road to socialism" (or Titoism) was ruthlessly suppressed.

Just as the Federal Republic became firmly joined to the West, the Democratic Republic became an integral part of the eastern communist bloc. In 1950 it joined COMECON, the communist answer to the Marshall Plan and OEEC, and in 1955 it became a member of the Warsaw Pact, the counterpart of NATO. In 1950 East Germany concluded border treaties with Poland and Czechoslovakia, the first of which recognized the Oder-Neisse frontier, and the latter the "resettlement" of the Sudeten Germans. East Germany's relations with its fellow members in the Soviet sphere, all of them victims of Nazi aggression, continued to be touchy, and Moscow had to use occasional pressure to assure harmony among its satellites. In 1955 the Soviet Union officially recognized the sovereignty of the DDR in all questions of domestic and foreign policy, and nine years later the two concluded a treaty of friendship and brotherhood. This meant that the German Democratic Republic remained closely tied to its big brother, following every twist and turn in Russia's relations with the West and the Federal Republic.

At home the main concerns of the DDR were economic. The trend toward socialization in industry and collectivization in agriculture continued through the 1950s, although wholesale collectivization did not start until 1959. By 1963 all but 2.4 percent of industry, 11 percent of commerce, and 10 percent of agriculture were state controlled. As in all communist states, economic life was regulated by five- or seven-year plans, with private initiative curtailed and all activity subjected to complicated bureaucratic control. Such a system should have endeared itself to a people that admired and was used to the intricacies of bureaucracy, but it did not work. There were other reasons for the Democratic Republic's failure to equal the economic miracle of its West German rival—the burden of Soviet reparations amounting to billions of dollars, the absence of anything comparable to Marshall Plan aid, the constant drain of skilled labor through flight to the West, and the inefficiency of small-scale farming resulting from the initial land reform (see chapter 7). But the dead hand of bureaucratization was the major factor in retarding East Germany's economic recovery.

As a result, life in the Democratic Republic was dismal and dull. With the emphasis on capital industries, there were few consumer goods, and with thousands of farmers defecting, food remained in short supply, and rationing was not discontinued until 1958. To spur the lagging economy, the government resorted to production contests and awards for workers who exceeded their norms; when this did not work, it raised the daily work load by 10 percent.

It was the resulting discontent among the construction workers of East Berlin that sparked the most dramatic event in the early history of the Democratic Republic—the abortive uprising of June 17, 1953. It began on June 16 with a work stoppage, escalated into a general strike the next day, and spread to other industrial centers. Although the initial causes were economic, the protesters also voiced political grievances. They burned communist flags and demanded free elections. The people's police was unable to cope with the situation, and Soviet forces finally intervened, easily subduing the unarmed rebels. More than eleven hundred persons were convicted; about a hundred were given death sentences, and a similar number life imprisonment. The western powers, taken entirely by surprise, did nothing. The West Germans protested and subsequently declared June 17 a national day of remembrance. But in time its meaning was forgotten, and it became just another holiday. Yet the fact that it had been a band of Germans, albeit small, that first rose against communist tyranny in eastern Europe should not be forgotten. Their action may well have inspired the protests in Poland and Hungary three years later.

In part all these uprisings were results of the thaw following Stalin's death. But while Stalinists gave way to more moderate leaders in the other communist countries, Ulbricht was able to rid himself of potential anti-Stalinist rivals and critics. After the June uprising Wilhelm Zaisser, minister for state security, and Rudolf Herrnstadt, editor of the official party organ *Neues Deutschland,* were let go. In 1958 there was another purge of dissenters around Ernst Wollweber and Karl Schirdewan. None of these men was punished, however, and some were given nonpolitical jobs. Ulbricht might be a tyrant, but he was not bloodthirsty. Intellectual critics were dealt with more harshly, however. The best-known example was Wolfgang Harich, a professor of Marxist philosophy, who in 1957 was sentenced to ten years in the penitentiary for having advocated a more humane type of socialism and respect for intellectual freedom.

Ulbricht's survival was a sign of his usefulness to the Russians and his own skill in combining repression and propaganda. In 1950 a political police, the SSD (Staatssicherheitsdienst) had been established. But as political opposition declined and the penal code and administration of justice were tightened, repression became part of regular legal procedure, with the notorious Hilde Benjamin, minister of justice since 1953, as the most dreaded guardian of state security and political orthodoxy. In 1956 the militarized people's police was transformed into the National People's Army (Nationale Volksarmee). Universal military service, however, was not introduced until 1962, after the Berlin wall had put an end to the threatened exodus of draftees.

The wall was a turning point in the history of the Democratic Republic, and events since then will be discussed later (see Chapter 11). The major reasons for sealing off the DDR were economic, as was shown by the sudden economic boom of the sixties. At the moment the Berlin wall further emphasized the separation of the two Germanies. During the past fifteen years, people on both sides of the heavily guarded frontier have steadily drifted apart, or as the Germans would say, *"sich auseinandergelebt."* And while the East Germans were able to follow the progress of their West German cousins via radio and television with a mixture of envy and admiration, the West Germans knew little and seemed to care less and less about what went on in East Germany. Political separatism led to human estrangement. To many Germans the wall was merely a symbol of what they had long felt in their hearts.

9 | From Adenauer to Brandt
1963–1974

I F THE KEYNOTE of the Adenauer era was stability, the next few years were characterized by movement and change. In domestic affairs the predominance of the CDU ebbed. At first it was forced to share power with the SPD, then in 1969, the SPD emerged first as the governing, and after 1972, as the largest party. During this time the Federal Republic found its second great leader in Socialist chairman Willy Brandt, whose major contribution was to find a way out of the rigid impasse that had developed in West Germany's relations with its eastern neighbors, especially the German Democratic Republic. In foreign relations the Federal Republic under Ludwig Erhard at first continued its close adherence or even subservience to the policies pursued by the United States. But as America continued to search for détente with its Soviet rival, Bonn increasingly wanted to become an equal partner rather than a mere ward of Washington. This *Wille zur Selbständigkeit* (will for independence), already evident in Adenauer's collaboration with de Gaulle, became a marked feature of German-American relations.

For the United States, Germany had always been one of many issues in the worldwide contest with communism. During the sixties and early seventies, America was primarily concerned with Asia, where the war in Vietnam was escalating into a major drain on its military and economic resources. Surprisingly, Vietnam did not interfere with the trend toward détente between the two superpowers, nor did any of the other crises of the period—the war between India and Pakistan in 1965, the Middle East war in 1967, the Czech crisis of 1968, and the energy crisis of the early seventies—interrupt what President Nixon called "the era of negotiation." Although most of these events did not affect relations between Washington and Bonn, they must be kept in mind to understand the seeming neglect with which some Germans charged the United States.

On the face of it, Ludwig Erhard was the ideal successor to Adenauer. The rotund and ebullient chancellor seemed the very embodiment of the *Wirtschaftswunder* he had masterminded. His kind and democratic manner made him popular both at home and abroad, especially in the United States. But in the rough-and-tumble game of politics, kindness can be more hindrance than help. Adenauer, when forced to resign, had not relinquished his leadership of the CDU, and he now used this position to undercut his successor. Allying himself with the German Gaullists, especially Franz Josef Strauss, Adenauer openly criticized Erhard's neutral stand toward France and ostentatiously continued to visit the French president. Just as Bismarck had lowered himself by attacking the men who succeeded him, Adenauer's intrigues against Erhard hardly improved the ex-chancellor's image. It was not the way elder statesmen should act.

The election campaign of 1965 called for a brief truce in Adenauer's anti-Erhard agitation, and actually the CDU did better in that election than it had done under Adenauer. The major losers were the FDP and the remaining splinter parties, the latter receiving a mere 3.6 percent of the total vote. But despite his victory, the chancellor's fortunes continued to wane, for foreign as well as domestic reasons. Abroad, the Erhard government had to steer a middle course between America's Atlantic and France's European policies, a thankless task at best. At home, economic growth had leveled off into a temporary recession, requiring higher taxes in 1967. Ironically, it was this economic issue that caused Erhard's downfall. In October 1966 the FDP withdrew its four members from the cabinet, and when efforts to mend the coalition failed, the CDU forced Erhard's withdrawal. As his successor, the party chose the minister president of Baden-Württemberg, Kurt Georg Kiesinger, who as a former Nazi had been subject to automatic arrest by the Allies in 1945. By all accounts Kiesinger had not been a rabid party member, and the fact that an ardent anti-Nazi like Willy Brandt was willing to serve as his foreign minister was held in Kiesinger's favor. Still, he was hardly the best choice. He formed a new government in coalition with the SPD.

Kiesinger was not the first former Nazi to win cabinet rank.

Brandt's predecessor as foreign minister, Gerhard Schröder, likewise had been involved with Nazism. Schröder had been appointed by Adenauer and had proved himself an able advocate of good relations with the United States (see chapter 8). At the same time he had been able to keep alive the tie between Bonn and Paris, without unduly falling under the influence of de Gaulle. These aims were the two main concerns of German foreign policy under Erhard, who visited the United States six times in three years and established close contacts with President Lyndon Johnson. Both men had assumed office almost simultaneously, and both had little prior experience with foreign affairs. Johnson, while vice-president, had visited Berlin during the wall crisis in 1961, but as president his main attention focused on domestic reforms and the deteriorating situation in Vietnam. Erhard, on the other hand, as a firm believer in the Atlantic community, hoped to maintain the closest possible relations with the United States. He went out of his way to support American policy in Asia, and when requested, canceled the sale of strategic materials to Russia and a steel plant to China, favors that were apparently taken very much for granted by Washington.

The issues that loomed largest in German-American relations during the Erhard years were offset payments and the MLF (Multilateral Force). The first involved Germany's promise to share in the cost of stationing American troops on German soil. In 1961 the two governments had signed an agreement under which Germany was to buy large quantities of American military equipment, thus helping to support America's balance of payments. This seemed a sensible and mutually satisfactory arrangement, but by 1966 Germany had fallen behind in its purchases, and Secretary of Defense Robert McNamara, supported by a faction in Congress, asked that the Germans live up to their agreement or else face a reduction of American forces. The Erhard government, though in financial straits at the time, had little choice. The chancellor pleaded with President Johnson during his last visit to Washington in September 1966 for a reduction in offset payments, but he was turned down. Because these payments were partly responsible for the tax rise that brought about Erhard's downfall, the United States bore some indirect responsibility for that event.

Another major disappointment for Erhard and Schröder was America's shelving of plans for a Multilateral Force, an idea that had been discussed in Adenauer's time (see chapter 8). Adenauer had supported it then but had since changed his mind. Its main opponent among the NATO allies was President de Gaulle, although support in Britain was also divided. The only two powers wholeheartedly in favor of the MLF were the United States and Germany, and most of the discussions about it were between McNamara and Germany's defense minister, Kai-Uwe von Hassel. In view of the mixed reaction to it, President Johnson in late 1964 decided not to push MLF but instead to sponsor a Nuclear Planning Group (NPG) of defense ministers to consult on matters of nuclear policy. Germany, although a nonnuclear power, was to be a member of this body and thus have a voice in the nuclear planning of the alliance. But Bonn would have preferred, and continued to hope for, the MLF.

While America was the center of Erhard's concern, there were also the commitments to France that he had inherited from Adenauer. Both Germany and the United States had troubles with de Gaulle, the former because of France's boycott of the European Economic Community in 1965–66, the latter because of the French president's withdrawal from NATO around the same time. Even though the nature of these problems differed, their common cause created a community of interest between Bonn and Washington in their dealings with the difficult old man in Paris.

A similar community of interest also developed on the subject of improved relations with the nations of eastern Europe. During the 1950s, the most important issue in West German foreign policy had been reunification, about which there had been endless plans, debates, and conferences. Solving the German problem was then seen as the sine qua non for improved western relations with the communist bloc. Beginning in the early sixties and especially after the Cuban missile crisis, a different view gained ground in the United States, namely that the only way to achieve peaceful reunification was through détente—a complete reversal of priorities. This was in substance what President Johnson told Erhard and Schröder during their second visit to America in 1964. There were to be no more initiatives or soundings by the western powers on the German question. It was up to the West Germans themselves to pursue further the flexible "policy of movement" on which Schröder had already embarked and to try to find a *modus vivendi* with the nations of eastern Europe, including the DDR.

Such sentiments were also heard in Germany, especially within the SPD. In 1963 Egon Bahr, close adviser to Willy Brandt, had coined the phrase *Wandel durch Annäherung* (change through contact) to describe his program for bridging the gap between the two German states. Gerhard Schröder had done his share by arranging for the exchange of trade missions with Poland, Rumania, Hungary, and Bulgaria, and early in 1965 there were signs that he might even consider establishing diplomatic relations with these countries. Meanwhile voices outside the government also began advocating a more flexible policy. In January 1965 the SPD's chief spokesman on foreign policy, Fritz Erler, suggested that the Federal Republic normalize its relations with Poland and recognize the Oder-Neisse frontier. In October the Evangelical Church took a similar stand, and certain prominent figures, like the philosopher Karl Jaspers, and some of the leading newspapers also spoke out for a less rigid policy toward eastern Europe. The time had clearly come for the government to move.

On March 25, 1966, Bonn addressed a "peace note" to the east European states, assuring these countries that the Federal Republic "was pursuing neither a policy of revenge nor of revision" and offering to sign agreements with the nations of eastern Europe, renouncing the use of force. The German question, the note said, should be resolved "by giving the whole German people the right to decide freely its political life [*Lebensform*] and fate." Nothing was said about diplomatic relations, recognition of the Oder-Neisse line, or the DDR.

The action of the Erhard government was welcomed in Washington as a contribution to détente. As expected, the reply to the peace note came from the Soviet Union, the only member of the Warsaw Pact with which the Federal Republic maintained diplomatic relations. Obviously annoyed at Bonn's mention of reunification, the Russians did not concern themselves with the specifics of the German note, but instead made a number of counterproposals dealing with general European security, disengagement, nuclear nonproliferation, and so on. By insisting on recognition of existing borders, furthermore, the Soviets also brought up West Germany's recognition of the Democratic Republic.

Recognition, of course, was the crux of Bonn's eastern policy. As a first attempt to bring about change through contact, the SPD and SED in the spring of 1966 discussed a possible exchange of speakers who would present each other's positions to public audiences. The plan never materialized, but while it was being debated, it became obvious that there was still much resistance in West Germany to normalization of relations between the two German states. In a talk between Erhard and leading members of the three main parties in April, the participants agreed that recognition of the DDR was out of the question, for the CDU-FDP coalition and the SPD opposition alike. Actually, the Federal Republic's position on the German question had become more flexible than this suggests. In a speech shortly before Erhard left office, President Johnson again placed détente ahead of reunification. "We must improve the East-West environment," he told a New York audience in October 1966, "in order to achieve the unification of Germany in the context of a larger, peaceful, and prosperous Europe." A few years earlier, such a statement would have caused alarm and raised protests in Germany. There were none this time.

The government of Kurt Georg Kiesinger was a "grand coalition" of the two leading parties, Christian Democrats and Socialists. Their combined delegates gave them an overwhelming majority in the Bundestag, but each party still hoped to defeat the other in the federal elections scheduled for 1969. The closer that time came, therefore, the more they asserted their rivalry. Of the nineteen cabinet members, nine belonged to the SPD, first and foremost among them Willy Brandt, who served as vice-chancellor and foreign minister. Other prominent Socialists were Herbert Wehner, a former Communist and one of the authors of the Godesberg program, who served as minister for all-German (*gesamtdeutsche*) affairs; Gustav Heinemann, who had left the CDU and who was to become the Federal Republic's third president in 1969, now minister of justice; and Karl Schiller, a former member of the Nazi party, who became minister of economics. On the CDU side, the main changes were the "demotion" of Gerhard Schröder from foreign to defense minister and the comeback of Franz Josef Strauss as minister of finance. Erhard was relegated to the ranks, though he continued as nominal head of the CDU.

The most impressive member of the new cabinet, far more so than the nondescript Kiesinger, was Willy Brandt. The man who in 1969 was to become Germany's first Socialist chancellor in thirty years was born Herbert Frahm in 1913 (he was illegitimate, a fact to which Adenauer, inexcusably, referred during the 1961 campaign). Frahm was too young during the Weimar Republic to become politically prominent, but he early became active on the radical left. He spent the Hitler years in Norway and Sweden, became a Norwegian citizen, and fought against the Nazis, at which time he took the name Willy Brandt. After the war he represented the SPD in West Berlin, where he became mayor in 1957. In 1961 and again in 1965 Brandt was his party's candidate for the chancellorship. However, the hope that his youthful charm and good looks would help the SPD break the 40 percent barrier proved vain. Willy Brandt emerged from these defeats a more mature, patient, and experienced man, ready to learn from and listen to his colleagues at home and his negotiating partners abroad. These qualities were to stand him in good stead during the years to come.

The Kiesinger-Brandt coalition was concerned mainly with domestic affairs, in particular with the creeping recession that had been Erhard's undoing. Surprisingly enough, despite their different party affiliations, the combination of Schiller (economics) and Strauss (finance) worked well at first. In 1967 German economic growth had slowed to 0.6 percent from its earlier record highs. But thanks to careful budgetary planning, government contracts, and tax incentives, Germany's economy in 1968 again showed a 9.4 percent growth rate. For the first time, however, inflation and rising living costs also became serious problems. Germany's overflowing balance of payments for some time had led its western partners to ask for an upward valuation of the deutsche mark. One such revaluation had already taken place in 1961, but further steps were resisted by industry and the government. Only during the 1969 election campaign did Strauss and Schiller part ways, with the former opposing and the latter supporting revaluation.

Disagreement between the two coalition partners also developed over the question of electoral reform. Both parties originally wanted to change election procedures so that small parties would be curtailed further and one of the two major ones would win a clearcut majority. But the SPD had second thoughts, and various legislative proposals by the CDU's interior minister Paul Lücke were turned down, finally leading to his resignation. The only controversial legislation passed during the coalition was the *Notstandsverfassung* of 1968, a detailed set of laws against political unrest. Because of their sweeping nature, these emergency decrees aroused heated opposition outside of parliament.

With both major parties in power, extraparliamentary opposition (*ausserparlamentarische Opposition,* or APO) became an important factor. Protest came from both right and left, although the rightist opposition was extraparliamentary only in fact, not in intent. The National Democratic Party (NDP) was founded in 1964. Its leaders and many of its followers came from various small neo-Nazi and expellee groups that had fallen victims to the 5 percent clause. Its platform smacked of Nazism—it denied collective guilt and demanded a general amnesty for ex-Nazis; it disclaimed German responsibility for both world wars; it denounced *Amerikanisierung* and communism; it laid claim to eastern Germany and the Sudetenland; and it opposed department stores and foreign workers. Its führer was a muddleheaded Junker, Adolf von Thadden. The NDP did not attract much attention until the recession of 1966, when it made sizable gains in various Land elections. On the federal level it broke the 5 percent barrier in four states in 1969, but this was not enough to gain it admission to the Bundestag. By 1970 it had run its course. What accounted for the NDP's brief success? Economic discontent mostly, plus the appeal it had for unregenerate survivors of the Nazi past. Another contributing factor may have been opposition to the simultaneous protest from the left, the real APO or "new left."

Most of this leftist protest was centered in the German universities. It was part of a larger student revolt extending from Berkeley to Berlin and from Paris to Prague, which reached its climax in 1968. Its aims were similar everywhere—opposition to authority, injustice, oppression, materialism, conformity, in short, the establishment. In time the war in Vietnam became the focal point of protest. Student unrest in Germany went back to the early sixties, caused by dissatisfaction with the ossified, hierarchical, and authoritarian structure of German universities, a system under which the *Ordinarius* (full professor) wielded virtually absolute power in matters of curriculum, examinations, appointments, and promotions. The rapid increase of student enrollment, from 244,000 in 1961 to 316,000 in 1968, and the inability of many graduates to find suitable employment created added tension, making student demonstrations the order of the day.

In 1967 peaceful demonstrations escalated into bloody riots. They were touched off during a rally in West Berlin against the Shah of Iran when a student, Benno Ohnesorg, was shot and killed by a policeman. From Berlin rioting spread to other universities. The unrest was led by various activist groups within the APO, foremost among them the Sozialistischer Deutscher Studentenbund (SDS), founded shortly after World War II, which had been supported by the SPD until 1960. After that the SDS had become more and more radical. In 1968 a second wave of violence erupted when a young leftist sociologist, Rudi Dutschke, was seriously wounded in an assassination attempt by an opponent of the protest movement. The resulting street fighting by protesters in almost all major cities of the Federal Republic eroded whatever sympathy people may have felt for the protesters after the attack on Dutschke. Except among a small group of radical and Marxist intellectuals, the student revolt never found much outside support. The workers in particular not only proved indifferent to the new left, they actually joined the Berlin authorities in 1968 in a public demonstration against the protesters.

After 1968 student protests in Germany, as elsewhere, died down as the attention of the rebels again focused on academic issues. In that area some tangible results were achieved. Most of the Länder introduced educational reforms that curtailed the powers of the full professors and gave not only the lower ranks but students and even employees a voice in running their universities. Such democratization or codetermination, however, did not solve the most burning problem of Germany's universities, the continuing rise in the student population, which was eventually choked off by a restrictive *numerus clausus* (see chapter 10).

During the Kiesinger-Brandt years much time and effort were spent on ironing out differences between the two coalition partners. In this process the leaders of the two parliamentary delegations, Rainer Barzel for the CDU and Helmut Schmidt for the SPD, played an important part. With the approach of elections in 1969, differences became more open and the conduct of government more difficult, for foreign as well as domestic affairs.

Under the coalition Germany's relations with the United States were not as close as they had been under Erhard. Kiesinger's Nazi past made him less welcome in America, and both he and Brandt gave priority to good relations with France. In the United States, President Johnson was still preoccupied with domestic reforms and the war in Vietnam, and a powerful section in Congress continued to call for substantial reductions of American forces in Europe. This issue, as we have seen, was tied in with the question of German offset payments. In 1967 another showdown over these payments was avoided when Germany, instead of buying large quantities of American arms, agreed to invest in some half billion dollars' worth of U.S. government securities. Similar arrangements were concluded in 1968 and 1969, each time accompanied by hard bargaining, which showed that the Germans had outgrown their earlier subservience to Washington. Under the offset agreements the Federal Republic made up about 80 percent of America's currency drain caused by forces stationed in West Germany. It should be noted that none of America's other European allies made similar contributions.

The question of offset costs was only one aspect of the larger balance of payments problem shared by all the western powers. While the deutsche mark was growing stronger, the dollar was getting weaker. Suggestions in 1967 that West Germany revalue its currency upward and thus aid American exports were to no avail. As more and more capital flowed into Germany in expectation of revaluation, Britain, which had already devalued the pound, and France in 1968 joined the United States in bringing pressure upon Bonn. The Germans, however, remained firm in their refusal to revalue. In 1969 the influx of foreign money into Germany continued, and the French franc followed the example of the pound.

In September 1969, shortly before the end of the grand coalition, the German government finally allowed the D-mark to float and then revalued it at 9 percent above its earlier parity. Meanwhile the drawn-out currency controversy, mainly between Economics Minister Karl Schiller and Secretary of the Treasury Henry Fowler, dampened the usual cordiality of American-German relations.

A still more serious cause of disagreement between the two countries was the nuclear nonproliferation treaty completed between the United States and the Soviet Union in 1968. The Bonn government, as on earlier occasions, complained that it had not been kept sufficiently informed about the negotiations, and when shown a draft of the treaty, found serious faults with it. The majority of the cabinet realized that the Federal Republic could hardly refuse to sign without running the risk of isolation, but there were strong voices of criticism and opposition. Kiesinger himself called the treaty "a form of complicity" between the two superpowers; Strauss compared it to the Treaty of Versailles; and Adenauer, shortly before his death, referred to it as a "Morgenthau Plan *im Quadrat*" (squared).

The Germans objected to the nonproliferation treaty for several reasons. They feared that it might hinder the creation of a multilateral or some other form of European nuclear force, for which they still had hopes; they objected to the treaty's provisions for inspection by the International Atomic Energy Agency, which the Russians might use for industrial espionage; and they wanted to be sure that East Germany's accession to the treaty did not imply diplomatic recognition by the other signatories. Some of these reservations were either met or dispelled, but by then the nonproliferation treaty had become an issue in the German elections, which further delayed its signature. The Soviet Union, meanwhile, insisted that it would not ratify the treaty unless Germany signed, but the United States, now under President Richard Nixon, was not ready to apply the necessary pressure in Bonn. So Germany did not sign the nonproliferation treaty until November 1969, shortly after the elections, in which Willy Brandt had become chancellor.

Although in their attitude toward Washington Kiesinger and Brandt were far less compliant than Erhard and Schröder had been, in their relations with Paris they were more so. The main issue between France and Germany in this period was the renewed request by Britain, in May 1967, for admission to the EEC. President de Gaulle again raised objections, although somewhat less categorically than when he had vetoed Britain's application in 1963. The French president was at least ready to discuss some arrangement with Britain, but at that point the May crisis of 1968 in Paris intervened,

France's counterpart to Germany's student unrest, which was a major factor in de Gaulle's resignation a year later. His successor, Georges Pompidou, was far readier to explore the possibility of British membership, but it did not materialize until 1972. Meanwhile the United States, despite occasional economic conflicts with the EEC, strongly supported West Germany's efforts on behalf of Britain.

The most important initiatives in German foreign policy continued to be toward eastern Europe, in particular the DDR. There were no major breakthroughs, but during the grand coalition the term *neue Ostpolitik* (new eastern policy) gained currency. In his speech to the Bundestag launching the coalition in December 1966, Kiesinger returned to Erhard's peace plan of the previous March but remained vague on such key issues as the Oder-Neisse line or the establishment of diplomatic relations with the countries of eastern Europe. The chancellor once again insisted that the Federal Republic was the only legally constituted German state and stressed the desire for reunification. He did speak of closer human, economic, and cultural relations with "the other part of Germany" but warned that such contacts would not mean "recognition of a second German state."

Germany's new Ostpolitik was directed toward three different but related areas: the smaller states of eastern Europe; the Soviet Union; and the German Democratic Republic. In the first of these some early progress was made. In January 1967 diplomatic relations were established with Rumania; in August trade missions were exchanged with Czechoslovakia; and in December diplomatic relations with Yugoslavia were resumed. The agreements with Rumania and Yugoslavia were noteworthy because they ignored the Hallstein Doctrine against relations with any country that recognized the DDR (see chapter 8).

Attempts to enter into an exchange of views with the Soviet Union were more discouraging. In various memoranda during 1967, the Russians insisted that Bonn recognize the "inviolability of existing frontiers in Europe [including those of the DDR]" and made other unacceptable demands. West Germany in 1968 repeated its earlier proposals for renunciation-of-force agreements, but Russian intervention in Czechoslovakia in August 1968 showed that the Soviet Union was hardly ready to thus tie its hands. In 1969 a meeting of the Warsaw Pact powers in Budapest endorsed a general European security conference rather than bilateral agreements to bring about détente. By then the earlier consensus between the two coalition parties on Ostpolitik had begun to wear thin, and it was chiefly the SPD and Willy Brandt who still hoped for signs of Soviet readiness to negotiate. On the eve of the elections in the summer of 1969, these hopes suddenly came true. In July Soviet Foreign Minister Andrei Gromyko told the Supreme Soviet that Russia wished for peaceful collaboration with the Federal Republic and was also ready to discuss the Berlin question with the western powers. In September the Kremlin agreed to consider German proposals for mutual renunciation of force and suggested a conference in Moscow. Brandt agreed to take part in such negotiations if he should become chancellor. At long last the road for negotiating an eastern détente seemed to have been cleared.

In the third and most difficult area of Ostpolitik, relations between the two Germanies, little progress was made between 1966 and 1969. There were numerous exchanges between Chancellor Kiesinger and Minister President Willi Stoph and between Brandt and Ulbricht as heads of their respective parties, but these netted nothing. While the West Germans made proposals for removing specific obstacles and tensions between the two states, the East Germans replied with sweeping demands for diplomatic recognition, West German withdrawal from NATO, renunciation of the Hallstein Doctrine, and such. They also suggested meetings between the two chief executives. In the spring and summer of 1968, the DDR once again began interfering with access to West Berlin, and in March 1969 it threatened to prevent the meeting of the West German federal assembly in West Berlin to elect President Gustav Heinemann. The threat turned out to be an empty one, but it emphasized the importance of West Berlin as a hostage or pawn in East-West relations.

The Berlin question was really an issue between the western Allies and the Soviet Union rather than between East and West Germany. Any crisis that the Ulbricht regime provoked over Berlin clearly had to have the approval of the Russians. It was seen as significant, therefore, that the threat of preventing the presidential election did not materialize. The western powers had asked the Federal Republic not to provoke the Russians by scheduling the event in West Berlin, but Bonn had ignored the request, once again showing its independence. The East Germans obviously did not enjoy similar independence, and their failure to act was interpreted as a sign that the Russians were ready to negotiate about Berlin. This was borne out four months later by Gromyko's Moscow speech. In early August the three western powers replied that they would welcome talks "that might prevent further crises in and around Berlin." Berlin was to be the keystone of the complicated structure usually referred to as Brandt's Ostpolitik.

The Socialist leader certainly deserves most of the credit for carrying to completion a veritable revolution in his country's foreign policy. To sacrifice reunification on the altar of détente, or at least to bury it at the altar's base, took great political courage, because in a democracy such a major change requires the approval of the electorate. That approval Brandt received twice, first in the elections of 1969, on the eve of his rapprochement with eastern Europe, and then again more triumphantly in the 1972 elections, after the completion of his Ostpolitik. But the acceleration of events and the array of agreements during this period must not make us forget their antecedents. What appeared as a revolution at the time was in reality the outcome of a slow and often painful evolution. Although Ostpolitik has become closely associated with Willy Brandt, other names—Egon Bahr, Fritz Erler (whose premature death in 1967 was a major tragedy), and Gerhard Schröder—should not be forgotten. And finally it should be remembered that the United States also played an important role behind the scenes, first by abandoning the Adenauer-Dulles policy of "reunification from strength" and then by encouraging and supporting Bonn's search for an eastern détente. Ostpolitik did much to maintain and cement the close relations between Washington and Bonn.

Campaigning under the slogan "twenty years are enough," the SPD emerged from the 1969 elections with twenty-two additional seats in the Bundestag, finally breaking the 40 percent barrier (42.7 percent). The CDU-CSU lost three seats, but with 46.1 percent of the vote was still the largest party. The poorest showing was by the FDP, which lost nineteen mandates, and with only 5.8 percent of the vote came dangerously close to the 5 percent limit. A new coalition government, this time between SPD and FDP, was quickly formed, and Brandt became chancellor; he had made no secret during the campaign of the fact that he wanted that post. Consensus by the new partners, especially on Ostpolitik, had been manifested earlier, in the spring of 1969, when Helmut Schmidt of the SPD and Walter Scheel, the leader of the FDP, had been invited to Moscow together, where they had found the Russians ready for discussion on substantive issues. Jointly the SPD and FDP had a majority of only twelve seats, giving the FDP a disproportionate influence, which was to prove a major headache to the Brandt-Scheel government, especially because some FDP delegates would have preferred an alliance with the CDU. In a cabinet reduced to fifteen members, the Free Democrats held three posts, including the foreign ministry under Walter Scheel.

I shall focus here on foreign rather than domestic problems, because most of the latter remained unresolved under Brandt and were carried over into the post-1973 period. The new chancellor and his foreign minister saw eye to eye on most foreign policy issues, so collaboration was more harmonious than it had been under Kiesinger and Brandt. But the grand coalition had at least muted the opposition within the CDU on the key issue of Ostpolitik; that restriction was now gone. The central figure among the Christian Democrats during the Brandt-Scheel years was Rainer Barzel, an able and intensely ambitious man in his mid-forties. Barzel had been one of the leading contenders for the chancellorship when Erhard stepped down in 1966, but he had lost out to Kiesinger. With the latter's defeat in 1969 the road was clear. (Like Erhard before him, Kiesinger remained party chairman for two years, after which he faded into oblivion.) As the CDU's chairman after 1971 and the leader of its delegation in the Bundestag, Barzel was clearly his party's candidate for chancellor in the next elections. Meanwhile he used his considerable talent as a speaker and debater in the Bundestag to attack the government's reformist efforts at home and détente policy abroad. One major weakness of the CDU was internal dissension, especially with its Bavarian branch, the CSU, led by Franz Josef Strauss. But on critical issues, the party closed ranks.

The keynote of international relations in the early 1970s continued to be détente, both on a global scale—the strategic arms limitation and other agreements between the United States and the Soviet Union, exchange of visits between Nixon and Brezhnev, rapprochement between Washington and Peking—and within Europe—expansion of the Common Market, Ostpolitik. In the larger arena America was the moving force; within Europe, Germany took the lead. The differences between the two countries in preoccupations and priorities might have led to conflict, but mutual trust prevented all but occasional misunderstandings. The simultaneous rise to power of a Socialist government in Bonn and a Republican administration in Washington also might have spelled trouble, yet neither regime was true to its image. And each was so deeply involved in domestic difficulties that it fully understood and sympathized with the other's desire to divert attention from troubles at home by reaping successes abroad.

Personalities, as always, played an important part in American-German relations. The leaders, Brandt and Nixon, got along tolerably, although Brandt, as architect of Ostpolitik, was more popular in America than Nixon, bête noire of the Vietnam War, was in Germany. The president's chief adviser on foreign and security matters, Henry Kissinger, had a unique position. Because of his German past and his intimate knowledge of American and German affairs, he seemed destined to serve as mediator. After he became secretary of state in 1973, Kissinger achieved greater power and influence than any German-born American had ever had before. But the experiences of his youth hardly disposed him in favor of his native land, and like most refugees from Hitler's Germany, he had become thoroughly and loyally American. The fact that he was never accused of being either pro- or anti-German speaks well for him.

There were other officials whose understanding of both countries did much to keep relations on an even keel—on the American side Martin Hillenbrand, assistant secretary for European affairs, and Kenneth Rush, ambassador to Bonn; on the German side Helmut Schmidt, close associate and successor-to-be to Brandt, and Rolf Pauls, ambassador to Washington. There were also critics on both sides of the "special relationship" (Hillenbrand's term) between the two countries. But the prevailing attitude was one of patience with and tolerance of each other's problems, with Germany at times more tolerant than the United States.

Offset payments continued to be a biennial headache. With America's annual payments deficit running into billions of dollars, the cost of American military commitments in Europe was under constant attack, and Congressional demands for troop withdrawals never ceased. Most of these troops, some 310,000 in 1971, were stationed in Germany. Not unreasonably, the Germans argued that these forces were for the protection of all NATO members, including the United States, and suggested that part of the offset costs be shared by the other nations of western Europe. Some Germans, especially among the new left, even suggested that the Americans withdraw altogether, to ease East-West tensions. Americans, on the other hand, felt that their country had paid for the defense of Europe (and much of the rest of the world) far too long, and that it was high time for the countries that owed their economic recovery to the United States, to aid their long-term benefactor. When thus translated into moral terms, the offset issue became an emotional one. At the government level, despite some heated exchanges, cool heads as usual prevailed, and compromises were worked out in 1971 and again in 1973.

In the more general area of arms limitation, American-German relations in the past had often been tense, or at least testy. The latest efforts in this direction had divided the grand coalition, and the nuclear nonproliferation treaty was not signed until November 1969, shortly after Brandt became chancellor. Its ratification was delayed for more than two years until early 1973, chiefly because the CDU opposed the treaty's alleged discrimination against Germany as a nuclear *Habenichts* (have not).

The Federal Republic was not the only western country to watch signs of American-Soviet détente with apprehension; the French and British also did. Much of this uneasiness stemmed from America's tendency to negotiate with the Russians without consulting its allies. The next step, the strategic arms limitations (SALT) talks, was concluded with an agreement signed by Nixon and Brezhnev in Moscow in May 1972. It caused less of a stir because the United States kept its friends better informed, but any bilateral arrangements between their most powerful friend and their most dangerous enemy could only alarm the western nations, including Germany.

To emphasize America's continued interest in Europe, Henry Kissinger in early 1973 proposed to make that the "Year of Europe." But such a slogan was more easily coined than carried out. Relations between the United States and the Common Market were not always the best, particularly in the economic sphere. America continued to welcome the trend toward European integration, but it did so to its own economic detriment. American agriculture in particular found the Common Market quite inhospitable to its products, and industry complained of EEC competition in third-world markets. The Federal Republic by now had emerged as the most powerful member of the EEC, and its main concerns, naturally, were with its own economic advantage. But it also tried to look after the interests of the United States, so much so that West Germany has been called "America's 'Trojan horse' inside the Community." * In August 1971 President Nixon, in a drastic set of moves to improve his country's worsening payments imbalance, imposed a 10 percent surcharge on all American imports and stopped the free convertibility of the dollar into gold. His unilateral action led to protests, less from Germany than from the rest of America's allies. In December 1971 the Germans again revalued their currency, in part to help American exports compete with their own. Economic contact and competition between the United States and the Common Market in general and Germany in particular remained a complicated and controversial subject.

If America's attitude toward European integration was ambivalent, the same held true for its views on German Ostpolitik. Washington unquestionably favored Bonn's improved relations with eastern Europe; its only concern was the speed with which that rap-

* R. Morgan, *The United States and West Germany 1945–1973* (London, 1974), p. 252.

prochement proceeded. Some people, such as Dean Acheson, feared that the Russians might get the better of the Germans in their "mad race to Moscow," while others worried that domestic disagreement over Ostpolitik might weaken West Germany's political stability. Ostpolitik, in other words, was all right as long as it went slowly and the Germans kept their American friends informed at every step. But this was not to be; it all happened incredibly fast.

The prerequisite for any lasting West German détente with eastern Europe was improved relations with the Soviet Union. To find out the terms on which the Russians would be willing to negotiate a renunciation-of-force agreement, Brandt in early 1970 sent his Staatssekretär and closest adviser, Egon Bahr, to Moscow for intermittent talks with Andrei Gromyko. Much of their discussion centered upon West Germany's recognition of East Germany and of the Oder-Neisse line. By early summer the two sides had agreed on a detailed list of issues to be discussed. When this so-called *Bahr-Papier* was leaked to the public, it caused considerable commotion among opponents of Ostpolitik. In the ensuing debate the Bonn government agreed that a satisfactory solution to the Berlin question must be a precondition for a treaty with Moscow and that such a treaty would not affect "the right of the Germans for self-determination," that is, for reunification.

The German-Soviet treaty was signed in the Kremlin on August 12, 1970, by Brandt, Scheel, Kosygin, and Gromyko, with Brezhnev present. The agreement stressed the desire for normalization and peaceful relations among all European states and called for the pacific resolution of all differences between the two signatories. All existing frontiers in Europe were recognized, specifically along the Oder-Neisse line and the border between the two German states. Reunification was not mentioned, but a separate letter on German unity, which Scheel addressed to Gromyko the same day, stated that the treaty did not change the Federal Republic's aim that "the German people regain its unity in free self-determination." The Russians accepted the letter.

In February 1970, simultaneously with the Bahr-Gromyko negotiations, a round of talks began between Georg Duckwitz, Staatssekretär in the Bonn foreign ministry, and Josef Winievicz, Poland's deputy foreign minister. The main issue on the Polish side was Germany's recognition of the Oder-Neisse line, and on the German side, the repatriation of thousands of Germans still living under Polish rule. These were touchy questions, but discussions were dispassionate and frank. The German-Polish treaty, signed in Warsaw on December 7, 1970, confirmed the inviolability of Poland's borders, renounced the threat or use of force, stressed the readiness for normalization (implying the exchange of ambassadors), and called for collaboration in economic, scientific, and cultural matters. In a separate note the repatriation issue was relagated to the Polish and German Red Cross. As in the case of the German-Soviet treaty, the Federal Republic informed its western allies of the text of the agreement with Poland before it was signed and assured them that nothing in it affected any prior arrangements among the victors of World War II, including the Soviet Union.

Of all the various *Ostverträge* (eastern treaties), the Warsaw treaty with Poland was the most difficult for Germans to adjust to. The regions thus lost, probably forever, meant a great deal to every German, not just to those who were born there. It was as though Americans were suddenly asked to give up their southwestern states to Mexico, or New England to Canada. Territorial changes that not only affect economic interests but touch emotional chords as well are rarely forgotten—we need only think of France and Alsace-Lorraine before 1918. In the past such grievances have often been kept alive by politicians trying to capitalize on nationalistic nostalgia. Willy Brandt's spontaneous act of kneeling down during a wreath-laying ceremony for the victims of the Warsaw ghetto did more than any proclamation, or treaty to dispel Polish suspicions that the Germans were not sincere in atoning for the suffering they had inflicted during the war. What Adenauer had earlier done toward the French in the West, Brandt had now done toward the Poles in the East.

After the Moscow and Warsaw treaties were signed, they had to be ratified, which the Brandt-Scheel government all along had insisted could be done only after the western powers and Russia had resolved their differences over Berlin. Desultory conversations between the two sides began in March 1970 but made little headway. The Soviets hoped to curtail whatever political ties existed between West Berlin and Bonn. The western allies wanted the opposite— recognition of existing connections between the Federal Republic and Berlin, secure access, improved communications between the two parts of the city, in short, as close integration between West Germany and West Berlin as possible. The German states were not officially involved in the negotiations, but each made its influence felt through its respective allies. The East Germans stood to lose most if curtailed in their capacity to cause trouble for the West. The Russians, therefore, seemed in no great hurry to come to terms, but because of the interdependence of all the Ostverträge, a decision could not be postponed indefinitely.

The Berlin negotiations, whose details need not concern us,

dragged on through 1970 and were not concluded until August 1971. In the end the western powers were the definite gainers, chiefly at the expense of the DDR, and Ulbricht's resignation in 1971 may have been related to the defeat he suffered over Berlin (see chapter 11). Under the agreement signed on September 3, 1971, the western powers were confirmed in their right to be in Berlin and were guaranteed free access to the city. West Berlin's ties to the Federal Republic also were recognized, although the number of federal agencies in the city was restricted to a single liaison office. The Russians were granted a consulate general in West Berlin to make their continued presence felt. They also insisted that the Berlin agreement would become valid only after the other Ostverträge had been ratified, reversing the order insisted on by the West Germans but underlining the fact that all the eastern treaties had to stand or fall together.

While these various negotiations were going on in Moscow, Warsaw, and Berlin, the most crucial phase of Ostpolitik—détente between the two Germanies—was also being tackled. In the opening statement of his new government, Brandt had referred to the "two states in Germany," something none of his predecessors had dared do. The problem was how to get into a discussion with East Germany without granting it de jure recognition and thus locking the door to reunification. Both sides clearly were ready to talk, but it took several exploratory exchanges before Brandt and Stoph finally agreed to meet.

The conferences of the two leaders at Erfurt, East Germany, in March 1970 and again at Kassel, West Germany, in May were disappointing. Brandt's reception by the East German public was decidedly cordial, but Stoph's in West Germany was marred by right- and left-wing protests. The most each side was able to do was to present its position to the other. Serious negotiations did not begin until November 1970, with Egon Bahr once again representing the Federal Republic and Staatssekretär Michael Kohl, speaking for the DDR. In March 1971 a parallel set of talks began between representatives of West Berlin and East Germany, with the immediate purpose of regulating access to and communications within Berlin. Once these matters had been settled at the four-power level in the summer of 1971, agreements between East and West Germany over Berlin were signed in December 1971.

Two years after he had assumed office, Willy Brandt's Ostpolitik thus seemed to be nearing its goal. All that was needed was a comprehensive settlement with East Germany, on which Bahr and Kohl were hard at work. There was only one flaw in what had been accomplished thus far—none of the agreements had been ratified. To complete his Ostpolitik, Brandt needed parliamentary support, and that support had become quite shaky.

Many of the coalition's difficulties were due to domestic problems, chiefly financial and economic. There had been several resignations from the cabinet and a gradual loss of government popularity and prestige. Along with the always active opposition of the CDU-CSU, there was unrest within the SPD and the FDP. As a result the government found it difficult or even impossible to adopt the most urgent remedial legislation, especially tax reform. Beginning in 1970 some delegates, mostly from the FDP, began defecting to the opposition, thus decreasing the coalition's majority in the Bundestag to two and ultimately to zero. At the same time the government parties managed to hold on to only the slimmest majority in the Bundesrat. This was the situation the opposition had been waiting for. In late April 1972 Rainer Barzel and the CDU introduced the first "constructive vote of no confidence" in the history of the Bundestag, hoping to gain a majority and oust the Brandt-Scheel coalition. In this they did not succeed, but parliamentary business reached a virtual standstill.

On May 17, 1972, the Ostverträge with the Soviet Union and Poland came up for their final vote in the Bundestag. They passed, thanks to the abstention of most of the CDU-CSU, but only barely. Two weeks later the four-power agreement on Berlin also went into effect. Throughout, the opposition continued its pressure on Brandt to resign, but fearing for the completion of his Ostpolitik, he decided on a different course. After asking for and losing a vote of confidence in September, the chancellor had President Heinemann dissolve the Bundestag and call for new elections.

The campaign of 1972 was the hardest fought, and the turnout on November 19 of over 91 percent of the electorate was the largest in the history of the Federal Republic. The result was a triumph for Willy Brandt and his policy. For the first time the SPD received the largest vote, and together with a strengthened FDP the coalition commanded a safe majority of forty-five delegates. This enabled Brandt to put the finishing touches on his Ostpolitik by having Bahr and Kohl sign the Grundvertrag between the Federal and Democratic republics on December 21, 1972.

The Grundvertrag was a short document of ten articles, supplemented by a large number of additions, protocols, exchanges of letters, and other instruments elaborating its provisions. Both partners agreed to respect each others' territorial integrity and to renounce the use of force. Neither could henceforth speak for the other or for Germany as a whole, as West Germany had claimed to do in the past. The two states were to exchange "permanent representations," and they were to collaborate on a large number of "practical and humanitarian questions," from trade and traffic to athletics and environmental protection. The reunion of families was to be made easier, as were day-trips from West to East (but not the other way around). The Grundvertrag carefully avoided the "national question," (reunification) except to say in its preamble that the "high contracting parties" held "different views" on it. What these views were was not made clear, except by Willy Brandt. In his public statements the chancellor said that he viewed the treaty as an effort to keep alive the national idea in the hope that some day it might become a reality again. On the night the Grundvertrag was signed, Brandt told the West Germans (and the many East Germans who no doubt listened in over the radio), "The treaty does not do away with the wall and barbed wire; it does not bring freedom of movement or other things. For all that we will have to continue working stubbornly and patiently. But making progress in this direction justifies leaving our illusions behind. It confirms the insight that motivates us and rewards the reasonableness that guides our course. Given our situation, this is the only way in which we can preserve our nation." For a man speaking in his hour of triumph, these were sober words, but then, Willy Brandt was a pragmatist with few illusions. "We have organized the *Nebeneinander* [alongside each other]," he said elsewhere. "Now we must learn the *Miteinander* [being together]."

Willy Brandt's election victory in November 1972 was clearly the high point of his political career. It coincided with the equally rousing success of Richard Nixon in his campaign for reelection. Although Nixon's opponent, George McGovern, was closer to Brandt in his outlook on domestic issues, in foreign affairs the senator favored the reduction of American forces in Europe, as proposed by his colleague Mike Mansfield, chairman of the Senate Foreign Relations Committee, an issue of deep concern to the West Germans. Brandt and Nixon, of course, did not enjoy their electoral triumphs for long; both resigned in 1974 over scandals in their respective governments. When an East German spy was discovered in the German chancellor's office, Brandt assumed full responsibility for what had been gross negligence. The chancellor had been unhappy for some time about squabbles with his coalition partners, differences within the European Community, and continued difficulties with East Germany, so his resignation provided relief. By acting promptly, Brandt cleared the air and was able to continue as leader of his party and much-respected elder statesman. This was in marked contrast to

Richard Nixon, who, though deeply involved in the far more sordid Watergate scandal, clung to his office tenaciously and mendaciously until he was forced to retire in disgrace.

American-German relations during the remainder of the Nixon-Brandt period remained close, though not always cordial. On the issue of détente the two sides agreed. In 1973 both leaders had separate meetings with Brezhnev, an indication of improved East-West relations, and in September of that year both German republics were admitted to the UN. Each country still worried, however, that the other might become too friendly with the Russians. The Federal Republic felt uneasy about the continuing SALT talks between the two superpowers and about possible American concessions during the Mutual and Balanced Force Reductions negotiations (MBFR) begun in October 1973 in Vienna. The United States, on the other hand, was disturbed by reports that Brandt's close adviser, Egon Bahr, envisaged his Ostpolitik as ultimately leading to the neutralization of both Germanies and the dissolution of NATO and the Warsaw Pact. Mutual trust between Bonn and Washington and awareness of their common interests, however, were strong enough to help overcome such occasional doubts.

Another problem that cast a shadow on American-German relations was the war in Vietnam. The German government in the past had loyally, albeit reluctantly, supported its ally's involvement in that unhappy country. Public opinion, however, especially among the young in Germany as in the United States, became increasingly critical of American intervention. In January 1973 Brandt's finance minister and party colleague, Helmut Schmidt, in a speech delivered in Washington, regretted the bombing of North Vietnam during Christmas. Shortly thereafter, when President Nixon ordered a cease-fire and U.S. troops were withdrawn, this impediment to German-American friendship was removed. But anti-American feeling in Germany had gained ground, not only among the extraparliamentary opposition but within the SPD itself, where a radical wing of Young Socialists (*Jusos*) opposed Bonn's contribution to the maintenance of American troops in Germany and demanded their withdrawal.

The cost of American forces continued to be a sore point, as the devaluation of the dollar, combined with rising inflation, increased the expense of stationing troops in what was easily the most expensive country in Europe. The Germans still paid their share, but with obvious reluctance, and voices in Congress continued to call for the withdrawal of American troops.

Many of the controversial issues between the two countries were part of the more general differences between the United States and the European Community. The most serious crisis between the alliance partners arose during the early 1970s, in connection with the brief but bloody Yom Kippur war in the Middle East. When Egyptian and Syrian forces in October 1973 invaded territories held by Israel, the United States immediately rushed substantial amounts of military aid to that country and at one point even put its nuclear forces on alert. These unilateral actions were sharply criticized by America's European allies who, because of their greater dependence on Arab oil, took a more neutral or even pro-Arab stand. West Germany tried to steer a middle course between its Atlantic and European partners. Only when the United States continued to send supplies to Israel from the German port of Bremerhaven did the Federal Republic protest, fearing for its own relationship with the Arab states.

Like earlier incidents, this tense confrontation was also resolved without leaving any permanent scars on the American-German partnership. The United States in late 1973 was having serious political and economic difficulties at home, with Watergate nearing its climax and the Arab ban on oil exports touching off the energy crisis. These events made Washington more ready to compromise on outstanding differences. The Germans, on the other hand, had come to consider their alliance with the United States as the second Basic Law (Grundgesetz) of the Federal Republic. Realization of mutual interdependence did much to maintain the stability that had characterized American-German relations in the past.

10 | The German Federal Republic since 1974

THERE WAS LITTLE QUESTION as to who would succeed Willy Brandt when the chancellor stepped down in May 1974. Helmut Schmidt, fifty-five years old, was known as a *Macher* (doer) and a troubleshooter. He had served ably under Brandt, first as defense minister and later as minister of finance, and he had made no secret of his readiness to take over. The new chancellor had a thorough background in economics, a subject on which he liked to lecture his foreign colleagues. In manner he was self-assured, sometimes aggressively so, and given to impatience. Schmidt lacked the contemplativeness and charisma of his predecessor, but he was an attractive and forthright person who inspired confidence and respect.

In another important change, Walter Scheel, Brandt's foreign minister, was sworn in as the fourth president of the Federal Republic, a largely ornamental post, in which he performed ably and with dignity. The number-two position in a coalition cabinet is usually reserved for the leader of the second party, so the office of vice-chancellor and foreign minister went to Scheel's successor as head of the FDP, Hans-Dietrich Genscher. The new foreign minister, who was forty-six at the time, had been minister of the interior since 1969 and was therefore responsible for the lax security that led to Brandt's resignation. He was an able administrator and shrewd negotiator but had little knowledge of world affairs, a shortcoming he tried to remedy by frantic travels abroad.

The rotund and jovial Genscher never achieved the stature

of his predecessors, chiefly because he was overshadowed not only by
Helmut Schmidt but by Willy Brandt as well. The ex-chancellor,
holder of the 1971 Nobel Peace Prize, added further to his international standing by being elected president of the Socialist International in 1976. In domestic affairs Brandt used his prestige far
more wisely and constructively than Adenauer had done a decade
earlier. But abroad he let himself be used at times to undercut
Genscher, as in 1975, when he accepted an invitation from Brezhnev
to visit Moscow, where he was received in a manner reserved for
very special visitors.

The change of the guard in Bonn was followed three months
later by the resignation of Richard Nixon and the accession of Gerald Ford as president of the United States. The new regime in Washington was to be of short duration and thus had little lasting effect
on American-German relations. The new president and the new
chancellor got on well with each other. They maintained close contact by frequent telephone calls, in which Ford proved a ready lis-
tener to Schmidt's liberally tendered advice. In June 1975 President
Scheel paid a state visit to Washington, and in July Ford stopped in
Bonn on his way to Helsinki. In 1976 Schmidt clearly hoped for
Ford's reelection, in which case Henry Kissinger would have remained secretary of state. Kissinger and Schmidt were on the best
of terms, and good relations between the two countries would easily
have continued.

But the "well-tried partnership," as President Scheel called
American-German relations during his Washington visit, faced readjustment when Jimmy Carter won the 1976 election by a very
narrow margin. Schmidt had just been through an election himself,
achieving an equally slim victory. The opposition CDU-CSU, with
243 seats against the SPD's 214, again emerged as the strongest party
in the Bundestag, and the governing coalition, including the FDP's
39 mandates, now had a majority of only 10 seats. When Schmidt
came up for reelection as chancellor in December, he won by only
a single vote.

As it turned out, winning by the skin of their teeth was the
only thing Carter and Schmidt had in common. At a time when summit meetings have become a preferred method of diplomacy, personal relations between leading statesmen are important. The two
men, both self-assertive, were otherwise quite different in outlook
and temperament. Schmidt the calculating pragmatist was baffled
and at times annoyed by Carter, the moralizing idealist. The president complained that the chancellor was obstinate and didactic; the
chancellor found the president erratic and inexperienced. Both tried

to overcome their differences, but they never quite succeeded. To Carter, Schmidt was "Helmut" from the start; it took Schmidt a while before he could reciprocate with "Jimmy." The two met frequently, four times in less than two years. Despite an outward show of cordiality on these occasions, observers always sensed a note of constraint or, some would say, antipathy.

Carter's secretary of state, Cyrus Vance, also was somewhat of a disappointment to the Germans. In contrast to the domineering and flamboyant Kissinger, Vance was a quiet and competent negotiator, an implementer rather than innovator. On major issues and pronouncements he was overshadowed by his president. On the ambassadorial level the resignation, during Ford's administration, of Martin Hillenbrand was a great loss. He was succeeded as ambassador to Bonn by Wa¹ter Stoessel, who was less experienced in German affairs. The Federal Republic was ably represented in Washington by Berndt von Staden, who was close to President Carter's security adviser, Zbigniew Brzezinski, whom he had known for many years.

If we turn from personalities to issues, the problems facing the United States and Germany during the mid-1970s remained substantially unchanged. They may be summarized under three main headings: nuclear policy, détente, and economic stagnation. The most important was the epidemic economic crisis, which in varying degrees affected all the major industrial nations of the free world. Beginning in 1975 the United States, Canada, West Germany, Britain, France, Italy, and Japan held periodic economic summits to discuss solutions to their mutual economic problems. More than ever before, German-American relations became intertwined with wider mutilateral issues.

Nuclear policy became a problem as more and more nonnuclear powers asked for, and were supplied with, atomic materials, which created the danger that such materials might be used for warlike rather than peaceful purposes. Canada's sale of uranium to India, which the Indians used to manufacture an atomic bomb, was seen as a case in point. In 1975 the issue arose between Bonn and Washington when the Federal Republic negotiated the biggest international business deal in its history, arranging for the sale of close to five billion dollars' worth of advanced nuclear equipment to Brazil over a period of fifteen years. Because Brazil had not signed the nuclear nonproliferation treaty, the American Congress and press voiced fears that this transaction might lead to a Brazilian bomb. The issue became heated in March 1977 when President Carter asked the German government to cancel the Brazilian deal. The Germans naturally resented this interference in their affairs and charged that the United States was motivated by envy of German competition rather than fear of nuclear proliferation. The matter was settled when Carter agreed to submit the problem to an international study group, and Bonn promised not to grant any further export permits for sensitive nuclear equipment.

On the question of détente, both countries continued to seek ways to ease East-West tensions. The United States doggedly pursued its second round of SALT talks and its MBFR negotiations with the Soviet Union. West Germany tried to improve relations with its East German neighbor despite occasional confrontations, especially over West Berlin. With some eight million West Germans visiting their eastern relatives each year, normalization of relations could not help but make some progress. On the official level, negotiations for joint road and railroad repairs and the construction of a new autobahn between Hamburg and Berlin promised to ease communications. From 1973 to 1978, 42,000 families were reunited under the Basic Treaty of 1972, and 187,000 Germans moved to the Federal Republic from Poland and eastern Europe.

These tangible effects of Ostpolitik made the Bonn government look askance at anything that might interfere with détente. Russia and the United States were still at odds in some areas, especially in Africa, but the issue over which the two met head on was President Carter's staunch stand on human rights.

The human rights issue arose out of the Conference on European Security and Cooperation held at Helsinki in 1975. In a declaration adopted by the thirty-five participating nations, including the United States and the Soviet Union, the signatories pledged themselves to respect the "fundamental freedoms, including the freedom of thought, conscience, religion or belief." It was among the citizens of the communist countries of eastern Europe that the Helsinki agreement had the most immediate effect by encouraging dissidents in Moscow and elsewhere to voice their grievances and demand their freedom to emigrate. With laudable intent, Jimmy Carter made human rights a key issue, thus injecting, like Woodrow Wilson before him, a moral principle into American foreign policy.

As Wilson had learned earlier, in a world still operating according to the rules of realpolitik, moral judgments soon run into immoral realities. When the American government began to make foreign aid dependent on the recipients' respect for human rights, it was accused of following a selective policy guided by national rather than humanitarian interests. President Carter's insistence on human rights caused particular dismay among America's western allies, especially France and West Germany, who feared that his policy might endanger the further progress of détente, especially in the military field and, in Germany's case, might halt the westward migration of thousands of Germans still under communist rule. Helmut Schmidt hoped that remaining silent on human rights would facilitate that migration, but Jimmy Carter felt that speaking out might make possible the exodus of the equally large number of Soviet Jews. There can be no question that both men were deeply concerned about human rights, but they differed over the best way to go about liberating the largest number of people—by secret negotiation or through open confrontation. To the German chancellor, Carter's outspoken position on human rights was another example of the president's naïve, amateurish, and zigzagging approach to foreign policy. American critics of that policy tended to agree with Schmidt.

The charge of pursuing a zigzagging course was also leveled by West Germany against another of Carter's actions, his announcement in April 1978 that America was abandoning its planned production of the neutron bomb. The abrupt and unilateral manner in which the president made his decision, without consulting his domestic advisers and foreign allies, was rightly criticized. But the decision was caused in no small measure by West Germany's reaction to the bomb. There had been widespread agitation by the left wing of the SPD against a weapon that killed humans but left their property intact. Schmidt's adviser, Egon Bahr, had called the neutron bomb "a symbol for the perversion of human thinking." The Bonn government actually favored the bomb, but because of domestic opposition, raised objections to having it stored on German soil, although if it was to serve as a deterrent, that was the only place for it. The Germans, it seemed, wanted to be pressured into accepting the neutron bomb, but President Carter was not ready to do that. If he hoped that abandoning the neutron bomb would lead the Russians to make commensurate concessions during the ongoing SALT negotiations, he was disappointed. Had there been such concessions, his action no doubt would have been praised as a further contribution to détente.

As I said earlier, the most important problem facing the United States and West Germany during the 1970s was the drawn-out stagnation of economic growth combined with rising inflation, or stagflation, as the jargon went. It began with the "October Revolution" of 1973, when the OPEC nations started raising the price of oil. After that, economic diplomacy overshadowed political diplomacy. The high points of economic diplomacy were the four economic summits, at Rambouillet in 1975, Puerto Rico in 1976, London in 1977, and Bonn in 1978, none of which accomplished very much. Each time the participants suggested different remedies for overcoming the prolonged economic malaise, with the United States and West Germany usually setting the tone and often finding themselves on opposite sides. References to the Bonn meeting as the German-American summit were not unjustified.

In 1975 Chancellor Schmidt urged the United States to stimulate its economy through budget deficits and expansion of its money supply in order to help the other industrial nations increase their sales on the American market. But President Ford and Secretary Kissinger resisted what was clearly an inflationary program. Since then the scenario has been completely reversed, with the Americans urging the Germans to engage in the same policy they themselves had turned down earlier. But for Germany to embark on an inflationary course, while perhaps economically sound, would be politically suicidal because of the never-forgotten experience with inflation in the 1920s. This, at least, was the most frequently cited reason given by the Schmidt government.

The United States and West Germany, which with Japan were the leading industrial nations of the noncommunist world, were closely linked economically, commercially, and financially. America's gross national product in 1975 was still more than three times that of the German Federal Republic, but on a per capita basis the Germans had almost caught up. Between 1968 and 1978 their mutual trade declined, but they were still among each other's best customers. One of the major trends since World War II has been the growing investment of American capital in Germany and the increase in multinational companies. West Germany ranked in third place, after Canada and Britain, as a field for American investment. By 1975 America had invested some $8 billion there. Meanwhile German capital, attracted by the falling value of the dollar, had also found its way into the American market, thus further intertwining the economies of the two countries.

Because of their similarly highly industrialized systems, both countries were seriously affected by the economic crisis of the mid-seventies, although the Federal Republic on the whole was less hard hit. For reasons already stated, every possible effort was made to contain inflation, which was held near 3 percent, compared to America's 6 percent. Unemployment also ran higher in the United States; but because the Germans had had so little, a 5 percent unemployment rate caused great concern. One of America's biggest problems, its unfavorable balance of payments, Germany did not share. While the United States had an annual trade deficit of $20 billion, Germany in 1977 still had a trade surplus of $18 billion and held twice that much in gold and foreign currency reserves. As the dollar became softer, the D-mark became harder. Between 1968 and 1978 the dollar declined to half its value on the German market.

The Bonn government, under pressure from Washington, tried to halt this decline by offset payments amounting to some $11 billion over the years, but to no avail. To Helmut Schmidt the root of the trouble lay in America's "irresponsible" waste of energy. If the United States curtailed its imports of oil, its imbalance of payments would be rectified, the dollar would be stabilized, and exports would thrive. To President Carter and his experts, the way out of economic stagnation was to have Germany (and Japan) serve as a "locomotive" and fire up their economies by reflation, in that way draining off surplus capital, providing markets for foreign imports, and correcting existing imbalances.

The problems of the seventies, of course, were far more complex, and the proposed solutions far less simplistic than here described. The situation was not unlike that of the 1930s, the decade of the Great Depression, a parallel that the leaders at their periodic summits were very much aware of. The main advantage of these get-togethers was the opportunity they provided for frank exchange. But while there were often heated debates during the weeks and months before a summit, the meetings themselves were always cordial, and the results usually quite meaningless.

This was the case with the Bonn summit of 1978. As at the meeting in London the year before, the participants promised to work for an increase in economic growth; in the past only the United States had lived up to that promise. President Carter assured his colleagues that he would continue hammering away at his energy program, which he hoped would bring a reduction in American oil imports. The dominant figure at the conference was its host, Helmut Schmidt, who made it quite plain that West Germany was not going to risk its low inflation rate by any extraordinary stimulation of its economy. The German chancellor's self-assurance was a clear indication of his country's growing international stature.

The Bonn summit held added interest for American-German relations because it was preceded by President Carter's state visit to Germany. The occasion provided an interesting barometer on how these relations were viewed from the German side. At the highest level the situation was unchanged, with Schmidt obviously more reserved than Carter. The American president traveled widely across the land, and in West Berlin he tried to recapture some of the excitement that had marked earlier presidential visits. In imitation of

John F. Kennedy, he even attempted some clumsy German, assuring Berliners that, *"Was immer sei, Berlin bleibt frei"* ("Whatever may be, Berlin stays free"). Popular reaction to the president's visit was polite and curious rather than admiring and emotional. This was not because Carter personally was unpopular, but was rather a sign that in German eyes the nimbus of the American presidency had begun to wear thin.

Having close and stable relations between nations requires not only common interests but some mutual affinity as well. Since World War II Germans and Americans have become better acquainted than at any time in their history, and their simplistic notions of each other have given way to more realistic judgments. Still the stereotyped images of the uncultured and materialistic Americans and the overbearing and militaristic Germans have never been entirely laid to rest and are apt to resurface.

We have already seen how German views of the United States were affected by the war in Vietnam, and withdrawal from that conflict only briefly improved America's image. Watergate, revelations about undercover CIA activities, and the Lockheed scandals kept alive anti-American sentiment in Germany, more strongly among the new left than among conservatives and the general population. From guardians of liberty and protectors of the weak, Americans became champions of imperialism and ringleaders of capitalist exploitation. The term most commonly used by these detractors to describe American society was fascist. Citing the warnings and apprehensions of Bertolt Brecht and Thomas Mann during the McCarthy era of the 1950s, these killers of the American dream described daily life in the United States as permeated with fascist practices, as in Reinhard Lettau's pamphlet *US = Täglicher Faschismus* (1970). Even so respected a literary figure as the poet Hans Magnus Enzensberger in 1968 drew parallels between contemporary America and the Germany of the 1930s. It is possible that such comparisons, and the German historian Ernst Nolte's equating of Vietnam with Auschwitz, in 1974, were motivated unconsciously by the hope of mitigating Germany's own past crimes. It is worth noting, however, that similar criticisms of American imperialism were heard among intellectuals and revisionists of the new left in the United States.

But anti-Americanism was not the dominant note in Germany, as was shown by the amount of goodwill toward America during the American Bicentennial in 1976. That year saw more celebrations—more than four thousand—in Germany than anywhere else except the United States. There were endless rounds of commemorative parties, exhibitions, and receptions, and the Bonn gov-

ernment spent several million dollars endowing exchange fellow-
ships and guest professorships. Helmut Schmidt paid his first visit
to Washington as chancellor, and Vice-President Nelson Rockefeller,
whose forebears had come from the Rhineland in 1723, represented
the United States at a Bicentennial ceremony in Frankfurt's restored
Paulskirche, the church made famous by the 1848 revolution and
destroyed by American bombers in 1944.

In retrospect 1976 appears as the high-water mark of good
feeling between the two countries. Ambassador Hillenbrand in Bonn
referred to "ties of friendship," and Ambassador von Staden in
Washington even used the term *herzlich* (heartfelt) to describe the
American-German relationship, a term not lightly used in German
diplomatic parlance. Since then, relations have again become more
formal. Americans never quite reciprocated the German effusions of
cordiality, and to some, Chancellor Schmidt's assertion that "We
are all Americans" seemed somehow presumptuous. The relative
standing of the two partners within the international community
also affected their attitudes. As America became economically weaker
and West Germany stronger, readjustments became necessary and
strains were unavoidable.

Fortunately, the grass-roots contacts that have developed between the two countries over the last thirty years did much to lessen
possible tensions. At no time have there been so many personal contacts between the two peoples. The number of Americans who have
spent time in Germany as members of the armed forces, although
that is not the best way to get to know a country, or as tourists must
by now run into the millions; and with the devaluation of the dollar, there has been a stream of German visitors to the United States.
In addition, numerous exchange programs have brought more than
twenty-five thousand Germans to the United States and more than
fifteen thousand Americans to Germany for varying lengths of time,
not only students and professors, but publicists, politicians, businessmen, labor leaders, persons from all walks of life. Organizations
devoted to such exchanges and to furthering mutual understanding
have multiplied. Besides official agencies, the United States Information Service (USIS) in Germany and the German Information Center and the Goethe Houses in the United States, there are the semi-
official academic exchanges of the German Academic Exchange Service (DAAD) and the American Fulbright program. Unofficial groups
include the American Council on Germany, Atlantik Brücke (Atlantic Bridge), the Conference Group for German Politics, the German Marshall Plan, the John J. McCloy Foundation for German-
American Exchange, and lesser organizations, all intended to foster

better American-German understanding. Never have more time and money been spent on interpreting two cultures and peoples to each other. It is impossible to assess the results of these efforts, but it seems that they have been more successful in explaining America to the Germans, than Germany to the Americans.

Amerikanisierung has always worried the Germans, but to debate its pros and cons is futile, since it has become a fact. Perhaps the Germans are more easily foreignized than other peoples, witness the Frenchification of the Rhineland during the Napoleonic period. West Germany today is certainly the most Americanized country in Europe, so much so that the natives hardly realize the American invasion of their manners, mores, and (most regrettably) their language.

There has been no comparable Germanization of American culture. The few German words that have become part of the American vocabulary—from kindergarten and sauerkraut to ersatz, putsch, and weltanschauung—have survived because they are untranslatable. Most of the American terms so freely used in Germany today, on the other hand, have perfectly good German equivalents. While many Germans speak English well, and many more know at least some English, few Americans know German, and fewer still speak it with ease. English is the leading foreign language taught in West German schools; German in American schools runs a poor third to Spanish and French. Since most Americans can neither speak the language nor afford to travel, what they know about Germany is what they read in their newspapers or see on television.

Germans visiting the United States are distressed by the meager coverage their country receives in the American press. It would be difficult to find any German paper that does not regularly devote some space to news about the United States. In contrast, references to German events in the American press are few, even in the cosmopolitan *New York Times.* The reason lies in America's worldwide interests and involvements and in the ethnic diversity of its readers. On occasion Germany does make the headlines, but usually with unfavorable news on war-crimes trials, terrorism, neo-Nazism, and such. To correct this situation, the West German government distributes a semiofficial weekly review of their press, *The German Tribune,* and Germany's most prestigious weekly, *Die Zeit,* publishes an overseas edition. But these publications are read chiefly by Americans already familiar with German affairs.

Television is the chief source of information for the average American, but here again the accent is almost wholly negative. Rarely does a week go by without some major network showing one of the many documentary series dealing with one of the two world wars. Their quality is always excellent, but they are hardly objective. The same is true of the frequent reruns of feature films, many of them dating from World War II and showing almost exclusively "bad" Germans. And finally there is that truly funny and very popular situation comedy, *Hogan's Heroes,* a caricature of life in a Nazi prisoner-of-war camp, which because of its oversimplified presentation of German character has been called "easily the most important program [dealing with Germany] in American television today." The Germans it depicts are either evil or stupid or both, hardly an objective picture of the German people, even under Hitler.

In 1978 one television series caused a particular stir, more in America than in Germany—*Holocaust,* a fictionalized account of Hitler's persecution and extermination of the Jews. In keeping alive the memory of these horrible events, the series served a valuable purpose, but in doing so, *Holocaust* also helped to refurbish the negative image of the Germans, even though a few of them were shown in a positive light. Reaction in Germany on the whole was surprisingly positive, especially among the young. Some of the debate, both in Germany and the United States, centered on the way in which the story of *Holocaust* was presented. Many survivors claimed that the death camps were far more terrible than depicted.

More serious in its implications was the reaction to *Holocaust* by the few remaining German-American groups, mostly in the traditional areas of German immigration of the Middle West. Asserting that the showing of *Holocaust* led to ethnic slurs and attacks against the children of German-Americans, the Chicago *Abendpost-Sonntagpost* (circulation 10,000) came out against introducing holocaust studies in the public schools. Similar sentiments were voiced by the German-American Committee in Philadelphia and by the president of the German-American Citizens' League in Cincinnati. The latter suggested that the holocaust, if taught at all, should be presented in conjunction with comparable historical incidents of genocide, as if there had ever been any. Organized German-Americans were few, however, and they are of more interest to the folklorist than to the historian. They are not Nazis, of course. Like most of their former compatriots, they merely want to forget about the Nazi past, hoping that by doing so, they may get the rest of the world to do the same.

But most Americans are not ready to do so. Any reports of Nazi activities, by the minuscule and crackpot National Socialist Party of America or by groups and individuals in Germany, arouse immediate attention and apprehension. In the early 1970s, radical right-wing activities in the Federal Republic showed a marked decline. Since 1974, however, they have been on the rise again, despite an overall drop in the membership of right-wing groups. The National Democratic Party (NDP), the only rightist party still in existence, declined from its high of 28,000 members in 1969 to below 9,000 in 1977, and its votes in Federal elections during the same period fell from 4.3 percent to 0.3 percent of the total. The same decrease was noted among the many small radical rightist organizations, whose membership in 1978 was estimated at no more than 10,000. The number of these splinter groups, however, increased from 123 in 1973 to 142 in 1976 and were attracting a larger number of young people. Another change was the increase in violent right-wing crimes—bank robbery, theft of weapons, assassination threats. The majority of neo-Nazi incidents still consisted of acts of hoodlumism—the painting of swastikas, desecration of Jewish cemetaries, and general harassment of Germany's approximately thirty thousand Jews. Incidents involving the painting of swastikas increased tenfold between 1974 and 1976; in 1976 there were eighty criminal investigations of extreme rightists, while in 1977 there were more than three hundred.

The German government was clearly worried over this apparent revival of Nazism. In 1977 Willy Brandt, in a published letter to Helmut Schmidt, expressed his concern and called for "heightened vigilance" against the neo-Nazi extremists. His warnings were echoed in 1978 by Minister of the Interior Werner Maihofer, who pledged strong countermeasures and warned of the growing militancy among the right-wing extremists. One encouraging sign was the decline in rightist votes, not only on the federal level, but in regional and local elections as well, which brings up the question of the average German's reaction to neo-Nazism.

Public opinion polls were hopeful. In 1968 50 percent of the people interviewed still thought that national socialism had been a good thing; by 1977 that percentage had dropped to 26. In 1950 every tenth person had agreed that Hitler "had done most for Germany"; by 1975 only one in fifty thought so. But there was also a noticeable upsurge of interest in Nazism and its leader, amounting to a veritable *Hitlerwelle* (Hitler wave). Along with Hitler biographies, there were the serialized memoirs of his henchmen, recordings of his and their speeches, and a long documentary film about the führer which, some critics felt, inspired nostalgia rather than aversion. In 1977 the German Jewish Central Council called this wave of Nazi nostalgia a "very menacing" phenomenon. Anti-Jewish jokes of the most macabre kind were making the rounds among the young, and at the German army school in Munich some drunken young lieutenants played a "game" of burning pieces of paper with *Jude* (Jew) written on them. The most sensational event recalling the Hitler years occurred in 1977, when a former SS general and war criminal, Herbert Kappler, was helped to escape from a prison hospital in Rome and return to his home town in Germany, where he subsequently died of cancer. The rousing demonstrations in his favor were seen as a further indication of the *NS-Renaissancebewegung* (National Socialist renaissance) and the Bonn government was censured abroad for not returning Kappler to Italy, even though extradition of German citizens is prohibited under the constitution.

Observers in Germany and elsewhere differed in their evaluation of neo-Nazism. Some saw it as a mere survival that in time would fade away, while others felt that it was a revival that might easily escalate in time of national crisis. Egon Bahr, SPD executive secretary and close to Helmut Schmidt, described the Federal Republic in 1978 as *stinknormal* (thoroughly normal), and *Die Zeit* stated categorically, "The Federal Republic is not threatened by danger from the right." The historian Karl Dietrich Bracher, on the other hand, recalled that during the 1920s there had been a similar rash of extreme rightist groups, and he warned that in a time of social and economic crisis such groups, now as then, might grow into a large movement. Historians in the past have often been more prescient than politicians or publicists. We would do well to remember that Hitler, after all, started with merely a handful of followers.

A more immediate threat than neo-Nazism to the internal security of the Federal Republic was the rise of terrorism on the left. Between 1970 and 1978 leftist terrorists in Germany killed 28 people, wounded 93, and took 162 hostages. The most noted victims were the federal prosecutor Siegfried Buback, the Frankfurt banker Jürgen Ponto, and the prominent industrialist Hanns-Martin Schleyer. All three were killed in 1977. There also were three bombings (in 1972 and 1976) of American military installations in Heidelberg and Frankfurt, causing four deaths and twenty-nine wounded. The most spectacular event in the fight against terrorism occurred in 1978, when a specially trained force of German antiterrorists freed a planeload of hostages aboard a Lufthansa jet on the airfield of Mogadishu, Somalia. The determination shown by Chancellor Schmidt on that occasion earned him more applause in America than in Europe.

Who were the terrorists? Most of the hard core, some forty or fifty, came from the upper middle class. They were between twenty-two and thirty-seven years old and might be classified "intellectuals," since two-thirds had attended a university. About half had lived for some time in a commune and more than half were women. All of them considered themselves Marxists. There have been endless attempts to explain "Hitler's children," as one author called them, but no explanation has been really satisfactory. The best-known group among them was the Baader-Meinhof gang. Andreas Baader, born in 1943, was a semi-intellectual drifter who had never held a real job. In 1968 he was sent to prison for having set fire to some Frankfurt department stores, and in 1970 Baader was freed by a band led by Ulrike Meinhof, a journalist. Beginning in 1972 the leading members of the gang were arrested and put on trial for the numerous holdups and bombings they had committed. Most of the subsequent acts of terrorism, by members still at large, were intended to help free the prisoners. The group then called itself the Red Army Faction (RAF). Throughout their long series of trials, the Baader-Meinhof group obstructed the proceedings in various ways, ranging from noncooperation to hunger strikes. Before it was over, several had committed suicide, including Meinhof and Baader, but the majority of the members have never been caught.

Terrorism was not restricted to Germany, of course. Similar acts by self-styled social revolutionaries were committed in Italy, Japan, and the United States, and far more violent deeds were done by nationalist-separatist groups in Northern Ireland and Palestine. But foreign observers concentrated their attention on the way Germany handled its major security problem. In 1972 while he was still chancellor, Willy Brandt and the minister presidents of the various Länder adopted the *Berufsverbot* (ban on employment), or *Radikalenerlass* (decree against radicals) as it was usually called, which banned radicals or members of extremist organizations from public employment. The measure was chiefly aimed at the DKP, the German Communist Party, successor to the KPD, which had been banned earlier. To its sponsors, the *Berufsverbot* seemed a simple and sensible way of preventing radicals from infiltrating the government. But because of its vague and sweeping provisions, the employment ban led to snoopings and denunciations and was soon seen as a violation of basic rights. Liberals in Germany and elsewhere charged that the law was applied more freely to radicals of the left than of the right, which in some states was true, and that its practices smacked of Nazism. Other government measures for curbing the spread of terrorism were similarly branded, among them the *Kontaktsperre* (prohibition of contact) and other restrictions imposed on contacts between accused terrorists and their attorneys, which the latter had misused to further their clients' cause. One factor contributing to the spread of terrorism was sympathy by non-terrorists, especially among the young and among leftist intellectuals. As terrorism became more murderous and public indignation grew, some of this indignation turned against these *Sympathisanten* (sympathizers). A hard-hat, law-and-order climate developed, not unlike what America had experienced during the McCarthy era.

The Federal Republic was thus attacked from two sides, its radical enemies and its liberal friends, both making the same nebulous charge of fascism. In 1978 the Russell Tribunal, a self-appointed international watchdog committee on human rights, held a much-publicized session in Frankfurt, at which the Federal Republic was found guilty of various violations. Many Germans wondered why they should thus be singled out for censure, when violations of human rights were the order of the day in other countries. There is no doubt that West Germany's mood has become more authoritarian, but it is also true that German observers are aware of this development and that a responsible press and well-functioning judicial system provide opportunities to make their concern known.

Terrorism was only the most extreme manifestation of general unrest among Germany's younger generation. Much of that unrest originated in the universities during the late 1960s (see chapter 9). Only a few members of the extraparliamentary opposition from that period, however, joined the terrorist RAF of the 1970s. The Socialist Student League (SDS) dissolved itself in 1970, and some of its more radical members joined the DKP or various communist splinter groups. What had appeared as the beginning of a revolutionary student movement in 1967-68 soon thereafter lost its momentum. There were occasional demonstrations at the more radicalized universities, but they remained local. In 1977 some excitement was caused when a radical faction at the University of Göttingen published an "anti-obituary" attacking the recently assassinated federal prosecutor Siegfried Buback. Not long afterward a student strike at a number of universities seemed to herald the beginning of a second student revolt. But unlike the outbreaks ten years earlier, this wave of unrest was not ideologically motivated and not addressed to big issues like social injustice, alienation, or the Vietnam War. The students had specific grievances against the situation inside the universities, not in the world outside.

The root cause of their discontent was the explosion of the student population. Between 1967 and 1977 university enrollments more than doubled. By 1977, to accommodate the growing number of new students each year, seventeen new universities had been built and existing ones had been substantially enlarged. Even so, there was not enough room for everyone, so under a *numerus clausus,* a central computer selected the applicants to be admitted. Once inside the university, students felt lost in overcrowded classes that afforded little contact with their professors. Furthermore, under the financial stringency of the 1970s, the stipends that half the students received did not keep up with inflation. And finally, with rising unemployment, the future after graduation looked increasingly uncertain.

The event that touched off the strikes in 1977 was the *Hochschulrahmengesetz* (general framework for university legislation). This 1975 law, which became effective at the time of the strikes, laid down guidelines for a uniform university policy in the various states. Students feared that some of the gains they had made in the 1960s would be taken away again. They specifically objected to proposals for stricter discipline within the universities, for limits on the length of study, and for changes in university governance. The Federal Constitutional Court had recently ruled that the tripartite system of group rule by professors, students, and employees was unconstitutional, which might mean a return to traditional professorial oligarchy.

The group system had been a mixed blessing. It had democratized university life, but in doing so had also politicized it, and together with vast enrollments, that had led to a marked lowering of academic standards. Qualifications required for tenured appointments at many German universities were far below those required in the United States, and the quality of students' work left much to be desired. On the positive side it must be noted that higher education in Germany since the 1960s has become far less elitist than in the past. With the abolition of tuition and the granting of government stipends, everyone had the opportunity to go to a university, but even so, the number of students from working-class families was less than 20 percent.

With ever-larger numbers of high school graduates applying for the limited number of available university places, a high degree of competitiveness has been injected into German secondary education. There have been many reforms at the high school level, not all of them necessarily for the better. The underlying aim has been to give all children an equal opportunity to realize their potential abilities. There has been much experimentation with new types of schools and curricula in the various Länder, and there are considerable differences of standards and requirements. In contrast to the United States, Germany has several types of secondary schools, only one of which, the gymnasium, entitles its graduates to enter a university. There are other differences between the German and American systems: German schools have no homerooms or study periods; they provide few extracurricular activities; and their teachers have civil-servant status and tenure. The Parents' Advisory Councils in most schools are modeled on the American parent-teacher organizations. It is difficult to compare two systems so different in many ways, but it is probably correct to say that while American university education is superior to Germany's, German secondary education is at least equal to, if not better than, that of the United States.

It is well to remember that unrest among students and the young is a worldwide phenomenon and that in Germany, as elsewhere, it is limited to a minority within the age group of, say, thirteen to twenty-four. The younger generation in Germany today is more like its American counterpart, in outlook and appearance, manners and mores, than any earlier generation ever was. In this process of assimilation the Germans have become more like Americans rather than the other way round. Only in some areas of youth culture—music (rock) and sports (soccer)—has the influence been in both directions. If the majority of young Germans are reproached for being more interested in sports than in politics, the same can be said for most young Americans.

Aside from schools and universities, another organization that involves mostly young people has been the object of much attention in the United States: the Bundeswehr, Germany's armed forces. With close to 500,000 men, it is the largest military force in western Europe. It was consciously organized as a democratic army of citizens in uniform (see chapter 8). About half of its members are career soldiers and long-term volunteers, the rest are young draftees between the ages of eighteen and twenty-five. About sixteen hundred German jet pilots are regularly trained in the United States, providing additional ties between the two countries. The Federal Republic's minister of defense since 1972, Georg Leber, a former labor leader, was very popular with his American colleagues, and his resignation in 1978 over security leaks, wiretapping, and other scandals in his department, was much regretted in Washington.

The Bundeswehr has never enjoyed the public support that the army had in earlier periods of German history, which may be just as well, but it has created a morale problem. Since 1977 the substitution of civilian social work for military service by conscientious objectors has become virtually automatic, and close to forty thousand young men have availed themselves of this opportunity each year (the Basic Law exempts women from military service). The Bundeswehr has been plagued by its lack of tradition. Because all German wars of the last hundred years have been wars of aggression, they have produced few military or naval figures worth commemorating. There are still seven Hindenburg barracks in West Germany, but they are leftovers from earlier times. This obliteration of the past created difficulties in naming new military installations, ships, and such. With the possible exception of Field Marshal Rommel and some members of the resistance against Hitler, there were no suitable candidates. In 1965 the defense ministry issued a *Traditions-erlass* (tradition decree), laying down what could and could not be commemorated, but the decree did not solve the problem. In his inaugural address in 1976, Helmut Schmidt advised the Bundeswehr to look to its own tradition of the last twenty years rather than to history for inspiration.

There has been occasional concern over signs of neo-Nazism in the German army, such as the incident involving some lieutenants at the Bundeswehr's school in Munich. But when one of Hitler's air aces, Colonel Hans-Ulrich Rudel, visited an army training camp in 1976, delivering speeches and distributing his pro-Nazi books, the resulting protests led to the premature retirement of the generals who had invited him. On the whole, the 210 generals and admirals of the Bundeswehr are unpretentious, hard-working, well-trained professionals, not unlike their American counterparts. Some of them have held leading positions within NATO. As for the rank and file, the average German soldier, again like his American counterpart, is truly a civilian in uniform. Parades with goose step and army bands are a thing of the past. To a nostalgic older generation, this lack of military glamour may be a loss, but the younger generation does not seem to miss it.

Another sphere in which traditional German attitudes and practices have changed is the role of women in society. When announcing his program in December 1976, Helmut Schmidt referred to the *zahlreichen Benachteiligungen* (numerous disadvantages) still suffered by German women, a situation the chancellor promised to change. The Federal Republic at the time had a ratio of thirty-two million women to thirty million men. Of the total number of employed persons, 37 percent are women. The constitution calls for complete legal equality of the sexes, but in practice, many inequities persist. While women provide between 86 and 96 percent of the work force in the textile and clothing industries and in hospital and secretarial work, women make up only 5 percent of the lawyers, 10 percent of the judges, and 20 percent of the doctors. The rule of equal pay for equal work, furthermore, is rarely observed, and managerial positions are still predominantly filled by males. Less than 10 percent of the seats in local and regional parliaments and 7 percent in the Bundestag are held by women. The position of minister for youth, family, and health, comparable to America's secretary of health, education, and welfare, is usually held by a woman, and there have been some other high-level appointments, but far too few.

Still, the situation today is a far cry from the old cliché that women's place was with *Kinder, Kirche, Küche* (children, church, kitchen), so dear to critics of Germany in the past. Actually, the position of Germany's women is little different from, and in some instances better than, that of their sisters in the United States. There are still glaring injustices in both societies. Legalization of abortion has made progress in Germany as in the United States, and the fact that it is hedged about by various restrictions is understandable in a country that is almost half Catholic. Male chauvinism survives on both sides of the Atlantic, and the remark of a German airline official, that it would be easier for a woman to become boxing champion than captain of a Lufthansa jet, would be heartily cheered by his American colleagues. Given the far more deeply ingrained tradition of male supremacy in Germany, however, the shift to genuine partnership between the sexes has been an encouraging trend. Few German families thus far have availed themselves of the opportunity to use the wife's name, but such conservatism is due as much to wives as to husbands. In many other respects, such as sharing household chores, doing the marketing, and taking care of the children, male participation, once rare, has become almost as common in Germany as it has long been in the United States.

There are many other ways in which German society has changed, more during the last ten years than during the previous twenty. Germany's birthrate is the lowest among the western powers, including the United States, and if it remains at its present level, West Germany's population in fifty years will be reduced to forty million. Germans now marry younger, but they also get divorced in greater numbers. The leading characteristics of social change have been mobility and prosperity. There are still distinctions and differences between classes, but they have become less obvious. As for prosperity, West Germany in the mid-seventies had all the earmarks of a *Wohlstandsgesellschaft*. Average hourly wages in 1975 were close to those in the United States, and more than half of the working population made more than DM 16,000 (about $7,000). Most of this new wealth went into private consumption—54 percent of the gross national product in 1975. Between 1956 and 1976 the number of automobiles and labor-saving appliances increased more than tenfold. More than 33 percent of the annual income was spent on food. When a national opinion survey asked about New Year's resolutions in 1976, most people replied, *"Weniger essen"* ("To eat less"). But despite the fact that they had lost virtually all their savings twice in this century, Germans still saved more than 15 percent of their income, compared to the average 5 percent saved by Americans.

The creeping recession that hit the industrialized nations of the West during the mid-1970s, however, also upset the Federal Republic by causing a marked leveling-off in economic growth. Economic decline did not affect Germany as much as some countries, but after decades of almost uninterrupted economic growth, its psychological effect was all the more serious. As elsewhere the most important manifestations of stagflation were inflation and unemployment. Prior to 1973 there had been a shortage of workers; suddenly there was an overabundance. The causes of Germany's economic difficulties were manifold. The energy crisis, so crucial in the United States, was mitigated by the fact that in Germany the rise in the cost of oil was balanced by increased exports to the oil-producing nations. More serious was the overall drop in German exports, due in part to the upward revaluation of the D-mark. Within Germany the sector hardest hit by economic stagnation was the building industry. The sudden stop of the building boom in 1973 had far-reaching repercussions, including thousands of bankruptcies in related industries and even some banks, a situation reminiscent of the depression year of 1931. Other causes of unemployment were the sudden influx of young people into the labor market as a result of the postwar baby boom and the decrease in manpower needs due to rationalization and automation. Still, stagflation hit the Federal Republic less hard than the other members of the EEC, who looked to Bonn for help.

One major cause of inflation almost everywhere was the recurrent demand, backed by strikes, for higher wages, and in this respect, too, West Germany was better off. I have discussed the early phase of the German labor movement and its leading organization, the German Trade Union Federation or DGB (see chapter 8). In 1975 its president, Heinz Oskar Vetter, proudly asserted that "never before in the history of the German trade union movement has so much been achieved for workers in such a short time as in the years after the total destruction of the economic basis of our country." Between 1960 and 1975 hourly wages of industrial workers increased sevenfold, while the cost of living only doubled. The forty-hour week and four weeks' paid vacation became general practice, and a large measure of job security was won. Some of these achievements were the result of collective bargaining, and others grew out of a unique system of *Konzertierte Aktion* (concerted action) begun in 1967 by Federal Minister of Economics Karl Schiller, who instituted periodic round-table discussions among representatives of government, management, and labor. The DGB was still not satisfied with labor's share in economic decision making. Its leadership expected further reforms from the social-liberal SPD-FDP coalition in 1969, but these hopes were disappointed.

The most crucial issue between workers and industrialists continued to be codetermination, that is, labor's participation on a parity basis in all economic, social, and personnel aspects of industrial policy. Such participation, as we have seen, had been granted in 1951 for iron, steel, and coal. In other sectors of the economy, employees were given only one-third of *Aufsichtsrat* (supervisory board) seats. The debate over parity codetermination continued for more than twenty years and was not resolved until 1976, then by compromise. The codetermination law, which affects about 85 percent of the work force, calls for equal representation of employees and stockholders on the supervisory boards of all large firms. But executives are included among the employees, and the chairman of the board, who is usually elected by the shareholders, has the deciding vote, so the employees' share in company management remains less than equal. Employers' organizations, furthermore, have gone to court to challenge codetermination as a violation of the right of property guaranteed under the constitution. American firms in Germany have claimed that the law should not apply to them.

The most effective antidote to working-class discontent continued to be the Federal Republic's comprehensive system of social insurance (see chapter 8). Covering every segment of the population and every conceivable type of emergency, Germany's *Sozialbudget*, the annual amount spent on social services, has grown by leaps and bounds. Between 1965 and 1975 it increased from DM 113 billion to DM 335 billion, which constituted 32.2 percent of the gross national product. It was estimated that by 1982 it would reach DM 500 billion. Social welfare ranked far ahead of defense as the largest item in the federal budget. About 59 percent of this staggering sum was contributed by the insured and their employers, with the remainder from public funds. Growing unemployment, rising costs of health care, and the annual increase of old-age pensions to keep up with inflation created budgetary problems not faced by any earlier governments. Schmidt's attempt in late 1976 to gain a breathing spell by postponing for six months the pension rise he had promised for July 1, 1977, caused a wave of protest and had to be abandoned. Over a period of ten years, the cost of social insurance pensions had doubled.

One group in West Germany posed a special problem, the *Gastarbeiter* (guest workers), who made up almost 10 percent of the working population. Between 1961 and 1973 more than two and a half million workers from the less developed countries of the Mediterranean region, notably Turkey, came to the Federal Republic. As unemployment became a problem, the government tried to stop and ultimately reverse this influx. By 1978 the number of foreign workers had been reduced to under two million, but by then many of the foreigners, most of whom had been in Germany for several years, had been joined by their families, so that their actual number was close to four million. In some urban centers like Frankfurt and Munich, one out of every five inhabitants was non-German.

The situation of this underprivileged minority was far from enviable, even though most were better off economically than they had been back home. They were restricted mostly to the dirtier menial jobs that German workers did not want; they were victimized by unscrupulous landlords; and they had virtually no social contacts with Germans. There was much official talk about integrating these outsiders, but little was done. The million or so foreign workers' children, six hundred thousand of whom had been born in Germany (but were not thereby German citizens), faced special problems. Unable to keep up with the requirements of German schools and without adequate schooling in their native tongue, they grew up "illiterate in two languages." Unlike the earlier problem of integrating millions of eastern German refugees, the assimilation of the foreign workers has thus far made little progress. Government and religious leaders are concerned to find remedies for the *Gastarbeiter* problem. But the majority of Germans seem indifferent or outright discriminatory toward this large number of less fortunate people in their midst.

Many of the economic and social problems discussed here, including the influx of foreign workers, have parallels in other industrialized countries. This also applies to the problem of environmental protection, which was a key issue in Germany as elsewhere, especially among the young. Because of the country's population density, air and water pollution posed particularly serious threats, and the Bundestag adopted some sweeping regulatory measures. On one issue—the building of nuclear reactors—the government and the environmentalists did not agree. In a series of protest demonstrations, groups of irate citizens, *Bürgerinitiativen* (citizens' initiatives), tried to prevent the construction of additional power plants to alleviate the energy shortage. The infiltration of these protest movements by radical elements of the right and left complicated the situation, as did opposition to nuclear development within the chancellor's party.

The marginal success of the SPD-FDP coalition in the 1976

252 / Germany and the United States

elections was seen as a sign that Schmidt had failed to fulfill the hopes aroused by Brandt in 1972 (see chapter 9). The economic recession doubtless had something to do with the outcome also. Even so, the total vote for the radical parties of both right and left was only 0.9 percent, despite the fact that unemployment was near the one million mark. In contrast to 1972, domestic issues overshadowed foreign policy during the campaign. The resulting Bundestag was the second youngest in the history of the BRD, with an average age of 47.3 years. Of its 518 members (including 22 nonvoting delegates from West Berlin), 148 held doctorates, more than 50 percent belonged to trade unions, at least 40 percent came from the public sector, and less than 2 percent were blue-collar workers.

More and more, German elections have become contests between individuals rather than parties, so the victory of the SPD-FDP coalition, in the last analysis, was a victory of Helmut Schmidt. The leader of the opposition, Helmut Kohl, while more popular than his predecessor Rainer Barzel, was no match for Schmidt. The CDU-CSU coalition was an uneasy one. As a member of the liberal wing of the CDU, Kohl was less stridently antileft than his partner, Franz Josef Strauss, head of the CSU. Shortly after the election, Strauss threatened that in the future his party would campaign separately from the CDU. An open split was avoided, but differences remained. Meanwhile, as the Schmidt regime continued to find the going tough, especially economically, the CDU and CSU showed increasing gains in Länder elections. The image of the opposition became seriously tarnished, however, when it supported too strongly and for too long Hans Filbinger, the Christian Democratic minister president of Baden-Württemberg. Filbinger resigned under pressure in 1978 when it was found that during World War II, while a navy judge, he had handed down several death sentences against German sailors, one of them several weeks after Germany's capitulation. Another grim reminder of the Nazi past.

Schmidt's performance during his second term was mixed. He made a poor start by trying to postpone the increase of pensions, a mistake that lost him much of his popularity. But the chancellor regained public confidence through his decisive and courageous handling of the terrorist crisis in 1977 when the hostages at Mogadishu were liberated. A public opinion poll in November 1977 gave him a rating of 58 percent. But Schmidt was working under a number of handicaps. First of all, he had to get along with his coalition partners in the FDP. Even though the Free Democrats held only four of the fifteen cabinet posts, they were important ones—the ministries of foreign affairs, economics, the interior, and food. Although the chancellor worked well with his FDP colleagues, his own party did not always approve of their policies.

A second difficulty was that Schmidt himself was not overly popular with the SPD. Its ranks still included a Marxist (or neo-Marxist) faction, whose members criticized the government's policy as social-liberal, rather than Socialist. Had it not been for support by Willy Brandt as party leader and by Herbert Wehner as chief of the SPD's Bundestag delegation, underlying differences might have led to an open split. The unity that the SPD had shown after Godesberg in 1959 was clearly a thing of the past. Finally, the CDU-CSU promised a policy of "energetic opposition," although differences between its two components weakened the opposition's effectiveness. But the dominant position of the opposition parties in a majority of the Länder gave them control of the federal chamber, the Bundesrat, enabling them to defeat or delay some important legislation.

The fact that the Federal Republic was able to function despite such signs of divisiveness was an indication of its political maturity. Democracy has taken a firm hold in Germany. One of the most encouraging aspects of the German political scene has been its stability. In the past a change of the guard has brought no startling changes in policy at home or abroad, and there is no reason to fear that this stability will not last.

To round out this brief sketch of West Germany in the 1970s, a few words must be said about the cultural scene, an area in which considerable American influence can be found. There is no cultural center, such as Berlin was during the Weimar Republic or New York is for the United States, but any visitor to Germany would be impressed with the richness of cultural offerings, not only in the larger cities, but in medium-sized towns as well. Much of Germany's cultural life derives from artistic works and institutions already in existence before 1945. The classics in literature and the arts still flourish, although when it comes to new creations and trends, the years after World War II cannot compare with the years after World War I. Compared to Weimar culture, Bonn culture has been rather thin.

One of the main differences between the cultural life of the United States and that of Germany is that German cultural institutions are always publicly subsidized. Without the substantial sums spent by the municipalities and Länder on theaters, opera companies, and symphony orchestras, the German cultural scene would be barren indeed. Most German performing artists belong to repertory companies, some of them world famous, like the Stuttgart Ballet. These municipal organizations provide steady employment to thousands of artists, including many Americans, in opera and music. Germans are very fond of *Festspiele* (festivals), from the traditional Richard Wagner Festivals at Bayreuth and the passion plays at Oberammergau to the Ruhrfestspiele and the Berlin Jazz Festivals. Like most major countries, Germany has an abundance of museums and art galleries, most of them rebuilt since World War II. Increased interest in cultural roots has spurred a search for Roman and early Germanic remains, many of which have been impressively assembled in one of the most popular new collections, the Roman-Germanic Museum in Cologne.

In the category of ongoing rather than innovative culture, radio and television have played a major part. An important difference between Germany and the United States is that neither of these media in Germany has ever been privately owned and operated. Radio before 1945 was government controlled with, under Hitler, disastrous consequences. Since then both radio and television have been set up as independent, semipublic enterprises, controlled by boards of governors made up of representatives from political, economic, social, and cultural groups and financed by listeners' and viewers' fees collected by the state. The intricate organization of German radio and television need not concern us. Suffice it to say that freedom from sponsors' pressure to cater to the lowest common denominator makes the German media more educational but also less entertaining than their American counterparts. Some American television series, ranging from "Kojak" to "Sesame Street," are also shown in Germany, where they have a wide following.

Another barometer of culture, the German press, is doing very well. As in the United States, there has been a tendency toward consolidation, with Hamburg's Axel Springer emerging as the leading press lord and target of attacks. The political press, so prominent in the past, today plays a secondary role. The most important supraregional dailies are *Die Welt, Frankfurter Allgemeine Zeitung,* and *Süddeutsche Zeitung,* each with a circulation of between a quarter and a third of a million. The most popular paper, the tabloid *Bild* (Picture), sells more than four million copies each day. In addition there are some twenty large regional dailies and several widely read weeklies, most prominently *Die Zeit* and *Der Spiegel.* The latter, modeled after America's *Time* magazine, specializes in sensational exposés. German newspapers do not draw as clear a line between news and editorial content as does the American press, and most papers have a decided slant, from conservative (*Die Welt*) to liberal (*Die Zeit*) to left-wing liberal (*Frankfurter Rundschau*). The German press on the whole has taken the task of serving democracy seriously, and freedom of the press, guaranteed under the constitution, is carefully guarded by a self-regulating board, the Deutscher Presserat (German Press Council).

As we turn from the performing arts and the news media to the creative arts and literature, the picture becomes more uneven. In music, where Germany has excelled in the past, one looks in vain for worthy successors to Richard Strauss, Paul Hindemith, or Kurt Weill. The name best known in the United States is that of Karl-heinz Stockhausen, a pioneer in electronic music. Among more conservative composers, Carl Orff and Werner Egk stand out. In the pictorial arts there is also a dearth of outstanding talent. Some of the expressionists who survived the Nazi years, Oskar Kokoschka, Emil Nolde, and Otto Dix, have continued to paint, but they really belong to the pre-1933 period. In contemporary trends, such as op art, pop art, *tachisme,* American influence has been strong. Several German museums have excellent collections of modern American art. There is a wide variety of artistic styles in Germany, from new realism to surrealism, and artists like Paul Wunderlich, Günther Fruhtrunk, Otto Piene, Mac Zimmermann, and a host of others have achieved national renown.

One area in which postwar Germany offered virtually unlimited opportunities was architecture. With thousands of public buildings and millions of private dwellings in ruins, new construction flourished. By 1977 the number of new homes reached fifteen million, but the results were not as innovative as one might have wished. During the Weimar Republic, Germany had been a leader in modern architecture, and some of its outstanding figures, notably Walter Gropius and Ludwig Mies van der Rohe, were exiled under Hitler, thus transferring this leadership to the United States. After the war Mies van der Rohe designed the National Gallery in West Berlin. Among contemporary German architects, Hans Scharoun, Egon Eiermann, Wassili Luckhardt, and Max Taut have won international acclaim. The most exciting examples of modern architecture in Germany since World War II have been the many new theater buildings and the thousands of churches that had to be newly built or restored. At first after 1945 there was a tendency toward demolition; but in time restoration, not only of historic but of nineteenth-century buildings, became a growing trend.

Industrial and urban architecture, with some exceptions (the headquarters of the Thyssen firm in Düsseldorf, for instance), has been quite unimaginative, and most German cities have a uniformly American look. Because of the high cost of land, high-rise apartments have become the vogue, not only in cities but in the countryside, where they are out of place. A prime example of a skyscraper in the wrong place is the administrative building of the Bundestag, the "tall Eugen" (after Eugen Gerstenmaier, the Bundestag's president at the time of its construction), which sits in the middle of the Rhine valley and spoils forever one of the Federal Republic's most beautiful views.

One art form in which, it is agreed, Germany had excelled before Hitler, was films. Not surprisingly, therefore, the world looked expectantly to see what the new Germany would produce. For almost twenty years there was nothing except some soft pornography, some *Heimat* kitsch, and an occasional documentary. The situation changed in the late sixties and early seventies, when a number of new directors, including Werner Herzog, Rainer Werner Fassbinder, Wim Wenders, Jürgen Syberberg, and others, produced a score of innovative and exciting movies. These young men of the post-1945 generation experimented with new approaches and techniques, and their messages, invariably dealing with large social and moral issues, did not always come across. Also, humor and laughter were unknown ingredients in their creations. But by 1978 some of these film-makers, especially Fassbinder, received wide publicity among the avant-garde in New York, where festivals of their films were more common than in the country of their origin.

In literature the scene became brighter earlier. In 1947 a group of young writers founded the Gruppe 47 to discuss and criticize one another's work. Some of its early members subsequently were among Germany's leading authors: Heinrich Böll, Günter Grass, Martin Walser, Ingeborg Bachmann, and Günter Eich. Ten years later the group had become an institution, and to be invited to its meetings meant being "in." Another ten years later in 1967, Gruppe 47 came to a sudden end. The previous year its annual meeting had been held, by invitation, at Princeton. A number of authors at that time refused to read from their works; several others did not attend, even though all expenses were paid; and one of the younger writers, Peter Handke (an Austrian), used the Princeton meeting for some ill-tempered criticism of the group. This was the beginning of the end. The last meeting, which took place near Erlangen in 1967, was picketed by students who demanded that Gruppe 47 associate itself with their radical protests against Axel Springer's newspapers. Efforts by some writers to politicize the organization was one reason for its demise. Others were differences in age and the growing conservatism of some of the more famous authors. But while it lasted, Gruppe 47 was a most constructive influence on the German literary scene.

By the mid-1960s, several German authors had become well

known abroad. The most successful of them was Heinrich Böll, who won the Nobel Prize for literature in 1972, and whose books, translated into thirty-five languages, sold more than twenty million copies. They included *Billiards at Half Past Nine, Group Portrait with Lady,* and *The Lost Honor of Katharina Blum.* Another prominent writer was Günter Grass, author of *The Tin Drum* and *Dog Years.* Other writers of international reputation are Uwe Johnson and Siegfried Lenz. There have been fewer successful playwrights. Best known among them are Peter Weiss, Peter Handke, and Rolf Hochhuth, the latter for his play *The Deputy,* dealing with Pope Pius XII's ambivalent attitude toward the Jews during World War II.

Writers and books hold an important place in German cultural life. With almost forty thousand titles published annually, West Germany holds third place in world book production (behind the Soviet Union and the United States). Every German city has several well-stocked bookstores managed by unusually knowledgeable personnel. The annual Frankfurt Book Fair is a major event in international publishing, and its Peace Prize of the German Book Trade is one of the most prestigious international awards. The prize has been won by foreigners as well as Germans, among them Thornton Wilder, whose plays, especially *Our Town,* have found enthusiastic audiences in Germany.

Much of the German culture here described unfortunately remains unknown to most Americans. Of the large number of German books published annually, less than a thousand are translated into English. And while 10 percent of Germany's sizable book exports go to the United States, their bulk consists of scientific and other specialized literature. In the visual arts, contacts are more frequent, but much more could be done, for instance by rebroadcasting German television shows in the United States. The Federal Republic beams a shortwave program across the Atlantic as part of its overseas service, *Deutsche Welle* (German wave), but its audience in the United States is minimal. More important is the German Information Center in New York, which performs a valuable service in providing up-to-date information about the Federal Republic. Despite these and other efforts, however, much remains to be done to bring the two peoples as close together culturally as their governments have been brought together politically.

11 | The German Democratic Republic since 1961

I HAVE SAID very little thus far about the German Democratic Republic (DDR). Relations between the United States and "the other Germany" were nonexistent until 1974. Before that time Washington strictly adhered to the policy of nonrecognition adopted by West Germany under Adenauer. As far as America was concerned, East Germany was to remain in limbo until the two Germanies were reunited. But in 1972, when the two German states recognized each other and concluded their Basic Treaty, the United States could no longer put off joining in the general move toward recognition of the DDR. Even so, it was almost two years before the first exchange of ambassadors took place between Washington and East Berlin.

After that event the expected normalization of relations was slow to materialize. Almost thirty years of mutual suspicions and recriminations could not be forgotten overnight. Exchange of persons, so important in American–West German relations, remained slow, with American tourists preferring more hospitable countries and East German tourists prohibited by their government from visiting the United States. Since personal contacts were few and the gathering of information restricted, we know far less about the eastern than about the western republic. As has long been the case with the Soviet Union, DDR-watching has become a favorite pastime, yet DDR-watchers are usually no more correct in their speculations about Erich Honecker than Kremlinologists are in their predictions about Leonid Brezhnev.

Erich Honecker succeeded Walter Ulbricht in 1971, when Ulbricht relinquished his position as first secretary of the SED. Ulbricht's decision to build the Berlin Wall in 1961, mainly to stop the drain of manpower, had initiated a wholly new phase in the history of the DDR. There were still escapees from East Germany, as many as six thousand per year (leaving through other communist countries rather than West Berlin), but they were a mere trickle compared to earlier years. Having made the Democratic Republic a virtual prison, Ulbricht then concentrated on conciliating the inmates. Under a New Economic System introduced in 1963, economic controls were relaxed, managerial initiatives encouraged, and profit incentives introduced. As a result the DDR experienced its own belated economic miracle; but beginning in the late 1960s, its ambitious economic plans began to fall short of their goals. A happy marriage between bureaucratic planning and individual initiative, it seemed, was difficult to achieve.

The reasons Ulbricht gave for his retirement were old age and declining health; he died two years later. But economic difficulties at home and differences with his Soviet masters abroad may have hastened his decision. If West Germany was closely tied to the United States in its foreign policy, East Germany was wholly subservient to the Soviet Union. In 1964, Khrushchev and Ulbricht signed a twenty-year treaty of friendship and mutual assistance. On the key issue of relations with West Germany, Ulbricht's hard-line stand during the 1960s found consistent Russian support. The close DDR-USSR relationship had been openly proclaimed when East German forces invaded Czechoslovakia during the 1968 crisis. In the subsequent phase of Ostpolitik, however, Ulbricht and Brezhnev had not always seen eye to eye on making concessions, for the sake of détente, in the Soviet–West German treaty and in the four-power agreement on Berlin. Those agreements clearly showed that the DDR enjoyed far less independence vis-à-vis the Soviet Union than did the BRD vis-à-vis the United States and its western allies.

Honecker had long been known as Ulbricht's heir apparent, so his "election" by the SED's central committee came as no surprise. Upon Ulbricht's death in 1973, Honecker's chief rival, Willi Stoph, who had been prime minister, became chairman of the council of state, or head of state. But after a major reorganization in 1976, Honecker took over that position as well, so that once again the DDR's two most important posts were combined. The new East German leader was born in 1912, the son of a coal miner. He had been an ardent communist since his youth, spent many years in prison under the Nazis, and had been active in the youth section of

his party after the war. An unpretentious and pedestrian functionary, Honecker projected a man-of-the-people image. Despite his reputation as a hard-liner and a loyal servant of the Soviet Union,
Honecker has proved to be somewhat more pliable than his predecessor.

This was the man with whom the United States had to deal
when official relations were established, but Washington was in no
hurry to send an ambassador to the DDR after the 1971 agreement
on Berlin had cleared the way. Britain and France did so in early
1973, but the United States waited until late in 1974. The East German press had been especially malicious about Watergate ("it ex-
presses the rottenness of the whole democratic system and the American way of life"), which did not ease the situation. America's first
ambassador to East Berlin was John Sherman Cooper, who had spent
some time in American military government in Germany in 1946.
His successor in 1977 was David B. Bolen, a career diplomat who had
been economic counselor in Bonn some years earlier. The East German ambassador to Washington was Rolf Sieber, a respected professor of economics. Both Bolen and Sieber had backgrounds in
economics, indicating where they would be most active.

There were no state visits in either direction, of course. It
was hardly conceivable that President Carter, after viewing the "wall
of shame" in 1978, would cross to East Berlin to say hello to Chairman Honecker. In 1977 East Germany's foreign minister, Oskar
Fischer, made a little-noticed trip to the United States, and in an
address to the Foreign Policy Association called for "unbiased [sach-
lich] collaboration" between the two countries and for efforts "to get
to know each other better." But there were few occasions for this,
since intercourse in Washington and East Berlin remained purely
formal. It was virtually impossible to gain any unbiased, up-to-date
information on the DDR in the United States. An American Society
for the Study of the German Democratic Republic, founded in 1965
by a group of journalists and scholars, was later taken over by its
communist members, and its purpose thus defeated. By 1976 about
one hundred DDR official representatives lived in Washington, but
in strict and self-imposed isolation. The same held true for the East
German mission to the UN in New York.

There were no major political issues between the two countries except for occasional differences over Berlin, which Washington
preferred to discuss with Moscow. As a precondition to the establishment of diplomatic ties, the East Germans had promised to negotiate any economic claims by Americans for properties confiscated
or nationalized by the communist regime. However, when it came

to making restitution for Jewish property lost during the Nazi period, the DDR authorities played a delaying game. In 1976 they finally offered to pay one million dollars to Jewish organizations, which was turned down as far too little, especially in view of the fact that West Germany had paid a total of twenty-five *billion* dollars in restitution since 1952. Other disputes arose from Congressional complaints that East Germany served as a link in the heroin trade that supplied American servicemen stationed in West Germany and from accusations that the DDR was sympathetic to international terrorists and secretly supported guerrilla actions in Africa, notably Zaïre. Some Americans ran into trouble by trying to help East Germans escape to the West. By 1977 some fifty East Germans who wanted to join relatives in the United States had been given permission, and the remaining small number would probably be allowed to follow.

If in the political sphere American–East German relations remained correct at best, in the economic sector the two countries became more cooperative. In 1972 economic links between them were practically nonexistent; total trade amounted to only $25 million. Between 1972 and 1974 that figure doubled, but compared to American trade with West Germany, it was still minuscule. The main initiative for stepping up economic exchange came from the East Germans. The first major developments happened in 1976, when representatives of American business for the first time visited the German Democratic Republic in appreciable numbers, when American ports were opened to East German ships, and when some American firms started exhibiting at the annual Leipzig Fair. The first large American company to open an office in East Berlin was Dow Chemical, but others soon followed.

In 1977 a formal U.S.–East German trade agreement was signed, setting up joint committees to facilitate dealings between their diametrically opposed economic systems. There were still innumerable difficulties to overcome, most of them created by the United States, which refused to conclude a consular treaty with the East Germans or to grant them most-favored-nation treatment. But each side had goods to offer that the other needed—machine tools, optics, and electronics for the United States from East Germany, and chemicals, electrical goods, and especially feed grains for East Germany from the United States. Under an agreement signed in 1976, the DDR contracted to import close to two million tons of American grain each year, and the amounts actually imported were far larger.

Economic self-interest thus proved the most effective magnet drawing the United States and East Germany together; neither Adam Smith nor Karl Marx would have been surprised. But some inhibitions still prevented the easy give-and-take that had developed over the years between American businessmen and their West German partners. How could relations be eased between American capitalists and East German communists? By "getting to know each other better," of course.

To bring about rapprochement through mutual acquaintance was the purpose of cultural exchange. But there was very little of this. The East Germans, able to watch Western television, could gain some impression, albeit distorted, of American life, but there was no comparable source of information for Americans on life in East Germany. Academic exchange of students and professors, so helpful in bringing the United States and West Germany together, hardly existed. Some American scholars were permitted to do research in East German archives, but the rules governing their admission were haphazard. In 1975 East Germany concluded an agreement with the International Research and Exchange Board (IREX) for the exchange of ten scholars from both sides over a period of two years, but this was a mere gesture. Occasionally an individual German scholar was permitted to accept an invitation from an American university, or some musicians performed in the United States. The only event causing national American attention was "The Splendor of Dresden," an exhibition of art treasures from that East German city, which toured the United States in 1978. It was intended, the East Germans said, as a contribution to "peace, détente, and cooperation." But its priceless art had been collected by the kings of Saxony centuries ago, and its relation to the DDR was tenuous at best.

Another link was provided by the translations of some East German authors, Stefan Heym, Christa Wolf, Jurek Becker, Wolf Biermann, Reiner Kunze, and others. But because their writings were highly critical of life in the DDR, they were hardly the kind of cultural ambassadors the East German government would have chosen. The Helsinki agreement on human rights found a particularly strong echo in East Germany (see chapter 10). When thousands of citizens applied for permission to leave the DDR, and scores of writers began criticizing the repression of individual rights and freedoms, the Honecker regime took strong countermeasures. In 1975 Wolf Biermann, a well-known political poet and folk singer, was deprived of his citizenship for having "slandered socialism in the DDR." This unprecedented action set up a wave of protest among his fellow writers, as a result of which many others were imprisoned or forced to leave. In 1977 the poet Reiner Kunze was expelled for his sardonic sketches of East German oppressiveness, *The Wonderful Years.*

But it was not only writers who spoke out. In 1978 the West German magazine *Der Spiegel* published an opposition manifesto by a group calling itself the League of Democratic Communists, assumed to be lower-level functionaries within the DDR. Around the same time another East German functionary, Rudolf Bahro, was sentenced to eight years in prison for his book *Die Alternative,* published in West Germany, which denounced the East German system and advocated a more humane kind of socialism. I will have more to say on dissent in the DDR later. Considering America's outspoken position on human rights, the suppression in East Germany could not help but affect relations between the two countries. It would take more than "The Splendor of Dresden" to hide the squalor of East Berlin.

There is no need here to stress the close relationship between the German Democratic Republic and the Soviet Union. Its outward manifestations are well known, and its inner workings we can only guess at. In 1975 the treaty of friendship concluded eleven years earlier was revised in the direction of aligning the foreign policy of the two partners still more closely. East Germany is generally considered the Soviet Union's most loyal satellite, and the two remain each other's best customers. There have been occasional reports of East German complaints concerning the high prices of Russian raw materials and about Soviet failures to live up to trade agreements. According to rumor, relations between Chairman Honecker and Russia's ambassador to East Berlin, Pyotr Abrassimov, are none too good, either. The Soviet troops stationed in East Germany are, by all accounts, far from popular, and at a demonstration of some one thousand young people on East Berlin's Alexanderplatz in 1977, cries of "Out with the Russians" were heard. But then, in East Germany as in the Soviet Union, the people do not count. The leaders at the top appeared to be in perfect harmony. When Brezhnev turned seventy in 1976, Honecker visited his Russian master and bestowed on him the Hero's Star of the DDR and the Great Star of International Friendship. The next year, during the sixtieth anniversary celebration of the Russian revolution, Honecker stood among the Soviet bigwigs reviewing the parade, proudly displaying his Order of Lenin.

If the German Democratic Republic's relations with the Soviet Union were close and with the United States distant, its dealing with its German sister republic ranged somewhere in between. We have seen how, as a result of Ostpolitik, relations had become somewhat easier during the early 1970s. Official diplomatic ties were not established until 1974, when the two German states exchanged permanent representatives, not ambassadors, since in West German eyes at least, the two states are not foreign countries to each other. East Germany sent to Bonn Michael Kohl, who in 1972 had been its chief negotiator for the Basic Treaty that regulated intercourse between the two Germanies. West Germany was represented in East Berlin by Günter Gaus. There were no formal meetings between Honecker and Schmidt, except when they both happened to be at some international function, such as the Helsinki conference or the opening of the UN. Any high-level personal contacts were between Honecker and Herbert Wehner, the SPD's grand old man, who knew Honecker from the days when he himself had been a communist.

The most perennial and painful problem in East–West German relations, and a source of endless incidents, was the border between the two states. "The boundary which runs through the middle of Germany," Chancellor Schmidt said in his inaugural address in 1976, "which separates people and at which people are shot again and again, hurts us ... The actions of the DDR along the border through Germany are without parallel in Europe. We do not endanger or threaten the security of that frontier. Responsibility for the use of guns lies entirely with the DDR." The security system along East Germany's western border has been perfected until it is virtually airtight: a three-mile-wide death strip with land mines, automatic guns, watchtowers, patrols, and police dogs. Even so, thousands of East Germans managed to escape and many more tried to but were caught (the number in the latter category between 1961 and 1977 was estimated at forty thousand). The zeal, not to say brutality, with which the East German border guards performed their grim duty led to a never-ending series of ugly incidents: West Germans shot for inadvertently straying onto East German territory; a child drowned because West German rescuers were prevented at gun point from saving her; and most common, East Germans killed while trying to escape. Their number since 1961 is estimated at close to two hundred.

But there has also been legal exodus from the DDR through emigration. It is difficult to obtain exact figures, but by the late 1970s it was estimated that several thousand left East Germany this way each year. Most of these emigrants were old-age pensioners who for obvious reasons have always been allowed to go. For economically active people, especially doctors, permission to emigrate was usually withheld. Many East Germans who were prevented from leaving, including some political prisoners (estimated to total six thousand in 1977), were quietly "bought free" by West Germany at a cost of as much as $20,000 per person. By 1977 about fifteen thousand East Germans had thus found asylum in the West. The most visible exiles, of course, and the most damaging to the reputation of the DDR, were the dissidents. Every time a famous writer, artist, or academician defected or was expelled, the news was greeted as a propaganda victory for the West, even though some of the dissidents, Wolf Biermann for instance, were as critical of life in the West as they had been of things in the East.

Relations between the two Germanies also were periodically disturbed by espionage scandals uncovered in various government agencies, mostly in West Germany. With at least three million East Germans living in the Federal Republic, infiltration of critical organizations by carefully selected agents was almost impossible to control. The most famous case was that of Günter Guillaume, whose unmasking as an East German spy in the immediate entourage of Willy Brandt led to the chancellor's resignation in 1974. In 1976 sixteen suspected spies were arrested in West Germany, some of whom had relayed important NATO plans to the DDR, and in 1977 a secretary in the chancellery was found to be in East German pay. Spying was not a one-way operation, of course. Some West German agents were also arrested in the DDR, but often on trumped-up charges and in retaliation against earlier arrests in the West. In spying, as in general police work, East Germany clearly held the upper hand.

Despite the deep-seated differences and antagonisms between the two Germanies, they somehow managed to get along. Their relations are correct rather than cordial, with mutual economic interests helping to bridge ideological and political gaps. Trade between the two states showed a marked increase in the mid-seventies, and the BRD was the DDR's main western trade partner. Still, the bulk of East Germany's foreign trade continued to be with the members of COMECON, just as West Germany's continued with the members of the Common Market.

A word should be said here about Berlin. The agreement of 1971, which was concluded by the great powers rather than by the two Germanies, was not very specific on the relation of East Berlin to East Germany, so there remained an area of possible disagreement. The Berlin problem will not be definitely resolved until Germany is reunited, if ever. Until then, in the words of Egon Bahr, the former German capital will remain "the touchstone [*Prüfstein*] of détente." Meanwhile the western allies continue to protest the DDR's claims that East Berlin is its capital and that the four-power agreement applies only to West Berlin.

The issue of reunification, so central during the 1960s, has been dead or dormant during the 1970s, especially in the DDR. To Erich Honecker the Federal Republic is a bourgeois, imperialist, and foreign country. To play down the linguistic and historical ties of the two Germanies, the use of the adjective "German" has been consciously deemphasized. The term used to describe the DDR's policy vis-à-vis the BRD has been *Abgrenzung* (fencing off), that is, a purposeful suppression of whatever common German feelings still exist in East Germany. Not only does the Honecker regime not share Willy Brandt's hope that increased contacts will transform an indifferent *Nebeneinander* into a cordial *Miteinander,* it actually tries by every possible means, as we have seen, to prevent contacts. Yet economic needs call for détente, and détente calls for contacts, which in turn will weaken the regime's ideological hold over its people. The incompatibility of *Abgrenzung* with détente presents the DDR with an insoluble dilemma, which accounts for much of the vacillation in its foreign and domestic policy.

I have already sketched the outlines of the DDR's political system as it evolved during the fifties and sixties (see chapters 7, 8). In 1968 the results of these developments were laid down in a new constitution. The underlying principles of the DDR's government are *Gewalteneinheit* (unity of powers) and "democratic centralism," one of those self-contradictory euphemisms of which communists are so fond. It means that people can democratically discuss issues and vote for candidates, as long as their discussion does not stray from the general outlines laid down by their superiors at the center, and as long as the candidates they vote for are the ones approved by their leaders. As for unity of powers, there is no division among legislative, executive, and judiciary as there is in most democratic countries. Under the DDR constitution, the Volkskammer is the "supreme organ of state power," but in reality, the Volkskammer has very little influence. It meets only a few times each year to pass, usually by unanimous vote and without debate, the few laws put before it.

Most of the Volkskammer's constitutional powers are wielded by its executive organ, the twenty-four-member Staatsrat, whose chairman (Erich Honecker since 1976) is also head of state. The Staatsrat introduces and passes on the constitutionality of legislation and also issues decrees. The cabinet, or Ministerrat, is primarily an administrative organ. Its chairman (Willi Stoph, again since 1976) is officially head of government, but the Ministerrat's functions are largely in economic policy and planning. Defense and security matters have been relegated to a separate body, the Nationaler Verteidigungsrat (National Defense Council), also headed by Honecker.

There were times during the 1970s when, according to DDR-watchers, the Ministerrat seemed to overshadow the Staatsrat; however, the ultimate political power lies with neither of these bodies but with the leading party of East Germany, the SED. Despite the continued existence of some bourgeois parties, the DDR is essentially a one-party state. Within the SED the Politbüro of about twenty-five members and the Sekretariat of about twelve members are in control. Erich Honecker, as chairman of the Politbüro and first secretary of the Sekretariat, is the most powerful man in the SED and thus the most powerful man in East Germany.

The SED under Honecker has lost the last vestiges of its Stalinist past. About one in every six adults belongs to it. More than half of the members are workers, or at least of working-class origin, and about 30 percent are women. The members are carefully selected, dues are high, and strict discipline, together with time-consuming party work, helps to discourage opportunists. Party membership and ideological orthodoxy are the prerequisites for holding any leading political position in the German Democratic Republic. In the economic sphere, on the other hand, pragmatic technocrats at times have clashed with dogmatic ideologists. Such clashes have led to some adjustments, but not to any basic changes, in East Germany's socialist economy.

The main characteristic of that economy, as in most communist states, has been long-range planning. Periodic five-year plans, drafted by the SED and adopted by the Volkskammer are carried out under the central direction of the Ministerrat. During the 1960s, the bureaucratic control inherent in this procedure was sufficiently relaxed to permit lower-echelon functionaries some independence in implementing long-term planning. But by 1970 it became clear that such liberalization threatened to undercut the influence of the party bureaucracy, and a partial return to centralized direction was made. Since then the incompatibility of central planning with individual initiative has remained East Germany's major economic problem. The Honecker regime has tried to overcome these difficulties by improved planning and management and by creating ever larger combines of *Volkseigene Betriebe* (people-owned companies), responsible directly to members of the Ministerrat. Even so, plans have continued to fall short of their goals due to waste and inefficiency in production, and there have been growing reports of listlessness and indifference among factory managers and workers.

To boost morale and to improve the economic situation, the government has followed a twofold course of ideological indoctrination and material inducements, neither of which has worked. East German workers reportedly are tired of the ceaseless ideological peptalks to which they have to listen after work. As for the material advantages offered under Honecker's brand of *Konsum-Kommunismus,* only a small number of East Germans can afford to enjoy them. To be sure, the supply of domestic consumer goods has increased, and if one is willing to wait eight years, one may even get a car. But imported "luxuries" continue to be beyond the reach of the average consumer. In early 1978 in a much publicized move, the DDR imported ten thousand Volkswagen Rabbits (called Golf in Germany), to be sold at two or three times their West German price. In addition, a large number of state-run Intershops have sprung up all over the country, where western goods can be bought at a stiff price, paid in West German D-marks. But few East Germans have the necessary western currency, so this "Intershop Socialism" has tended only to increase the discontent of the majority.

East Germany's slower growth during the 1970s was due not only to the cumbersomeness of its state-run economy, but to other handicaps as well. We must remember that the DDR has had to build up much of its heavy industry from scratch and that except for lignite and potash, it has no sizable supplies of raw materials; the expected exhaustion of both resources by the end of the century is cause for much concern. Lignite serves as the basis for East Germany's chemical and energy industries, and its heavy use for industrial and home heating accounts for the drab, dirty look of many East German towns.

Added to the lack of raw materials is a shortage of manpower. The human drain before the construction of the Berlin Wall and the virtually stagnant birthrate are the main reasons for this deficiency. The large-scale employment of women (about 45 percent of the work force) and of pensioners beyond retirement provides a partial remedy. In comparison to West Germany, few foreign workers (mostly Poles) are employed in the DDR, and they do not perform the menial tasks of the *Gastarbeiter* in the West. Here is a further factor to explain the grimy appearance always commented upon by foreign visitors.

One way in which East Germany hopes to overcome its relative economic backwardness and win the loyalty of its citizens is through education. Because the educational system of the DDR is uniform and carefully planned, it has been free from the periodic crises that have plagued West German education. The system is also far simpler than the educational programs in the various West German Länder. It starts out with three years of voluntary kindergarten, followed by the compulsory *Zehnklassenschule* (ten-class school) for ages six to sixteen, and ends with two or three years of *Erweiterte Oberschule* (extended upper school) for the most able students intending to go on to a university. The emphasis of East German education, aside from ideology, is on mathematics and the natural sciences. Its quality and standards are generally high, and the student-teacher ratio is better than in the West. And despite what some outsiders think, the educational system is not intended to separate children from their parents. On the contrary, it tries to bring families closer together by encouraging parental participation in school affairs.

The main purposes of East German education are ideological and economic, to instill in the young the socialist values and maxims of the SED and to prepare them for maximum usefulness to the country's economic development. The ideological component is evident at every stage. It begins in kindergarten, where toddlers are first introduced to the collectivist or communal mode of life characteristic of socialism, and it ends at the universities, where students have to devote part of their studies to *Gesellschaftswissenschaften* (social sciences), a euphemism for the intensive study of dialectical and historical materialism. Ideological indoctrination in the schools takes many forms, from daily discussions of current events and instruction in civics to glorification of communist heroes and celebration of national holidays. Special stress is laid on friendship with the Soviet Union, and learning Russian is compulsory. To ensure strict adherence to the party line, the majority of teachers are members of the SED. Furthermore, education is not limited to the schools, but is supplemented by the extracurricular activities of East Germany's youth organization, the Freie Deutsche Jugend (Free German Youth, or FDJ), to which almost all schoolchildren belong.

On the more strictly academic side, East German education trains the young for the economic role they are best qualified to play in their society. Each school is associated with an industrial *Patenbetrieb* (sponsor company), in which the children spend one day each week. In judging a student's qualifications, especially for a possible leadership position in the future, three criteria are applied: ability, a positive attitude toward the socialist state, and social origin. In the early years of the DDR, social origin was the most important of these criteria, especially for admission to a university. Since then, however, the emphasis has changed. Although children of workers or peasants are still favored over children of equal ability from bourgeois backgrounds, academic standing, or ability, now ranks higher than social class. Class differences, in any case, will gradually become extinct under an egalitarian socialist society. In East Germany, as in the West, only about 10 percent of the eighteen-year-olds can go directly to a university. But alternate routes to gaining a degree are through correspondence courses or adult education. The majority of East German students, after the tenth grade, continue in various vocational or technical schools, commercial or rural academies, or in a number of other special schools, all of which offer opportunities for further advancement. *Weiterbildung* (continuing education) is far more common in the DDR than in West Germany.

How successful has East Germany been in reaching its educational goals? In the technical and scientific area, education in the East is judged superior to that in the West, although superiority is gained at the expense of more liberal and humanistic pursuits. In its ideological indoctrination, on the other hand, East Germany has been less successful. Many of the young share their elders' aversion to the constant propaganda barrage to which they are subjected. With old and young equally critical of the government, there is less of a generation gap than in West Germany or the United States. Honecker, who was at one time chief of the FDJ, has shown some understanding of youthful concerns, and such symbols of youth culture as long hair, rock and roll, and jeans, once frowned upon as "western," are now tolerated. Still, there are frequent reports of restlessness and protests among East German youth, of passive withdrawal from politics or active clashes with the police. This dissatisfaction, it seems, is directed not so much against East Germany's underlying ideology as against the rigid and paternalistic manner in which that ideology is applied by the ruling SED.

Another aspect of East German education has aroused some attention. Beginning in the 1950s, schoolchildren were given instruction in elementary military subjects—map reading, airplane spotting, close-order drill, and such. These activities started at age fourteen and included both boys and girls. Training became more intensive at the upper-school level, where members of the regular army took over as instructors. University students spent several weeks in military camp, and they welcomed this paramilitary training as a change from classroom routine. In 1978 these premilitary activities were intensified, and *Wehrunterricht* (military instruction) is now an integral part of the East German curriculum. Agitation against the western enemies of communism is stressed as the underlying motive for the militarization of East Germany's youth. It is this *Erziehung zum Hass* (education to hate) that has aroused strong opposition from the otherwise quiescent Protestant churches of the DDR, expressed most vehemently in the death by self-immolation of an elderly pastor, Oskar Brüsewitz, as a protest against the state's efforts to teach young people to hate. The incident caused widespread indignation, but it did not seriously alter the government's policy.

The emphasis on military preparedness is part of the German Democratic Republic's general policy of *Abgrenzung* against the dangers of too much *Annäherung* (rapprochement) with West Germany. The dual purpose of East Germany's Nationale Volksarmee (National People's Army, NVA) is to protect the state against attacks from within and without. Among potential foreign enemies, the Federal Republic ranks first. The NVA (army, navy, air force, and border troops) numbers approximately 180,000 men. Since 1962 they have been recruited by conscription for terms of eighteen months. Conscientious objectors do not officially exist but are tolerated on occasion. With its emphasis on discipline and punctuality, the NVA is more reminiscent of Prussian militarism than is its West German counterpart. But the emphasis in the East as in the West, is on technical training in the use of advanced modern weaponry (mostly Russian in this case), rather than on traditional drill. Military training in the NVA is said to be tougher, and the quality of its units somewhat higher, than in the West German Bundeswehr. The East German army proved its readiness for action during the invasion of Czechoslovakia in the summer of 1968, to help restore that country's "socialist gains."

Like every other agency in East Germany, the army is under the firm control of the SED. The minister of defense, General Heinz Hoffmann, is a member of the Politbüro, and virtually all officers are SED members. The party, furthermore, maintains its own branches within the armed forces, and each unit has a special *Politoffizier* in charge of political education. Most officers are of working-class origin, and relations between officers and men are reported to be more democratic than in the old Wehrmacht or even in the Bundeswehr. The NVA is subject to the supreme command of the Warsaw Pact and thus ultimately of the Soviet Union.

The continued presence of Russian troops on East German soil and the proximity of the remaining Soviet forces may explain the smaller size of the NVA as compared to that of the Bundeswehr. There are other military or paramilitary organizations, notably the Volkspolizei (People's Police), which includes some militarized units, and the Kampfgruppen (Fighting Units), which the SED organized in the larger factories after the abortive uprisings of 1953 (see chapter 8). These units are estimated at about 400,000 men and are intended mainly for use against domestic disturbances. The fighting power of this militia is not very great, although its training has been upgraded in recent years. Finally, there is the Gesellschaft für Sport und Technik (Society for Sports and Technics), which engages in paramilitary activities. The East German government, in contrast to its West German rival, is clearly trying to imbue its people with a spirit of military preparedness, but there is no evidence that the majority of East Germans are any more militaristic than their West German brethren. Both Germanies have learned the lessons of the past.

It is difficult for outsiders to imagine what everyday life in the German Democratic Republic is like. Until the early 1960s western accounts of the DDR were mostly negative; since then they have become less one-sided. Some people hope that by stressing the similarities between the two German states, their differences may become fewer. But observers who have known life in East Germany do not share this wishful thinking.

Let us take a brief look first at the way East Germans work. In their collectivist mode of life, their jobs play a more central role in their everyday existence than jobs do elsewhere, because economic mobility is restricted and professional and social activities are often intertwined; one's colleagues are also one's friends. Official slogans emphasize everyone's working for the good of the whole, and some of this propaganda has taken hold. Periodic contests in factories and on farms to work harder toward fulfilling economic norms ahead of schedule have a twofold appeal: they help boost individual income through premiums and prizes, and they further the common good— a combination of egoism and altruism.

The workers' employment is regulated by the Free German Trade Union Federation (Freier Deutscher Gewerkschaftsbund, or FDGB). This large organization, which includes blue- and white-collar workers, concerns itself with wages, hours, working conditions, and other questions on which the worker is heard. But codetermination does not extend to basic economic planning, which is reserved for the Politbüro, nor can workers exert pressure through strikes. The FDGB is thus a labor union in name only. What it *does* provide is absolute job security. To a people accustomed to discipline and hard work, the lack of a few economic freedoms may seem a small price to pay for a guaranteed economic place in a society in which few are rich and none are destitute.

This brings up the question of wages and prices. While it is difficult to make any valid comparisons, the real wage level in the DDR is estimated at about 25 to 30 percent below that in the BRD. Income is more evenly distributed—few people earn more than $1,000 per month, and the lowest welfare rate is $120 per month. Government controls and subsidies maintain the price levels of basic goods and services. In general, prices for staple foods in East Germany are lower, and for luxuries and imports higher than in the West. The cost of household appliances and clothing is almost double, in part due to shortages, which are being gradually overcome. Housing in the East is much cheaper but also more primitive than in the West. Because there was never as great a housing shortage, large-scale construction did not get seriously under way until the 1960s, and much remains to be done. One of the most frequently cited advantages of East Germany is its low rents, which are only about one-quarter of what they are in the West. These savings help to offset the higher cost of consumer goods.

The aim of the East German government is to assure the modest well-being of its people and to care for them in sickness and old age. Health services are excellent, with emphasis as much on prevention as on cure. Despite the heavy exodus of physicians prior to the construction of the Berlin Wall in 1961, the doctor-patient ratio is almost the same in the two Germanies. Virtually the entire population is covered by social insurance, which is free of charge. Old-age pensions are a heavier financial burden in the East, where the percentage of people over sixty-five is higher than in the West. The government urges pensioners to work beyond retirement, and it also permits them to emigrate to West Germany.

One area in which the DDR is considerably more advanced than both West Germany and the United States is women's rights. Women make up almost half of the East German work force, and while few of them hold top-level positions, they all receive equal pay for equal work. In the political sphere the picture is even more impressive compared to the West. About a third of the Volkskammer members are women, and women mayors and judges are common. Abortion has been legalized, and liberal provisions for day-care centers allow mothers to pursue their own careers. Despite these various measures and the easing of divorce, the family continues to play a central role in East German life, probably because it serves as a private refuge from the public demands of a collectivized society.

The constant pressure to work together with one's colleagues or neighbors for the greater glory of socialism makes life trying for many East Germans. There is little escape from this emphasis on togetherness. The information media—press, radio, and television—are state (meaning SED) controlled, with the newspaper *Neues Deutschland* laying down the party line. The resulting news coverage is not only selective and slanted but also extremely dull. Surprisingly, there is no ban on receiving western radio and television broadcasts, although western newspapers and magazines are forbidden. Still, there is more freedom of opinion and expression (oral, not written!) in the DDR than outsiders imagine. As long as the basic aims of the SED state are not attacked, self-criticism is actually encouraged as a means of letting off steam.

When such criticism oversteps certain boundaries, however, the state acts with ruthless repression, as it has done with the dissidents of recent years. Even so, the DDR is not a police state, as Germany was under Hitler, or Russia under Stalin. It is impossible to obtain any reliable information on the number of political prisoners in East Germany. The figure of six thousand has been mentioned, including a thousand young people between the ages of fifteen and twenty. If one includes minor "crimes," such as attempting to leave the country illegally, the number of prisoners becomes much higher. The government's ban on travel to the West is one of the main causes of discontent. East Germans see in it a lack of confidence in their loyalty and an indirect admission that the achievements of the communist East cannot stand comparison with the attractions of the capitalist West.

One of the favorite pastimes of DDR-watchers has been to gauge the support that the East German government enjoys among its people. In 1970 loyal supporters and die-hard opponents were thought to be about equal, with 20 percent in each category. The remaining 60 percent of the population were classified as politically indifferent. Since then it has been estimated that the number of supporters is nearing 30 percent and of opponents declining from 20 percent, leaving the "silent majority" still close to 60 percent.

This gradual shift away from opposition and toward support seems plausible, despite occasional reports of unrest in the DDR. Many of the hard-core opponents by now have left, and the bourgeois element of the population is gradually dying out. The most important component, of course, is the uncommitted majority. Just because these people are not enthusiastic about the present East German system, they should not be classified as opponents of socialism per se. Quite the contrary, most of them are said to be in favor of the "socialist achievements" in education, social security, full employment, and health care. What they do not like is the way their socialist state is run, the SED's didactic and schoolmasterish emphasis on planning and indoctrination. With a more humane regime, an ample supply of consumer goods, and freedom to travel to the West, most members of this silent majority would probably be perfectly content to live in a state where diligence, discipline, and order prevail, where everyone is given their rightful place in society.

One cannot write about the two Germanies without trying to speculate about their future—separately or together. Such speculation, to have any validity, must be free from the wishful thinking that has long dominated the discussion of German affairs. A joint future, or reunification, is clearly out of the question for now and for an unforeseeable time to come. Whether the two German states will continue to drift apart depends on the contacts they maintain or regain. Here the decision lies entirely with the East German government, that is, with the SED. The question is, will Honecker or his successors give the East Germans the *Freizügigkeit* (freedom of movement) they so ardently desire?

The answer must be no. Unless East Germany is prepared to change its system into a less rigid kind of Eurocommunism, the restrictions of *Abgrenzung* must be maintained. Modifying its orthodoxy would constitute an admission of failure and an abdication of power on the part of the ruling SED and would run into forceful opposition from the Soviet Union, as events in Czechoslovakia have shown. The willing dependency of the SED upon its Russian "friends" remains the most important factor in the life of the German Democratic Republic. East Germany's satellite status restricts its contacts not only with West Germany, but with the United States as well. Relations between Washington and East Berlin are merely a function of relations between Washington and Moscow. When Americans speak of Germany, they mean only the West; the East, through its own fault, has been virtually forgotten. Such oblivion is deplorable for both sides.

12 | Conclusion
A "Special Relationship"?

T
HE REMARKABLE IMPROVEMENT in American–West German relations since World War II has been the subject of much discussion and speculation. Until the early 1970s, these relations were usually described as a partnership. Since then the more cordial term friendship has come into use. Most recently one even encounters the expression "special relationship," hitherto reserved for American-British friendship. The labeling of relations between nations is, of course, quite arbitrary. The Germans in particular have always been eager to rank their friends and foes. But while the term *Erbfeind* (hereditary enemy) has virtually disappeared, one is tempted to coin a new term, *Erbfreund* (hereditary friend), to describe how the United States is viewed from Bonn. The question is, how accurately does this verbal escalation of cordiality reflect the true state of American-German relations? Is it really correct to say that the two countries are each other's best friends?

For a close relationship to exist between two nations, three conditions are often seen as essential: (1) common interests, political and economic; (2) identity of basic aims, ideals, and values; and (3) personal acquaintance and empathy between the two peoples. For the relationship to be lasting, moreover, these ties must be firmly rooted in the past. My brief survey of relations between the United States and Germany prior to 1945 and the more detailed account of events since should help us to reach some conclusions about the firmness and stability of American-German friendship.

276

Advocates of that friendship, to provide a historic foundation, have often presented American-German relations during the nineteenth century as far more intimate than they actually were. The two countries did face many similar problems, but they had few common concerns, and even before the turn of the century, they had a number of conflicting interests, especially economic. More important still, in their political traditions and institutions, the United States as the world's most liberal democracy and Imperial Germany as one of Europe's staunchest autocracies, they had little or nothing in common. Close ethnic ties resulted from the several waves of German immigration, but as we have seen, the German-Americans, while contributing much to the growth of their new country, did not serve as the bridge to their old country that one might have expected. There was mutual admiration between Americans and Germans, but there was also mutual condescension. And as international crises became more common before 1914, American opinion frequently sided with Germany's European rivals. On the eve of World War I, America's relationship with Germany was still amicable, but it hardly deserved to be called friendship.

World War I was a major dividing line, a turning point in American-German relations. From playing a merely peripheral role in each other's international affairs, each briefly came to occupy a central position in the other's life. For the United States, Germany's threat to the balance of power overshadowed all other concerns and justified America's departure from traditional isolationism. For Germany the United States emerged as the major obstacle on the road to European hegemony. The brief and relatively unbloody confrontation between the two powers had a curious effect on America's attitude toward Germany: on the one hand, wartime propaganda helped to root the image of the "bad" German—arrogant, militaristic, domineering, and incapable of understanding the blessings of democracy—in the American mind. On the other hand, by joining in the war against Germany, America hoped to correct that image and make Germany "safe for democracy." When the war was over, the United States once again withdrew from its European involvements, but less so from Germany than from the rest of the powers. America's decisive role in causing Germany's defeat seemed to have created a special bond between the two. Not only did American-German relations become more active after World War I, they also became more cordial. It was during the 1920s that the term friendship first became current in both countries to describe that relationship.

In retrospect the decade following World War I appears as

a period of lost opportunities. The Allied failure to help the new Weimar Republic adjust to a lost war may have been shortsighted, but given Germany's past actions and its unwillingness to recognize defeat, it was understandable. The United States can be faulted for not recognizing its opportunity and responsibility to serve as mediator in European affairs. Still, America did more than any other country to help Germany get back on its feet. Without the Great Depression, followed by the rise of Hitler, relations between the two countries might have become still closer, and democracy might have taken a firm hold in Germany. Some Germans and Americans at the time thought that it had and that a community of ideals and values already existed between the two countries, but the rousing victory of Hitler showed they were wrong.

The Nazi years undid whatever progress toward American-German understanding had been made during the 1920s. By the time war came around in 1939, Germany's reputation in the United States had sunk to an all-time low. Everything bad that had ever been said about the Germans, individually and as a nation, suddenly seemed to be borne out by events in central Europe. There were still some Americans who tried to distinguish between Germans and Nazis, but their number became smaller as the threat of Nazism increased. Many Germans today do not realize the depth of contempt in which their nation was held, not only in the countries invaded by Germany but in the distant United States, *especially* there, where so many of Hitler's opponents and potential victims found asylum. It was because of these refugees that the hatred of Nazi Germany did not turn into a blanket indictment of all things German. Still, the Germanophobia of World War II, reinforced by the gruesome discoveries of Nazi atrocities at the end of the war, had become too deeply ingrained to be soon, if ever, forgotten.

The year 1945 for Germany, as for American-German relations, was a *Nullpunkt* (point zero). To present the gradual change since then, from hostility via détente to partnership and friendship, as a continuation of earlier trends going back to the nineteenth century would clearly be wrong. Comforting as it may be to some Germans and Americans to speak of hereditary or eternal friendship between their two countries, history has shown otherwise. It is the differences rather than the similarities between American-German relations before and after 1945 that make their study so interesting and rewarding. At the same time, the vacillation of relations in the past should caution us against taking the present stability too much for granted. Relations between nations are unpredictable and volatile, and terms like eternal friendship or special relationship are more readily used by politicians than by historians.

The most dramatic change in American-German relations after 1945 took place during the first ten years, when West Germany changed from adversary to ally, from pariah to partner. The most important factor in bringing about this change was the Allied need for German help against the rising threat of communism. The resulting rapprochement owed more to cold war pressures than to American planning, and ever since, common interests have been the most important ingredient in the American-German relationship.

The second ingredient essential to close relations between nations, identity of basic values and ideas, was slower to assert itself, for concern over the survival or revival of Nazism continued to cast a shadow over West Germany's rapid recovery. Had it not been for the trust inspired by the stalwart figure of Konrad Adenauer, such concern might have prevented Germany's integration into the western community. Even so, there remained some doubts about the sincerity of West Germany's conversion to democracy.

A third element making for improved relations was the greatly increased personal contacts between Americans and Germans after World War II. Public opinion plays an important role in international affairs, especially among democracies. Its temper is difficult to measure, but without grass-roots support, foreign policy operates in a vacuum. At no time in their history have so many Americans and Germans been able to form an opinion about each other through personal experience. As long as the resulting impressions of each other were favorable, American-German relations profited greatly from this mutual acquaintance.

Relations between Washington and Bonn during the past thirty years have gone through several phases. Until the mid-sixties, West Germany was clearly a junior partner, not to say satellite, of the United States. Since then the relationship has become increasingly more equal, even though America's military strength and economic potential continue to outweigh those of West Germany. The reasons for this trend toward a more balanced partnership were the relative decline of American superiority and the simultaneous increase of West German influence within the western world. As Germany emerged the de facto leader of the European Community and, together with Japan, became a powerful factor on the world market, a more independent or even self-assertive stand on international issues was only natural. This changing balance could not help causing occasional misunderstandings. The United States, long used to having its way, found it difficult at first to adjust to the new situation. West Germany's leaders, on the other hand, obviously valued their close relations with the United States, so they tried to understand and reach compromises with their American partners. This spirit of accommodation was rarely found in German history before 1945.

This last statement again raises the question of whether Germany has really changed since World War II, whether it has really become democratic, whether it actually adheres to the same basic values as the United States. Community of ideals, as we have said, is the sine qua non for any lasting friendship. Some people, including Germans, continue to feel uneasy about this subject. The majority of Americans, however, seem ready to believe that West Germany by now has been made safe for democracy, not by outside pressure but by the willing acceptance of the Germans themselves. If there are still occasional incidents of neo-Nazism or anti-Semitism, they cause as much concern in Germany as elsewhere. A vigilant government aided by a responsible press keeps a watchful eye for any signs of radicalism by either right or left. One reason for the firm hold that democracy has taken, it is often said, has been the favorable economic climate in which it has grown. One can only guess at the viability of West German democracy in time of major economic crisis, but even for such an eventuality, the prognoses are optimistic.

With similar aims and values and with more personal contacts than ever before, American-German relations in the late 1970s continue to seem stable and close. Whether that stability will last depends on the continued congruity of American and German interests. And here the outlook is no longer as clear and simple as it was in the fifties and sixties.

Similarity of interests is most evident in the military field. The United States and Germany are the closest and most important of the NATO allies; without the participation of both, that alliance would collapse. Because the Germans are situated in the direct path of possible communist aggression, they are thought to be the prime beneficiaries of American military aid. But given the mobility of modern warfare, the rest of Europe is hardly in less danger than West Germany. The Germans, therefore, resent the occasional veiled threats by critics in Washington that American forces might be withdrawn unless Germany contributes more to their support. The possibility of American withdrawal, furthermore, injects a note of uncertainty into American-German relations, despite lip service on both sides to the stability of these relations.

The underlying cause of U.S.-German military collaboration, of course, has been common fear of and opposition to communism.

Anticommunism drew the two countries together in the first place and continues to be their strongest bond. With the advent of détente, however, and with growing signs of friction within the communist camp, especially between the Soviet Union and China, the fear of communism has diminished. And while the Germans are worried that détente might weaken American military readiness vis-à-vis the Soviet Union, Americans fear that Bonn and Moscow might draw closer together. The memory of Rapallo has never quite disappeared (see chapter 4), and there are still Germans who see their country's role as a bridge between East and West. More disturbing to the United States than German-Russian rapprochement is the possibility of "Finlandization," that is, the neutralization of West Germany and the rest of Western Europe and the emergence of a socialist Europe from the Atlantic to the Urals. To the Germans, Finlandization might bring about the reunification of the two German states, a development that would hardly be welcomed by Germany's neighbors or by the Soviet Union.

As these speculations show, the lineup of powers in the era of détente has become less rigid than it was in the days of the cold war. As a result, American-German relations under Carter and Schmidt are more ambiguous than they were under Eisenhower and Adenauer. Even then, West Germany was a member of two communities, Atlantic and European, although the close relations between Bonn and Washington never left any doubt where Germany's prime allegiance lay. With the decline of American preponderance in the Atlantic Community, however, and the rise of West Germany to pre-eminence in the European Community, Germany today enjoys more international options than does the United States. The term special relationship might as easily be applied to the entente between Bonn and Paris as to the partnership between Bonn and Washington.

The uncertainty, or fluidity, that has replaced stability in American-German military and political relations is also found in the economic sphere. Prior to 1945 the two countries were more often economic rivals than partners. Since then, American and German economic aims and policies, their belief in free enterprise and opposition to protectionism, have been virtually identical. America's and Germany's economies are complementary in many ways and closely intertwined. Although the United States, because of its size, natural wealth, and advanced technology, clearly holds the edge, West Germany in one generation has risen from abject poverty to assured affluence and has become America's leading partner in Europe. Germany's dominant role within the European Community further raises its standing vis-à-vis the United States and increases the chances for possible future rivalries between the two, both in Europe and in the third world. As long as the creeping economic crisis of the 1970s continues, competition rather than cooperation may become the keynote of American-German economic relations.

If I have dwelled here on the differences that have arisen in recent years and that may arise in the future between the United States and Germany, my intention is not to detract from the close ties that have developed between the two countries since 1945. It is rare that relations between nations are wholly harmonious and stable, and to ignore their negative aspects may lead to disappointments, which in turn may cause distrust. Given the numerous changes in governments over the past thirty years, the steadiness and reasonableness that has characterized American-German relations is a credit to both sides. Whether the relationship has been a matter of the head or of the heart, a marriage of convenience or a love match— on this, observers may differ. To categorize it as a special relationship certainly would be too restrictive. The Germans, in their desire to monopolize America's friendship, sometimes forget that Americans have come from, and feel a responsibility toward, other parts of Europe as well. Both Germans and Americans would do well to heed the words of Willy Brandt on the thirtieth anniversary of the Marshall Plan:

> In my opinion, the European responsibility of the United States, our own orientation and a permanent relationship of trust between the United States and the Federal Republic of Germany are part of the basic law of our ordered peace. It is the awareness of mutual dependence; it is the obligation to be considerate and forbearing; it is the will to listen to each other and not to rebuke, in which we remember this basic law.

Suggested Reading
Index

Suggested Reading

The following is a selective list of works in English that have proved particularly useful in writing this book. A large number of titles in German, as well as numerous journal articles, had to be omitted for lack of space. The suggestions are arranged under chapter headings, but many of them cut across several chapters. Most of the books have bibliographies.

Introduction

There is no satisfactory general work covering the whole range of American-German relations. Thomas Piltz, ed., *Two Hundred Years of German-American Relations, 1776–1976* (Munich, 1975), a bilingual coffee-table book produced for the Bicentennial, is beautifully illustrated but otherwise disappointing. The same holds true for Joachim H. Schwelien, *Encounter and Encouragement: A Bicentennial Review of German-American Relations* (Bonn, 1976), a brief survey by a German journalist. The most thoughtful history of Germany proper for the period is Golo Mann, *The History of Germany since 1789* (New York, 1968). Two other good treatments that complement each other are Agatha Ramm, *Germany 1789–1919: A Political History* (London, 1967), and A. J. Ryder, *Twentieth-Century Germany: From Bismarck to Brandt* (New York, 1973). Like no other country, Germany has been the object of sweeping analyses and efforts to determine what has made Germans different from other peoples. Two suggestive recent books on the German Problem are one by a German sociologist, Ralf Dahrendorf, *Society and Democracy in Germany* (Garden City, N.Y., 1967), and one by an American political scientist, David Calleo, *The German Problem Reconsidered: Germany and the World Order, 1870 to the Present* (New York, 1978). It should be noted that the German author is far harsher toward his compatriots than is his American colleague—times have changed indeed.

1 Germany: The Land and the People

Because Germany has changed more drastically over the past thirty years than any other western European country, it is difficult to find even recent

284

books dealing with German society that are not in need of some revision. The land, on the other hand, has changed much less than the people, and Robert E. Dickinson's admirably comprehensive *Germany: A General and Regional Geography* (New York, 1953) remains a standard work. See also E. H. Mellor, *The Two Germanies: A Modern Geography* (New York, 1978). As a general introduction to present-day Germany, Alfred Grosser, *Germany in Our Time: A Political History of the Post-War Years* (New York, 1973), by a German-born French political scientist, is critical but sympathetic. The same holds true of the entertaining book by Rudolf Walter Leonhardt, *This Germany: The Story since the Third Reich* (New York, 1964), which deals more with everyday life. The most up-to-date information on West Germany can be found in the various official and semi-official publications distributed by the German Information Center (410 Park Avenue, New York, N.Y. 10022). While it is interested in projecting a favorable image, its materials are nevertheless quite objective. Of special interest are two periodically revised publications: Federal Republic of Germany, *Germany—Facts and Figures about the Two German States: A Comparative Study,* and *Meet Germany,* a well-illustrated collection of articles by various specialists on every aspect of life in contemporary Germany. The latter is published by the Atlantik-Brücke, a nonpartisan group dedicated to furthering understanding between Germany and the United States.

Books on present-day East Germany include Hanns Werner Schwarze, *The GDR Today: Life in the "Other Germany"* (London, 1973); Hans Axel Holm, *The Other Germans: Report from an East German Town* (New York, 1970); and John Dornberg, *The Two Germanys* (New York, 1974). The last author has also recorded his views on today's Germans in *The New Germans: Thirty Years After* (New York, 1976). There are a number of such books, usually giving their authors' individual impressions, such as the critical report by an Israeli journalist, Amos Elon, *Journey through a Haunted Land: The New Germany* (New York, 1967), and the favorable and informative book by Adolph Schalk, *The Germans* (Englewood Cliffs, N.J., 1971). The large number of books on contemporary Germany may be a sign of increased American interest in that country. The same holds true for various writings dealing with everyday German life: Reginald Peck, *The West Germans: How They Live and Work* (New York, 1969); Robin Sawers, *Life in a West German Town* (London, 1974); and Jürgen Neven-DuMont, *After Hitler: A Report on Today's West Germans* (New York, 1970).

German folklore is the subject of Dietrich Kramer, *German Holidays and Folk Customs* (Hamburg, 1972), and Richard Thonger, *A Calendar of German Customs* (London, 1966). George D. Spindler et al., *Burgbach: Urbanization and Identity in a German Village* (New York, 1973), is a case study in cultural anthropology. The influence of English on the German language since World War II is examined in Werner F. Leopold, *English Influence on Postwar German* (Lincoln, Nebr., 1967). I discuss in later chapters of this book the German universities, the army, the churches, and other institutions, each of which is also discussed in the general works already mentioned.

The following are a few specialized studies: Gerhard Hess, *Universities in Germany, 1930–1970* (Bad Godesberg, 1968); Arthur Haernden, *Education in the Two Germanies* (Boulder, Colo., 1976); Walter Henry Nelson, *Germany Rearmed* (New York, 1972); and Frederic Spotts, *The Churches and Politics in Germany* (Middletown, Conn., 1973). On everyday life in East Germany, compare the depressing eyewitness reports by two Americans—Joseph Wechsberg, *Journey through the Land of Eloquent Silence* (Boston, 1964), and Steven Kelman, *Behind the Berlin Wall: An Encounter in East Germany* (Boston, 1972)—with the more positive account by Jean Edward Smith, *Germany beyond the Wall: People, Politics ... and Prosperity* (Bonn, 1969). The question of German *Nationalgefühl* is treated in Gebhard L. Schweigler, *National Consciousness in Divided Germany* (Beverly Hills, Calif., 1975).

2 GERMANY AND THE UNITED STATES, 1776–1914

There are no general books in English on American-German relations for the early nineteenth century, and for the later years the situation is not much better. The study by a German historian, Count Otto zu Stolberg-Wernigerode, *Germany and the United States of America during the Era of Bismarck* (Reading, Pa., 1937) is based on some German and American documents. Jeannette Keim, *Forty Years of German-American Relations* (Philadelphia, 1919) does not go much below the surface of events. Clara Eve Schieber, *The Transformation of American Sentiment toward Germany, 1870–1914* (Boston, 1923), is a traditional public-opinion study. For the earlier period, there are some good works on cultural and intellectual relations. Henry A. Pochmann, *German Culture in America: Philosophical and Literary Influences, 1600–1900* (Madison, Wis., 1957), presents a comprehensive survey. Horst Dippel, *Germany and the American Revolution, 1770–1800* (Wiesbaden, 1978), deals with political thinking on both sides of the Atlantic, and Carl Diehl, *Americans and German Scholarship, 1770–1870* (New Haven, 1978), throws new light on German academic influences in the United States. Paul C. Weber, *America in Imaginative German Literature* (New York, 1926), presents the United States through German eyes. Much useful information can also be gained from the biographies of noted Americans of German origin, such as John M. Palmer, *General von Steuben* (New Haven, 1937); Carl Wittke, *Against the Current: The Life of Karl Heinzen 1809–80* (Chicago, 1945); and Claude M. Fuess, *Carl Schurz, Reformer* (New York, 1932). For biographical references to other figures, see Dieter Cunz, *They Came from Germany* (New York, 1966). Joseph G. Rosengarten, *The German Soldier in the Wars of the United States* (Philadelphia, 1886), evaluates the contributions of German-Americans in the Revolutionary and Civil wars.

In contrast to the sparse literature on American-German relations, there is an abundance of writings on the German element in the United States. Most of these books have appeared since 1945, but all of them owe a considerable debt to the basic text by Albert B. Faust, *The German Element in the United States*, 2 vols. (Boston, 1909), which might be called the bible of German-American studies. Among the more recent studies, the following stand out: John A. Hawgood, *The Tragedy of German-America* (New York, 1940); Richard O'Connor, *The German-Americans: An Informal History* (Boston, 1968); and La Vern J. Rippley, *The German-Americans* (Boston, 1976). Robert H. Billigmeier, *Americans from Germany: A Study in Cultural Diversity* (Belmont, Calif., 1974), deals with the transformation of German immigrants into Americans. The best book on the German migration itself is Mack Walker's *Germany and the Emigration, 1816–1885* (Cambridge, Mass., 1964). Of the different waves of German immigrants, the Forty-Eighters have aroused the most interest. Carl Wittke, *Refugees of Revolution: The German Forty-Eighters in America* (Philadelphia, 1952), is by a leading American authority on the history of German-Americans. See also A. E. Zucker, *The Forty-Eighters* (New York, 1950).

Turning to the history of Germany during the nineteenth century, there are a number of good studies in English. On the period before 1871, the two books by Theodore S. Hamerow, *Restoration, Revolution, Reaction: Economics and Politics in Germany, 1815–1871* (Princeton, 1958), and *The Social Foundations of German Unification 1858–1871: Ideas and Institutions* (Princeton, 1969), deal primarily with domestic affairs. The diplomatic and military aspects of German unification are treated authoritatively in Otto Pflanze, *Bismarck and the Development of Germany: The Period of Unification, 1815–1871* (Princeton, 1963). The most recent biography of Bismarck is Alan Palmer, *Bismarck* (London, 1976). Walter M. Simon, *Germany in the Age of Bismarck* (London, 1968), is a good brief introduction. On Bismarck's foreign policy, William L. Langer, *European Alliances and Alignments*, 2nd ed. (New York, 1950), is a standard work. The definitive biography of William II remains to be written. Michael Balfour, *The Kaiser and His Times* (London, 1964), is readable but breaks no new ground. On the domestic policy of Wilhelmian Germany, Arthur Rosenberg, *Imperial Germany: The Birth of the German Republic 1871–1918* (Boston, 1964), a pioneering work by a German scholar, first published in 1928, is still the best general introduction. See also Alexander Gerschenkron, *Bread and Democracy in Germany* (New York, 1943). Both authors consider the agrarian-industrial alliance as the root cause of Germany's ills. Thorstein Veblen, *Imperial Germany and the Industrial Revolution*, new ed. (New York, 1939), is a classic. Volker R. Berghahn, *Germany and the Approach of War in 1914* (London, 1973), stresses the domestic roots of German foreign policy on the eve of World War I. Fritz Fischer, in *The War of Illusions* (New York, 1975), elaborates his thesis of Germany's major responsibility for the war. On American-British relations and their effect on Germany, see Bradford Perkins, *The Great Rapprochement: England and the United States, 1895–1914* (New York, 1968). There is no comparable study for Germany. For a brief resumé of American-German relations at the outbreak of World War I, see Hans W. Gatzke, "The United States and Germany on the Eve of World War I," in *Deutschland in der Weltpolitik des 19. und 20. Jahrhunderts: Fritz Fischer zum 65. Geburtstag,* eds. Imanuel Geiss and Bernd Jürgen Wendt, rev. ed. (Düsseldorf, 1974), pp. 271–286.

3 World War I: A Turning Point, 1914–1918

The controversy touched off by Fritz Fischer's writings on Germany's war aims and responsibility for World War I has been summarized in John A. Moses, *The Politics of Illusion: The Fischer Revolution in German Historiography* (New York, 1975). For the German historian's reply to his critics, see Fritz Fischer, *World Power or Decline: The Controversy over Germany's Aims in the First World War* (New York, 1974). The books by Hans W. Gatzke, *Germany's Drive to the West: A Study of Germany's Western War Aims during the First World War* (Baltimore, 1950), and Henry Cord Meyer, *Mitteleuropa in German Thought and Action, 1815–1945* (The Hague, 1955), are both pioneering works. The career of Germany's wartime chancellor is treated sympathetically in Konrad H. Jarausch, *The Enigmatic Chancellor: Bethmann Hollweg and the Hubris of Imperial Germany* (New Haven, 1973). His military counterparts are the subject of Martin Kitchen, *The Silent Dictatorship: The Politics of the German High Command under Hindenburg and Ludendorff, 1916–1918* (New York, 1977). See also Gerald D. Feldman, *Army, Industry, and Labor in Germany, 1914–1918* (Princeton, 1966). The best study on the German element in the United States during the war is Frederick C. Luebke, *Bonds of Loyalty: German-Americans and the World War* (De Kalb, Ill., 1974). Carl Wittke, *German-Americans and the World War* (Columbus, Ohio, 1936), deals mostly with Ohio. See also Niel M. Johnson, *George Sylvester Viereck: German-American Propagandist* (Urbana, Ill., 1972). The memoirs of Germany's ambassador in Washington, Johann Heinrich Graf von Bernstorff, *My Three Years in America* (New York, 1920), compare favorably with those of the American ambassador in Berlin, James W. Gerard, *My Four Years in Germany* (New York, 1917).

Like the origins of all modern wars, the causes of America's intervention in World War I have been the subject of a large body of "revisionist" literature, of which C. Hartley Grattan, *Why We Fought* (New York, 1929) was the first example, and Charles C. Tansill, *America Goes to War* (Boston, 1938), the most impressive. The best and most judicious book on the subject is Ernest R. May, *The World War and American Isolation 1914–1917* (Cambridge, Mass., 1959). Ross Gregory, *The Origins of American Intervention in the First World War* (New York, 1971), is a good brief summary. The literature on Woodrow Wilson is vast. The most solid work has been done by America's leading Wilson scholar, Arthur S. Link: *Woodrow Wilson and the Progressive Era, 1910–1917* (New York, 1954); *Wilson the Diplomatist: A Look at His Foreign Policies* (Baltimore, 1957); and *Wilson: The Struggle for Neutrality* (Princeton, 1960). John M. Blum, *Woodrow Wilson and the Politics of Morality* (Boston, 1956) is a very good short introduction. The immediate sequence of events leading to the outbreak of war between the United States and Germany has been studied by Karl E. Birnbaum, *Peace Moves and U-Boat Warfare: A Study of Im-*

perial Germany's Policy towards the United States, April 18, 1916–Jan. 9, 1917 (Stockholm, 1958). See also Lancelot L. Farrar, Jr., *Divide and Conquer: German Efforts to Conclude a Separate Peace, 1914–1918* (New York, 1978), and Maurice Prendergast and R. H. Gibson, *The German Submarine War, 1914–1918* (New York, 1931). On other causes of the American-German confrontation, see Henry Landau, *The Enemy Within: The Inside Story of German Sabotage in America* (New York, 1937); H. C. Peterson, *Propaganda for War: The Campaign against American Neutrality, 1914–1917* (Norman, Okla., 1939); and Barbara Tuchman, *The Zimmermann Telegram* (New York, 1958). Germany's last all-out military effort is treated in Joseph Gies, *Crisis 1918: The Leading Actors, Strategies and Events in the German Gamble for Total Victory on the Western Front* (New York, 1974). On Germany's peace treaty with Russia, John W. Wheeler-Bennett, *Brest-Litovsk: The Forgotten Peace, March 1918* (London, 1938), is still the best.

The end of the war has been dramatically, though not always accurately, described by Richard M. Watt, *The Kings Depart—The Tragedy of Germany: Versailles and the German Revolution* (New York, 1968). America's thoughts about the future of Central Europe are the subject of Victor Mamatey, *The United States and East Central Europe 1914–1918* (Princeton, 1957), and David F. Trask, *The United States in the Supreme War Council: American War Aims and Inter-Allied Strategy, 1917–1918* (Middletown, Conn., 1961). Arno Mayer, *Political Origins of the New Diplomacy 1917–1918* (New Haven, 1959) puts Wilson's Fourteen Points in historical perspective. See also Lawrence E. Gelfand, *The Inquiry: American Preparations for Peace, 1917–1919* (New Haven, 1963), and Arthur Walworth, *America's Moment: 1918* (New York, 1977). The curtain on the war is lowered in Harry R. Rudin, *Armistice 1918* (New Haven, 1944).

4 THE WEIMAR REPUBLIC: A DEMOCRATIC INTERLUDE, 1918–1933

The standard general history of the Weimar Republic is Erich Eyck, *A History of the Weimar Republic*, 2 vols. (Cambridge, Mass., 1962). S. William Halperin, *Germany Tried Democracy: A Political History of the Reich from 1918 to 1933* (New York, 1946) is an adequate survey, and Hugh Quigley and R. T. Clark, *Republican Germany: A Political and Economic Study* (London, 1928) is still useful. Among writings in English on the German revolution, A. J. Ryder, *The German Revolution of 1918* (Cambridge, England, 1967), is good, though uninspired. The army's counterrevolutionary activities are treated in Robert G. L. Waite, *Vanguard of Nazism: The Free Corps Movement in Postwar Germany 1918–1923* (Cambridge, Mass., 1952). On the army's influence through the remaining years of the republic, see F. L. Carsten, *The Reichswehr and Politics, 1918 to 1933* (Oxford, 1966). Among the many books on the Paris Peace Conference, Arno J. Mayer's monumental *Politics and Diplomacy of Peacemaking. Containment and Counterrevolution at Versailles* (New York, 1967) stands out. George Goldberg, *The Peace to End Peace: The Paris Peace Conference of 1919* (New York, 1969), is a brief popularized account. The eyewitness story by Harold Nicolson, *Peacemaking 1919* (New York, 1933), is a classic. The best evaluation of the Treaty of Versailles is still Paul Birdsall, *Versailles Twenty Years After* (New York, 1941). Étienne Mantoux, *The Carthaginian Peace, or the Economic Consequences of Mr. Keynes* (London, 1946), is a reply to Keynes's earlier indictment of the peace settlement.

American foreign policy in the interwar period is treated by Selig Adler, *The Uncertain Giant: American Foreign Policy between the Wars, 1921–1941* (New York, 1966). Sidney Brooks, *America and Germany, 1918–1925* (New York, 1925), is out of date. Keith L. Nelson, *Victors Divided: America and the Allies in Germany, 1918–1923* (Berkeley, Calif., 1975) is an important contribution. On America's economic and financial involvement in Europe and Germany, see: Herbert Feis, *The Diplomacy of the Dollar, 1919–1932* (New York, 1966); Joan Hoff Wilson, *American Business and Foreign Policy, 1920–1933* (Lexington, Ky., 1971); and Derek H. Aldcroft, *From Versailles to Wall Street: The International Economy in the 1920's* (Berkeley, Calif., 1976). Two recent studies deal with the early postwar crises culminating in the French occupation of the Ruhr and the subsequent adoption of the Dawes Plan: Walter A. McDougall, *France's Rhineland Diplomacy, 1919–1924: The Last Bid for a Balance of Power in Europe* (Princeton, 1978), and Stephen A. Schuker, *The End of French Predominance in Europe: The Financial Crisis of 1924 and the Adoption of the Dawes Plan* (Chapel Hill, N.C., 1976). The latter in particular stresses America's involvement in Europe's economic problems. Germany's relations with Russia before and after Rapallo are effectively presented in Gerald Freund, *Unholy Alliance: Russo-German Relations from the Treaty of Brest-Litovsk to the Treaty of Berlin* (New York, 1957). The best recent study in English on the Locarno era is Jon Jacobsen, *Locarno Diplomacy: Germany and the West 1925–1929* (Princeton, 1972). The career of Gustav Stresemann during the Weimar Republic is examined by Hans W. Gatzke, *Stresemann and the Rearmament of Germany* (Baltimore, 1954), and Henry A. Turner, *Stresemann and the Politics of the Weimar Republic* (Princeton, 1963). The latter emphasizes Stresemann's role in domestic politics. Hindenburg's fateful influence is the subject of a critical but fair assessment by Andreas Dorpalen, *Hindenburg and the Weimar Republic* (Princeton, 1964). One of the few occasions of American involvement in European political affairs during the 1920s is treated in Robert H. Ferrell, *Peace in Their Time: The Origins of the Kellogg-Briand Pact* (New Haven, 1952). The book by James W. Angell, *The Recovery of Germany*, rev. ed. (New Haven, 1932), is interesting for the optimism of its author, a noted American economist, in the midst of the depression. The best book on the cultural flowering during the Weimar period is Peter Gay, *Weimar Culture* (New York, 1968); see also Walter Laqueur, *Weimar: A Cultural History, 1918–1933* (New York, 1975).

There are some good diplomatic studies on the period just before Hitler came to power. Robert H. Ferrell, *American Diplomacy in the Great Depression: Hoover-Stimson Foreign Policy, 1929–1933* (New Haven, 1957),

tells the American story. The major problems facing statesmen at the time
—reparations and disarmament—are analyzed in two superb studies by
Edward W. Bennett, *Germany and the Diplomacy of the Financial Crisis,*
1931 (Cambridge, Mass., 1962), and *German Rearmament and the West,*
1932–1933 (Princeton, 1979). Most of the key figures in Germany at the
time, including Brüning, still await their biographers. John A. Leopold,
Alfred Hugenberg: The Radical Nationalist Campaign against the Weimar
Republic (New Haven, 1977), throws interesting new light on one of the
major gravediggers of the republic. There are numerous accounts, mostly
in German, of the final agony of Weimar. Arnold Brecht, *Prelude to Si-*
lence: The End of the German Republic (New York, 1944), deserves special mention; the author was a high Prussian civil servant who lived through
the period before leaving Germany in 1933. Another contemporary view
is by Edgar Ansel Mowrer, *Germany Puts the Clock Back* (New York, 1933),
an eyewitness account by a noted American journalist who had to leave
Germany as a result of his book.

5   HITLER AND THE "THIRD REICH," 1933–1939

The number of books on Hitler by now runs into the thousands, and more
are appearing almost daily. One of the earliest biographies, Alan Bullock's
Hitler: A Study in Tyranny, rev. ed. (New York, 1962), is still one of the
best. Another excellent book is Joachim C. Fest, *Hitler* (New York, 1974),
which takes into account more recent research. The best general study of
the Nazi years is Karl Dietrich Bracher, *The German Dictatorship* (New
York, 1970). William L. Shirer, *The Rise and Fall of the Third Reich: A*
History of Nazi Germany (New York, 1959), has been criticized for some of
its interpretations but is still a gold mine of information. See also the same
author's *Berlin Diary: The Journal of a Foreign Correspondent, 1934–1941*
(New York, 1941). The final stage of Hitler's rise is seen from the grass roots
by William S. Allen, *The Nazi Seizure of Power: The Experience of a*
Single German Town 1930–1935 (Chicago, 1965). Other good introductions
to life in Nazi Germany are David Schoenbaum, *Hitler's Social Revolution:*
Class and Status in Nazi Germany 1933–1939 (Garden City, N.Y., 1966), and
Joachim Remak, ed., *The Nazi Years: A Documentary History* (Englewood
Cliffs, N.J., 1969). The best books on the völkisch ideology are Fritz Stern,
The Politics of Cultural Despair (Garden City, N.Y., 1965), and Klemens
von Klemperer, *Germany's New Conservatism: Its History and Dilemma in*
the Twentieth Century (Princeton, 1957). German anti-Semitism during the
1930s is treated in Karl A. Schleunes, *The Twisted Road to Auschwitz: Nazi*
Policy toward German Jews 1933–1939 (Urbana, Ill., 1970). On the back-
ground and causes of anti-Semitism in Germany, see Eva G. Reichmann,
Hostages of Civilization: The Social Causes of Anti-Semitism in Germany
(Boston, 1951), and George L. Mosse, *Germans and Jews: The Right, the*
Left, and the Search for a "Third Force" in Pre-Nazi Germany (New York,
1970).

In contrast to earlier periods, relations between the United States
and Germany during the Nazi years have been the subject of several good

books. Arnold A. Offner, *American Appeasement. United States Foreign Policy and Germany, 1933–1938* (Cambridge, Mass., 1969) is critical of American policy; Alton Frye, *Nazi Germany and the American Hemisphere 1933–1941* (New Haven, 1967), deals also with Latin America; and James V. Compton, *The Swastika and the Eagle: Hitler, the United States, and the Origins of World War II* (Boston, 1967), discusses U.S.-German relations as seen from Berlin. The papers of America's ambassadors to Germany during the 1930s have been published by their children: William E. Dodd, Jr., and Martha Dodd, *Ambassador Dodd's Diary, 1933–1938* (New York, 1941); and Hugh R. Wilson, Jr., ed., *Hugh R. Wilson, A Career Diplomat, the Third Chapter: The Third Reich* (New York, 1960). See also Robert Dallek, *Democrat and Diplomat: The Life of William E. Dodd* (New York, 1968). There are no comparable books on Germany's ambassadors to the United States. On the machinations of Hjalmar Schacht, his own account, *Confessions of "the Old Wizard"* (Boston, 1956), must be read in conjunction with Edward N. Peterson, *Hjalmar Schacht: For and against Hitler* (Boston, 1954), and Amos E. Simpson, *Hjalmar Schacht in Perspective* (The Hague, 1969).

Several books have been written on German attempts to export Nazism to the United States, the best of which is Sander A. Diamond, *The Nazi Movement in the United States, 1924–1941* (Ithaca, N.Y., 1974). On Nazi propaganda activities in America, see Arthur L. Smith, Jr., *The Deutschtum of Nazi Germany and the United States* (The Hague, 1965); O. John Rogge, *The Official German Report* (New York, 1961); and Donald M. McKale, *The Swastika outside Germany* (Kent, Ohio, 1977). The other side of the coin, the contributions of anti-Nazi German refugees to American life and culture, have also been frequently recorded, sometimes as part of a larger story, as in Laura Fermi, *Illustrious Immigrants: The Intellectual Migration from Europe 1930–1941* (Chicago, 1968), and Donald Fleming and Bernard Bailyn, eds., *The Intellectual Migration, Europe and America, 1930–1960* (Cambridge, Mass., 1969); and sometimes as in the United States alone, as in Donald P. Kent, *The Refugee Intellectual: The Americanization of the Immigrants of 1933–1941* (New York, 1953); Eric E. Hirshler, *Jews from Germany in the United States* (New York, 1955); and Robert E. Cazden, *German Exile Literature in America, 1933–1950* (Chicago, 1970).

The debate on Hitler's foreign policy and its aims, touched off by A.J.P. Taylor's *Origins of the Second World War* (London, 1961), has been ably summarized in Wm. Roger Louis, ed., *The Origins of the Second World War: A.J.P. Taylor and His Critics* (New York, 1972). One of the best brief analyses of Hitler's plans and policies is Klaus Hildebrand, *The Foreign Policy of the Third Reich* (Berkeley, Calif., 1973). The most authoritative treatment of the early years of Nazi foreign policy is Gerhard L. Weinberg, *The Foreign Policy of Hitler's Germany: Diplomatic Revolution in Europe, 1933–36* (Chicago, 1970), which is to be followed by a second volume on the later period. The best brief account on the major steps to war is still Christopher Thorne, *The Approach of War, 1938–1939* (London, 1967).

William R. Rock, *British Appeasement in the 1930's* (New York, 1977), is an excellent brief assessment of that elusive subject. Other noteworthy recent books on British policy are Maurice Cowling, *The Impact of Hitler: British Politics and British Policy, 1933–1940* (Chicago, 1977); Sidney Aster, *1939: The Making of the Second World War* (New York, 1973); Keith Middlemas, *Diplomacy of Illusion: The British Government and Germany, 1937–1939* (London, 1972); and Corelli Barnett, *The Collapse of British Power* (London, 1972). On France, see Anthony Adamthwaite, *France and the Coming of the Second World War* (London, 1977); and Robert J. Young, *In Command of France: French Foreign Policy and Military Planning, 1933–1940* (Cambridge, Mass., 1978). The literature on the German resistance to Hitler before and during World War II is extensive, and more is yet to come. The best and most comprehensive study thus far is the massive volume by Peter Hoffman, *The History of German Resistance, 1933–1945* (Cambridge, Mass., 1976). Briefer, less scholarly, but more readable is the sympathetic account by a noted British journalist and authority on Germany, Terence Prittie, *Germans against Hitler* (Boston, 1964).

6 WORLD WAR II: THE END OF THE GERMAN REICH, 1939–1945

A good brief history of World War II, with an excellent bibliography, is Gordon Wright, *The Ordeal of Total War 1939–1945* (New York, 1968). John Lukacs, *The Last European War, September 1939–December 1941* (Garden City, N.Y., 1976), deals brilliantly with the early phase, before America's and Japan's entry converted the war into a world conflict. On German-Italian relations, see Elizabeth Wiskemann, *The Rome-Berlin Axis*, rev. ed. (London, 1966), and F. W. Deakin, *The Brutal Friendship* (New York, 1962). The short-lived German-Soviet alliance and Hitler's decision to invade Russia are treated in Gerhard L. Weinberg, *Germany and the Soviet Union 1939–1941* (Leiden, 1954). America's entry into the war is most comprehensively covered in the two-volume study by William L. Langer and S. Everett Gleason, *The Challenge to Isolation, 1937–1940* (New York, 1952), and *The Undeclared War, 1940–1941* (New York, 1953). Robert A. Divine, *The Reluctant Belligerent: American Entry into World War II* (New York, 1965), is a readable brief account. See also the same author's *Roosevelt and World War II* (Baltimore, 1969). The best study on the coming of the war in the Pacific is Herbert Feis, *The Road to Pearl Harbor* (Princeton, 1962). American-German relations during the first two years of war are the subject of Saul Friedländer, *Prelude to Downfall: Hitler and the United States, 1939–1941* (New York, 1967). On relations between Germany and Japan, see Johanna M. Meskill, *Hitler and Japan: The Hollow Alliance* (New York, 1966), and Paul Schroeder, *The Axis Alliance and Japanese-American Relations 1941* (Ithaca, N.Y., 1958).

As happened after World War I, America's entry into World War II again gave rise to a number of revisionist works. Charles A. Beard, *President Roosevelt and the Coming of the War* (New Haven, 1948), began the assault, followed by William H. Chamberlin, *America's Second Crusade* (Chicago, 1950), and Charles C. Tansill, *Back Door to War: The Roosevelt*

Foreign Policy, 1933–1941 (Chicago, 1952). See also Bruce M. Russett, *No Clear and Present Danger: A Skeptical View of the United States Entry into World War II* (New York, 1972). The domestic debate surrounding America's going to war is perceptively analyzed in Wayne S. Cole, *America First: The Battle against Intervention, 1940–1941* (Madison, Wis., 1953) and less objectively in Walter Johnson, *The Battle against Isolation* (Chicago, 1944). On German propaganda activities in the United States, see Niel M. Johnson, *George Sylvester Viereck: German-American Propagandist* (Urbana, Ill., 1972).

Germany's administration of its conquered territories is the subject of Norman Rich, *The Establishment of the New Order*, vol. 2 of *Hitler's War Aims* (New York, 1974). Jan T. Gross, *Polish Society under German Occupation: The Generalgouvernement, 1939–1944* (Princeton, 1979), is a recent case study. Robert Koehl, *RKFDV: German Resettlement and Population Policy, 1939–1945* (Cambridge, Mass., 1957) deals with the demographic changes brought about under the direction of Heinrich Himmler. The best book on the mass murder of the Jews is Raul Hilberg, *The Destruction of the European Jews*, rev. ed. (Chicago, 1967). See also Gerald Reitlinger, *The Final Solution* (New York, 1953). Arthur D. Morse, *While Six Million Died: A Chronicle of American Apathy* (New York, 1968), charges that America could have done more to help Europe's Jews.

A great deal has been written about the diplomacy of World War II, much of which concerned the future of Germany. Most of the general works go beyond the war into the cold war period. Two of the best treatments are Walter LaFeber, *America, Russia, and the Cold War, 1945–1966* (New York, 1967), and Stephen E. Ambrose, *Rise to Globalism: American Foreign Policy, 1938–1976* (New York, 1976). On the war proper, Herbert Feis, *Churchill, Roosevelt, Stalin: The War They Waged and the Peace They Sought* (Princeton, 1957), is a standard work. Gaddis Smith, *American Diplomacy during the Second World War* (New York, 1965), is a brief survey. Much of the writing on wartime and postwar diplomacy has been revisionist, that is, holding the United States responsible for the cold war. A good example is Gabriel Kolko, *The Politics of War: The World and United States Foreign Policy, 1943–1945* (New York, 1968). See also John L. Gaddis, *The United States and the Origins of the Cold War, 1941–1947* (New York, 1972). The future of Germany as an issue in wartime diplomacy is discussed in John E. Snell, *Wartime Origins of the East-West Dilemma over Germany* (New Orleans, 1959). See also Tony Sharp, *The Wartime Alliance and the Zonal Division of Germany* (Oxford, 1975). Two controversial issues affecting Germany are treated in Raymond G. O'Connor, *Diplomacy for Victory: FDR and Unconditional Surrender* (New York, 1971), and Warren F. Kimball, *Swords into Ploughshares? The Morgenthau Plan for Defeated Nazi Germany, 1943–1946* (Philadelphia, 1976). The best book on the Yalta conference is by Diane Shaver Clemens, *Yalta* (New York, 1970), which corrects the view held by many Americans that the Russians got the better part of the bargain. See also Arthur Conte, *Yalta* (London, 1970). The standard work on the Potsdam conference is Herbert

Feis, *The Potsdam Conference* (Princeton, 1960). Alfred M. de Zayas, *Nemesis at Potsdam: The Anglo-Americans and the Expulsion of the Germans— Background, Execution, Consequences* (Boston, 1977), deals with a dark chapter in the transition from war to peace. H. R. Trevor-Roper, *The Last Days of Hitler* (London, 1947), is a suitably dramatic epilogue to the history of the "Thousand-Year Reich."

7 ONE GERMANY OR TWO? OCCUPATION, 1945–1949

The best study on the beginnings of the cold war is Daniel Yergin, *Shattered Peace: The Origins of the Cold War and the National Security State* (Boston, 1977). See also the books mentioned for chapter 6, as well as Lynn E. Davis, *The Cold War Begins: Soviet-American Conflict over Eastern Europe* (Princeton, 1974). The tug-of-war between the United States and Russia over Germany is ably and judiciously presented in R. Morgan, *The United States and West Germany 1945–1973* (Oxford, 1975). See also Bruce Kuklick, *American Policy and the Division of Germany: The Clash with Russia over Reparations* (Ithaca, N.Y., 1972). Good general works on the West German Federal Republic are Alfred Grosser, *Germany in Our Time* (New York, 1973), as seen from France and Aidan Crawley, *The Rise of Western Germany 1945–1972* (London 1973), a British view. The Nuremberg trials of the Nazi war criminals are reassessed in Eugene Davidson, *The Trial of the Germans: An Account of the Twenty-Two Defendants before the International Military Tribunal at Nuremberg* (New York, 1966). The most recent and best book on the subject is Bradley F. Smith, *Reaching Judgment at Nuremberg: The Untold Story of How the Nazi War Criminals Were Judged* (New York, 1977). For other joint activities of the four powers, see M. Balfour and J. Mair, *Four-Power Control in Germany and Austria, 1945–1946* (London, 1956). On the first Berlin crisis and blockade, see Daniel J. Nelson, *Wartime Origins of the Berlin Dilemma* (University, Ala., 1977); W. Phillips Davison, *The Berlin Blockade: A Study in Cold War Politics* (Princeton, 1958); Robert Rodrigo, *Berlin Airlift* (London, 1960); and the account of the American commander on the spot, Frank L. Howley, *Berlin Command* (New York, 1950).

There are several good general treatments of the American occupation of Germany. The most recent are Edward N. Peterson, *The American Occupation of Germany—Retreat to Victory* (Detroit, 1978), and Earl F. Ziemke, *The US Army in the Occupation of Germany, 1944–1946* (Washington, 1975). John Gimbel, *The American Occupation of Germany: Politics and the Military, 1945–1949* (Stanford, 1968), is a standard work; see also by the same author, *A German Community under American Occupation* (Stanford, 1961). Harold Zink, *The United States in Germany, 1944–1955* (Princeton, 1957), is by the former chief historian of the U.S. high commissioner for Germany. Eugene Davidson, *The Death and Life of Germany: An Account of the American Occupation* (New York, 1959), is quite critical of America's performance. On the role of General Clay, we have his own story, Lucius D. Clay, *Decision in Germany* (Garden City, N.Y., 1950), and *The Papers of General Lucius D. Clay* (Bloomington, Ind.,

1974). Another key figure during the occupation period, Secretary of State James F. Byrnes, reminisces in *Speaking Frankly* (New York, 1947) and in *All in One Lifetime* (New York, 1958). Special studies on the major activities of military government include: Constantine FitzGibbon, *Denazification* (London, 1969); H. Lidell, *Education in Occupied Germany* (New York, 1949); Nicholas Balabkins, *Germany under Direct Controls: Economic Aspects of Industrial Disarmament, 1945–1948* (New Brunswick, N.J., 1964); and John H. Barker, *Priming the German Economy* (Durham, N.C., 1971). See also the latter's *The Decision to Divide Germany: American Foreign Policy in Transition* (Durham, N.C., 1978), an authoritative study by a former member of the U.S. military government's economic administration.

The emergence of the West German Federal Republic is dealt with in most of the general works cited above, as well as in John F. Golay, *The Founding of the Federal Republic of Germany* (Chicago, 1958), and Peter H. Merkl, *The Origins of the West German Republic* (New York, 1963). The standard work on the French occupation of Germany is F. Roy Willis, *The French in Germany, 1945–1949* (Stanford, 1962). On the British zone, see Raymond Ebsworth, *Restoring Democracy in Germany: The British Contribution* (New York, 1961). J. P. Nettl, *The Eastern Zone and Soviet Policy in Germany 1945–1950* (London, 1951), is useful, though hampered by restricted access to information. Henry Krisch, *German Politics under Soviet Occupation* (New York, 1974), deals mainly with the first two postwar years.

There are a number of books by journalists and other observers familiar with Germany and concerned about its future, which are still worth reading for the atmosphere they convey of that crucial period in American-German relations. Hans Habe, *Our Love Affair with Germany* (New York, 1953), is by the former editor of the military-government-sponsored *Neue Zeitung*. William L. White, *Report on the Germans* (New York, 1947), and Drew Middleton, *Struggle for Germany* (Indianapolis, 1949), are by noted American journalists. W. E. Hocking, *Experiment in Education: What We Can Learn from Teaching Germany* (Chicago, 1954), is by a Harvard philosopher critical of American policy. Also critical is Freda Utley, *High Cost of Vengeance* (Chicago, 1949), an ill-tempered attack by an American publicist. Ernst von Salomon, *Fragebogen* (New York, 1954), is a vitriolic indictment of denazification by one of its "victims," a well-known German author and former Free Corps fighter. The book caused quite a stir at the time. Some of the best and most judicious contemporary discussions of the German question came from a long-time observer of the German scene, J. P. Warburg, *Germany, Bridge and Battleground* (New York, 1947), and *Germany: Key to Peace* (Cambridge, Mass., 1953).

8 The Germany of Konrad Adenauer, 1949–1963

A useful guide to the literature in English on the German Federal Republic is Arnold H. Price, ed., *The Federal Republic of Germany: A Selected Bibliography of English-Language Publications,* 2nd rev. ed. (Washington, 1978), published by the Library of Congress and citing articles as well as books. Richard Hiscocks, *The Adenauer Era* (Philadelphia, 1966), is a very good general history. On the central figure, Terence Prittie, *Konrad Adenauer, 1876–1967* (Chicago, 1972), is critical but sympathetic. Of the chancellor's own recollections, only the first of four volumes, *Memoirs, 1945–1953* (Chicago, 1966), has been translated. The emergence of the Federal Republic as an active participant in international affairs is traced in Wolfram Hanrieder, *West German Foreign Policy 1949–1963* (Stanford, 1967), and by the same author, *The Stable Crisis: Two Decades of German Foreign Policy* (New York, 1970). Philip Windsor, *German Reunification* (London, 1969), and Frederick H. Hartmann, *Germany between East and West: The Reunification Problem* (Englewood Cliffs, N.J., 1965), address themselves to the major issue in German foreign policy. Another important problem, German rearmament, is the subject of Robert McGeehan, *The German Rearmament Question: American Diplomacy and European Defense after World War II* (Urbana, Ill., 1971). The major obstacle to Franco-German rapprochement is treated in Jacques Freymond, *The Saar Conflict, 1945–1955* (London, 1960). Two critical assessments of de Gaulle's German policy are contained in Wladyslaw W. Kulski, *De Gaulle and the World: The Foreign Policy of the Fifth French Republic* (Syracuse, N.Y., 1966), and Lois Pattison De Ménil, *Who Speaks for Europe? The Vision of Charles de Gaulle* (London, n.d., 1977?). There are several studies of the second Berlin crisis. Robert M. Slusser, *The Berlin Crisis of 1961: Soviet-American Relations and the Struggle for Power in the Kremlin, June–November 1961* (Baltimore, 1973), traces its domestic Soviet roots. Jack M. Schick, *The Berlin Crisis 1958–1962* (Philadelphia, 1971), paints a broader picture. See also Glen D. Camp, *Berlin in the East-West Struggle, 1958–1961* (New York, 1971), and Eleanor L. Dulles, *The Wall: A Tragedy in Three Acts* (Columbia, S.C.,1972).

On West Germany's government, Guido Goldman, *The German Political System* (New York, 1974), and Kurt Sontheimer, *The Government and Politics of West Germany* (New York, 1973), are good introductions. See also Arnold J. Heidenheimer, *Adenauer and the C.D.U.* (The Hague, 1960). The chancellor's great rival is the subject of Lewis J. Edinger, *Kurt Schumacher: A Study in Personality and Political Behavior* (Stanford, 1965). Several works deal with the changes in Schumacher's party during the Adenauer years: David Childs, *From Schumacher to Brandt: The Story of German Socialism, 1945–1965* (New York, 1966); Harold K. Schellinger, *The SPD and the Bonn Republic: A Socialist Party Modernizes* (The Hague, 1968); and Douglas A. Chalmers, *The Social Democratic Party of Germany: From Working-Class Movement to Modern Political Party* (New Haven, 1964).

On the beginnings of Germany's economic recovery, see Herbert C. Mayer, *German Recovery and the Marshall Plan, 1948–1952* (New York, 1969). Henry C. Wallich, *Mainsprings of German Revival* (New Haven, 1955) is an important contribution. Walter H. Nelson, *Small Wonder: The Amazing Story of the Volkswagen,* rev. ed. (Boston, 1970), deals with the main symbol of the economic miracle. See also Ludwig Erhard, *Germany's*

Comeback in the World Market (New York, 1954). Labor's search for co-determination is treated in Abraham Shuchman, *Codetermination: Labor's Middle Course in Germany* (Washington, 1957), and in Herbert J. Spiro, *The Politics of German Codetermination* (Cambridge, Mass., 1958).

The problem of assimilating the millions of German refugees and expellees from the East is discussed in Hans W. Schoenberg, *Germans from the East: A Study of Their Migration, Resettlement, and Subsequent Group History since 1945* (The Hague, 1970), and in Bertram G. Lattimore, *The Assimilation of German Expellees in the West German Polity and Society since 1945: A Case Study of Eutin, Schleswig-Holstein* (The Hague, 1974). Nicholas Balabkins, *West German Reparations to Israel* (New Brunswick, N.J., 1971), deals with another positive aspect of the Adenauer era. See also Rolf Vogel, ed., *The German Path to Israel: A Documentation with a Foreword by Konrad Adenauer* (Chester Springs, Pa., 1969). On the Jews in West Germany today, see Leo Katcher, *Post-Mortem: The Jews in Germany Today* (New York, 1968), and Karen Gershon, ed., *Postscript: A Collective Account of the Lives of Jews in West Germany since the Second World War* (London, 1969).

The first years of the new German army are discussed in Eric Waldman, *The Goose Step Verboten: The German Army Today* (New York, 1964). The *Spiegel* affair, which darkened the closing years of Adenauer's career, is analyzed by Ronald F. Bunn, *German Politics and the Spiegel Affair: A Case Study of the Bonn System* (Baton Rouge, La., 1968); see also David Schoenbaum, *The Spiegel Affair* (Garden City, N.Y., 1968). The attitudes and views of the West Germans toward their new state are examined in two valuable collections: Elisabeth Noelle-Neumann and Erich P. Neumann, *The Germans: Public Opinion Polls 1947–1966* (Allensbach, 1967), a basic survey by the directors of Germany's leading institute of opinion research; and Walter Stahl, ed., *Education for Democracy in West Germany: Achievements, Shortcomings, Prospects* (New York, 1961), the contributions made by schools, universities, the mass media, etc., toward strengthening civic attitudes.

The literature in English on East Germany is scarce. Carola Stern, *Ulbricht: A Political Biography* (New York, 1965), is the only full-length study of East Germany's counterpart to Adenauer. Arthur M. Hanhardt, *The German Democratic Republic* (Baltimore, 1968), is a standard work. On the economic problems of the German Democratic Republic, see Wolfgang F. Stolper, *The Structure of the East German Economy* (Cambridge, Mass., 1960). Arnulf Baring, *Uprising in East Germany: June 17, 1953* (Ithaca, N.Y., 1972), recounts an elevating, though tragic, episode in the history of postwar Germany.

9 From Adenauer to Brandt, 1963–1974

The decade covered by this chapter was the crucial period in the rise of West Germany to full-fledged partnership with the United States. Relations between the two countries are clearly and expertly presented in Roger Morgan, *The United States and West Germany 1945–1973* (New York,

1975). Karl Kaiser, *German Foreign Policy in Transition: Bonn between East and West* (New York, 1968), examines West Germany's foreign policy options on the eve of Ostpolitik. See also Eleanor L. Dulles, *One Germany or Two: The Struggle at the Heart of Europe* (Stanford, 1970). F. Roy Willis, *France, Germany, and the New Europe, 1945–1967* (London, 1968), deals with Germany's Westpolitik. There are several biographies of Willy Brandt: David Binder, *The Other German: Willy Brandt's Life and Times* (Washington, 1975); Terence Prittie, *Willy Brandt: Portrait of a Statesman* (New York, 1974); and the profile by a close Brandt associate, Klaus Harpprecht, *Willy Brandt* (Los Angeles, 1971). For the chancellor's own views on the most important period of his life, see Willy Brandt, *People and Politics: The Years 1960–1975* (Boston, 1978). Henry Kissinger, the leading figure in the making of American foreign policy, has also been the subject of preliminary assessments: David Landau, *Kissinger: The Uses of Power* (Boston, 1972), and Marvin and Bernard Kalb, *Kissinger* (Boston, 1974). See also Henry A. Kissinger, *The Troubled Partnership: A Reappraisal of the Atlantic Alliance* (New York, 1965).

The most important events of the Brandt era dealt with the complex negotiations and treaties subsumed under the term Ostpolitik. The chancellor's preliminary outline of his eastern policy is given in Willy Brandt, *A Peace Policy for Europe* (New York, 1969). Several books written while the negotiations were still in progress stress the major significance of Brandt's policy within the general framework of East-West détente: Philip Windsor, *Germany and the Management of Détente* (New York, 1971); Frederick A. Becker, *The Development of an Eastern Policy in West Germany's Foreign Relations* (Claremont, Calif., 1971); Michael Freund, *From Cold War to Ostpolitik: Germany and the New Europe* (London, 1972); and Lawrence L. Whetten, *Germany's Ostpolitik: Relations between the Federal Republic and the Warsaw Pact Countries* (New York, 1971). Roger Tilford, *The Ostpolitik and Political Change in Germany* (Lexington, Mass., 1975), examines the long-range results of Ostpolitik in Germany, and Kenneth A Myers, *Ostpolitik and American Security Interests in Europe* (Washington, 1972), deals with its effects on American policy. See also Walter F. Hahn, *Between Westpolitik and Ostpolitik: Changing West German Security Views* (Beverly Hills, Calif., 1975). The most important of the eastern treaties, the one between West Germany and Poland, has attracted special attention: Wladyslaw W. Kulski, *Germany and Poland: From War to Peaceful Relations* (Syracuse, N.Y., 1976); Louis L. Ortmayer, *Conflict, Compromise, and Conciliation: West German–Polish Normalization 1966–1976* (Denver, 1975); and Henry K. Rosenthal, *German and Pole: National Conflict and Modern Myth* (Gainesville, Fla., 1976). The agreement between the western powers and the Soviet Union, defusing the tense situation over Berlin, has been exhaustively studied by Honoré M. Catudal, *The Diplomacy of the Quadripartite Agreement on Berlin: A New Era in East-West Politics* (Berlin/West, 1978). On relations between the two Germanies under the Basic Treaty, see Karl E. Birnbaum, *East and West Germany: A Modus Vivendi* (Lexington, Mass., 1973).

10 THE GERMAN FEDERAL REPUBLIC SINCE 1974

Most of the events discussed in this chapter are too recent to have given rise to any book-length studies, but a number of general works are useful in trying to understand the German Federal Republic in the late 1970s. David P. Conradt, *The German Polity* (New York, 1978), is an informative introduction to West German politics and policy making. Viola H. Drath, ed., *Germany in World Politics* (New York, 1978), presents a collection of essays on contemporary Germany by authors of differing qualifications. See also Günther Kloss, *West Germany: An Introduction* (New York, 1976), and Geoffrey Pridham, *Christian Democracy in Western Germany* (New York, 1977). Karl Dietrich Bracher, *The German Dilemma: The Relationship of State and Democracy* (New York, 1975), confronts the problem of rising authoritarianism. On American-German relations, many of the works cited for the previous chapter also apply to this one. David Calleo, *The German Problem Reconsidered: Germany and the World Order, 1870 to the Present* (New York, 1978), offers insightful speculations on the possible future course of German policy. Werner Höfer, ed., *Favored Forever?: A Critical Dialogue on America and Germany Today and Tomorrow* (Düsseldorf, 1976), has essays on life in both countries by ten German and ten American journalists.

There are books on some of the domestic developments discussed in this chapter: Kurt P. Tauber, *Beyond Eagle and Swastika: German Nationalism since 1945*, 2 vols. (Middletown, Conn., 1967), is an impressive performance. Ivor Montagu, *Germany's New Nazis* (London, 1967), is more polemical. John D. Nagle, *The National Democratic Party: Right Radicalism in the Federal Republic of Germany* (Berkeley, Calif., 1970) presents a careful analysis of the NPD. The most readable and disturbing account of terrorism in West Germany is Jillian Becker, *Hitler's Children: The Story of the Baader-Meinhof Terrorist Gang* (Philadelphia, 1977). On the situation in the universities, see *Report on German Universities* (New York, 1977), by the International Council on the Future of the University. F. C. Hunnius, *Student Revolts: The New Left in West Germany* (London, 1968), is a brief pamphlet sympathetic to the protesters.

The German school system is the subject of: Theodore Huebener, *The Schools of West Germany: A Study of German Elementary and Secondary Schools* (New York, 1962); Robert F. Lawson, *Reform of the West German School System, 1945–1962* (Ann Arbor, Mich., 1965); and Arthur Haernden, *Education in the Two Germanies* (Boulder, Colo., 1976). Walter H. Nelson, *Germany Rearmed* (New York, 1972), discusses developments in the Bundeswehr. The West German economy is treated in Frank Vogl, *German Business after the Economic Miracle* (New York, 1973), and Horst Mendershausen, *Coping with the Oil Crisis: French and German Experiences* (Baltimore, 1976). See also Klaus Conrad and Dale W. Jorgenson, *Measuring Performance in the Private Sector of the Federal Republic of Germany, 1950–1973* (Tübingen, 1975). On the German labor movement, see Martin Peltzer, *The German Labour Management Relations Act* (London, 1972). See also G. Hallett, *The Social Economy of West Germany* (New York, 1974). Franz Flamm, *Social Welfare Services and Social Work in the Federal Republic of Germany* (Cologne, 1974), is a good introduction. Dieter Schewe, Karlhugo Nordhorn, and Klaus Schenke, *Survey of Social Security in the Federal Republic of Germany* (Bonn, 1972), is a comprehensive government-sponsored report.

The literature on West German cultural developments since 1945 is quite plentiful. Good general introductions are: Charles E. McClelland and Steven P. Scher, eds., *Postwar German Culture: An Anthology* (New York, 1974), and Paul Schallück, ed., *Germany: Cultural Developments since 1945* (Munich, 1971). On the mass media, see John Sanford, *The Mass Media in the German-Speaking Countries* (London, 1976), and Arthur Williams, *Broadcasting and Democracy in West Germany* (Bradford, Mass., 1976). Günther Feuerstein, *New Directions in German Architecture* (New York, 1968); John Burchardt, *The Voice of the Phoenix: Postwar Architecture in Germany* (Cambridge, Mass., 1966); and Wolfgang Pehnt, *German Architecture, 1960–1970* (New York, 1970), all testify to Germany's architectural revival. Roger Manvell and Heinrich Fraenkel, *The German Cinema* (New York, 1971), is by two noted film historians and writers on recent German history. Contemporary German literature is brilliantly presented by Peter Demetz, *Postwar German Literature: A Critical Introduction* (New York, 1970), and competently by H. M. Waidson, *The Modern German Novel, 1945–1965*, 2nd. ed. (London, 1971). See also R. H. Thomas and K. Bullivant, *Literature in Upheaval: West German Writers and the Challenge of the 1960s* (New York, 1974), and Siegfried Mandel, *Group 47: The Reflected Intellect* (Carbondale, Ill., 1973). On the contemporary German theater, see Michael Patterson, *German Theatre Today* (London, 1976), and M. Benedikt and G. E. Wellwarth, eds., *Postwar German Theatre* (New York, 1968).

11 THE GERMAN DEMOCRATIC REPUBLIC SINCE 1961

Except for a few general works, not much information in English is available on the German Democratic Republic. Some of the best studies are by a well-known West German political scientist, Peter Christian Ludz, who is a leading authority on East Germany: *The German Democratic Republic from the Sixties to the Seventies* (Cambridge, Mass., 1970); *Two Germanys in One World* (Paris, 1973); and *The Changing Party Elite in East Germany* (Cambridge, Mass., 1972). Other good general works are Arthur M. Hanhardt, *The German Democratic Republic* (Baltimore, 1968), and David Childs, *East Germany* (London, 1969). On East Germany's leaders, Carola Stern, *Ulbricht: A Political Biography* (New York, 1965), and Heinz Lippmann, *Honecker and the New Politics of Europe* (New York, 1972), are useful. There are no books on American–East German relations, because there is not much to tell. What longer studies there are on foreign policy deal with East German–Soviet relations: Gerhard Wettig, *Community and Conflict in the Socialist Camp: The Soviet Union, East Germany and the German Problem, 1965–1972* (New York, 1975), and Welles Hangen, *The Muted Revolution: East Germany's Challenge to Russia and the West* (New York, 1966). Relations between the two Germanies are treated in Karl E. Birnbaum, *East and West Germany: A Modus Vivendi* (Lexington, Mass., 1973); and Peter H. Merkl, *German Foreign Policies, East and West: On the Threshold of a New European Era* (Santa Barbara, Calif., 1974). See also David Shears, *The Ugly Frontier* (New York, 1970).

The existence of two German states naturally invites comparisons on various aspects of their respective political, economic, and social systems. Some examples are: John Dornberg, *The Two Germanys* (New York, 1974); Martin Schnitzer, *East and West Germany: A Comparative Economic Analysis* (New York, 1972); Arthur Haernden, *Education in the Two Germanies* (Boulder, Colo., 1976); Ingrid Sommerkorn et al., *Women's Careers: Experience from East and West Germany* (London, 1970); and M. Donald Hancock, *The Bundeswehr and the National People's Army: A Comparative Study of German Civil–Military Polity* (Denver, Colo., 1973). For more on the East German army, see D. R. Herspring, *East German Civil–Military Relations: The Impact of Technology, 1949–1972* (New York, 1973). On everyday life in East Germany, Hans Axel Hohn, *The Other Germans: Report from an East German Town* (New York, 1970), and Hanns Werner Schwarze, *The GDR Today: Life in the "Other Germany"* (London, 1973), while somewhat out of date, still convey an impression of what it is like.

Index

Abrassimov, Pyotr, 263
Acheson, Dean, 161, 183, 223
Adenauer, Konrad, 172, 175, 177, 203;
  as chancellor, 11, 87, 92, 177, 179–194,
  202, 207–210, 218, 224, 231, 258, 279,
  281
Africa: German ambitions in, 40–42, 54
America First Committee, 130, 136
Anti-Comintern Pact (1936), 134
Anti-Semitism: pre-Hitler, 21–22, 41,
  64, 70, 87; under Hitler/Nazis, 21–22,
  104–113 passim, 134, 135, 141–142,
  148, 202–203, 240; U.S. reaction to,
  109, 110–111, 121, 123; postwar re-
  surgence of, 190, 241–242, 280. *See
  also* Jews
Appeasement, 117, 124, 151; and
  Munich crisis, 118, 119, 123
Arendt, Hannah, 112
Argentina, 122–123
Army, German, 41, 43, 55, 90, 108;
  inter- and postwar, 20, 78, 194, 200–
  201, 206, 246–247, 271; Freikorps, 76–
  77, 98, 111; Reichswehr, 77, 90, 99,
  101, 200. *See also* Militarism, German
Atlantic Charter, 131, 134
Attlee, Clement, 147
Augstein, Rudolf, 194
Austria, 27, 30, 33-36, 115, 128;
  anschluss, 54, 83, 99, 119, 123;
  German annexation of, 115, 123

Austria-Hungary, 42, 51, 72

Baader, Andreas, 243
Bachmann, Ingeborg, 256
Badoglio, Marshal Pietro, 143
Bahr, Egon, 210, 219, 223, 225, 226, 228,
  234, 242, 265
Bahro, Rudolf, 263
Balkan states, 42, 51, 72, 128, 129, 150
Baltic states, 128, 141
Bancroft, George, 35, 38
Barnes, Harry Elmer, 52, 95
Baruch, Bernard, 162
Barzel, Rainer, 215, 220, 226, 252
Baudissin, Count Wolf Heinrich von,
  201
Bavaria, 4, 11–12, 13, 75
Beard, Charles A., 136
Becher, Johannes R., 171
Becker, Jurek, 262
Belgium, 86, 91; in World Wars I and
  II, 54, 57, 58, 66, 72, 127, 139
Benedict XV (pope), 56
Benjamin, Hilde, 206
Berlin: as capital, 3, 10, 265–266; Wall,
  24, 25, 191, 206, 209, 259, 268, 273;
  Allied occupation of, 147, 150; block-
  ade and airlift, 154, 156, 160–161, 173,
  187–188, 190, 191; negotiations, 224–
  225, 226, 260. *See also* Reunification
  of Germany

Bernhardi, Friedrich von, 57
Bernstorff, Count Johann von, 46–50
　passim, 61–68
Bethmann Hollweg, Theobald von, 55,
　56, 61, 62, 66, 67, 68
Bevin, Ernest, 157, 158, 161, 183
Bidault, Georges, 157, 161
Biermann, Wolf, 262, 265
Bismarck, Otto von, 105, 116, 179, 194,
　208; and "Second" Reich, 3, 13, 35,
　36–38; domestic and foreign policies
　of, 33–38, 40–43, 78, 178, 197–198
Bliss, General Tasker, 81
Bloc of Expellees and Disfranchised
　(BHE), 198–199
Blomberg, General Werner von, 108
Böckler, Hans, 197
Böll, Heinrich, 256, 257
Bolen, David B., 260
Bolshevik party, 70, 71, 75, 100, 104.
　See also Communism
Borah, William E., 102
Bötticher, General Friedrich von, 119,
　133
Boxer Rebellion, 44
Bracher, Karl Dietrich, 242
Brandt, Willy, 199–200, 208–215 passim,
　241, 253, 266; as chancellor, 207, 216–
　231, 243, 252, 265, 282
Brazil, 39, 49, 122, 232
Brecht, Bertolt, 112, 237
Brentano, Heinrich von, 191, 194
Brezhnev, Leonid, 220, 222, 223, 228,
　231, 258, 259, 263
Briand, Aristide, 91, 92, 118, 188; and
　Kellogg-Briand Pact, 93
Brockdorff-Rantzau, Count Ulrich von,
　78
Brüning, Heinrich, 98–100, 101, 102,
　112
Brüsewitz, Oskar, 270
Bryan, William Jennings, 60, 65
Bryce, Lord, 31
Brzezinski, Zbigniew, 232
Buback, Siegfried, 242
Bulganin, Nikolai, 187
Bulgaria, 139, 210
Burgess, John W., 60
Butler, Nicholas Murray, 112
Butler, R., 138
Byrnes, James F., 157–158, 159, 163, 173

Canada, 64, 232, 235
Carter, Jimmy, 231–234, 236–237, 260,
　281
Casement, Sir Roger, 64
Castle, William R., 93
Cavell, Edith, 58
Chamberlain, Austen, 91, 118
Chamberlain, Houston Stewart, 106
Chamberlain, Neville, 118
Chaplin, Charlie, 103, 107
Chéradame, André, 58
Chichester, Captain (at Manila Bay), 44
China, 44, 46, 132, 151; People's Re-
　public of, 155, 188, 192, 209, 281
Christian-Democratic Union (CDU),
　171–172, 175, 177, 194, 207–208, 212–
　213, 215, 219–220, 226, 231, 252–253
Christian-Social Union (CSU), 172, 177,
　219, 220, 226, 231, 252–253
Churches, see Religion
Churchill, Winston, 90, 127, 131, 144,
　147–152, 184
Class, Heinrich, 48
Clay, General Lucius D., 159, 163, 165,
　191
Clemenceau, Georges, 78, 81, 91
Cold war, 2, 3, 24, 154–155, 172, 187,
　188, 279
COMECON, 204, 265
Common Market (European Economic
　Community, EEC), 186, 189, 210, 216–
　217, 220, 222, 249, 265
Communism, 125, 188, 191, 198, 199,
　260; fears of, 70, 75–76, 81, 85, 87,
　117, 129, 155, 280; in German elec-
　tions (1930s), 99, 100; and anticom-
　munism, 142, 179, 181, 205, 207, 213,
　234, 279, 281; postwar expansion of,
　150, 155, 157, 203, 204, 205, 280;
　German communist Party (KPD),
　171, 172, 243; and COMECON, 204,
　265. See also Bolshevik party; Soviet
　Union
Conant, James B., 180
Coolidge, Calvin, 89, 93
Cooper, John Sherman, 260
Creel, George, 71
Croly, Herbert, 49
Cuban missile crisis, 192, 210
Czechoslovakia, 8, 9, 92, 204, 217; Ger-
　man conquest and loss of, 115, 118,

123–124, 147; Soviet Union and, 128, 155, (1968 crisis) 208, 259, 271, 275

D'Abernon, Lord, 1
Dahrendorf, Ralf, 145
Daladier, Édouard, 118
Darlan, Admiral Jean, 144
Dawes, Charles G., and Dawes Plan, 89, 90, 92, 93
de Gaulle, Charles, 92, 188–193 passim, 207, 208, 209–210, 216–217
de Lagarde, Paul, 105
Democracy in Germany, 18, 22–23, 158, 167, 171, 215; failure/lack of, 38, 41 85, 90, 98, 100, 102, 106, 108, 110, 278; Wilson and, 72, 73, 74, 81; Weimar Republic, 75–102; German Federal Republic, 145, 193, 253, 254, 279, 280; East Germany, 172
Denmark, 30, 34, 35, 45, 127, 139
Depression, economic: *1873*, 38–39; *1930s* (Great), 85, 89, 97, 99, 104, 108, 113, 116, 236, 278; *1960s and 1970s*, 208, 213, 232, 235, 249, 252, 282
Dernburg, Bernhard, 63
Détente, 191, 232, 233–234, 266, 281; U.S.-Soviet, 207, 210–212, 220, 222, 228, 262; West German-Soviet, 217–219, 223, 228, 259
Deutsche Partei (DP), 177
Dewey, Admiral George, 44, 49
Dieckhoff, Hans, 119, 123
Diederichs, Vice Admiral Otto von, 44
Dix, Otto, 225
Dodd, William E., 110, 123
Donelson, Andrew J., 30
Dönitz, Karl, 156
Duckwitz, Georg, 223
Dulles, John Foster, 80, 180, 188, 219
Dumba, Constantin, 65

East German Democratic Republic (Deutsche Demokratische Republik, DDR), 3; geography and character of, 8–13; refugees from, 8, 9, 25, 172, 191, 195, 198–199, 205, 206, 213, 259–268 passim, 273, 274; army (NVA) of, 20, 206, 271; -U.S. relations, 23, 258, 260–261, 263, 275; emergence and economic/political development of, 24–26, 159, 161, 171–172, 177–178,

185–187, 203–206, 259, 261, 266–268, 272–275; 1953 uprising in, 205; -West German Basic Treaty, 226–227, 233, 258, 264; culture and dissent in, 262–263
Ebert, Friedrich, 69–70, 76, 90
Eden, Anthony, 185, 187
Education: democratization of, 18, 215; and student protest, 19, 214, 217, 244–246; in U.S., German contributions to and exchange with, 39, 47, 94, 112, 238–239, 262; and reeducation in postwar Germany, 165, 166–167, 171, 201–202; of foreign workers, 251; East German goals of, 269–271
Edward VII, king of England, 48
Egk, Werner, 255
Egypt, 128
Ehard, Hans, 174
Eich, Günter, 256
Eiermann, Egon, 255
Einstein, Albert, 112
Einstein, Lewis, 49
Eisenhower, General Dwight D., 165, 187, 190, 381
Engels, Friedrich, 171
Enzensberger, Hans Magnus, 237
Erhard, Ludwig, 193–195, 196, 207–217, 220
Ericson, Leif, 29
Erler, Fritz, 200, 211, 219
Erzberger, Matthias, 87
Ethiopian war, 121, 128
Eucken, Walter, 195
European Community, 229, 279, 281; Coal and Steel (ECSC), 182, 186; Defense (EDC), 183, 184–185. *See also* Common Market; Marshall Plan

Falkenhayn, General Erich von, 55, 62–63
Fassbinder, Rainer Werner, 256
Faure, Edgar, 187
Fay, Sidney B., 52, 95
Federal Republic of West Germany, *see* West German Federal Republic
Filbinger, Hans, 252
Finland, 128, 129, 139; and "Finlandization," 281
Fischer, Fritz, 15–16, 53
Fischer, Oskar, 260

Ford, Gerald, 231, 232, 235
.Ford, Henry, 96
"Forty-eighters," *see* Immigration,
 German
Fourteen Points, 69, 71–74, 144
Fowler, Henry, 216
France, 44, 88, 95, 192; alliances of, 42,
 51, 82, 83, 86, 89, 91, 128, 222, 233;
 and World War II, 54, 115–117, 121,
 125, 127, 135; fall of, 127, 130, 133.
 See also Franco-German relations
Francis Ferdinand, archduke of Austria,
 77
Francke, Kuno, 47, 59, 60
Franco-German relations, 35, 42, 45;
 World War I and interwar, 54, 72,
 73, 80, 82, 92, 96, 99; Hitler and, 114,
 123, 124, 139; postwar, 145, 156–158,
 161–173 passim, 182–192 passim, 209,
 210, 215–217, 224, 260. *See also* Ruhr,
 the
Franco-Prussian War, 35, 42, 78
Frederick the Great, 29, 45, 105
Frederick William IV, 30, 34
Frederick III, 41
Free Democratic Party (FDP), 172, 177,
 194, 208, 219, 226, 230, 231, 252
Fruhtrunk, Günther, 255
Fulbright, William, 188

Gannett, Lewis S., 95
Gaus, Günter, 264
Genoa Conference (1922), 86
Genscher, Hans-Dietrich, 230–231
Gerard, James, 60
German-American Economic Associa-
 tion, 50, 95
German-Americans: cultural contribu-
 tions of, 28–29, 36, 39, 47, 48, 94, 112;
 German sympathies of, 36, 46–47,
 58–61, 84, 88, 111–112, 114, 122, 136;
 in U.S. army, 138, 163; postwar, 240,
 277. *See also* Immigration, German
German Communist Party (KPD), 99,
 100, 171–172, 177, 243
German Confederation or Bund, 27,
 30–31, 34
German Democratic Republic, *see* East
 German Democratic Republic
German history: "continuity" of, 15–
 16, 53, 76–77, 126; revisionism and,

52, 95, 150, 162; Nazism and, 119,
 138; effect of U.S. policy on, 150–153.
 See also "Responsibility"
German language, 13, 14, 23, 163, 164;
 in U.S., 29, 94, 110, 239
German Reich ("First" and "Second"),
 3, 4, 7, 9, 13, 27, 38; navy of, 41, 42,
 44, 49, 50, 78; and pre-World War I
 alliances, 42, 45, 46, 51; in World
 War I, 52–74, 107; war aims of, 54,
 56, 57, 66, 68; reform demands and
 postwar revolutions in, 56, 69–70,
 76–77, 107. *See also* Bismarck, Otto
 von; Imperialism
German views of United States and
 Americans: condescension/contempt,
 5, 27, 48, 82, 97, 113, 114, 119, 124,
 168, 213, 228, 237, 277; stereotyped,
 33, 97, 237; admiration, 38, 48, 95–
 97, 101, 113; misconceptions of policy
 and strength, 46, 60–61, 68, 113, 114,
 116, 119, 123, 125, 129, 133, 137. *See
 also* Hitler, Adolf
Germany, postwar: Allied plans for,
 143–178, 184; and war reparations,
 145, 148–149; economic situation in,
 169–170, 171–172, 174. *See also* East
 German Democratic Republic; Reunification of Germany; West German Federal Republic
Gerstenmaier, Eugen, 256
Gilbert, Parker, 89, 93
Globke, Hans, 202
Gobineau, Count Joseph Arthur, 106
Godesberg program (1959), 194, 199–
 200, 212, 253
Goebbels, Joseph, 109, 124, 133, 144, 156
Göring, Hermann, 109, 114, 119, 136,
 142, 156
Grass, Günter, 256, 257
Great Britain, 59, 63–66 passim, 132,
 149, 155, 196, 235; -U.S. relations, 22,
 44–51 passim, 60, 61, 65, 83, 135, 222,
 (Atlantic Charter) 131 134; -Ger-
 many relations, 40–51 passim, 82, 86–
 91 passim, 260, (blockade) 61, 62, 65,
 71, (Hitler and) 114–117, 123, 124;
 -France relations, 86, 89, 91; and
 World War II, 115, 116, 121 124, 127,
 129–135, 143; U.S. aid to (and Lend-
 Lease), 127, 129–131, 133–134, 136;

and postwar Germany, 145, 149, 151, 157–159, 163–175 passim, 215; and Common Market, 189, 216–217. *See also* Appeasement
Greece, 128, 154, 155
Greenland, 131, 134
Grewe, Wilhelm, 192
Grey, Sir Edward, 66
Groener, General Wilhelm, 76
Gromyko, Andrei, 191, 218, 223
Gropius, Walter, 255
Grotewohl, Otto, 171, 177
Guillaume, Günter, 265

Hague conferences (1899, 1907), 50
Hallstein, Dr. Walter, and Hallstein Doctrine, 186, 217, 218
Handke, Peter, 256, 257
Hanfstaengl, Ernst "Putzi," 113
Harding, Warren G., 88
Harich, Wolfgang, 206
Harlan, Veit, 202
Hassel, Kai-Uwe von, 210
Haussmann, Manfred, 96
Hay, John, 44
Hayek, Friedrich, 195
Heiden, Konrad, 112
Heinemann, Gustav, 182, 212, 218, 226
Heinzen, Karl, 36
Helsinki (human rights) Conference (1975), 233, 262, 264
Henry, prince of Prussia, 45
Herrnstadt, Rudolf, 205
Herter, Christian, 188; and Herter Plan, 190
Herzog, Werner, 256
Heuss, Theodor, 177, 193, 201
Hexamer, Dr. Charles J., 58
Heym, Stefan, 262
Hillenbrand, Martin, 221, 232, 238
Himmler, Heinrich, 109, 136, 139, 141, 156
Hindemith, Paul 112, 255
Hindenburg, Oskar von, 100
Hindenburg, Field Marshal Paul von, 55–56, 61, 63, 70, 78, 93; as president of Weimar Republic, 90, 92, 98–100, 101–102, 108
Hindenburg disaster, 94
Hitler, Adolf, 8, 83, 151, 168, 198, 241; rise of, 1, 12, 35, 64, 77, 85, 87, 97, 98–

102, 106–109, 242, 278; and "Greater Germany," 3, 9, 13, 118, 124, 139, 141, 154; racism of, 15; and Versailles Treaty, 80, 84, 114–116, 124; para-military organizations of, 90, 101, 108–109; character of, 103–105; *Mein Kampf* and *Second Book,* 107, 113, 114–115; and German-American re-lations, 110–114, 180; attitude of, toward U.S., 113, 114, 119, 133, 134–135, 137; foreign policy of, 115–119, 121–125; German resistance to, 118–119, 144, 145; -Stalin pact (1939), 125, 128–129; 147, 150; and "Hitler's war," 126–127; Four-Year Plan and New Order of, 136, 139, 142; suicide of, 143, 152, 156. *See also* Anti-Semi-tism; German views of United States and Americans; National Socialist (Nazi) party; Propaganda
Hochhuth, Rolf, 257
Hoffman, Theodore, 111
Hoffmann, General Heinz, 271
Holy Roman Empire, 27
Honecker, Erich, 258–270 passim, 275
Hoover, Herbert 81, 96, 99, 101, 102, 163
Houghton, Alanson B., 88, 92, 97
House, Colonel Edward M., 50–51, 60, 65–66, 71, 73, 81
Hugenberg, Alfred, 98, 101, 106
Hughes, Charles Evans, 88–89, 95
Hull, Cordell, 120, 124, 132, 147, 148, 151
Hungary, 139, 187, 205, 210
Hutchins, Robert M., 112

Iceland, 131
Ickes, Harold, 110
Immigration, German: into U.S., 2, 29, 31–33, 36, 38–39, 112, 163, 255; "Forty-eighters," 31, 36; into South America, 39, 49, 122; East-to-West Germany, 233, 234. *See also* East Ger-man Democratic Republic; German-Americans
Imperialism: colonial clashes, 40–45, 122; German territorial ambitions, 49–50, 54–58 passim, 66, 69, 72, 122, 139, 141–142; and German postwar

territorial losses, 78, 82, 91, 92, 147; U.S., 237
India, 64, 155, 207, 232
Indochina, 132, 155, 185
Ireland: U.S. immigrants from, 32, 48; and Irish-Americans, 59, 64, 135
Isolationism (U.S.), 95, 113, 114, 121, 123; World War I, 60–61, 68, 277; inter- and postwar, 84, 151, 162; World War II, 119, 124, 125, 126, 130, 131, 133, 135–136
Israel, 202–203, 229
Italy, 32, 72, 86; and alliances, 42, 91, 139; Hitler and, 114, 116, 127, 139, in World War II, 128, 130, 135, 139, 143

Jäckh, Ernst, 97
Japan, 44, 123; and Tripartite Pact, 116, 132, 134, 137; U.S. relations and war with, 122, 132–133, 137, 141, 149, 151, 152; postwar economy of, 235, 236, 270
Jaspers, Karl, 211
Jefferson, Thomas, 94
Jews, 21, 59, 63, 70, 104, 111, 112, 234, 261. See also Anti-Semitism
Johns Hopkins University, 39
Johnson, Alvin, 112
Johnson, Lyndon B., 191, 209–212, 215
Johnson, Uwe, 257
Joint Chiefs of Staff (JCS) directives, 162, 165, 167
Jünger, Ernst, 105, 106

Kapp, Friedrich, 36
Kappler, Herbert, 242
Kellogg, Frank B., 93, 95
Kennedy, John F., 188, 190–193, 237
Keynes, John Maynard, 84
Khrushchev, Nikita, 187–188, 190, 191, 192, 259
Kiesinger, Kurt Georg, 166, 208, 212–213, 215–218, 220
Kissinger, Henry, 220–222, 231, 232, 235
Kohl, Helmut, 252
Kohl, Michael, 225, 226, 264
Kokoschka, Oskar, 255
Konoye, Prince Fumimaro, 132
Korean War, 182, 184, 195

Kosygin, Aleksei, 223
Kroll, Hans, 191
Kuh, Fritz, 111
Kunze, Reiner, 262, 263

Labor: unions, 108, 196–197, 249, 272; foreign (guest) workers, 250–251, 268
Langbehn, Julius, 105
Lansing, Robert, 60, 81
Lasker, Eduard, 40
Lausanne conference (1932), 90, 99
Laval, Pierre, 102
Lea, Homer, 49
League of Nations, 82; Germany and, 72, 83–84, 91, 93, 115, 122; U.S. and, 83–84, 87; Soviet Union and, 128
Leber, Georg, 246
Leisler, Jacob, 29
Lenin, V. I., 71
Lenya, Lotte, 112
Lenz, Siegfried, 257
Lettau, Reinhard, 237
Lewis, Fulton, Jr., 136
Lewis, Sinclair, 94
Ley, Robert, 156
Lincoln, Abraham, 33
Lima conference (1938), 122
Lindbergh, Charles, 103, 136
Lippman, Walter, 71
Lloyd George, David, 71, 81, 91, 103
Locarno, see Treaty(ies)
Lodge, Henry Cabot, 74
Luckhardt, Wassili, 255
Ludwig, Emil, 112
Lübke, Heinrich, 193
Lücke, Paul, 213
Ludendorff, General Erich, 55–56, 61, 63, 69, 73, 76, 107
Lusitania crisis, 60, 62, 63, 66, 78
Lüth, Erich, 203
Luther, Hans, 110, 119
Luther, Martin, 105

McCloy, John J., 163, 165, 180
McGovern, George, 227
McGovern, W. M., 138
McKinley Tariff Act (1890), 40
McNamara, Robert, 209, 210
McNarney, Joseph T., 165
Mahan, Alfred Thayer, 49
Maihofer, Werner, 241

Maltzan, Baron Ago von, 93
Mann, Heinrich, 112
Mann, Thomas, 94, 105, 112, 237
Mansfield, Mike, 227
Mao Tse-tung, 155
Marshall, General George, 159, 161, 163
Marshall Plan, 155, 159, 170, 174, 195, 204, 205, 282
Marx, Karl, 171, 262; and Marxism, 14, 37–38, 181, 199, 203, 214, 243, 253
Max (of Baden), Prince, 69, 73, 76
MBFR negotiations, 228, 233
Meinhof, Ulrike, 243
Mencken, Henry L., 60
Metternich, Count (German ambassador), 46
Metternich, Prince Clemens von, 27
Mexico, 35, 64, 68
Michaelis, Georg, 56
Mies van der Rohe, Ludwig, 255
Militarism, German, 20, 97; "Prussian," 5, 19, 110, 148, 271; of William II, 41, 42, 44–45; and responsibility for war, 61, 70, 71, 80; and disarmament violations, 85, 90; postwar paramilitary organizations, 90, 270–271; inter- and postwar fears of, 95, 183–184, 200. See also Army, German; Hitler, Adolf; "Responsibility"
Minuit, Peter, 29
Mitteleuropa, Mittelafrika, 54
Moeller van den Bruck, Arthur, 105, 106
Molotov, Vyacheslav, 158, 159, 161, 185
Moltke, General Helmuth von, 35, 36
Morgenthau, Henry, Jr., 110, 162; and Morgenthau Plan, 148–149, 216
Morocco: Algeciras conference, 45, 48
Motley, John Lothrop, 33, 38
Mowrer, Edgar Ansel, 121
Müller, Hermann, 98
Munich crisis, see Appeasement
Münsterberg, Hugo, 47, 59, 60
Mussolini, Benito, 123, 124, 127–128, 143, 152

Napoleon Bonaparte, 27, 129
Napoleon III, 35
National Democratic Party (NDP): East, 204; West, 213–214, 241

National German-American Alliance, 58, 59
Nationalism, 43, 54, 55, 93, 150, 202; and German "national character," 15–17, 103; Hitler and, 87, 101, 107, 115, 119; German resurgence feared, 90, 95
National Socialist (Nazi) party, 94, 97, 172, 196, 252; rise of, 85, 99, 100, 105, 107, 108–109, 115, 119, 278; U.S. attitude toward, 95, 110–112, 114, 121–125, 136–138, 144–145, 152, 278; völkisch ideology of, 105, 106, 111; ethnic policy and anti-Semitism of, 141–142, 148, 202–203, 278; and German denazification, 145, 152, 156, 165–167, 171, 201, 208; postwar neo-Nazism, 213–214, 240–243, 247, 279, 280. See also Anti-Semitism; Hitler, Adolf; "Responsibility"
Nativism (in U.S.), 32–33
Naumann, Friedrich, 58
Netherlands, the, 127, 135, 139
Neurath, Constantin von, 113
Nixon, Richard, 208, 216, 220, 222, 227–228, 231
Nolde, Emil, 255
Nolte, Ernst, 237
North Atlantic Treaty Organization (NATO), 161, 185–186, 189, 199, 201, 218, 221, 228, 247, 265, 280; and multilateral force (MLF), 192, 209–210
Norway, 127, 135, 139
Nuclear weapons, 152; and nuclear policy, 187, 192, 210, 216, 221–222, 232–233, 234, 251
Nuremberg Laws (1935), 109, 202
Nuremberg trials, 145, 156

Oberländer, Theodor, 199, 202
Ollenhauer, Erich, 199
Orff, Carl, 255
Organization for European Economic Cooperation (OEEC), 155, 182, 204
"Ostpolitik," 210–212, 216, 219, 222–227

Pacifism, 20, 50, 68, 117
Panama Canal, 45, 49, 122–123
Pan-American (Inter-American Neutrality) Conference (1939), 123

Pan-German League, 48
Papen, Franz von, 64, 100–102, 106, 156
Paris Peace Conference, *see* Versailles
  Treaty
Pastorious, Franz, 29
Pauls, Rolf, 221
Pétain, Marshal Henri-Philippe, 127
Pieck, Wilhelm, 171, 177, 203
Piene, Otto, 255
Pius XII (pope), 257
Pleven, René, and Pleven Plan, 183, 185
Poincaré, Raimond, 89
Poland, 8, 9, 57, 135, 233; annexes Ger-
  man lands (1945), 3, 7, 145, 147, 196;
  post-World War I, 72, 78, 82; and
  Polish Corridor, 91, 102; German
  treaties with, 115, 124, 204; German
  invasion of (1939), 115, 116, 117, 124–
  127, 139, 142; Soviet Union and, 128,
  147, 154, 205, 224; West German re-
  lations with, 210–211, 223–224
Pompidou, Georges, 217
Ponto, Jürgen, 242
Population, 8, 9, 39–40, 247, 248, 251
Portugal, 139
Potsdam conference, 143, 147, 148, 149,
  156–157, 159, 168
Press, radio, and television: pro-Ger-
  man/Nazi (in U.S.), 47, 60, 63, 101–
  103, 111; anti-Americanism of (German), 48, 59, 124, 133, 159, 260;
  censorship of, 55; pro-Allied/anti-
  German (in U.S.), 59, 88, 123, 135;
  inter- and postwar German, 78, 159,
  167–168, 202, 239, 254–255, 274, 280;
  Hitler and, 110, 124; television (U.S.
  and German), 206, 239–240, 254, 257,
  262, 274. *See also* Propaganda
Prittwitz und Gaffron, Baron Friedrich
  von, 102
Propaganda, 49, 265; World War I, 57–
  58, 61, 63, 64, 71, 88, 114, 135, 277;
  interwar, against Germany's "oppressors," 80, 81; Hitler/Nazi, 107–109,
  110–111, 114, 120, 124, 134–137, 144,
  148, 168, 254; "Jewish," 111; Auswärtiges Amt and, 113, 114; East
  German, 272. *See also* Anti-Semitism;
  Press, radio, and television
Prussia, kingdom of, 27, 33–37, 43, 56,
  109, 171; disappearance of, 4, 13,

159; U.S. trade agreements with, 29–
  30, 40; and Prusso-German Empire,
  75; and Polish Corridor, 91–92.
  See also Franco-Prussian War; Militarism, German

Raeder, Admiral Erich, 133, 134
Rapacki, Adam, and Rapacki Plan, 187
Rathenau, Walther, 87
Reinhardt, Max, 112
Religion, 21, 37, 115, 248; Catholic-
  Protestant antagonism, 4, 20; perse-
  cution of, 29, 31, 37–38; and politics,
  37, 211
Remarque, Erich Maria, 94
Reparations, German: World War I,
  78–93 passim, 98, 99, 101–102; World
  War II, 145, 148–149, 156–159, 168–
  169, 172, 260–261; and Reparations
  Commission, 149
"Responsibility": for Nazism, 15, 17,
  21, 105–106, 201–202; for World War
  I, 51–54, 59, 61, 70, 71, 80, 82, 88,
  94–95; for World War II, 126, 213
Reunification of Germany, 24, 178, 227,
  265–266, 275; German desire and
  efforts for, 4, 175, 184–185, 192, 210,
  217, 219, 223, 225; Soviet Union and,
  161, 186–187, 191, 192, 223, 281; U.S.
  and, 162, 190, 212, 219; difficulties
  preventing, 172, 173–174. *See also*
  Berlin
Revolutions of 1848, 30–31
Rhineland, 4, 12; reoccupation of
  (1936), 115, 117, 122
Ribbentrop, Joachim von, 113, 119, 123,
  133–134, 156
Rockefeller, Nelson, 238
Röhm, Captain Ernst, 108, 122
Roosevelt, Franklin D., 120, 126, 132,
  137, 152; and relations with Hitler/
  Germany, 109–110, 122, 123, 124–125,
  135; and neutrality acts/arms em-
  bargo, 121, 124, 134, 136; and aid to
  Britain, 130–131, 134; -Churchill
  meetings, 131, 144, 148; and postwar
  Germany, 144, 147–151
Roosevelt, Theodore, 45, 46, 50, 73–74,
  94; -kaiser relations, 47–49, 60
Röpke, Wilhelm, 195
Rudel, Colonel Hans-Ulrich, 247

Ruhr, the: France invades (1923), 85, 86–89, 91, 107; postwar control of, 157, 158, 159, 160, 161, 169, 182
Rumania, 67, 69, 129, 139, 210, 217
Rush, Kenneth, 221
Rusk, Dean, 190, 191, 192
Russia, 42, 57, 59, 63, 68–69, 95, 150; German territorial ambition in, 54, 72. See also Bolshevik party; Communism; Soviet Union
Russo-Japanese War, 45

Sabotage, 61, 64, 138; and fifth column activity, 59, 111, 138. See also Propaganda
Sackett, Frederic M., 102
SALT negotiations, 222, 234
Samoan Islands crisis, 40–41, 44
Schacht, Dr. Hjalmar, 93, 120, 156
Schäffer, Dr. Fritz, 172
Scharoun, Hans, 255
Scheel, Walter, 219–220, 223, 224, 226, 230, 231
Scheidemann, Philipp, 70, 80
Schiller, Karl, 212, 213, 216, 249
Schirdewan, Karl, 205
Schleicher, General Kurt von, 100–101, 106
Schleyer, Hanns-Martin, 242
Schlieffen Plan, 53
Schmidt, Helmut, 215, 219, 221, 228; as chancellor, 230–242 passim, 247, 250, 252–253, 264, 281
Schmitt, Bernadotte, 58
Schröder, Gerhard, 191, 193, 194, 209, 210, 212, 216, 219
Schubert, Carl von, 95
Schumacher, Kurt, 177, 181, 182, 199
Schuman, Robert, 161, 182; and Schuman Plan, 183
Schurman, Jacob Gould, 1, 5, 92–93, 96, 97
Schurz, Carl, 31, 33, 36, 38, 180; and Memorial Foundation, 111
Schurz, Mrs. Carl, 39
Seebohm, Hans-Christoph, 202
Seeckt, General Hans von, 77
Seyss-Inquart, Arthur von, 156
Shirer, William L., 121
Sieber, Rolf, 260
Smith, Captain John, 29

Social Democratic Party (SPD), 37, 75–76, 98–99, 171–172, 175, 177, 181–183 passim, 194, 199–200, 207–208, 212–213, 215, 216, 219, 226, 231, 252–253
Socialist Unity Party (SED), 171, 178, 203–204
Sokolovsky, Marshal Vasili, 160
South America: German immigration into, 39, 49, 122; German expansion in, 41, 45, 49, 50, 122–123
Soviet Union, 90; annexation of German lands by (1945), 3, 7, 196; and treaties with Germany, 86, 91, 115; Hitler and, 114, 125, 128; German invasion of, 128–129, 131–143 passim; and Winter War, 128, 129; and Japan, 134, 137, 151; German defeat in, 143, 144, 148, 151; and occupation of Germany, 145, 147, 149–151, 157–174 passim, 184; German reparations to, 149, 156–159, 169, 172; and East German Republic, 171–172, 178, 185–187, 204–205, 259, 263, 269, 271, 275; and West German Republic, 187, 191, 209, 211, 217–218, 223, 224; and nuclear policy, 216; and China, 281. See also Communism; East German Democratic Republic; Russia; Stalin, Joseph
Spain, 139; Civil war in, 115, 121, 128
Spanish-American War, 44
Spanknöbel, Heinz, 111
Speer, Albert, 142, 156
Spiegel affair, 194, 201
Spengler, Oswald, 97, 105, 106
Speyer, James, 47
Springer, Axel, 254, 256
Spring Rice, Sir Cecil, 48
Staden, Berndt von, 232, 238
Stalin, Joseph, 205; -Hitler pact, 125, 128–129, 147, 150; and postwar Germany, 143, 147–151, 154, 171, 184
Sternburg, Speck von, 45, 46
Steuben, General Friedrich von, 29, 180
Steuben Society (U.S.), 59, 95, 111, 136
Stimson, Henry L., 102, 147, 148
Stockhausen, Karlheinz, 255
Stoessel, Walter, 232
Stoph, Willi, 218, 225, 259, 267
Strauss, Franz Josef, 192, 194, 201, 208, 212, 213, 216, 220, 252

Strauss, Richard, 255
Stresemann, Gustav, 85, 87, 90–92, 95–96, 98, 116, 118, 180, 188
Submarine warfare: World War I, 55, 57, 58, 61–63, 64, 66–68, 131; World War II, 130, 131, 133, 134, 137, 138
Suez crisis, 187
Syberberg, Jürgen, 256

Taft, William Howard, 49, 50, 74
Taut, Max, 255
Taylor, A. J. P., 116
Teheran conference (1943), 143, 147
Television, see Press, radio, and television
Terrorism, postwar, 242–244, 252, 261
Thadden, Adolf von, 213
"Third Reich," 7, 22, 108; trends (völkisch) toward, 105–106, 111; -U.S. relations, 110–114, 129, 131–135; and crises leading to war, 115–119, 122, 124–125; in World War II, 126–153; territorial seizures and losses, 127, 139, 141–142, 147; and Tripartite Pact, 132, 134, 137; defeat and surrender of, 143–145, 148–149, 152, 154, 155
Third world, 82, 282. See also Imperialism
Thompson, Dorothy, 94, 121
Thomsen, Hans, 134
Tillich, Paul, 112
Tirpitz, Admiral Alfred von, 41, 61
Tocqueville, Alexis de, 31
Toynbee, Arnold, 103
Trade, 122, 123; U.S.-German agreements, 29–30, 40, 43, 50, 120, 261; protectionism, 30, 40, 43; East-West German, 265, 268
Treaty(ies): Brest-Litovsk (1918), 68–69, 72; secret, of Allies, 70; Rapallo (1922), 86, 87, 91, 281; Berlin, (1921, with U.S.) 87, (1926, with Soviet Union) 91, 115; Locarno (1925), 90–91, 96, 117, 118; Kellogg-Briand (Pact of Paris, 1928), 93; Brussels Treaty Organization, 155; Franco-German (1963), 189; Paris (1955), 190; German-Soviet and German-Polish (Ostverträge, 1970), 223–224, 226; Basic East-West German (Grundvertrag),

226–227, 233, 258, 264. See also Versailles Treaty
Tripartite Pact, 132, 134, 137
Truman, Harry S, 147, 162
Truman Doctrine (1947), 155, 159
Turkey, 72, 154, 155, 251
Twain, Mark, 94

Ulbricht, Walter, 171, 178, 203, 205–206, 218, 225, 259
"Unconditional Surrender," 144
United Nations, 151, 184, 228, 260, 264
United States, 89, 94; official diplomatic relations of, with Germany, 2, 36, 39–41, 44–50, 87–88, 89, 92–93, 96, 110, 119–125, 133, 173, 180, 196, 222–223, 237–238, 258, 260, 261–263, 279, (severance of) 55, 62, 63, 65, 67; prohibition in, 32, 58; Civil War in, 33, 35, 38; Espionage and Sedition Acts (1917, 1918), 71; investments of, in Germany, 93, 120, 235; Nazi activities in, 111, 122, 136; neutrality and neutrality legislation of, 113, 121, 124, 125, 129, 130, 132, 137; arms embargo by, 121, 124, 129–130, 133; and postwar Germany, 145, 147–153, 157–170 passim, 172–174, 184, 188–193, 207–229 passim. See also German-Americans; Great Britain; Immigration, German; Isolationism; Japan; Trade; World War I; World War II
United States views of Germany and Germans: nonfraternization orders, 1–2, 152–153, 165, 170; stereotyped, 5, 97, 138, 237; during World War I, 5, 32, 36, 45, 47, 57–59, 62, 63–65, 71, 73–74, 77–78, 88, 136, 138, 277; respect and admiration, 32, 38, 47, 57, 81, 92–94, 103, 136; immigration restrictions sought, 39; colonial/economic clashes and, 40–41, 43–45, 49–50, 122; alarm at naval expansion, 41, 49; revisionism and, 52, 95, 150; and Nazi/Hitler cause, 95, 110–112, 114, 121–125, 129, 136–138, 144–145, 152, 180, 278; postwar, 147–149, 162, 167, 170, 190, 192–193, 212, 221, 223, 228, 277
Usher, Roland G., 49

Vance, Cyrus, 232
Venezuela, 45
Versailles Treaty (1919), 52, 85, 97, 104, 216; revision of, 1, 78, 81, 82, 92, 102, 116, 124; Paris Peace Conference and, 12, 77–78, 81–83, 86, 91, 117; Hitler and, 80, 84, 114–116, 124; U.S. fails to ratify, 83, 87–88, 91. *See also* Treaty(ies)
Vetter, Heinz Oskar, 249
Viereck, George Sylvester, 59, 60, 63, 114, 136
Viereck, Peter, 138
Vietnam War, 207, 209, 214, 215, 220, 228, 237, 244
Villard, Oswald Garrison, 60
Vishinsky, Andrei Y., 161

Waldersee, Field Marshal Alfred von, 44
Waldseemüller, Martin, 29
Wallace, Henry, 162
Walser, Martin, 256
"War guilt," *see* "Responsibility"
Warsaw Pact, 186, 204, 211, 217, 228, 271
Washington, George, 29
Wehner, Herbert, 199, 212, 253, 264
Weill, Kurt, 112, 255
Weimar Republic, 35, 75–76, 104, 106, 199, 200; putsch against, 77, 107; territorial losses of, 78, 82, 91, 92; and war reparations, 78–93 passim, 98, 99, 101–102; occupation of, by Allies, 80, 85, 86–89, 91, 92; –U.S. reciprocal sentiments, 80–81, 82, 84, 92–97, 100–101, 120, 278; economic conditions in, 85–87, 89, 93, 94, 98, 99, 108, 195; and treaties with Russia, 86, 91; in League of Nations, 91, 93; and "Weimar culture," 93–94, 105, 252, 253; constitution of, 176
Weiss, Peter, 257
Welles, Sumner, 110, 162
Wenders, Wim, 256
West German Federal Republic (Bundesrepublik Deutschland, BRD), 3, 145, 261; geography and character of, 7–13, 196; army (Bundeswehr) of, 20, 183–184, 194, 200–201, 246, 247, 271; attitude of, toward East Germany, 25, 172, 186–187, 203–207 passim, 210–211, 216, 217, 223, 225, 264, democracy in, 145, 193, 253, 279, 280; emergence and economic/political development of, 158–160, 166, 169, 172–177, 179–203, 207–229, 281–282; constitution of, 175–176, 229; –Soviet relations, 187, 191, 209, 211, 217–218, 223, 224; as U.S. "partner," 207, 215, 222–223, 229, 231, 238, 276, 279–282; and Basic Treaty with East Germany, 226–227, 233, 258, 264; since 1974, 230–257; culture in, 253–257. *See also* Adenauer, Konrad; Common Market
Wiedemann, Captain Fritz, 122
Wiedfeldt, Dr. Otto, 88, 93, 96
Wilder, Thornton, 257
William I, 34, 35, 36
William II, 41–46, 51, 111; and Theodore Roosevelt, 47–49, 60; as war leader and "criminal," 54, 56, 67, 80; abdication of, 69, 73, 75, 78
Willkie, Wendell, 130, 151
Wilson, Hugh, 123
Wilson, Woodrow, 51, 59, 62, 233; pro-British sentiments of, 50, 60, 70; mediation attempts by, 56–57, 65–67, 69, 70, 72–73; Fourteen Points program of, 69, 71–74, 144; and League of Nations, 72, 82–84, 91; German obloquy toward, 80–81, 82, 96
Winievicz, Josef, 223
Wolf, Christa, 262
Wolfe, Thomas, 94
Wollweber, Ernst, 205
Women, 17, 246–248, 268, 273
World War I, 111, 117, 120; U.S. feeling toward Germans during, 32, 45, 47, 59, 136, 138, 277; U.S. intervention in, 54, 57, 61, 68, 70, 71, 126, 131, 277; German sabotage during, 61, 64; armistice negotiations, 68–70, 73–74, 82, 87, 127, 144. *See also* German Reich; Propaganda; "Responsibility"; Submarine warfare
World War II, 111; crises leading to, 115–119, 122, 124–125; responsibility for, 126, 213; U.S. intervention in, 126, 132–138, 143–144
Wunderlich, Paul, 255

Yalta conference (1945), 143, 147–151
   passim
Young, Owen D., 97; and Young Plan,
   90, 93, 98, 101
Yugoslavia, 128, 139, 217

Zaisser, Wilhelm, 205
Zenger, John Peter, 29
Zimmermann, Mac, 255
Zimmermann telegram, 61, 68

The American Foreign Policy Library

The United States and the Andean Republics: Peru, Bolivia, and Ecuador
Frederick B. Pike

The United States and the Arab World THIRD EDITION William R. Polk

The Balkans in Our Time REVISED EDITION Robert Lee Wolff

The United States and Burma John F. Cady

The United States and Canada Gerald M. Craig

The United States and the Caribbean REVISED EDITION Dexter Perkins

The United States and China FOURTH EDITION John King Fairbank

Germany and the United States: A "Special Relationship"? Hans W. Gatzke

The United States and India, Pakistan, Bangladesh W. Norman Brown

The United States and Ireland Donald Harman Akenson

The United States and Italy THIRD EDITION, ENLARGED H. Stuart Hughes

The United States and Japan THIRD EDITION Edwin O. Reischauer

The United States and Malaysia James W. Gould

The United States and North Africa: Morocco, Algeria, and Tunisia
Charles F. Gallagher

The United States and Poland Piotr S. Wandycz

Scandinavia REVISED EDITION, ENLARGED Franklin D. Scott

The United States and the Southern Cone: Argentina, Chile, and Uruguay
Arthur P. Whitaker